# SIX CENTURIES OF GREAT POETRY

The wide selection of poems collected here by Robert Penn Warren and Albert Erskine is the finest in British lyrics written between the mid-1300s and the early 1900s. The selections are taken from the lyric tradition: generally short, reflective poems expressing the thoughts of a single speaker but conveying a wide range of styles and themes, from the romantic poets' passionate view of nature to twentieth-century poets' search for meaning in troubled times. A comprehensive selection of enduring work by over one hundred acknowledged masters, this extraordinary collection is the definitive anthology of great poetry.

ROBERT PENN WARREN taught English at Yale University and is the winner of the Pulitzer prize for fiction and one for poetry, and of the National Book Award for poetry. He is the author, with Cleanth Brooks, of *Understanding Fiction,* and of the novels *All the King's Men, World Enough and Time, Band of Angels,* and *Flood,* as well as many other works of fiction, poetry, and literary criticism. He died in 1989.

ALBERT ERSKINE was a vice president and executive editor at Random House in New York. He was also on the staff of *The Southern Review* and was associated with the Louisiana State University Press.

# SIX
# CENTURIES
# OF GREAT
# POETRY

*Edited by*

ROBERT PENN WARREN

*and*

ALBERT ERSKINE

Published by
Dell Publishing
a division of
Random House, Inc.
New York, New York

The trademark Laurel® is registered in the U.S. Patent and Trademark Office and in other countries.

The trademark Dell® is registered in the U.S. Patent and Trademark Office.

ISBN: 978-0-440-21383-3

Printed in the United States of America

Published simultaneously in Canada

November 1992

21  20  19  18  17

OPM

# INDEX OF POETS

# INTRODUCTION

This book is intended for the general reader of poetry—the person who, though he may or may not be a specialist in literature, enjoys poetry as part of his natural enjoyment of life.

There are many kinds of anthologies. There is, for instance, the historical anthology often used in schools, which gives good representative examples, period by period, of the sort of poetry written in the past. The primary obligation of the maker of such an anthology is to keep the record straight, to give samples of the work of all periods, even work with which he, or his age, may be unsympathetic, and to mark the fluctuations of taste. Again, there are anthologies illustrating some critical principle —for instance George Moore's anthology of "pure" poetry. There are anthologies of special forms—of ballads, of odes, of sonnets, and so on. Or anthologies of topics—poems of love, poems of friendship, poems of patriotism, poems of childhood, even anthologies for dog lovers and devoted gardeners. And there is the personal anthology in which the maker indulges his tastes, his whims, his accidental preferences and prejudices, his eccentricities, with a shameless, and sometimes delightful, contempt of public opinion.

Our anthology is not quite like any of these. No form or topic dominates this book. We could simply ignore such concerns, but we could not quite so readily ignore—and did not wish to ignore—some of the problems of historical representation. Our book is, in fact, historical; it begins with Chaucer and comes down into our century, and we hope that it does give a picture of the long sweep of English poetry. Our emphasis is, however, more on the "poetry" than on the "sweep." In other words, we intended to select the best English poems of a certain scale and put them in their historical sequence.

The "best," we say. But the best on whose authority? On nobody's authority, not even the authority of Time, that most reverend critic, but on our own responsibility. This may sound as though we have made a personal anthology, after all, and in one sense that is true. We have read or reread the body of poetry that falls within our province and have tried to scrutinize honestly our own reactions to it. We have found, of course, some need to revise old opinions. Some poems have lost their morning glister, others shine more brightly than ever before. Some that we, and many anthologists, have previously ignored appear on our pages to solicit now the franchise of general approval—for instance, certain poems by Skelton, Clare, and Barnes.

This anthology, then, is personal in that we take the risk of our taste and judgment. But whose else can we take? And as we take that risk we can only hope that our own experience of life and poetry is not too gross or too whimsical, and that we are not too ignorant or too doctrinaire.

But in another sense this book is not personal. It is the fruit of a collaboration, a long and careful collaboration full of wrangles and debates as well as happy enthusiasms. No collaboration can make the purely personal anthology. What may give the personal anthology its charm—the sentimental attachment, the accidental association, the crankiness of taste, the flavor of an individual life—these things are subdued in a collaboration. Eccentricities and accidents belonging to one collaborator tend to be canceled by those of the other. We must confess that occasionally we have not been above bargaining with each other, and perhaps now and then have compounded rather than canceled eccentricity and accident, but ordinarily a veto has been carried, and the poem in question laid away for somebody's truly personal anthology.

This book represents not only the limitations of our taste and judgment, but other limitations as well. For one thing, we have a limited number of pages. English poetry has a long and rich history, and simply on grounds of space, many fine poems have been laid regretfully aside. For the same reason, long poems have been passed by. This is a collection of short pieces, chiefly lyrical—taking *lyric* in its broadest significance. It is true that we do have here Coleridge's *Ancient Mariner*, with its 625 lines, but without it Coleridge could scarcely be said to be represented at all, and the poem itself has its affiliations with characteristically short rather than long poems, the ballad and not the epic, the personal cry and not the extended argument.

As another limitation we have ruled out excerpts from poems. We use only whole poems, or occasionally such parts of longer works as are self-contained units that can stand alone without explanation—for instance, songs from plays or certain units from Tennyson's *In Memoriam*. There are thrilling and beautiful passages from epics, plays, and other long works, but they are not for us now. Excerpts may tease the reader to further acquaintance, or if he already knows the full work, may revive it for him with peculiar poignancy, as a scrap of overheard music may revive the massiveness of a past experience. Or the excerpt, by reason of its very lack of mooring and context, may give the joy of a free flash of poetry—somehow purer, finer, more nearly absolute than ordinarily. But there is another more human, sober, and lasting joy in watching, as it were, the poetry derive from the whole poem, in seeing poetry accept its untranscendental condition of a poem, in seeing it flow, sometimes, from the unpromising lines that would never be quoted in a collection of brilliant excerpts.

The fact that the size of this book prevents the use of long poems, and that we have discarded excerpts, does, however, work certain inequities. Pope suffers, as do Thomson, Johnson, and Crabbe—and that may again tell us something we already knew about the eighteenth century. Shelley and Byron suffer too; for a different reason.

But within our plan, what poets do have here the fullest exhibits? In asking this question we remember that some poets of highest quality have a relatively small body of work, or achieve this quality in only a few poems. Even so the answer to our question may say something about English poetry—and about us, the editors. When our work was done we found that Shakespeare—Shakespeare as lyric poet—dominated the field with 942 lines. Wordsworth is second with 688 lines. Milton, Browning, and Tennyson, as is customary, occupy impressive positions. To some poets we have allotted significantly more space than they usually receive in anthologies of this scope: Skelton, Wyatt, Campion, Donne, Herrick, Marvell, Blake, Clare, and Barnes.

It is easy to choose Chaucer as a starting point. But it is not quite so easy to choose an ending point. In an anthology that covers some centuries there is always a problem when contem-

porary writers are reached. For it is inevitable that our judg-
ments of our own time should be somewhat interested and spe-
cial. And it is inevitable that there be some temptation to shift
scale—a feeling that if we represent our age at all we ought to
do it as it appears to us, a rank, rich, undifferentiated hurly-
burly without benefit of history. If we don't shift scale, how
perfunctory and wrong-headed the contemporary section is
likely to seem! We need only look back at a few anthologies to
be convinced of this. There is no happy solution for the prob-
lem, and there is no solution that is not more or less arbitrary.
Our solution is arbitrary: to represent no poet born in this cen-
tury and no poet who is now alive.

In the beginning we said that we had set out to print the best
English poems—with all the risks of our choosing the best. But
some shadows fell across that bright intention. One shadow was
the need for some proportion in representation. If we had been
absolutely rigorous in fulfilling that intention we should have
had fewer poets in our 570 pages. Though we have made a point
of giving fuller showings of the big poets than has been custom-
ary in anthologies of this scale, we have sometimes been forced
to omit impressive pieces to make a place at all for smaller but
attractive, or even indispensable, poems. Out of the massive
reservoir of Donne or Wordsworth or Tennyson some pieces
have been passed by to make room for, shall we say, Leigh
Hunt. Another shadow was the matter of publishers' permission
for work still in copyright. The holders of copyrights restricted
us to the number of poems here exhibited by several poets—
Yeats and Hardy among them. For us at least, these would de-
mand many more, even in a book of this size.

The texts used have been drawn from the best available
sources. As our work of compilation progressed, we were sur-
prised to find how little consistency in such mechanical matters
as spelling, punctuation, capitalization, etc., exists—not only
among the various editions of an early poet, but sometimes
within the pages of a single volume. Varying degrees of modern-
ization have been employed by various editors, and sometimes
by the same editor. Had we followed what seemed to us the

most authoritative edition of each poet, our text would have had no consistent approach to these questions at all.

We have tried, therefore, to follow this principle: to use a modern system in all cases where meter and meaning are not violated by so doing. Though the general reader can, with the help of a glossary, take pleasure in Chaucer, his language, and that of the poets for a century or so thereafter, is so different from ours that modernization would alter its poetic quality; we have therefore left the texts as we found them. We have likewise respected dialectal peculiarities in the work of certain later poets—as for example Allan Ramsay, Burns, and William Barnes. When dealing with a poet like Blake, whose text seems to represent an eccentric personal quality and not merely the convention of a period, we have not tampered with it except in certain trivial respects.

After Skelton, with some self-evident exceptions, we are dealing with the language of our own time. Donne's line, "Who saies my teares have overflow'd his ground?" is not in any way changed by this version: "Who says my tears have overflowed his ground?"

It was long the practice to print the past participles of verbs, when the *-ed* had no independent syllabic value, thus: *drown'd,* which is pronounced, of course, the same way as *drowned*—one syllable. By the same practice, when poets needed to make an extra foot with such a verb form, the participle was given in full: *drowned,* pronounced *drownèd.* We have consistently printed the full form and have marked the accent when it seemed to be the poet's intention.

And to anyone who feels that by changing "Who saies my teares . . ." we have destroyed something called "the flavor of the original," we can only say we don't believe the "flavor" was a part of the original but something added to it by a modern response to the funny spelling. Presumably, "Who *faies* . . ." would be even more flavorful.

R. P. W.
A. E.

# GEOFFREY CHAUCER/1340?–1400

*Merciles Beautè*

### I. CAPTIVITY

Your yën two wol slee me sodenly,
I may the beautè of hem not sustene,
So woundeth hit through-out my herte kene.

And but your word wol helen hastily
My hertes wounde, whyl that hit is grene,
   *Your yën two wol slee me sodenly,*
   *I may the beautè of hem not sustene.*

Upon my trouthe I sey yow feithfully,
That ye ben of my lyf and deeth the quene;
For with my deeth the trouthe shal be sene.
   *Your yën two wol slee me sodenly,*
   *I may the beautè of hem not sustene,*
   *So woundeth hit through-out my herte kene.*

### II. REJECTION

So hath your beautè fro your herte chaced
Pitee, that me ne availeth not to pleyne;
For Daunger halt your mercy in his cheyne.

Giltles my deeth thus han ye me purchaced;
I sey yow sooth, me nedeth not to feyne;
   *So hath your beautè fro your herte chaced*
   *Pitee, that me ne availeth not to pleyne.*

Allas! that nature hath in yow compassed
So greet beautè; that no man may atteyne
To mercy, though he sterve for the peyne.
  *So hath your beautè fro your herte chaced*
  *Pitee, that me ne availeth not to pleyne;*
  *For Daunger halt your mercy in his cheyne.*


### III. ESCAPE

Sin I fro Love escaped am so fat,
I never thenk to ben in his prison lene;
Sin I am free, I counte him not a bene.

He may answere, and seye this or that;
I do no fors, I speke right as I mene.
  *Sin I fro Love escaped am so fat,*
  *I never thenk to ben in his prison lene.*

Love hath my name y-strike out of his sclat,
And he is strike out of my bokes clene
For ever-mo; ther is non other mene.
  *Sin I fro Love escaped am so fat,*
  *I never thenk to ben in his prison lene;*
  *Sin I am free, I counte him not a bene.*


## Truth

### BALADE DE BON CONSEYL

Flee fro the prees,[1] and dwelle with sothfastnesse,
Suffyce unto thy good, though hit be smal;
For hord hath hate, and climbing tikelnesse,[2]
Prees hath envye, and wele blent overal;
Savour no more than thee bihove shal;

---

[1] press, crowd   [2] uncertainty

Werk wel thy-self, that other folk canst rede;
And trouthe shal delivere, hit is no drede.

Tempest[1] thee noght al croked to redresse,
In trust of hir that turneth as a bal:
Gret reste stant in litel besinesse;
And eek be war to sporne ageyn an al;
Stryve noght, as doth the crokke with the wal.
Daunte thy-self, that dauntest otheres dede;
And trouthe shal delivere, hit is no drede.

That thee is sent, receyve in buxumnesse,[2]
The wrastling for this worlde axeth a fal.
Her nis nor hoom, her nis but wildernesse;
Forth, pilgrim, forth! Forth, beste, out of thy stall
Know thy contree, look up, thank God of al;
Hold the hye wey, and lat thy gost thee lede:
And trouthe shal delivere, hit is no drede.

### ENVOY

Therfore, thou vache,[3] leve thyn old wrecchednesse
Unto the worlde; leve now to be thral;
Crye him mercy, that of his hy goodneese
Made thee of noght, and in especial
Draw unto him, and pray in general
For thee, and eek for other, hevenlich mede;
And trouthe shal delivere, hit is no drede.

### *The Compleint of Chaucer to His Empty Purse*

To you, my purse, and to non other wight
Compleyne I, for ye be my lady dere!
I am so sory, now that ye be light;
For certes, but ye make hevy chere,

[1] disturb  [2] submission  [3] cow

Me were as leef be leyd up-on my bere;
For whiche un-to your mercy thus I crye:
Beth hevy ageyn, or elles mot I dye!

Now voucheth sauf this day, or hit be night,
That I of you the blisful soun may here,
Or see your colour lyk the sonne bright,
That of yelownesse hadde never pere.
Ye be my lyf, ye be myn hertes stere,[1]
Quene of comfort and of good companye:
Beth hevy ageyn, or elles mot I dye!

Now purs, that be to me my lyves light,
And saveour, as doun in this worlde here,
Out of this toune help me through your might,
Sin that ye wole nat been my tresorere;
For I am shave as ny as any frere.
But yit I pray un-to your curtesye:
Beth hevy ageyn, or elles mot I dye!

LENVOY DE CHAUCER

O conquerour of Brutes Albioun!
Which that by lyne and free eleccioun
Ben verray king, this song to you I sende;
And ye, that mowen al our harm amende,
Have minde up-on my supplicacioun!

## Balade

Hyd, Absolon, thy gilte tresses clere;
Ester, ley thou thy meknesse al adown;
Hyd, Jonathas, al thy frendly manere;
Penalopee and Marcia Catoun,
Make of youre wifhod no comparisoun;

[1] guide

Hyde ye youre beautes, Ysoude and Eleyne:
My lady cometh, that al this may disteyne.[1]

Thy faire body, lat hit nat appere,
Lavyne; and thou, Lucresse of Rome toun,
And Polixene, that boghte love so dere,
And Cleopatre, with al thy passioun,
Hyde ye your trouthe of love and your renoun;
And thou, Tisbe, that hast for love swich peyne:
My lady cometh, that al this may disteyne.

Herro, Dido, Laudomia, alle yfere,[2]
And Phillis, hangyng for thy Demonphoun,
And Canace, espied by thy chere,
Ysiphile, betrayed with Jasoun,
Maketh of your trouthe neyther boost ne soun;
Nor Ypermystre or Adriane, ye tweyne:
My lady cometh, that al this may disteyne.


# ANONYMOUS

*Ich Am of Irlonde*

Ich am of Irlonde,
   Ant[3] of the holy londe
      Of Irlonde.
Gode sire, pray ich thee,
   For of sainte charite,
Come ant dance wit me,
      In Irlonde.

[1] bedim   [2] together   [3] and

# ANONYMOUS ·

## *I Sing of a Maiden* ·

I sing of a maiden
　That is makeles;[1]
King of alle kinges
　To here sone che[2] ches.[3]

He cam also[4] stille
　Ther his moder was,
As dew in Aprille
　That fallith on gras.

He cam also stille
　To his moderes bowr,
As dew in Aprille
　That fallith on the flowr.

He cam also stille
　Ther his moder lay,
As dew in Aprille
　That fallith on the spray.

Moder and maiden
　Was never non but che;
Wel may swich a lady
　Godes moder be.

[1] matchless　[2] she　[3] chose　[4] as

# WILLIAM DUNBAR/1460?–1520?

### Lament for the Makers

I that in heill[1] wes[2] and gladnes,
Am trublit now with gret seiknes,
And feblit with infermitie;
*Timor mortis conturbat me.*[3]

Our plesance heir[4] is all vaneglory,
This fals warld is bot transitory,
The flesche is brukle,[5] the Fend is sle;
*Timor mortis conturbat me.*

The stait of man dois change and vary,
Now sound, now seik, now blith, now sary,
Now dansand mery, now like to dee;
*Timor mortis conturbat me.*

No stait in erd[6] heir standis sickir;[7]
As with the wind wavis the wickir,[8]
Wavis this warldis vanite;
*Timor mortis conturbat me.*

On to the ded gois all Estatis,
Princis, Prelotis, and Potestatis,[9]
Baith riche and pur of al degre;
*Timor mortis conturbat me.*

He takis the knichtis into feild,
Anarmit under helme and scheild;
Victour he is at all melle;[10]
*Timor mortis conturbat me.*

[1] health   [2] was   [3] the fear of death disturbs me   [4] here   [5] brittle   [6] earth   [7] firm
[8] twig   [9] potentates   [10] melee

That strang unmercifull tyrand
Takis, on the moderis[1] breist soukand,[2]
The bab full of benignite;
  *Timor mortis conturbat me.*

He takis the campion in the stour,[3]
The capitane closit in the towr,
The lady in bowr full of beute;
  *Timor mortis conturbat me.*

He spairis no lord for his piscence,[4]
Na clerk for his intelligence;
His awfull strak may no man fle;
  *Timor mortis conturbat me.*

Art-magicianis, and astrologgis,
Rethoris, logicianis, and theologgis,
Thame helpis no conclusionis sle;
  *Timor mortis conturbat me.*

In medicine the most practicianis,[5]
Lechis, surrigianis, and physicianis,
Thamself fra ded may not supple;[6]
  *Timor mortis conturbat me.*

I se that makaris[7] amang the laif[8]
Playis heir ther pageant, sine[9] gois to graif;[10]
Sparit is nocht ther faculte;
  *Timor mortis conturbat me.*

He hes done petuously devour
The noble Chaucer, of makaris flowr,
The Monk of Bery, and Gower, all thre;
  *Timor mortis conturbat me.*

---

[1] mother's   [2] sucking [3] battle  [4] puissance  [5] practiced  [6] deliver  [7] poets  [8] rest
              [9] then   [10] grave

The gude Sir Hew of Eglintoun,
.And eik Heriot, and Wintoun,
He hes tane out of this cuntre;
   *Timor mortis conturbat me.*

That scorpion fell hes done infek
Maister Johne Clerke, and James Afflek,
Fra balat-making and tragidie;
   *Timor mortis conturbat me.*

Holland and Barbour he hes berevit;[1]
Allace! that he nocht with us levit
Schir Mungo Lokert of the Le;
   *Timor mortis conturbat me.*

Clerk of Tranent eik he has tane,
That maid the Anteris[2] of Gawane;
Schir Gilbert Hay endit hes he;
   *Timor mortis conturbat me.*

He hes Blind Hary and Sandy Traill
Slaine with his Schowr of mortall haill,
Qwhilk[3] Patrik Johnestoun might nocht fle;
   *Timor mortis conturbat me.*

He hes reft Merseir his endite,[4]
That did in luf so lifly[5] write,
So schort, so quik, of sentence hye;
   *Timor mortis conturbat me.*

He hes tane Roull of Aberdene,
And gentill Roull of Corstorphin;
Two bettir fallowis did no man se;
   *Timor mortis conturbat me.*

In Dumferline he hes done roune[6]
With Maister Robert Henrysoun;

<hr>

[1] reft   [2] adventures   [3] which   [4] writing   [5] spritely   [6] whispered

Schir Johne the Ros enbrast hes he;
*Timor mortis conturbat me.*

And he hes now tane, last of aw,
Gud gentill Stobo and Quintine Schaw,
Of qwham[1] all wichtis[2] hes[3] pete;
*Timor mortis conturbat me.*

Gud Maister Walter Kennedy
In point of dede lyis veraly,
Gret reuth it wer that so suld be;
*Timor mortis conturbat me.*

Sen[4] he hes all my brether tane,
He will nocht lat me lif alane,
On forse[5] I man[6] his nixt pray be;
*Timor mortis conturbat me.*

Sen for the deid remeid is none,
Best is that we for dede dispone,
Eftir our deid that lif may we;
*Timor mortis conturbat me.*

# JOHN SKELTON/1460?–1529

### *To the Second Person*

O benign Jesu, my sovereign Lord and King,
   The only Son of God by filiation,
The Second Person withouten beginning,
   Both God and man, our faith maketh plain relation,
   Mary Thy mother, by way of incarnation,

---

[1] whom  [2] creatures  [3] have  [4] since  [5] perforce  [6] must

Whose glorious passion our soulès doth revive,
    Against all bodily and ghostly tribulation
Defend me with Thy piteous woundès five.

O peerless Prince, painèd to the death,
    Ruefully rent, Thy body wan and blo,[1]
For my redemption gave up Thy vital breath,
    Was never sorrow like to Thy deadly woe!
    Grant me, out of this world when I shall go,
Thine endless mercy for my preservative:
    Against the world, the flesh, the devil also,
Defend me with Thy piteous woundès five.

## Upon a Dèad Man's Head

*Sent to him from an honourable gentlewoman for a token,*
*he devised this ghostly meditation in English covenable,*
*in sentence commendable, lamentable, lacrimable, profitable for a soul.*

Your ugly token
My mind hath broken
From worldly lust:
For I have discust
We are but dust,
And die we must.
  It is general
To be mortal:
I have well espied
No man may him hide
From Death hollow-eyed,
With sinews witherèd,
With bonès shiverèd,
With his worm-eaten maw,
And his ghastly jaw
Gasping aside,
Naked of hide,

[1] livid

Neither flesh nor fell.[1]
    Then, by my counsell,
Look that ye spell
Well this gospell:
For whereso we dwell
Death will us quell,
And with us mell.[2]
    For all our pampered paunches
There may no fraunchis,[3]
Nor worldly bliss,
Redeem us from this:
Our days be dated
To be check-mated
With draughtès of death
Stopping our breath:
Our eyen sinking,
Our bodies stinking,
Our gummès grinning,
Our soulès brinning.[4]
To whom, then, shall we sue,
For to have rescue,
But to sweet Jesu
On us then for to rue?
    O goodly Child
Of Mary mild,
Then be our shield!
That we be not exiled
To the dun dale
Of bootless bale,
Nor to the lake
Of fiendès blake.
    But grant us grace
To see thy Face,
And to purchase
Thine heavenly place,
And thy palace
Full of solace

[1] skin  [2] meddle  [3] franchise  [4] burning

Above the sky
That is so high,
Eternally
To behold and see
The Trinitie!
  Amen.
Myrres vous y.


## Now Sing We, as We Were Wont

Now sing we, as we were wont,
*Vexilla regis prodeunt.*[1]

The King's banner on field is splayed,
The cross's mystery cannot be nayed.[2]
To whom our Saviour was betrayed,
  And for our sake.
Thus saith he:
I suffer for thee,
  My death I take.
    Now sing we, as we were wont,
    *Vexilla regis prodeunt.*

Behold my shanks, behold my knees,
Behold my head, arms, and thees,[3]
Behold of me nothing thou sees
  But sorrow and pine:[4]
Thus was I spilt,
Man, for thy guilt,
  And not for mine.
    Now sing we, as we were wont,
    *Vexilla regis prodeunt.*

Behold my body, how Jews it dong[5]
With knots of whipcord and scourges strong:

[1] the King's banners are displayed  [2] denied  [3] thighs  [4] pain  [5] struck

As streams of a well the blood outsprong
   On every side.
The knottès were knit
Right well with wit,
   They made woundès wide.
      Now sing we, as we were wont,
      *Vexilla regis prodeunt.*

Man, thou shalt now understand,
Of my head, both foot and hand,
Are four c. and five thousand
   Woundès and sixty;
Fifty and vii.
Were told full even
   Upon my body.
      Now sing we, as we were wont,
      *Vexilla regis prodeunt.*

Sith I for love bought thee so dear,
As thou may see thyself here,
I pray thee with a right good cheer
   Love me again:
That it likes me
To suffer for thee
   Now all this pain.
      Now sing we, as we were wont,
      *Vexilla regis prodeunt.*

Man, understand now thou shall,
Instead of drink they gave me gall,
And eisell[1] mingled therewithall,
   The Jewès fell.
Those pains on me
I suffered for thee
   To bring thee fro hell.
      Now sing we, as we were wont,
      *Vexilla regis prodeunt.*

[1] vinegar

Now for thy life thou hast mislead,
Mercy to ask be thou not adread:
The least drop of blood that I for thee shed
  Might cleanse thee soon
Of all the sin
The world within
  If thou haddest doon.
    Now sing we, as we were wont,
    *Vexilla regis prodeunt.*


I was more wrother with Judas
For he would no mercy ask
Than I was for his trespass
  When he me sold;
I was ever ready
To grant him mercy,
  But he none wold.
    Now sing we, as we were wont,
    *Vexilla regis prodeunt.*


Lo, how I hold mine arms abroad,
Thee to receive ready yspread!
For the great love that I to thee had
  Well may thou know.
Some love again
I would full fain
  Thou wouldest to me show.
    Now sing we, as we were wont,
    *Vexilla regis prodeunt.*


For love I ask nothing of thee
But stand fast in faith, and sin thou flee,
And pain[1] to live in honestie
  Both night and day;
And thou shalt have bliss

[1] strive

That never shall miss
　　Withouten nay.[1]
　　　　Now sing we, as we were wont,
　　　　*Vexilla regis prodeunt.*

Now, Jesu, for thy great goodness,
That for men suffered great hardness,
Save us from the devil's cruelness,
　　And to bliss us send,
And grant us grace
To see Thy Face
　　Withouten end:
　　　　Now sing we, as we were wont,
　　　　*Vexilla regis prodeunt.*


## Lullay, Lullay, Like a Child

With lullay, lullay, like a child,
Thou sleep'st too long, thou art beguiled.

My darling dear, my daisy floure,
　　Let me, quod he, lie in your lap.
Lie still, quod she, my paramoure,
　　Lie still hardlie,[2] and take a nap.
　　His head was heavy, such was his hap,
All drowsy dreaming, drowned in sleep,
That of his love he took no keep,
　　With hey lullay, lullay, like a child,
　　Thou sleep'st too long, thou art beguiled.

With ba,[3] ba, ba! and bas, bas, bas!
　　She cherished him both cheek and chin,
That he wist never where he was:
　　He had forgotten all deadly sin.
　　He wanted wit her love to win:
He trusted her payment and lost all his pay;

---

[1] assuredly　　[2] with confidence　　[3] kiss

She left him sleeping and stole away,
    With hey lullay, lullay, like a child,
    Thou sleep'st too long, thou art beguiled.

The rivers rough, the waters wan,
    She sparèd not to wet her feet;
She waded over, she found a man
    That halsèd[1] her heartily and kissed her sweet:
    Thus after her cold she caught a heat.
My love, she said, routeth[2] in his bed;
Ywis[3] he hath an heavy head,
    With hey lullay, lullay, like a child,
    Thou sleep'st too long, thou art beguiled.

What dream'st thou, drunkard, drowsy pate?
    Thy lust and liking is from thee gone;
Thou blinkard blowboll,[4] thou wakest too late,
    Behold thou liest, luggard, alone!
    Well may thou sigh, well may thou groan,
To deal with her so cowardly:
Ywis, pole hatchet,[5] she bleared thine eye.


### *To Mistress Isabel Pennell*

    By Saint Mary, my lady,
    Your mammy and your daddy
    Brought forth a goodly baby.

    My maiden Isabel,
    Reflaring[6] rosabel,
    The flagrant camomel,

    The ruddy rosary,
    The sovereign rosemary,
    The pretty strawberry,

[1] embraced    [2] snores    [3] assuredly    [4] blink-eyed drunkard    [5] a man who gossips around an ale-pole, the sign of an inn    [6] redolent

The columbine, the nept,[1]
The jelofer[2] well set,
The proper violet;

Ennewèd your colour
Is like the daisy flower
After the April shower.

Star of the morrow gray,
The blossom on the spray,
The freshest flower of May,

Maidenly demure,
Of womanhood the lure;
Wherefore I you assure,

It were an heavenly health,
It were an endless wealth,
A life for God himself,

To hear this nightingale
Among the birdès small
Warbling in the vale,

"Dug, dug,
Jug, jug!
Good year and good luck!"
With "Chuck, chuck, chuck, chuck!"


### To Mistress Margaret Hussey

Merry Margaret, as midsummer flower,
Gentle as falcon or hawk of the tower,
With solace and gladness,
Much mirth and no madness,
All good and no badness;

[1] mint   [2] gillyflower

So joyously,
So maidenly,
So womanly,
Her demeaning;
In every thing
Far far passing
That I can indite
Or suffice to write
Of merry Margaret, as midsummer flower,
Gentle as falcon or hawk of the tower.
As patient and as still,
And as full of good will,
As the fair Isyphill,
Coliander,[1]
Sweet pomander,
Good Cassander;
Steadfast of thought,
Well made, well wrought.
Far may be sought
Erst than ye can find
So courteous, so kind,
As merry Margaret, the midsummer flower,
Gentle as falcon or hawk of the tower.


SIR   THOMAS   WYATT/1503?–1542


*The Long Love*

The long love that in my thought doth harbour,
And in mine heart doth keep his residence,
Into my face presseth with bold pretence,
And therein campeth, spreading his banner.
She that me learneth to love and suffer,
And wills that my trust and lust's negligence

[1] coriander

Be reined by reason, shame, and reverence,
With his hardiness taketh displeasure.
Wherewithal, unto the heart's forest he fleeth,
Leaving his enterprise with pain and cry;
And there him hideth, and not appeareth.
What may I do when my master feareth
But in the field with him to live and die?
For good is the life ending faithfully.

## Whoso List to Hunt

Whoso list to hunt, I know where is an hind,
But as for me, *helas!* I may no more.
The vain travail hath wearied me so sore,
I am of them that furthest come behind.
Yet may I, by no means, my wearied mind
Draw from the deer; but as she fleeth afore
Fainting I follow. I leave off therefore,
Since in a net I seek to hold the wind.
Who list her hunt, I put him out of doubt,
As well as I, may spend his time in vain;
And graven with diamonds in letters plain
There is written, her fair neck round about,
*"Noli me tangere,* for Caesar's I am,
And wild for to hold, though I seem tame."

## Farewell, Love

Farewell, Love, and all thy laws forever:
Thy baited hooks shall tangle me no more;
Senec and Plato call me from thy lore,
To perfect wealth my wit for to endeavor.
In blind error when I did persevere,
Thy sharp repulse that pricketh aye so sore
Hath taught me to set in trifles no store
And scape forth, since liberty is liefer.
Therefore, farewell: go trouble younger hearts,

And in me claim no more authority;
With idle youth go use thy property
And thereon spend thy many brittle darts:
For hitherto though I have lost all my time,
Me lusteth no longer rotten boughs to climb.


### Some Fowls There Be

Some fowls there be that have so perfect sight
Again the sun their eyes for to defend,
And some, because the light doth them offend,
Do never peer but in the dark or night.
Others rejoice that see the fire so bright
And wene to play in it as they do pretend,
And find the contrary of it that they intend.
Alas, of that sort I may be by right,
For to withstand her look I am not able;
Yet can I not hide me in no dark place,
Remembrance so followeth me of that face,
So that with teary eyen swollen and unstable,
My destiny to behold her doth me lead;
Yet do I know I run into the glede.[1]


### My Galley

My galley, chargèd with forgetfulness,
Thorough sharp seas in winter nights doth pass
'Tween rock and rock; and eke mine enemy, alas!
That is my Lord, steereth with cruelness;
And every oar a thought in readiness,
As though that death were light in such a case.
An endless wind doth tear the sail apace
Of forcèd sighs, and trusty fearfulness;
A rain of tears, a cloud of dark disdain,
Hath done the wearèd cords great hinderance,

[1] live coal

Wreathèd with error and eke with ignorance.
The stars be hid that led me to this pain.
Drownèd is reason that should me comfort,
And I remain despairing of the port.


## They Flee from Me

They flee from me, that sometime did me seek,
With naked foot, stalking in my chamber:
I have seen them gentle, tame, and meek,
That now are wild, and do not remember
That sometime they put themselves in danger
To take bread at my hand; and now they range,
Busily seeking with a continual change.

Thankèd be fortune, it hath been otherwise
Twenty times better; but once, in special,
In thin array, after a pleasant guise,
When her loose gown from her shoulders did fall,
And she me caught in her arms long and small,
Therewithal sweetly did me kiss,
And softly said, "Dear heart, how like you this?"

It was no dream; I lay broad waking.
But all is turned, thorough my gentleness,
Into a strange fashion of forsaking;
And I have leave to go of her goodness,
And she also to use new-fangledness.
But since that I so kindly am served,
I would fain know what she hath deserved.


## Marvel No More

Marvel no more although
  The songs I sing do moan,
For other life than woe
  I never provèd none.

And in my heart also
   Is graven with letters deep
A thousand sighs and mo,
   A flood of tears to weep.

How may a man in smart
   Find matter to rejoice?
How may a mourning heart
   Set forth a pleasant voice?

Play who that can that part:
   Needs must in me appear
How fortune, overthwart,
   Doth cause my mourning cheer.

Perdy! there is no man
   If he never saw sight,
That perfectly tell can
   The nature of the light.

Alas! how should I than,
   That never taste but sour,
But do as I began
   Continually to lour.

But yet perchance some chance
   May chance to change my tune;
And when such chance doth chance
   Then shall I thank fortune.

And if such chance do chance,
   Perchance, ere it be long,
For such a pleasant chance
   To sing some pleasant song.

## My Lute, Awake!

My lute, awake! perform the last
Labour that thou and I shall waste,
  And end that I have now begun;
For when this song is sung and past,
  My lute, be still, for I have done.

As to be heard where ear is none,
As lead to grave[1] in marble stone,
  My song may pierce her heart as soon.
Should we then sigh, or sing, or moan?
  No, no, my lute, for I have done.

The rocks do not so cruelly
Repulse the waves continually,
  As she my suit and affection;
So that I am past remedy,
  Whereby my lute and I have done.

Proud of the spoil that thou hast got
Of simple hearts thorough love's shot,
  By whom, unkind, thou hast them won,
Think not he hath his bow forgot,
  Although my lute and I have done.

Vengeance shall fall on thy disdain,
That makest but game on earnest pain;
  Think not alone under the sun
Unquit[2] to cause thy lovers plain,
  Although my lute and I have done.

Perchance thee lie withered and old,
The winter nights that are so cold,
  Plaining in vain unto the moon;
Thy wishes then dare not be told.
  Care then who list, for I have done.

[1] engrave  [2] unrequited

And then may chance thee to repent
The time that thou hast lost and spent
   To cause thy lovers sigh and swoon;
Then shalt thou know beauty but lent,
   And wish and want as I have done.

Now cease, my lute! this is the last
Labour that thou and I shall waste,
   And ended is that we begun;
Now is this song both sung and past.
   My lute, be still, for I have done.

### *To Cause Accord*

To cause accord or to agree,
Two contraries in one degree,
And in one point, as seemeth me,
To all man's wit, it cannot be,
   It is impossible.

Of heat and cold when I complain,
And say that heat doth cause my pain,
When cold doth shake me every vein,
And both at once, I say again,
   It is impossible.

That man that hath his heart away,
If life liveth there, as men do say,
That he heartless should last one day
Alive, and not to turn to clay,
   It is impossible.

'Twixt life and death, say what who saith,
There liveth no life that draweth breath,
They join so near, and eke, i' faith,
To seek for life by wish of death,
   It is impossible.

Yet love that all thing doth subdue,
Whose power there may no life eschew,
Hath wrought in me that I may rue
These miracles to be so true,
    That are impossible.


### Tagus, Farewell

Tagus, farewell, that westward with thy streams
  Turns up the grains of gold already tried;
For I with spur and sail go seek the Thames,
  Gainward[1] the sun that showeth her wealthy pride,
And to the town that Brutus sought by dreams,
  Like bended moon, doth lean her lusty side.
    My king, my country, alone for whom I live,
Of mighty love the wings for this me give.


### My Pen

My pen, take pain a little space
To follow that which doth me chase,
  And hath in hold my heart so sore;
But when thou hast this brought to pass,
  My pen, I prithee, write no more.

Remember, oft thou hast me eased,
And all my pain full well appeased;
  But now I know, unknown before,
For where I trust I am deceived;
  And yet, my pen, thou canst no more.

A time thou hadst, as others have,
To write which way my hope to crave;
  That time is past, withdraw therefore.

[1] flowing against

Since we do lose that others save,
    As good leave off and write no more.

In worth to use another way,
Not as we would, but as we may;
    For once my loss is past restore,
And my desire is my decay,
    My pen, yet write a little more.

To love in vain who ever shall,
Of worldly pain it passeth all,
    As in like case I find. Wherefore
To hold so fast and yet to fall!
    Alas! my pen, now write no more.

Since thou hast taken pain this space
To follow that which doth me chase,
    And hath in hold my heart so sore,
Now hast thou brought my mind to pass.
    My pen, I prithee write no more.

### And Wilt Thou Leave Me Thus?

And wilt thou leave me thus?
    Say nay, say nay, for shame!
    To save thee from the blame
    Of all my grief and grame.[1]
And wilt thou leave me thus?
        Say nay! say nay!

And wilt thou leave me thus,
    That hath loved thee so long
    In wealth and woe among?
    And is thy heart so strong
As for to leave me thus?
        Say nay! say nay!

- [1] vexation

And wilt thou leave me thus,
　　That hath given thee my heart,
　　Never for to depart
　　Neither for pain nor smart;
And wilt thou leave me thus?
　　Say nay! say nay!

And wilt thou leave me thus,
　　And have no more pity
　　Of him that loveth thee?
　　*Helas!* thy cruelty!
And wilt thou leave me thus?
　　Say nay! say nay!

## Forget Not Yet

Forget not yet the tried intent
Of such a truth as I have meant;
My great travail so gladly spent
　　Forget not yet!

Forget not yet when first began
The weary life ye know, since whan
The suit, the service, none tell can;
　　Forget not yet!

Forget not yet the great assays,
The cruel wrong, the scornful ways,
The painful patience in denays,
　　Forget not yet!

Forget not yet, forget not this,
How long ago hath been, and is,
The mind that never meant amiss
　　Forget not yet!

Forget not then thine own approved,
The which so long hath thee so loved,

Whose steadfast faith yet never moved;
Forget not this!

## Blame Not My Lute

Blame not my lute! for he must sound
Of these and that as liketh me;
For lack of wit the lute is bound
To give such tunes as pleaseth me.
Though my songs be somewhat strange,
And speaks such words as touch thy change,
Blame not my lute!

My lute, alas! doth not offend,
Though that perforce he must agree
To sound such tunes as I intend
To sing to them that heareth me;
Then though my songs be somewhat plain,
And toucheth some that use to feign,
Blame not my lute!

My lute and strings may not deny,
But as I strike they must obey;
Break not them then so wrongfully,
But wreak thyself some wiser way;
And though the songs which I indite
Do quit thy change with rightful spite,
Blame not my lute!

Spite asketh spite, and changing change,
And falsèd faith must needs be known;
The fault so great, the case so strange,
Of right it must abroad be blown;
Then since that by thine own desert
My songs do tell how true thou art,
Blame not my lute!

Blame but thy self that hast misdone
   And well deservèd to have blame;
Change thou thy way, so evil begone,[1]
   And then my lute shall sound that same;
But if till then my fingers play
By thy desert their wonted way,
      Blame not my lute!

Farewell, unknown! for though thou break
   My strings in spite with great disdain,
Yet have I found out, for thy sake,
   Strings for to string my lute again.
And if, perchance, this silly rhyme
Do make thee blush at any time,
      Blame not my lute!

### What Should I Say

What should I say,
   Since faith is dead,
And truth away
   From you is fled?
   Should I be led
     With doubleness?
     Nay, nay, mistress!

I promised you,
   And you promised me,
To be as true,
   As I would be.
   But since I see
     Your double heart,
     Farewell my part!

Though for to take
   It is not my mind,

[1] conditioned

But to forsake
        One so unkind,
    And as I find
            So will I trust,
            Farewell, unjust!


Can ye say nay,
        But that you said
That I alway
        Should be obeyed?
        And thus betrayed,
            Or that I wist,
            Farewell, unkissed!


### Mine Own John Poins

Mine own John Poins, since ye delight to know
    The cause why that homeward I me draw,
And fly the press of courts whereso they go,


Rather than to live thrall, under the awe
    Of lordly looks, wrapped within my cloak,
To will and lust learning to set a law;


It is not for because I scorn and mock
    The power of them, to whom fortune hath lent
Charge over us, of right, to strike the stroke.


But true it is that I have always meant
    Less to esteem them than the common sort,
Of outward things that judge in their intent,


Without regard what doth inward resort.
    I grant some time that of glory the fire
Doth touch my heart; me list not to report

Blame by honour, and honour to desire.
　　But how may I this honour now attain,
That cannot dye the colour black a liar?

My Poins, I cannot frame my tune to feign,
　　To cloak the truth for praise without desert
Of them that list all vice for to retain.

I cannot honour them that sets their part
　　With Venus and Bacchus all their life long,
Nor hold my peace of them although I smart.

I cannot crouch nor kneel to do so great a wrong,
　　To worship them, like God on earth alone,
That are as wolves these silly lambs among.

I cannot with my words complain and moan,
　　Nor suffer nought, nor smart without complaint,
Nor turn the word that from my mouth is gone.

I cannot speak and look like as a saint;
　　Use wiles for wit, or make deceit a pleasure;
And call craft counsel, for profit still to paint.

I cannot wrest the law to fill the coffer
　　With innocent blood to feed myself fat,
And do most hurt where that most help I offer.

I am not he that can allow the state
　　Of high Caesar, and damn Cato to die,
That with his death did 'scape out of the gate

From Caesar's hands (if Livy do not lie),
　　And would not live when liberty was lost;
So did his heart the common weal apply.

I am not he such eloquence to boast
　　To make the crow singing as the swan;
Nor call the lion of coward beasts the most,

That cannot take a mouse as the cat can;
   And he that dieth for hunger of the gold,
Call him Alexander; and say that Pan

Passeth Apollo in music manifold;
   Praise Sir Thopas for a noble tale,
And scorn the story that the knight told;

Praise him for counsel that is drunk of ale,
   Grin when he laugheth that beareth all the sway,
Frown when he frowneth and groan when he is pale;

On others' lust to hang both night and day.
   None of these points would ever frame in me;
My wit is nought, I cannot learn the way.

And much the less of things that greater be,
   That asken help of colours of device
To join the mean with each extremity,

With the nearest virtue to cloak alway the vice.
   And as to purpose, likewise it shall fall
To press the virtue that it may not rise;

As drunkenness good fellowship to call;
   The friendly foe with his double face,
Say he is gentle, and courteous therewithal;

And say that favell[1] hath a goodly grace
   In eloquence; and cruelty to name
Zeal of justice, and change in time and place;

And he that suffereth offence without blame,
   Call him pitiful; and him true and plain
That raileth reckless to every man's shame;

[1] flattery

Say he is rude that cannot lie and feign;
   The lecher a lover; and tyranny
To be the right of a prince's reign.

I cannot, I. No, no, it will not be.
   This is the cause that I could never yet
Hang on their sleeves, that weigh, as thou mayst see,

A chip of chance more than a pound of wit;
   This maketh me at home to hunt and to hawk,
And in foul weather at my book to sit;

In frost and snow then with my bow to stalk.
   No man doth mark where so I ride or go;
In lusty leas at liberty I walk;

And of these news I feel nor weal nor woe,
   Save that a clog doth hang yet at my heel.
No force for that, for it is ordered so,

That I may leap both hedge and dyke full well.
   I am not now in France to judge the wine,
With savoury sauce the delicates to feel;

Nor yet in Spain where one must him incline,
   Rather than to be, outwardly to seem;
I meddle not with wits that be so fine.

Nor Flanders' cheer letteth not my sight to deem
   Of black and white, nor taketh my wit away
With beastliness, they beasts do so esteem.

Nor I am not where Christ is given in prey
   For money, poison and treason at Rome,
A common practice used night and day.

But here I am in Kent and Christendom,
  Among the Muses where I read and rhyme.
Where if thou list, my Poins, for to come,
  Thou shalt be judge how I do spend my time.


# THOMAS, LORD VAUX/1510–1556

*The Aged Lover Renounceth Love*

I loathe that I did love,
  In youth that I thought sweet,
As time requires for my behove,
  Methinks they are not meet.

My lusts they do me leave,
  My fancies all be fled,
And tract of time begins to weave
  Grey hairs upon my head.

For age with stealing steps
  Hath clawed me with his crutch,
And lusty life away she leaps
  As there had been none such.

My Muse doth not delight
  Me as she did before;
My hand and pen are not in plight,
  As they have been of yore.

For reason me denies
  This youthly idle rhyme;
And day by day to me she cries,
  "Leave off these toys in time."

The wrinkles in my brow,
  The furrows in my face,

Say, limping age will lodge him now
   Where youth must give him place.

The harbinger of death,
   To me I see him ride,
The cough, the cold, the gasping breath
   Doth bid me to provide

A pickaxe and a spade,
   And eke a shrouding sheet,
A house of clay for to be made
   For such a guest most meet.

Methinks I hear the clark
   That knolls the careful knell,
And bids me leave my woeful wark,
   Ere nature me compel.

My keepers knit the knot
   That youth did laugh to scorn,
Of me that clean shall be forgot
   As I had not been born.

Thus must I youth give up,
   Whose badge I long did wear;
To them I yield the wanton cup
   That better may it bear.

Lo, here the barèd skull,
   By whose bald sign I know
That stooping age away shall pull
   Which youthful years did sow.

For beauty with her band
   These crooked cares hath wrought,
And shippèd me into the land
   From whence I first was brought.

And ye that bide behind,
   Have ye none other trust:
As ye of clay were cast by kind,
   So shall ye waste to dust.


# HENRY HOWARD, EARL OF SURREY
## 1517?–1547


### *Prison in Windsor Castle*

So cruel prison how could betide, alas,
As proud Windsor, where I in lust and joy
With a king's son my childish years did pass
In greater feast than Priam's sons of Troy?
Where each sweet place returns a taste full sour;
The large green courts where we were wont to hove
With eyes cast up unto the maidens' tower,
And easy sighs, such as folk draw in love;
The stately sails, the ladies bright of hue,
The dances short, long tales of great delight,
With words and looks that tigers could but rue,
Where each of us did plead the other's right;
The palm-play where, despoilèd for the game,
With dazèd eyes oft we by gleams of love
Have missed the ball and got sight of our dame,
To bait her eyes, which kept the leads above;
The gravelled ground, with sleeves tied on the helm,
On foaming horse, with swords and friendly hearts,
With cheer, as though the one should overwhelm,
Where we have fought and chasèd oft with darts;
With silver drops the meads yet spread for ruth,
In active games of nimbleness and strength,
Where we did strain, trailed by swarms of youth,
Our tender limbs that yet shot up in length;
The secret groves which oft we made resound
Of pleasant plaint and of our ladies' praise,

Recording soft what grace each one had found,
What hope of speed, what dread of long delays;
The wild forest, the clothèd holts with green,
With reins avaled,[1] and swift ybreathèd horse,
With cry of hounds and merry blasts between,
Where we did chase the fearful hart a force;
The void walls eke that harboured us each night,
Wherewith, alas! revive within my breast
The sweet accord, such sleeps as yet delight,
The pleasant dreams, the quiet bed of rest,
The secret thoughts imparted with such trust,
The wanton talk, the divers change of play,
The friendship sworn, each promise kept so just,
Wherewith we passed the winter nights away.
And with this thought the blood forsakes my face,
The tears berain my cheeks of deadly hue,
The which as soon as sobbing sighs, alas!
Upsuppèd have, thus I my plaint renew:
"O place of bliss, renewer of my woes,
Give me account where is my noble fere,[2]
Whom in thy walls thou didst each night enclose,
To other lief,[3] but unto me most dear."
Echo, alas! that doth my sorrow rue,
Returns thereto a hollow sound of plaint.
Thus I alone, where all my freedom grew,
In prison pine with bondage and restraint;
And with remembrance of the greater grief
To banish the less, I find my chief relief.

## Description of Spring

The soote[4] season, that bud and bloom forth brings,
With green hath clad the hill and eke the vale.
The nightingale with feathers new she sings;
The turtle to her make[5] hath told her tale.
Summer is come, for every spray now springs.

[1] lowered   [2] company   [3] beloved   [4] sweet   [5] mate

The hart hath hung his old head on the pale;
The buck in brake his winter coat he flings;
The fishes float with new repairèd scale;
The adder all her slough away she slings;
The swift swallow pursueth the flies small;
The busy bee her honey now she mings;[1]
Winter is worn that was the flowers' bale.
And thus I see among these pleasant things
Each care decays; and yet my sorrow springs.


### A Complaint by Night

Alas! so all things now do hold their peace,
Heaven and earth disturbèd in no thing.
The beasts, the air, the birds their song do cease;
The nightès chare[2] the stars about doth bring;
Calm is the sea; the waves work less and less.
So am not I, whom love, alas! doth wring,
Bringing before my face the great increase
Of my desires, whereat I weep and sing,
In joy and woe, as in a doubtful ease:
For my sweet thoughts sometime do pleasure bring;
But by and by, the cause of my disease
Gives me a pang, that inwardly doth sting,
When that I think what grief it is again,
To live and lack the thing should rid my pain.


### Complaint of the Absence of Her Lover
### Being upon the Sea

O happy dames, that may embrace
    The fruit of your delight,
Help to bewail the woeful case
    And eke the heavy plight
Of me, that wonted to rejoice

---

[1] remembers[2]    chariot

The fortune of my pleasant choice;
Good ladies, help to fill my mourning voice.

In ship, freight with rememberance
    Of thoughts and pleasures past,
He sails that hath in governance
    My life while it will last;
With scalding sighs, for lack of gale,
Furthering his hope, that is his sail,
Toward me, the sweet port of his avail.

Alas! how oft in dreams I see
    Those eyes that were my food;
Which sometime so delighted me,
    That yet they do me good;
Wherewith I wake with his return,
Whose absent flame did make me burn:
But when I find the lack, Lord, how I mourn!

When other lovers in arms across
    Rejoice their chief delight,
Drowned in tears, to mourn my loss
    I stand the bitter night
In my window, where I may see
Before the winds how the clouds flee.
Lo! what a mariner love hath made me!

And in green waves when the salt flood
    Doth rise by rage of wind,
A thousand fancies in that mood
    Assail my restless mind.
Alas! now drencheth my sweet foe,
That with the spoil of my heart did go,
And left me; but, alas! why did he so?

And when the seas wax calm again
    To chase fro me annoy,
My doubtful hope doth cause me plain;
    So dread cuts off my joy.

Thus is my wealth mingled with woe,
And of each thought a doubt doth grow;
"Now he comes! Will he come? Alas, no, no!"


# NICHOLAS GRIMALD/1519–1562

### Virtue

What one art thou, thus in torn weed yclad?
"Virtue, in price whom ancient sages had."
Why poorly 'rayed? "For fading goods past care."
Why double-faced? "I mark each fortune's fare."
This bridle, what? "Mind's rages to restrain."
Tools why bear you? "I love to take great pain."
Why wings? "I teach above the stars to fly."
Why tread you death? "I only cannot die."


# RICHARD EDWARDS/1523?–1566

### Amantium Irae

In going to my naked bed, as one that would have slept,
I heard a wife sing to her child, that long before had wept;
She sighed sore, and sang full sweet to bring the babe to rest,
That would not rest but cried still, in sucking at her breast.
She was full weary of her watch, and grievèd with her child,
She rockèd it and rated it, until on her it smiled.
Then did she say, "Now have I found this proverb true to
    prove,
*The falling out of faithful friends, renewing is of love.*"

Then took I paper, pen, and ink, this proverb for to write,
In register for to remain of such a worthy wight.

As she proceeded thus in song unto her little brat
Much matter uttered she of weight, in place whereas she sat:
And provèd plain there was no beast, nor creature bearing life
Could well be known to live in love, without discord and
     strife.
Then kissèd she her little babe, and sware, by God above,
*The falling out of faithful friends, renewing is of love.*

She said that neither king, ne prince, ne lord could live
     aright,
Until their puissance they did prove, their manhood, and
     their might:
When manhood shall be matchèd so, that fear can take no
     place,
Then weary works make warriors each other to embrace,
And leave their force that failèd them, which did consume the
     rout
That might by force with love have lived the term of nature
     out.
Then did she sing, as one that thought no man could her
     reprove,
*The falling out of faithful friends, renewing is of love.*

She said she saw no fish, ne fowl, nor beast within her haunt
That met a stranger in their kind, but could give it a taunt.
Since flesh might not endure, but rest must wrath succeed,
And force the fight to fall to play in pasture where they feed,
So noble Nature can well end the work she hath begun,
And bridle well that will not cease her tragedy in some.
Thus in her song she oft rehearsed, as did her well behove,
*The falling out of faithful friends, renewing is of love.*

"I marvel much, pardy," quoth she, "for to behold the route,
To see man, woman, boy, and beast, to toss the world about,
Some kneel, some crouch, some beck, some check, and some
     can smoothly smile,
And some embrace others in arms, and there think many
     wile;

Some stand aloof at cap and knee, some humble, and some
    stout,
Yet are they never friends in deed until they once fall out!"
Thus ended she her song, and said, before she did remove,
*The falling out of faithful friends, renewing is of love.*


# BARNABE GOOGE/1540–1594

### An Epitaph of the Death of Nicholas Grimald

Behold this fleeting world, how all things fade,
How everything doth pass and wear away,
Each state of life by common course and trade
Abides no time but hath a passing day.
For look, as Life, that pleasant dame, hath brought
The pleasant years and days of lustiness,
So Death, our foe, consumeth all to nought,
Envying these, with dart doth us oppress,
And that which is the greatest grief of all,
The greedy gripe doth no estate respect,
But where he comes he makes them down to fall,
Nor stays he at the high, sharp-witted sect.
For if that wit or worthy eloquence,
Or learning deep, could move him to forbear,
O Grimald, then thou hadst not yet gone hence
But here hadst seen full many an agèd year.
Nor had the Muses lost so fine a flower,
Nor had Minerva wept to leave thee so;
If wisdom might have fled the fatal hour,
Thou hadst not yet been suffered for to go;
A thousand doltish geese we might have spared,
A thousand witless heads Death might have found
And taken them, for whom no man had cared,
And laid them low in deep, oblivious ground.
But Fortune favors fools, as old men say,
And lets them live, and takes the wise away.

## The Lullaby of a Lover

Sing lullaby, as women do,
Wherewith they bring their babes to rest,
And lullaby can I sing too,
As womanly as can the best.
With lullaby they still the child,
And if I be not much beguiled,
Full many wanton babes have I,
Which must be stilled with lullaby.

First lullaby my youthful years,
It is now time to go to bed,
For crooked age and hoary hairs
Have won the haven within my head:
With lullaby then youth be still,
With lullaby content thy will,
Since courage quails and comes behind,
Go sleep, and so beguile thy mind.

Next lullaby my gazing eyes,
Which wonted were to glance apace.
For every glass may now suffice
To show the furrows in my face:
With lullaby then wink awhile,
With lullaby your looks beguile:
Let no fair face, nor beauty bright,
Entice you eft with vain delight.

And lullaby my wanton will,
Let reason rule, now rein thy thought,
Since all too late I find by skill
How dear I have my fancies bought:
With lullaby now take thine ease,
With lullaby thy doubts appease:

For trust to this, if thou be still,
My body shall obey thy will.

Eke lullaby my loving boy,
My little Robin take thy rest,
Since age is cold and nothing coy,
Keep close thy coign, for so is best:
With lullaby be thou content,
With lullaby thy lusts relent,
Let others pay which hath more pence,
Thou art too poor for such expense.

Thus lullaby my youth, mine eyes,
My will, my ware, and all that was,
I can no more delays devise,
But welcome pain, let pleasure pass:
With lullaby now take your leave,
With lullaby your dream deceive,
And when you rise with waking eye,
Remember then this lullaby.

### A Farewell

"And if I did, what then?
    Are you aggrieved therefore?
The sea hath fish for every man,
    And what would you have more?"

Thus did my mistress once
    Amaze my mind with doubt;
And popped a question for the nonce,
    To beat my brains about.

Whereto I thus replied:
    "Each fisherman can wish,
That all the seas at every tide
    Were his alone to fish.

"And so did I in vain,
  But since it may not be,
Let such fish there as find the gain,
  And leave the loss for me.

"And with such luck and loss
  I will content myself,
Till tides of turning time may toss
  Such fishers on the shelf.

"And when they stick on sands,
  That every man may see,
Then will I laugh and clap my hands,
  As they do now at me."


# ANONYMOUS BALLADS


### Sir Patrick Spens


The king sits in Dumferling toune,
  Drinking the blude-reid wine:
"O whar will I get guid sailor,
  To sail this schip of mine?"

Up and spak an eldern knicht,
  Sat at the kings richt kne:
"Sir Patrick Spens is the best sailor,
  That sails upon the se."

The king has written a braid[1] letter,
  And signd it wi his hand,
And sent it to Sir Patrick Spens,
  Was walking on the sand.

[1] broad

The first line that Sir Patrick red,
   A loud lauch lauchèd[1] he;
The next line that Sir Patrick red,
   The teir blinded his ee.

"O wha is this has don this deid,
   This ill deid don to me,
To send me out this time o' the yeir,
   To sail upon the se!

"Mak hast, mak haste, my mirry men all
   Our guid schip sails the morne:"
"O say na sae, my master deir,
   For I feir a deadlie storme.

"Late, late yestreen I saw the new moone,
Wi the auld moone in hir arme,
And I feir, I feir, my deir master,
   That we will cum to harme."

O our Scots nobles wer richt laith[2]
   To weet their cork-heild schoone;[3]
Bot lang owre[4] a' the play wer playd,
   Thair hats they swam aboone.

O lang, lang may their ladies sit,
   Wi thair fans into their hand,
Or eir they se Sir Patrick Spens
   Cum sailing to the land.

O lang, lang may the ladies stand,
   Wi thair gold kems[5] in their hair
Waiting for thar ain deir lords,
   For they'll se thame na mair.

Half owre,[6] half owre to Aberdour,
   It's fiftie fadom deip,

---

[1] laughed   [2] loath   [3] shoes   [4] ere   [5] combs   [6] over

And thair lies guid Sir Patrick Spens,
  Wi the Scots lords at his feit.


### The Wife of Usher's Well

There lived a wife at Usher's Well,
  And a wealthy wife was she;
She had three stout and stalwart sons,
  And sent them o'er the sea.

They hadna been a week from her,
  A week but barely ane,
Whan word came to the carlin[1] wife
  That her three sons were gane.

They hadna been a week from her,
  A week but barely three,
Whan word came to the carlin wife
  That her sons she'd never see.

"I wish the wind may never cease,
  Nor fashes[2] in the flood,
Till my three sons come hame to me,
  In earthly flesh and blood."

It fell about the Martinmass,
  When nights are lang and mirk,
The carlin wife's three sons came hame,
  And their hats were o the birk.[3]

It neither grew in syke[4] nor ditch,
  Nor yet in ony sheugh;[5]
But at the gates o Paradise,
  That birk grew fair eneugh.

[1] old woman   [2] troubles   [3] birch   [4] trench   [5] furrow

"Blow up the fire, my maidens,
  Bring water from the well;
For a' my house shall feast this night,
  Since my three sons are well."

And she has made to them a bed,
  She's made it large and wide,
And she's taen her mantle her about,
  Sat down at the bed-side.

Up then crew the red, red cock,
  And up and crew the gray;
The eldest to the youngest said,
  " 'Tis time we were away."

The cock he hadna crawd but once,
  And clappd his wings at a',
When the youngest to the eldest said,
  "Brother, we must awa.

"The cock doth craw, the day doth daw,
  The channerin[1] worm doth chide;
Gin we be mist out o our place,
  A sair pain we maun bide.

"Fare ye weel, my mother dear!
  Fareweel to barn and byre!
And fare ye weel, the bonny lass
  That kindles my mother's fire!"

### The Laily Worm and the Machrel of the Sea

"I was but seven year auld
  When my mither she did dee,
My father married the ae warst woman
  The warld did ever see.

[1] devouring

"For she has made me the laily[1] worm
   That lies at the foot of the tree,
An' o' my sister Maisry
   The machrel of the sea.

"An' every Saturday at noon
   The machrel comes to me,
An' she takes my laily head,
   An' lays it on her knee,
An' kames it wi' a siller kame,
   An' washes it in the sea.

"Seven knights hae I slain
   Sin I lay at the foot of the tree;
An' ye war nae my ain father,
   The eighth ane ye should be."

"Sing on your song, ye laily worm,
   That ye sung to me."
"I never sung that song
   But what I would sing to ye.

"I was but seven year auld
   When my mither she did dee,
My father married the ae warst woman
   The warld did ever see.

"She changed me to the laily worm
   That lies at the foot of the tree,
And my sister Maisry
   To the machrel of the sea.

"And every Saturday at noon
   The machrel comes to me,
An' she takes my laily head,
   An' lays it on her knee,

[1] loathly

An' kames it wi' a siller kame,
    An' washes it i' the sea.

"Seven knights hae I slain
    Sin I lay at the foot o' the tree;
An' ye war nae my ain father,
    The eighth ane ye should be."

He sent for his lady
    As fast as send could he:
"Whar is my son,
    That ye sent frae me,
And my daughter,
    Lady Maisry?"

"Your son is at our king's court,
    Serving for meat an' fee,
And your daughter is at our queen's court,
    The queen's maiden to be."

"Ye lee, ye lee, ye ill woman,
    Sae loud as I hear ye lee,
For my son is the laily worm
    That lays at the foot of the tree,
And my daughter Maisry
    The machrel of the sea."

She has ta'en a silver wan'
    An' gi'en him strokes three,
And he started up the bravest knight
    Your eyes did ever see.

She has ta'en a small horn
    An' loud an' shrill blew she;
An' a' the fish came her untill
    But the machrel of the sea:
"Ye shaped me ance an unseemly shape,
    An' ye'll never mare shape me."

He has sent to the wood
   For hathorn an' whin,
An' he has ta'en that gay lady,
   An' there he did her burn.


### Lord Randal

"O where hae ye been, Lord Randal, my son?
  O where hae ye been, my handsome young man?"
   "I hae been to the wild wood; mother, make my bed soon,
   For I'm weary wi hunting, and fain wald lie down."

"Where gat ye your dinner, Lord Randal, my son?
  Where gat ye your dinner, my handsome young man?"
   "I dined wi my true-love; mother, make my bed soon,
   For I'm weary wi hunting, and fain wald lie down."

"What gat ye to your dinner, Lord Randal, my son?
  What gat ye to your dinner, my handsome young man?"
   "I gat eels boiled in broo;[1] mother, make my bed soon,
   For I'm weary wi hunting, and fain wald lie down."

"What became of your bloodhounds, Lord Randal, my son?
  What became of your bloodhounds, my handsome young
  man?"
   "O they swelld and they died; mother, make my bed soon,
   For I'm weary wi hunting, and fain wald lie down."

"O I fear ye are poisond, Lord Randal, my son!
  O I fear ye are poisond, my handsome young man!"
   "O yes! I am poisond; mother, make my bed soon,
   For I'm sick at the heart, and I fain wald lie down."

[1] broth

## Edward

"Why dois your brand sae drap wi bluid,
      Edward, Edward,
Why dois your brand sae drap wi bluid,
  And why sae sad gang[1] yee O?"
"O I hae killed my hauke sae guid,
      Mither, mither,
O I hae killed my hauke sae guid,
  And I had nae mair bot hee O."

"Your haukis bluid was nevir sae reid,
      Edward, Edward,
Your haukis bluid was nevir sae reid,
  My deir son I tell thee O."
"O I hae killed my reid-roan steid,
      Mither, mither,
O I hae killed my reid-roan steid,
  That erst was sae fair and frie O."

"Your steid was auld, and ye hae got mair,
      Edward, Edward,
Your steid was auld, and ye hae got mair,
  Sum other dule[2] ye drie[3] O."
"O I hae killed my fadir deir,
      Mither, mither,
O I hae killed my fadir deir,
  Alas, and wae is mee O!"

"And whatten penance wul ye drie for that,
      Edward, Edward,
And whatten penance will ye drie for that?
  My deir son, now tell me O."
"Ile set my feit in yonder boat,
      Mither, mither,
Ile set my feit in yonder boat,
  And Ile fare ovir the sea O."

[1] go   [2] grief   [3] suffer

"And what wul ye doe wi your towirs and your ha,[1]
      Edward, Edward?
And what wul ye doe wi your towirs and your ha,
    That were sae fair to see O?"
"Ile let thame stand tul they doun fa,
      Mither, mither,
Ile let thame stand tul they doun fa,
    For here nevir mair maun I bee O."

"And what wul ye leive to your bairns and your wife,
      Edward, Edward?
And what wul ye leive to your bairns and your wife,
    Whan ye gang ovir the sea O?"
"The warldis room, late them beg thrae life,
      Mither, mither,
The warldis room, late them beg thrae life,
    For thame nevir mair wul I see O."

"And what wul ye leive to your ain mither deir,
      Edward, Edward?
And what wul ye leive to your ain mither deir?
    My deir son, now tell me O."
"The curse of hell frae me sall ye beir,
      Mither, mither,
The curse of hell frae me sall ye beir,
    Sic counseils ye gave to me O."


## The Demon Lover

"O where have you been, my long, long love,
    This long seven years and mair?"
"O I'm come to seek my former vows
    Ye granted me before."

"O hold your tongue of your former vows,
    For they will breed sad strife;

[1] hall

O hold your tongue of your former vows,
  For I am become a wife."

He turned him right and round about,
  And the tear blinded his ee:
"I wad never hae trodden on Irish ground,
  If it had not been for thee.

"I might hae had a king's daughter,
  Far, far beyond the sea;
I might have had a king's daughter,
  Had it not been for love o thee."

"If ye might have had a king's daughter,
  Yer sel ye had to blame;
Ye might have had taken the king's daughter,
  For ye kend[1] that I was nane.

"If I was to leave my husband dear,
  And my two babes also,
O what have you to take me to,
  If with you I should go?"

"I hae seven ships upon the sea—
  The eighth brought me to land—
With four-and-twenty bold mariners,
  And music on every hand."

She has taken up her two little babes,
  Kissd them baith cheek and chin:
"O fair ye weel, my ain two babes,
  For I'll never see you again."

She set her foot upon the ship,
  No mariners could she behold;
But the sails were o the taffetie,
  And the masts o the beaten gold.

[1] knew

She had not sailed a league, a league,
   A league but barely three,
When dismal grew his countenance,
   And drumlie[1] grew his ee.

They had not saild a league, a league,
   A league but barely three,
Until she espied his cloven foot,
   And she wept right bitterlie.

"O hold your tongue of your weeping," says he,
   "Of your weeping now let me be;
I will shew you how the lilies grow
   On the banks of Italy."

"O what hills are yon, yon pleasant hills,
   That the sun shines sweetly on?"
"O yon are the hills of heaven," he said,
   "Where you will never win."

"O whaten a mountain is yon," she said,
   "All so dreary wi frost and snow?"
"O yon is the mountain of hell," he cried,
   "Where you and I will go."

He strack the tap-mast wi his hand,
   The fore-mast wi his knee,
And he brake that gallant ship in twain,
   And sank her in the sea.

### The Twa Corbies

As I was walking all alane,
I heard twa corbies[2] making a mane:
The tane unto the tither did say,
"Whar sall we gang and dine the day?"

___
[1] dark  [2] ravens

"In behint yon auld fail[1] dyke
I wot there lies a new-slain knight;
And naebody kens that he lies there
But his hawk, his hound, and his lady fair.

"His hound is to the hunting gane,
His hawk to fetch the wild-fowl hame,
His lady's ta'en anither mate,
So we may mak our dinner sweet.

"Ye'll sit on his white hause[2]-bane,
And I'll pike out his bonny blue e'en:
Wi' ae lock o' his gowden hair
We'll theek[3] our nest when it grows bare.

"Mony a one for him maks mane,
But nane sall ken whar he is gane:
O'er his white banes, when they are bare,
The wind sall blaw for evermair."

## The Three Ravens

There were three ravens sat on a tree,
  Downe a downe, hay downe, hay downe.
There were three ravens sat on a tree,
  With a downe.
There were three ravens sat on a tree,
They were as blacke as they might be.
  With a downe derrie, derrie, derrie, downe, downe.

The one of them said to his mate,
"Where shall we our breakefast take?"

"Downe in yonder greene field,
There lies a knight slain under his shield.

[1] turf   [2] neck   [3] thatch

"His hounds they lie downe at his feete,
So well they can their master keepe.

"His haukes they flie so eagerly,
There's no fowle dare him come nie."

Downe there comes a fallow doe,
As great with yong as she might goe.

She lift up his bloudy hed,
And kist his wounds that were so red.

She got him up upon her backe,
And carried him to earthen lake.[1]

She buried him before the prime,
She was dead herselfe ere even-song time.

God send every gentleman,
Such haukes, such hounds, and such a leman.[2]


### Barbara Allen

In Scarlet town, where I was born,
    There was a fair maid dwellin',
Made every youth cry *Well-a-way!*
    Her name was Barbara Allen.

All in the merry month of May,
    When green buds they were swellin',
Young Jemmy Grove on his death-bed lay,
    For love of Barbara Allen.

He sent his man in to her then,
    To the town where she was dwellin';

[1] pit   [2] loved one: sweetheart, wife

"O haste and come to my master dear,
    If your name be Barbara Allen."

So slowly, slowly rase she up,
    And slowly she came nigh him,
And when she drew the curtain by—
    "Young man, I think you're dyin'."

"O it's I am sick and very very sick,
    And it's all for Barbara Allen."—
"O the better for me ye'se never be,
    Tho' your heart's blood were a-spillin'!

"O dinna ye mind, young man," says she,
    "When the red wine ye were fillin',
That ye made the healths go round and round,
    And slighted Barbara Allen?"

He turned his face unto the wall,
    And death was with him dealin':
"Adieu, adieu, my dear friends all,
    And be kind to Barbara Allen!"

As she was walking o'er the fields,
    She heard the dead-bell knellin';
And every jow[1] the dead-bell gave
    Cried "Woe to Barbara Allen."

"O mother, mother, make my bed,
    O make it saft and narrow:
My love has died for me to-day,
    I'll die for him to-morrow.

"Farewell," she said, "ye virgins all,
    And shun the fault I fell in:
Henceforth take warning by the fall
    Of cruel Barbara Allen."

[1] toll

## Bonny George Campbell

Hie upon Hielands,
  And laigh[1] upon Tay,
Bonny George Campbell
  Rade out on a day:
Saddled and bridled,
  Sae gallant to see,
Hame cam his gude horse,
  But never cam' he.

Down ran his auld mither,
  Greetin[2] fu' sair;
Out ran his bonny bride,
  Reaving[3] her hair;
"My meadow lies green,
  And my corn is unshorn,
My barn is to bigg,[4]
  And my babe is unborn."

Saddled and bridled
  And booted rade he;
A plume in his helmet,
  A sword at his knee;
But toom[5] cam his saddle
  A' bluidy to see,
O hame cam his gude horse,
  But never cam he!

## The Bonny Earl of Murray

Ye Highlands, and ye Lawlands,
  O where have ye been?
They hae slain the Earl of Murray,
  And they layd him on the green.

[1] low   [2] crying   [3] tearing   [4] build   [5] empty

Now wae be to thee, Huntley!
And whairfore did you sae?
I bade you bring him wi' you,
    But forbade you him to slay.

He was a braw gallant,
    And he rid at the ring;
And the bonny Earl of Murray,
    O he might hae been a king!

He was a braw gallant,
    And he playd at the ba';
And the bonny Earl of Murray
    Was the flower amang them a'.

He was a braw gallant,
    And he playd at the gluve;
And the bonny Earl of Murray,
    O he was the Queen's luve!

O lang will his lady
    Look owre the castle Downe,
Ere she see the Earl of Murray
    Come sounding thro the town!

## Helen of Kirconnell

I wish I were where Helen lies,
Night and day on me she cries;
O that I were where Helen lies
    On fair Kirconnell lea!

Curst be the heart that thought the thought,
And curst the hand that fired the shot,
When in my arms burd Helen dropt,
    And died to succour me!

O think na ye my heart was sair,
When my Love dropt down and spake nae mair!
I laid her down wi' meikle care
  On fair Kirconnell lea;

As I went down the water-side,
None but my foe to be my guide,
None but my foe to be my guide
  On fair Kirconnell lea;

I lighted down my sword to draw,
I hacked him in pieces sma',
I hacked him in pieces sma',
  For her sake that died for me.

O Helen fair, beyond compare!
I'll make a garland o' thy hair
Shall bind my heart for evermair
  Until the day I dee!

O that I were where Helen lies!
Night and day on me she cries;
Out of my bed she bids me rise,
  Says, "Haste, and come to me!"

O Helen fair! O Helen chaste!
If I were with thee, I were blest,
Where thou lies low and takes thy rest,
  On fair Kirconnell lea.

I wish my grave were growing green,
A winding-sheet drawn ower my een,
And I in Helen's arms lying,
  On fair Kirconnell lea.

I wish I were where Helen lies!
Night and day on me she cries;
And I am weary of the skies,
  Since my Love died for me.

### Mary Hamilton

Word's gane to the kitchen,
 And word's gane to the ha',
That Mary Hamilton gangs wi' bairn
 To the highest Stewart of a'.

He's courted her in the kitchen,
 He's courted her in the ha',
He's courted her in the laigh[1] cellar.
 And that was warst of a'.

She's tyed it in her apron
 And she's thrown it in the sea;
Says, sink ye, swim ye, bonny wee babe!
 You'll neer get mair o me.

Down then cam the auld queen,
 Goud tassels tying her hair;
"O Marie, where's the bonny wee babe
 That I heard greet[2] sae sair?"

"There was never a babe intill my room,
 As little designs to be;
It was but a touch o my sair side,
 Come o'er my fair bodie."

"O Marie put on your robes o black,
 Or else your robes o brown,
For ye maun gang wi me the night,
 To see fair Edinbro town."

"I winna put on my robes o black,
 Nor yet my robes o brown;
But I'll put on my robes o white,
 To see fair Edinbro town."

[1] low [2] cry

When she gaed up the Cannogate,
  She laughed loud laughters three;
But whan she cam down the Cannogate
  The tear blinded her ee.

When she gaed up the Parliament stair,
  The heel cam aff her shee;
And lang or she cam down again
  She was condemned to dee.

When she cam down the Cannogate,
  The Cannogate sae free,
Many a lady lookd owre her window,
  Weeping for this ladie.

"Ye need nae weep for me," she says,
  "Ye need nae weep for me;
For had I not slain mine own sweet babe,
  This death I wadna dee.

"Bring me a bottle of wine," she says,
  "The best that ee ye hae,
That I may drink to my weil-wishers,
  And they may drink to me.

"Here's a health to the jolly sailors,
  That sail upon the main;
Let them never let on to my father and mother
  But what I'm coming hame.

"Here's a health to the jolly sailors,
  That sail upon the sea;
Let them never let on to my father and mother
  That I cam here to dee.

"O little did my mother think
  The day she cradled me,
What lands I was to travel through,
  What death I was to dee.

"O little did my father think
    The day he held up me,
What lands I was to travel through,
    What death I was to dee.

"Last night I washd the queen's feet,
    And gently laid her down;
And a' the thanks I've gotten the nicht
    To be hangd in Edinbro town!

"Last nicht there was four Maries,
    The nicht there'll be but three;
There was Mary Seton, and Marie Beton,
    And Marie Carmichael, and me."

# ANONYMOUS

## Western Wind

Western wind, when will thou blow,
The small rain down can rain?
Christ, if my love were in my arms
And I in my bed again!

# ANONYMOUS

## The Cherry-Tree Carol

Joseph was an old man,
    And an old man was he,
When he wedded Mary,
    In the land of Galilee.

Joseph and Mary walked
  Through an orchard good,
Where was cherries and berries,
  So red as any blood.

Joseph and Mary walked
  Through an orchard green,
Where was berries and cherries
  As thick as might be seen.

O then bespoke Mary,
  So meek and so mild:
"Pluck me one cherry, Joseph,
  For I am with child."

O then bespoke Joseph,
  With words most unkind:
"Let him pluck thee a cherry
  That brought thee with child."

O then bespoke the babe,
  Within his mother's womb:
"Bow down then the tallest tree,
  For my mother to have some."

Then bowed down the highest tree
  Unto his mother's hand;
Then she cried, "See, Joseph,
  I have cherries at command."

O then bespake Joseph:
  "I have done Mary wrong:
But cheer up, my dearest,
  And be not cast down."

Then Mary plucked a cherry,
  As red as the blood,
Then Mary went home
  With her heavy load.

Then Mary took her babe,
   And sat him on her knee,
Saying, "My dear son, tell me
   What this world will be."

"O I shall be as dead, mother,
   As the stones in the wall;
O the stones in the streets, mother,
   Shall mourn for me all.

"Upon Easter-day, mother,
   My uprising shall be;
O the sun and the moon, mother,
   Shall both rise with me."

# ANONYMOUS

## A Religious Use of Taking Tobacco

The Indian weed witherèd quite,
Green at morn, cut down at night,
   Shows thy decay;
   All flesh is hay:
Thus think, then drink tobacco.

And when the smoke ascends on high,
Think thou behold'st the vanity
   Of worldly stuff,
   Gone with a puff:
Thus think, then drink tobacco.

But when the pipe grows foul within,
Think of thy soul defiled with sin.
   And that the fire
   Doth it require:
Thus think, then drink tobacco.

The ashes that are left behind,
May serve to put thee still in mind
That into dust
Return thou must:
Thus think, then drink tobacco.


# ANONYMOUS


*Hierusalem*

Hierusalem, my happy home,
　When shall I come to thee?
When shall my sorrows have an end,
　Thy joys when shall I see?

O happy harbour of the saints,
　O sweet and pleasant soil,
In thee no sorrow may be found,
　No grief, no care, no toil.

There lust and lucre cannot dwell,
　There envy bears no sway;
There is no hunger, heat, nor cold,
　But pleasure every way.

Thy walls are made of precious stones,
　Thy bulwarks diamonds square;
Thy gates are of right orient pearl,
　Exceeding rich and rare.

Thy turrets and thy pinnacles
　With carbuncles do shine;
Thy very streets are paved with gold,
　Surpassing clear and fine.

Ah, my sweet home, Hierusalem,
    Would God I were in thee!
Would God my woes were at an end,
    Thy joys that I might see!

Thy gardens and thy gallant walks
    Continually are green;
There grows such sweet and pleasant flowers
    As nowhere else are seen.

Quite through the streets, with silver sound,
    The flood of life doth flow;
Upon whose banks on every side
    The wood of life doth grow.

There trees for evermore bear fruit,
    And evermore do spring;
There evermore the angels sit,
    And evermore do sing.

Our Lady sings *Magnificat*
    With tune surpassing sweet;
And all the virgins bear their part,
    Sitting about her feet.

Hierusalem, my happy home,
    Would God I were in thee!
Would God my woes were at an end,
    Thy joys that I might see!


# ANONYMOUS


*A Song of Ale*


Back and side go bare, go bare,
    Both foot and hand go cold;

But, belly, God send thee good ale enough,
   Whether it be new or old.
I cannot eat but little meat,
   My stomach is not good;
But sure I think that I can drink
   With him that wears a hood.
Though I go bare, take ye no care,
   I am nothing a-cold;
I stuff my skin so full within
   Of jolly good ale and old.
      Back and side go bare, go bare, etc.

I love no roast but a nutbrown toast,
   And a crab laid in the fire;
A little bread shall do me stead,
   Much bread I not desire.
No frost nor snow, no wind, I trow,
   Can hurt me if I would,
I am so wrapt, and throughly lapt
   Of jolly good ale and old.
      Back and side go bare, go bare, etc.

And Tib my wife, that as her life
   Loveth well good ale to seek,
Full oft drinks she, till ye may see
   The tears run down her cheek.
Then doth she troll to me the bowl,
   Even as a maltworm should;
And saith, "Sweetheart, I took my part
   Of this jolly good ale and old."
      Back and side go bare, go bare, etc.

Now let them drink, till they nod and wink,
   Even as good fellows should do;
They shall not miss to have the bliss
   Good ale doth bring men to.
And all poor souls that have scourëd bowls,
   Or have them lustily trolled,

God save the lives of them and their wives,
   Whether they be young or old.
      Back and side go bare, go bare, etc.


# ANONYMOUS


### Death

O death, rock me asleep,
   Bring me to quiet rest,
Let pass my weary guiltless ghost
   Out of my careful breast.
Toll on, thou passing bell;
Ring out my doleful knell;
Let thy sound my death tell.
   Death doth draw nigh;
   There is no remedy.

My pains who can express?
   Alas, they are so strong;
My dolour will not suffer strength
   My life for to prolong.
Toll on, thou passing bell;
Ring out my doleful knell;
Let thy sound my death tell.
   Death doth draw nigh;
   There is no remedy.

Alone in prison strong
   I wait my destiny.
Woe worth this cruel hap that I
   Should taste this misery!
Toll on, thou passing bell;
Ring out my doleful knell;

Let thy sound my death tell.
　　Death doth draw nigh;
　　There is no remedy.


Farewell, my pleasures past,
　　Welcome, my present pain!
I feel my torments so increase
　　That life cannot remain.
Cease now, thou passing bell;
Rung is my doleful knell;
For the sound my death doth tell.
　　Death doth draw nigh;
　　There is no remedy.



# ANONYMOUS


### Green Willow


The poor soul sat sighing by a sycamore tree;
　　Sing willow, willow, willow!
With his hand in his bosom, and his head upon his knee;
　　O! willow, willow, willow, willow,
　　O! willow, willow, willow, willow,
　　　Shall be my garland.
　Sing all a green willow, willow, willow, willow!
　Ay me, the green willow must be my garland.


He sight[1] in his singing, and made a great moan,
I am dead to all pleasure, my true love she is gone.


The mute bird sat by him was made tame by his moans;
The true tears fell from him would have melted the stones.

[1] sighed

Come all you forsaken, and mourn you with me;
Who speaks of a false love, mine's falser than she.

Let Love no more boast her, in palace nor bower,
It buds, but it blasteth, ere it be a flower.

Thou fair and more false, I die·with thy wound;
Thou hast lost the truest lover that goes upon the ground.

Let nobody chide her, her scorns I approve;
She was born to be false, and I to die for love.

Take this for my farewell and latest adieu;
Write this on my tomb, that in love I was true.


## ANONYMOUS


*Love Me Little, Love Me Long*

Love me little, love me long,
Is the burden of my song.
Love that is too hot and strong
    Burneth soon to waste:
Still, I would not have thee cold,
Not too backward, nor too bold,
Love that lasteth till 'tis old
    Fadeth not in haste.
        Love me little, love me long,
        Is the burden of my song.

If thou lovest me too much,
It will not prove as true as touch;
Love me little, more than such,
    For I fear the end:
I am with little well content,
And a little from thee sent

Is enough, with true intent
    To be steadfast friend.
        Love me little, love me long,
        Is the burden of my song.

Say thou lov'st me while thou live;
I to thee my love will give,
Never dreaming to deceive
    Whiles that life endures:
Nay, and after death, in sooth,
I to thee will keep my truth,
As now, when in my May of youth;
    This my love assures.
        Love me little, love me long,
        Is the burden of my song.

Constant love is moderate ever,
And it will through life persèver:
Give me that, with true endeavour
    I will it restore.
A suit of durance let it be
For all weathers that for me,
For the land or for the sea,
    Lasting evermore.
        Love me little, love me long,
        Is the burden of my song.

Winter's cold, or summer's heat,
Autumn's tempests, on it beat,
It can never know defeat,
    Never can rebel:
Such the love that I would gain,
Such the love, I tell thee plain,
Thou must give, or woo in vain:
    So to thee, farewell!
        Love me little, love me long,
        Is the burden of my song.

# NICHOLAS BRETON/1545-1626

### An Assurance

Say that I should say I love ye,
   Would you say 'tis but a saying?
But if love in prayers move ye,
   Will you not be moved with praying?

Think I think that love should know ye,
   Will you think 'tis but a thinking?
But if love the thought do show ye,
   Will ye lose your eyes with winking?

Write that I do write you blessed,
   Will you write 'tis but a writing?
But if truth and love confess it,
   Will ye doubt the true inditing?

No, I say, and think, and write it,
   Write, and think, and say your pleasure;
Love, and truth, and I indite it,
   You are blessed out of measure.


# EDMUND DE VERE, EARL OF OXFORD
# 1550-1604

### Of the Birth and Bringing up of Desire

When wert thou born, Desire?
   In pride and pomp of May.
By whom, sweet boy, wert thou begot?
   By Self Conceit, men say.
Tell me, who was thy nurse?
   Fresh Youth, in sugared joy.

What was thy meat and daily food?
  Sad sighs and great annoy.
What haddest thou to drink?
  Unfeigned lovers' tears.
What cradle wert thou rocked in?
  In hope devoid of fears.
What brought thee to thy sleep?
  Sweet thoughts, which liked me best.
And where is now thy dwelling-place?
  In gentle hearts I rest.
Doth company displease?
  It doth, in many one.
Where would Desire then choose to be?
  He loves to muse alone.
What feedeth most thy sight?
  To gaze on favour still.
Whom finds thou most thy foe?
  Disdain of my good will.
Will ever age or death
  Bring thee unto decay?
No, no! Desire both lives and dies
  A thousand times a day.


# EDMUND SPENSER/1552?–1599


### Prothalamion

Calm was the day, and through the trembling air
Sweet breathing Zephyrus did softly play,
A gentle spirit, that lightly did delay
Hot Titan's beams, which then did glister fair;
When I whose sullen care,
Through discontent of my long fruitless stay
In prince's court, and expectation vain
Of idle hopes, which still do fly away
Like empty shadows, did afflict my brain,

Walked forth to ease my pain
Along the shore of silver streaming Thames,
Whose rutty bank, the which his river hems,
Was painted all with variable flowers,
And all the meads adorned with dainty gems,
Fit to deck maidens' bowers,
And crown their paramours,
Against the bridal day, which is not long:
    Sweet Thames, run softly, till I end my song.

There, in a meadow, by the river's side,
A flock of nymphs I chancèd to espy,
All lovely daughters of the flood thereby,
With goodly greenish locks all loose untied,
As each had been a bride;
And each one had a little wicker basket,
Made of fine twigs entrailèd curiously,
In which they gathered flowers to fill their flasket,
And with fine fingers cropped full featously
The tender stalks on high.
Of every sort, which in that meadow grew,
They gathered some; the violet pallid blue,
The little daisy, that at evening closes,
The virgin lily, and the primrose true,
With store of vermeil roses,
To deck their bridegrooms' posies,
Against the bridal day, which was not long:
    Sweet Thames, run softly, till I end my song.

With that, I saw two swans of goodly hue
Come softly swimming down along the Lee;
Two fairer birds I yet did never see.
The snow, which doth the top of Pindus strew,
Did never whiter shew,
Nor Jove himself, when he a swan would be
For love of Leda, whiter did appear:
Yet Leda was they say as white as he,
Yet not so white as these, nor nothing near.
So purely white they were,

That even the gentle stream, the which them bare,
Seemed foul to them, and bade his billows spare
To wet their silken feathers, lest they might
Soil their fair plumes with water not so fair,
And mar their beauties bright,
That shone as heaven's light,
Against their bridal day, which was not long:
    Sweet Thames, run softly, till I end my song.

Eftsoons the nymphs, which now had flowers their fill,
Ran all in haste, to see that silver brood,
As they came floating on the crystal flood.
Whom when they saw, they stood amazèd still,
Their wondering eyes to fill.
Them seemed they never saw a sight so fair,
Of fowls so lovely, that they sure did deem
Them heavenly born, or to be that same pair
Which through the sky draw Venus' silver team;
For sure they did not seem
To be begot of any earthly seed,
But rather angels or of angels' breed:
Yet were they bred of Somers-heat[1] they say,
In sweetest season, when each flower and weed
The earth did fresh array,
So fresh they seemed as day,
Even as their bridal day, which was not long:
    Sweet Thames, run softly, till I end my song.

Then forth they all out of their baskets drew
Great store of flowers, the honour of the field,
That to the sense did fragrant odours yield,
All which upon those goodly birds they threw,
And all the waves did strew,
That like old Peneus' waters they did seem,
When down along by pleasant Tempe's shore,
Scattered with flowers, through Thessaly they stream,
That they appear through lilies' plenteous store,

---

[1] summer's heat = Somerset

Like a bride's chamber floor.
Two of those nymphs, meanwhile, two garlands bound,
Of freshest flowers which in that mead they found,
The which presenting all in trim array,
Their snowy foreheads therewithal they crowned,
Whilst one did sing this lay,
Prepared against that day,
Against their bridal day, which was not long:
    Sweet Thames, run softly, till I end my song.

"Ye gentle birds, the world's fair ornament,
And heaven's glory, whom this happy hour
Doth lead unto your lovers' blissful bower,
Joy may you have and gentle heart's content
Of your love's couplement:
And let fair Venus, that is queen of love,
With her heart-quelling son upon you smile,
Whose smile, they say, hath virtue to remove
All love's dislike, and friendship's faulty guile
For ever to assoil.
Let endless peace your steadfast hearts accord,
And blessed plenty wait upon your board,
And let your bed with pleasures chaste abound,
That fruitful issue may to you afford,
Which may your foes confound,
And make your joys redound,
Upon your bridal day, which is not long:
    Sweet Thames, run softly, till I end my song."

So ended she; and all the rest around
To her redoubled that her undersong,
Which said, their bridal day should not be long.
And gentle echo from the neighbour ground
Their accents did resound.
So forth those joyous birds did pass along,
Adown the Lee, that to them murmured low,
As he would speak, but that he lacked a tongue,
Yet did by signs his glad affection show,
Making his stream run slow.

And all the fowl which in his flood did dwell
'Gan flock about these twain, that did excel
The rest so far as Cynthia doth shend[1]
The lesser stars. So they, enrangèd well,
Did on those two attend,
And their best service lend,
Against their wedding day, which was not long:
    Sweet Thames, run softly, till I end my song.

At length they all to merry London came,
To merry London, my most kindly nurse,
That to me gave this life's first native source;
Though from another place I take my name,
An house of ancient fame.
There when they came, whereas those bricky towers,
The which on Thames' broad agèd back do ride,
Where now the studious lawyers have their bowers
There whilom wont the Templar Knights to bide,
Till they decayed through pride:
Next whereunto there stands a stately place,
Where oft I gainèd gifts and goodly grace
Of that great lord, which therein wont to dwell,
Whose want too well now feels my friendless case.
But ah! here fits not well
Old woes but joys to tell
Against the bridal day, which is not long:
    Sweet Thames, run softly, till I end my song.

Yet therein now doth lodge a noble peer,
Great England's glory and the world's wide wonder,
Whose dreadful name late through all Spain did thunder,
And Hercules' two pillars standing near
Did make to quake and fear.
Fair branch of honour, flower of chivalry,
That fillest England with thy triumph's fame,
Joy have thou of thy noble victory,
And endless happiness of thine own name

[1] shame

That promiseth the same:
That through thy prowess and victorious arms,
Thy country may be freed from foreign harms;
And great Elisa's glorious name may ring
Through all the world, filled with thy wide alarms,
Which some brave Muse may sing
To ages following,
Upon the bridal day, which is not long:
    Sweet Thames, run softly, till I end my song.

From those high towers this noble lord issuing,
Like radiant Hesper when his golden hair
In th' Ocean billows he hath bathèd fair,
Descended to the river's open viewing,
With a great train ensuing.
Above the rest were goodly to be seen
Two gentle knights of lovely face and feature
Beseeming well the bower of any queen,
With gifts of wit and ornaments of nature,
Fit for so goodly stature;
That like the twins of Jove they seemed in sight,
Which deck the baldric of the heavens bright.
They two forth pacing to the river's side,
Received those two fair birds, their love's delight,
Which at th'appointed tide
Each one did make his bride,
Against their bridal day, which is not long:
    Sweet Thames, run softly, till I end my song.

## CHIDIOCK TICHBORNE/?–1586

*Elegy*

My prime of youth is but a frost of cares,
    My feast of joy is but a dish of pain,

My crop of corn is but a field of tares,
  And all my good is but vain hope of gain;
    The day is past, and yet I saw no sun,
    And now I live, and now my life is done.

My tale was heard and yet it was not told,
  My fruit is fallen and yet my leaves are green,
My youth is spent and yet I am not old,
  I saw the world and yet I was not seen;
    My thread is cut and yet it is not spun,
    And now I live, and now my life is done.

I sought my death and found it in my womb,
  I looked for life and saw it was a shade,
I trod the earth and knew it was my tomb,
  And now I die, and now I was but made;
    My glass is full, and now my glass is run,
    And now I live, and now my life is done.


# SIR EDWARD DYER/?–1607

### I Would It Were Not As It Is

I would it were not as it is,
Or that I cared not yea or no;
I would I thought it not amiss,
Or that amiss might blameless go;
    I would it were, yet would I not;
    I might be glad, yet could I not.

I would desire to know the mean,
Or that the mean desire sought;
I would I could my fancy wean
From such sweet joys as love hath wrought;
    Only my wish is least of all:
    A badge whereby to know a thrall.

Oh happy man, which dost aspire
To what which seemly thou dost crave;
Thrice happy man, if thy desire
May win with hope, good hap to have;
 But woe to me, unhappy man,
 Whom hope nor hap acquiet can.

The buds of hope are starved with fear,
And still his foe presents his face;
My state, if hope and palm should bear
Unto my hap, would be disgrace;
 As diamond in wood were set,
 Or Irus rags in gold yfrett.

For lo, my tired shoulders bear
Desire's weary beating wings,
And at my feet a clog I wear,
Tied on with false disdaining strings;
 My wings to mount aloft make haste,
 My clog doth sink me down as fast.

That is our state, lo, thus we stand,
They rise to fall that climb too high;
The boy that fled King Mino's land
May learn the wise more low to fly;
 What gained his point against the sun,
 He drowned in seas, his noon that won.

Yet Icarus more happy was,
By present death his cares to end,
Than I, poor man, on whom, alas,
Ten thousand deaths their pains do send;
 Now grief, now hope, now love, now spite,
 Long sorrow mixed with short delight.

The fere and fellow of thy smart,
Prometheus, I am indeed,
Upon whose ever-living heart

The greedy gryphs do daily feed;
    But he that lifts his heart too high
    Must be content to pine and die.

### My Mind to Me a Kingdom Is

My mind to me a kingdom is,
    Such present joys therein I find,
That it excels all other bliss
    That world affords or grows by kind.
Though much I want which most would have,
Yet still my mind forbids to crave.

No princely pomp, no wealthy store,
    No force to win the victory,
No wily wit to salve a sore,
    No shape to feed a loving eye;
To none of these I yield as thrall,
For why my mind doth serve for all.

I see how plenty suffers oft,
    And hasty climbers soon do fall;
I see that those which are aloft
    Mishap doth threaten most of all;
They get with toil, they keep with fear:
Such cares my mind could never bear.

Content I live, this is my stay,
    I seek no more than may suffice;
I press to bear no haughty sway;
    Look, what I lack my mind supplies.
Lo! thus I triumph like a king,
Content with that my mind doth bring.

Some have too much, yet still do crave;
    I little have, and seek no more.
They are but poor, though much they have,
    And I am rich with little store.

They poor, I rich; they beg, I give;
They lack, I leave; they pine, I live.

I laugh not at another's loss;
  I grudge not at another's gain;
No worldly waves my mind can toss;
  My state at one doth still remain.
I fear no foe, I fawn no friend;
I loathe not life, nor dread my end.

Some weigh their pleasure by their lust,
  Their wisdom by their rage of will;
Their treasure is their only trust,
  A cloakèd craft their store of skill:
But all the pleasure that I find
Is to maintain a quiet mind.

My wealth is health and perfect ease,
  My conscience clear my choice defence;
I neither seek by bribes to please,
  Nor by deceit to breed offence.
Thus do I live; thus will I die;
Would all did so as well as I!

## A Modest Love

The lowest trees have tops, the ant her gall,
  The fly her spleen, the little sparks their heat;
The slender hairs cast shadows, though but small,
  And bees have stings, although they be not great;
Seas have their source, and so have shallow springs;
And love is love, in beggars as in kings.

Where rivers smoothest run, deep are the fords;
  The dial stirs, yet none perceives it move;

The firmest faith is in the fewest words;
    The turtles cannot sing, and yet they love:
True hearts have eyes and ears, no tongues to speak;
They hear and see, and sigh, and then they break.


# SIR  WALTER  RALEIGH/1552?-1618

### The Nymph's Reply to the Shepherd

If all the world and love were young,
And truth in every shepherd's tongue,
These pretty pleasures might me move,
To live with thee, and be thy love.

Time drives the flocks from field to fold,
When rivers rage, and rocks grow cold,
And Philomel becometh dumb,
The rest complains of cares to come.

The flowers do fade, and wanton fields,
To wayward winter reckoning yields,
A honey tongue, a heart of gall,
Is fancy's spring, but sorrow's fall.

Thy gowns, thy shoes, thy beds of roses,
Thy cap, thy kirtle, and thy posies,
Soon break, soon wither, soon forgotten:
In folly ripe, in reason rotten.

Thy belt of straw and ivy buds,
Thy coral clasps and amber studs,
All these in me no means can move,
To come to thee, and be thy love.

But could youth last, and love still breed,
Had joys no date, nor age no need,

Then these delights my mind might move,
To live with thee and be thy love.

## A Vision Upon This Conceit of the Faerie Queene

Methought I saw the grave, where Laura lay,
    Within that temple, where the vestal flame
Was wont to burn, and passing by that way,
    To see that buried dust of living fame,
Whose tomb fair Love and fairer Virtue kept,
    All suddenly I saw the Faerie Queene;
At whose approach the soul of Petrarch wept,
    And from thenceforth those graces were not seen,
For they this Queen attended, in whose stead
    Oblivion laid him down on Laura's hearse.
Hereat the hardest stones were seen to bleed,
    And groans of buried ghosts the heavens did pierce;
        Where Homer's spright did tremble all for grief,
        And cursed th' access of that celestial thief.

## Walsinghame*

"As you came from the holy land
    Of Walsinghame,
Met you not with my true love
    By the way as you came?"

"How shall I know your true love,
    That have met many one
As I went to the holy land,
    That have come, that have gone?"

"She is neither white nor brown,
    But as the heavens fair,

* Sometimes attributed to anonymous authorship.

There is none hath a form so divine
   In the earth or the air."

"Such an one did I meet, good Sir,
   Such an angelic face,
Who like a queen, like a nymph did appear
   By her gait, by her grace."

"She hath left me here all alone,
   All alone as unknown,
Who sometimes did me lead with herself,
   And me loved as her own."

"What's the cause that she leaves you alone
   And a new way doth take,
Who loved you once as her own
   And her joy did you make?"

"I have loved her all my youth,
   But now old as you see,
Love likes not the falling fruit
   From the withered tree.

"Know that Love is a careless child,
   And forgets promise past;
He is blind, he is deaf when he list
   And in faith never fast.

"His desire is a dureless content
   And a trustless joy;
He is won with a world of despair
   And is lost with a toy.

"Of womenkind such indeed is the love
   Or the word love abused,
Under which many childish desires
   And conceits are excused.

"But love is a durable fire
    In the mind ever burning;
Never sick, never old, never dead,
    From itself never turning."


### The Lie

Go, soul, the body's guest,
    Upon a thankless arrant:
Fear not to touch the best;
    The truth shall be thy warrant.
        Go, since I needs must die,
        And give the world the lie.

Say to the court, it glows
    And shines like rotten wood;
Say to the church, it shows
    What's good, and doth no good:
        If church and court reply,
        Then give them both the lie.

Tell potentates, they live
    Acting by others' action,
Not loved unless they give,
    Not strong but by their faction:
        If potentates reply,
        Give potentates the lie.

Tell men of high condition
    That manage the estate,
Their purpose is ambition,
    Their practice only hate:
        And if they once reply,
        Then give them all the lie.

Tell them that brave it most,
    They beg for more by spending,

Who, in their greatest cost,
    Seek nothing but commending:
        And if they make reply,
        Then give them all the lie.

Tell zeal, it wants devotion;
    Tell love, it is but lust;
Tell time, it is but motion;
    Tell flesh, it is but dust:
        And wish them not reply,
        For thou must give the lie.

Tell age, it daily wasteth;
    Tell honour how it alters;
Tell beauty how she blasteth;
    Tell favour how it falters:
        And as they shall reply,
        Give every one the lie.

Tell wit how much it wrangles
    In tickle points of niceness;
Tell wisdom, she entangles
    Herself in over-wiseness:
        And when they do reply,
        Straight give them both the lie.

Tell physic of her boldness;
    Tell skill, it is prevention;
Tell charity of coldness;
    Tell law, it is contention:
        And as they do reply,
        So give them still the lie.

Tell fortune of her blindness;
    Tell nature of decay;
Tell friendship of unkindness;
    Tell justice of delay:
        And if they will reply,
        Then give them all the lie.

Tell arts, they have no soundness,
　　But vary by esteeming;
Tell schools, they want profoundness,
　　And stand too much on seeming:
　　　If arts and schools reply,
　　　Give arts and schools the lie.

Tell faith, it's fled the city;
　　Tell how the country erreth;
Tell, manhood shakes off pity;
　　Tell, virtue least preferreth:
　　　And if they do reply,
　　　Spare not to give the lie.

So when thou hast, as I
　　Commanded thee, done blabbing,
Although to give the lie
　　Deserves no less than stabbing,
　　　Stab at thee he that will,
　　　No stab the soul can kill.


## To His Son

Three things there be that prosper up apace
And flourish, whilest they grow asunder far,
But on a day they meet all in one place,
And when they meet, they one another mar;
And they be these, the wood, the weed, the wag.
The wood is that which makes the gallow tree,
The weed is that which strings the hangman's bag,
The wag, my pretty knave, betokeneth thee.
Mark well, dear boy, whilest these assemble not,
Green springs the tree, hemp grows, the wag is wild,
But when they meet, it makes the timber rot,
It frets the halter, and it chokes the child.
Then bless thee, and beware, and let us pray
We part not with thee at this meeting day.

## *The Passionate Man's Pilgrimage*

Give me my scallop-shell of quiet,
My staff of faith to walk upon,
My scrip of joy, immortal diet,
My bottle of salvation,
My gown of glory, hope's true gage,
And thus I'll take my pilgrimage.

Blood must be my body's balmer,
No other balm will there be given,
Whilst my soul like a white palmer
Travels to the land of heaven,
Over the silver mountains,
Where spring the nectar fountains;
And there I'll kiss
The bowl of bliss,
And drink my everlasting fill
On every milken hill.
My soul will be a-dry before,
But after it will thirst no more.

And by the happy blissful way
More peaceful pilgrims I shall see,
That have shook off their gowns of clay
And go apparelled fresh like me.
I'll bring them first
To slake their thirst,
And then to taste those nectar suckets,
At the clear wells
Where sweetness dwells,
Drawn up by saints in crystal buckets.

And when our bottles and all we
Are filled with immortality,
Then the holy paths we'll travel,
Strewed with rubies thick as gravel,
Ceilings of diamonds, sapphire floors,
High walls of coral and pearl bowers.

From thence to heaven's bribeless hall
Where no corrupted voices brawl,
No conscience molten into gold,
Nor forged accusers bought and sold,
No cause deferred, nor vain-spent journey,
For there Christ is the King's Attorney,
Who pleads for all without degrees,
And he hath angels, but no fees.

When the grand twelve million jury
Of our sins and direful fury
'Gainst our souls black verdicts give,
Christ pleads his death, and then we live.
Be thou my speaker, taintless pleader,
Unblotted lawyer, true proceeder;
Thou movest salvation even for alms,
Not with a bribèd lawyer's palms.

And this is my eternal plea
To him that made heaven, earth, and sea:
Seeing my flesh must die so soon,
And want a head to dine next noon,
Just at the stroke when my veins start and spread,
Set on my soul an everlasting head.
Then am I ready, like a palmer fit,
To tread those blest paths which before I writ.

## What Is Our Life?

What is our life? A play of passion,
Our mirth the music of division.
Our mothers' wombs the tiring-houses be,
Where we are dressed for this short comedy.
Heaven the judicious sharp spectator is,
That sits and marks still who doth act amiss.
Our graves that hide us from the searching sun
Are like drawn curtains when the play is done.

Thus march we, playing, to our latest rest,
Only we die in earnest, that's no jest.

### Epitaph

Even such is Time, which takes in trust
Our youth, our joys, and all we have,
And pays us but with age and dust;
Who in the dark and silent grave,
When we have wandered all our ways,
Shuts up the story of our days:
And from which earth, and grave, and dust,
The Lord shall raise me up, I trust.

# ANTHONY MUNDAY/1553–1633

### I Serve a Mistress

I serve a mistress whiter than the snow,
  Straighter than cedar, brighter than the glass,
Finer in trip and swifter than the roe,
  More pleasant than the field of flowering grass;
More gladsome to my withering joys that fade,
Than winter's sun or summer's cooling shade.

Sweeter than swelling grape of ripest wine,
  Softer than feathers of the fairest swan,
Smoother than jet, more stately than the pine,
  Fresher than poplar, smaller than my span,
Clearer than beauty's fiery pointed beam,
Or icy crust of crystal's frozen stream.

Yet is she curster than the bear by kind,
  And harder-hearted than the agèd oak,

More glib than oil, more fickle than the wind,
   Stiffer than steel, no sooner bent but broke.
Lo! thus my service is a lasting sore;
Yet will I serve, although I die therefore.


# SIR PHILIP SIDNEY/1554–1586


## *Loving in Truth*

Loving in truth, and fain in verse my love to show,
That she, dear she, might take some pleasure of my pain,
Pleasure might cause her read, reading might make her know,
Knowledge might pity win, and pity grace obtain,
I sought fit words to paint the blackest face of woe;
Studying inventions fine, her wits to entertain,
Oft turning others' leaves to see if thence would flow
Some fresh and fruitful showers upon my sun-burned brain.
But words came halting forth, wanting Invention's stay;
Invention, Nature's child, fled step-dame Study's blows,
And others' feet still seemed but strangers in my way.
Thus, great with child to speak, and helpless in my throes,
Biting my truant pen, beating myself for spite,
"Fool," said my Muse to me, "look in thy heart and write."


## *With How Sad Steps, O Moon*

With how sad steps, O Moon, thou climb'st the skies!
How silently, and with how wan a face!
What! may it be that even in heavenly place
That busy archer his sharp arrows tries?
Sure, if that long-with-love-acquainted eyes
Can judge of love, thou feel'st a lover's case;
I read it in thy looks; thy languished grace
To me, that feel the like, thy state descries.
Then, even of fellowship, O Moon, tell me,

Is constant love deemed there but want of wit?
Are beauties there as proud as here they be?
Do they above, love to be loved, and yet
Those lovers scorn whom that love doth possess?
Do they call virtue there ungratefulness?

## Come, Sleep! O Sleep

Come, Sleep! O Sleep, the certain knot of peace,
The baiting-place of wit, the balm of woe,
The poor man's wealth, the prisoner's release,
Th' indifferent judge between the high and low;
With shield of proof shield me from out the prease[1]
Of those fierce darts Despair at me doth throw:
O make in me those civil wars to cease;
I will good tribute pay, if thou do so.
Take thou of me smooth pillows, sweetest bed,
A chamber deaf of noise and blind of light,
A rosy garland and a weary head:
And if these things, as being thine in right,
Move not thy heavy grace, thou shalt in me,
Livelier than elsewhere, Stella's image see.

## No More, My Dear

No more, my dear, no more these counsels try;
Oh, give my passions leave to run their race;
Let Fortune lay on me her worst disgrace;
Let folk o'ercharged with brain against me cry;
Let clouds bedim my face, break in mine eye;
Let me no steps but of lost labour trace;
Let all the earth with scorn recount my case;
But do not will me from my love to fly.
I do not envy Aristotle's wit,
Nor do aspire to Caesar's bleeding fame;

[1] press, crowd

Nor aught do care though some above me sit;
Nor hope nor wish another course to frame,
But that which once may win thy cruel heart;
Thou art my wit, and thou my virtue art.

## Highway, Since You My Chief Parnassus Be

Highway, since you my chief Parnassus be,
And that my Muse, to some ears not unsweet,
Tempers her words to trampling horses' feet
More oft than to a chamber-melody,
Now, blessèd you, bear onward blessèd me
To her, where I my heart, safe left, shall meet;
My Muse and I must you of duty greet
With thanks and wishes, wishing thankfully.
Be you still fair, honoured by public heed;
By no encroachment wronged, nor time forgot;
Nor blamed for blood, nor shamed for sinful deed;
And, that you know I envy you no lot
Of highest wish, I wish you so much bliss,
Hundreds of years you Stella's feet may kiss!

## My True Love Hath My Heart

My true Love hath my heart, and I have his,
By just exchange one for the other given:
I hold his dear, and mine he cannot miss;
There never was a better bargain driven.
His heart in me keeps me and him in one,
My heart in him his thoughts and senses guides:
He loves my heart, for once it was his own;
I cherish his because in me it bides.
His heart his wound receivèd from my sight,
My heart was wounded with his wounded heart;
For as from me, on him his hurt did light,
So still methought in me his hurt did smart.

Both, equal hurt, in this change sought our bliss:
My true Love hath my heart, and I have his.

## Leave Me, O Love!

Leave me, O Love, which reachest but to dust,
And thou, my mind, aspire to higher things;
Grow rich in that which never taketh rust:
Whatever fades, but fading pleasure brings.
Draw in thy beams, and humble all thy might
To that sweet yoke where lasting freedoms be,
Which breaks the clouds and opens forth the light
That doth both shine and give us sight to see.
Oh, take fast hold! Let that light be thy guide
In this small course which birth draws out to death,
And think how evil becometh him to slide
Who seeketh heaven, and comes of heavenly breath.
Then, farewell, world! thy uttermost I see.
Eternal Love, maintain thy life in me!

## Thou Blind Man's Mark

Thou blind man's mark, thou fool's self-chosen snare,
Fond fancy's scum, and dregs of scattered thought;
Band of all evils, cradle of causeless care;
Thou web of will, whose end is never wrought;
Desire, desire! I have too dearly bought,
With price of mangled mind, thy worthless ware;
Too long, too long, asleep thou hast me brought,
Who should my mind to higher things prepare.
But yet in vain thou hast my ruin sought;
In vain thou madest me to vain things aspire;
In vain thou kindlest all thy smoky fire;
For virtue hath this better lesson taught,
Within myself to seek my only hire,
Desiring nought but how to kill desire.

## A Litany

Ring out your bells, let mourning shows be spread;
For Love is dead.
  All Love is dead, infected
With plague of deep disdain;
  Worth, as nought worth, rejected,
And Faith fair scorn doth gain.
  From so ungrateful fancy,
  From such a female franzy,
    From them that use men thus,
    Good Lord, deliver us!

Weep, neighbors, weep! do you not hear it said
That Love is dead?
  His death-bed, peacock's folly;
His winding-sheet is shame;
  His will, false-seeming holy;
His sole executor, blame.
  From so ungrateful fancy,
  From such a female franzy,
    From them that use men thus,
    Good Lord, deliver us!

Let dirge be sung and trentals rightly read,
For Love is dead.
  Sir Wrong his tomb ordaineth
My mistress Marble-heart,
  Which epitaph containeth,
"Her eyes were once his dart."
  From so ungrateful fancy,
  From such a female franzy,
    From them that use men thus,
    Good Lord, deliver us!

Alas! I lie, rage hath this error bred;
Love is not dead.
  Love is not dead, but sleepeth

In her unmatchèd mind,
   Where she his counsel keepeth,
Till due desert she find.
   Therefore from so vile fancy,
   To call such wit a franzy,
     Who Love can temper thus,
     Good Lord, deliver us!

### The Nightingale

The nightingale, as soon as April bringeth
   Unto her rested sense a perfect waking,
While late bare earth, proud of new clothing, springeth,
   Sings out her woes, a thorn her song-book making;
   And mournfully bewailing,
Her throat in tunes expresseth
What grief her breast oppresseth
   For Tereus' force on her chaste will prevailing.
O Philomela fair, O take some gladness,
That here is juster cause of plaintful sadness.
   Thine earth now springs, mine fadeth;
   Thy thorn without, my thorn my heart invadeth.


Alas, she hath no other cause of anguish
   But Tereus' love, on her by strong hand wroken,
Wherein she suffering, all her spirits languish;
   Full womanlike complains her will was broken.
   But I, who daily craving,
Cannot have to content me,
Have more cause to lament me,
   Since wanting is more woe than too much having.
O Philomela fair, O take some gladness,
That here is juster cause of plaintful sadness.
   Thine earth now springs, mine fadeth;
   Thy thorn without, my thorn my heart invadeth.

*Solitariness*

O sweet woods, the delight of solitariness!
O, how much I do like your solitariness!
Where man's mind hath a freed consideration,
Of goodness to receive lovely direction;
Where senses do behold th' order of heavenly host,
And wise thoughts do behold what the Creator is.
Contemplation here holdeth his only seat,
Bounded with no limits, borne with a wing of hope,
Climbs even unto the stars; Nature is under it.
Nought disturbs thy quiet, all to thy service yields;
Each sight draws on a thought (thought, mother of
    science);
Sweet birds kindly do grant harmony unto thee;
Fair trees' shade is enough fortification,
Nor danger to thyself if be not in thyself.

O sweet woods, the delight of solitariness!
O, how much I do like your solitariness!
Here nor treason is hid, veiled in innocence;
Nor envy's snaky eye finds any harbour here;
Nor flatterers' venomous insinuations,
Nor cunning humourists' puddled opinions,
Nor courteous ruin of proffered usury,
Nor time prattled away, cradle of ignorance,
Nor causeless duty, nor cumber of arrogance,
Nor trifling title of vanity dazzleth us,
Nor golden manacles stand for a paradise.
Here wrong's name is unheard, slander a monster is.
Keep thy spright from abuse; here no abuse doth haunt.
What man grafts in a tree dissimulation?

O sweet woods, the delight of solitariness!
O, how well I do like your solitariness!
Yet, dear soil, if a soul closed in a mansion
As sweet as violets, fair as lily is,
Straight as cedar, a voice stains the canary bird's,
Whose shade safely doth hold, danger avoideth her;

Such wisdom that in her lives speculation;
Such goodness that in her simplicity triumphs;
Where envy's snaky eye winketh or else dieth;
Slander wants a pretext, flattery gone beyond;
O! if such a one have bent to a lonely life,
Her steps glad we receive, glad we receive her eyes,
   And think not she doth hurt our solitariness,
   For such company decks such solitariness.


## Who Is It That This Dark Night

   "Who is it that this dark night
Underneath my window plaineth?"
   It is one who from thy sight
Being, ah, exiled, disdaineth
   Every other vulgar light.

   "Why, alas, and are you he?
Be not yet those fancies changèd?"
   Dear, when you find change in me,
Though from me you be estrangèd,
   Let my change to ruin be.

   "Well, in absence this will die;
Leave to see, and leave to wonder."
   Absence, sure, will help, if I
Can learn how much myself to sunder
   From what in my heart doth lie.

   "But time will these thoughts remove;
Time doth work what no man knoweth."
   Time doth as the subject prove;
With time still the affection groweth
   In the faithful turtle-dove.

   "What if you new beauties see,
Will not they stir new affection?"
   I will think they pictures be,

(Image-like, of saints' perfection)
    Poorly counterfeiting thee.


  "But your reason's purest light
Bids you leave such minds to nourish."
    Dear, do reason no such spite:
Never doth thy beauty flourish
    More than in my reason's sight.


  "But the wrongs Love bears will make
Love at length leave undertaking."
    No, the more fools it do shake,
In a ground of so firm making
    Deeper still they drive the stake.


  "Peace! I think that some give ear,
Come, no more, lest I get anger."
    Bliss! I will my bliss forbear,
Fearing, sweet, you to endanger;
    But my soul shall harbour there.


  "Well, be gone; be gone, I say!
Lest that Argus' eyes perceive you."
    Oh, unjust is Fortune's sway,
Which can make me thus to leave you;
    And from louts to run away.


# JOHN LYLY/ 1554?–1606

### Cupid and Campaspe

Cupid and my Campaspe played
At cards for kisses, Cupid paid;
He stakes his quiver, bow, and arrows,
His mother's doves, and team of sparrows;
Loses them too; then, down he throws

The coral of his lip, the rose
Growing on 's cheek (but none knows how);
With these, the crystal of his brow,
And then the dimple of his chin:
All these did my Campaspe win.
At last, he set her both his eyes;
She won, and Cupid blind did rise.
　　O Love! has she done this to thee?
　　What shall (alas!) become of me?


### What Bird So Sings

What bird so sings, yet so does wail?
O, 'tis the ravished nightingale.
Jug, jug, jug, jug, tereu! she cries,
And still her woes at midnight rise.
Brave prick-song! who is 't now we hear?
None but the lark so shrill and clear;
How at heaven's gates she claps her wings!—
The morn not waking till she sings.
Hark, hark, with what a pretty throat
Poor robin redbreast tunes his note!
Hark how the jolly cuckoos sing
Cuckoo! to welcome in the spring!
Cuckoo! to welcome in the spring!


### Pan's Syrinx Was a Girl Indeed

Pan's Syrinx was a girl indeed,
Though now she's turned into a reed;
From that dear reed Pan's pipe does come,
A pipe that strikes Apollo dumb;
Nor flute, nor lute, nor gittern can
So chant it, as the pipe of Pan;
Cross-gartered swains, and dairy girls,
With faces smug, and round as pearls,
When Pan's shrill pipe begins to play,

With dancing wear out night and day;
The bagpipe's drone his hum lays by,
When Pan sounds up his minstrelsy;
His minstrelsy! O base! This quill,
Which at my mouth with wind I fill,
Puts me in mind, though her I miss,
That still my Syrinx' lips I kiss.

# FULKE GREVILLE, LORD BROOKE
## 1554–1628

### Epitaph on Sir Philip Sidney

Silence augmenteth grief, writing increaseth rage,
Staled are my thoughts, which loved and lost the wonder of
  our age:
Yet quickened now with fire, though dead with frost ere now,
Enraged I write I know not what; dead, quick, I know not
  how.

Hard-hearted minds relent, and rigour's tears abound,
And envy strangely rues his end, in whom no fault she found.
Knowledge her light hath lost; valour hath slain her knight.
Sidney is dead; dead is my friend; dead is the world's delight.

Place pensive wails his fall whose presence was her pride,
Time crieth out, "My ebb is come; his life was my spring
  tide."
Fame mourns in that she lost the ground of her reports;
Each living wight laments his lack, and all in sundry sorts.

He was (woe worth that word!) to each well-thinking mind
A spotless friend, a matchless man, whose virtue ever shined,
Declaring in his thoughts, his life, and that he writ,
Highest conceits, longest foresights, and deepest works of wit.

He, only like himself, was second unto none,
Whose death (though life) we rue, and wrong, and all in vain
   do moan.
Their loss, not him, wail they, that fill the world with cries,
Death slew not him, but he made death his ladder to the
   skies.
Now sink of sorrow I, who live, the more the wrong,
Who wishing death, whom death denies, whose thread is all
   too long;
Who tied to wretched life, who looks for no relief,
Must spend my ever-dying days, in never-ending grief.

Heart's ease and only I, like parallels run on,
Whose equal length keep equal breadth, and never meet in
   one;
Yet for not wronging him, my thoughts, my sorrow's cell,
Shall not run out, though leak they will, for liking him so
   well.

Farewell to you my hopes, my wonted waking dreams,
Farewell sometimes enjoyèd joy; eclipsèd are thy beams.
Farewell self-pleasing thoughts, which quietness brings forth;
And farewell friendship's sacred league, uniting minds of
   worth.

And farewell merry heart, the gift of guiltless minds,
And all sports which, for life's restore, variety assigns;
Let all that sweet is void; in me no mirth may dwell.
Philip, the cause of all this woe, my life's content farewell!

Now rhyme, the son of rage, which art no kin to skill,
And endless grief, which deads my life, yet knows not how to
   kill,
Go, seek that hapless tomb, which if ye hap to find,
Salute the stones, that keep the limbs, that held so good a
   mind.

# GEORGE PEELE/1558?–1597?

## His Golden Locks Time Hath to Silver Turned

His golden locks time hath to silver turned;
  O time too swift, O swiftness never ceasing!
His youth 'gainst time and age hath ever spurned,
  But spurned in vain; youth waneth by increasing:
Beauty, strength, youth, are flowers but fading seen;
Duty, faith, love, are roots, and ever green.

His helmet now shall make a hive for bees;
  And lovers' sonnets turned to holy psalms,
A man-at-arms must now serve on his knees,
  And feed on prayers, which are age's alms:
But though from court to cottage he depart,
His saint is sure of his unspotted heart.

And when he saddest sits in homely cell,
  He'll teach his swains this carol for a song:
"Blest be the hearts that wish my sovereign well,
  Curst be the souls that think her any wrong."
Goddess, allow this agèd man his right,
To be your beadsman now that was your knight.

# THOMAS LODGE/1558?–1625

## Love in My Bosom

Love in my bosom like a bee
    Doth suck his sweet;
Now with his wings he plays with me,
    Now with his feet.
Within mine eyes he makes his nest,
His bed amidst my tender breast;

My kisses are his daily feast,
And yet he robs me of my rest.
 Ah, wanton, will ye?

And if I sleep, then percheth he
  With pretty flight,
And makes his pillow of my knee
  The livelong night.
Strike I my lute, he tunes the string;
He music plays if so I sing;
He lends me every lovely thing;
Yet cruel he my heart doth sting.
  Whist, wanton, still ye!

Else I with roses every day
  Will whip you hence,
And bind you, when you long to play,
  For your offence.
I'll shut mine eyes to keep you in,
I'll make you fast it for your sin,
I'll count your power not worth a pin.
Alas! what hereby shall I win
  If he gainsay me?

What if I beat the wanton boy
  With many a rod?
He will repay me with annoy,
  Because a god.
Then sit thou safely on my knee,
And let thy bower my bosom be;
Lurk in mine eyes, I like of thee.
O Cupid, so thou pity me,
  Spare not, but play thee!

# GEORGE CHAPMAN/1559–1634

### *Muses That Sing Love's Sensual Empery*

Muses that sing Love's sensual empery,
And lovers kindling your enragèd fires
At Cupid's bonfires burning in the eye,
Blown with the empty breath of vain desires,
You that prefer the painted cabinet
Before the wealthy jewels it doth store ye,
That all your joys in dying figures set,
And stain the living substance of your glory,
Abjure those joys, abhor their memory,
And let my love the honoured subject be
Of love, and honour's complete history;
Your eyes were never yet let in to see
The majesty and riches of the mind,
But dwell in darkness; for your God is blind.

# ROBERT GREENE/1560?–1592

### *Weep Not, My Wanton*

Weep not, my wanton, smile upon my knee;
When thou art old there's grief enough for thee.
    Mother's wag, pretty boy,
    Father's sorrow, father's joy.
    When thy father first did see
    Such a boy by him and me,
    He was glad, I was woe:
    Fortune changèd made him so,
    When he left his pretty boy,
    Last his sorrow, first his joy.

Weep not, my wanton, smile upon my knee;
When thou art old there's grief enough for thee.
    Streaming tears that never stint,
    Like pearl drops from a flint,
    Fell by course from his eyes,
    That one another's place supplies:
    Thus he grieved in every part,
    Tears of blood fell from his heart,
    When he left his pretty boy,
    Father's sorrow, father's joy.

Weep not, my wanton, smile upon my knee;
When thou art old there's grief enough for thee.
    The wanton smiled, father wept;
    Mother cried, baby lept;
    More he crowed, more we cried;
    Nature could not sorrow hide.
    He must go, he must kiss
    Child and mother, baby bliss;
    For he left his pretty boy,
    Father's sorrow, father's joy.

Weep not, my wanton, smile upon my knee;
When thou art old there's grief enough for thee.

### The Palmer's Ode

    Old Menalcas on a day,
    As in field this shepherd lay,
    Tuning of his oaten pipe,
    Which he hit with many a stripe,
    Said to Coridon that he
    Once was young and full of glee:
    "Blithe and wanton was I then;
    Such desires follow men.
    As I lay and kept my sheep,
    Came the God that hateth sleep,
    Clad in armour all of fire,

Hand in hand with Queen Desire;
And with a dart that wounded nigh, ·
Pierced my heart as I did lie;
That when I woke I'gan swear,
Phillis' beauty palm did bear.
Up I start, forth went I,
With her face to feed mine eye:
There I saw Desire sit,
That my heart with love had hit,
Laying forth bright beauty's hooks
To entrap my gazing looks.
Love I did and 'gan to woo,
Pray and sigh; all would not do:
Women, when they take the toy,
Covet to be counted coy.
Coy she was, and I'gan court,
She thought love was but a sport.
Profound hell was in my thought,
Such a pain Desire had wrought,
That I sued with sighs and tears.
Still ingrate she stopped her ears,
Till my youth I had spent.
Last a passion of Repent
Told me flat that Desire
Was a brand of love's fire,
Which consumeth men in thrall,
Virtue, youth, wit, and all.
At this saw back I start,
Beat Desire from my heart, ·
Shook off love and made an oath,
To be enemy to both.
Old I was when thus I fled
Such fond toys as cloyed my head.
But this I learned at Virtue's gate,
The way to good is never late."

*The Description of Sir Geoffrey Chaucer*

His stature was not very tall,
Lean he was, his legs were small,
Hosed within a stock of red,
A buttoned bonnet on his head,
From under which did hang, I ween,
Silver hairs both bright and sheen.
His beard was white, trimmèd round,
His countenance blithe and merry found.
A sleeveless jacket large and wide,
With many plights and skirts side,
Of water camlet did he wear;
A whittle by his belt he bare,
His shoes were corned, broad before,
His inkhorn at his side he wore,
And in his hand he bore a book.
Thus did this ancient poet look.


# ROBERT SOUTHWELL/1561?–1595


*The Burning Babe*

As I in hoary winter's night stood shivering in the snow,
Surprised I was with sudden heat, which made my heart to
    glow;
And lifting up a fearful eye to view what fire was near,
A pretty Babe all burning bright, did in the air appear,
Who scorchèd with excessive heat, such floods of tears did
    shed,
As though His floods should quench His flames which with
    His tears were fed;
Alas! quoth He, but newly born, in fiery heats I fry,
Yet none approach to warm their hearts or feel my fire but I!
My faultless breast the furnace is, the fuel wounding thorns,

Love is the fire, and sighs the smoke, the ashes shame and
    scorns;
The fuel Justice layeth on, and Mercy blows the coals,
The metal in this furnace wrought are men's defilèd souls,
For which, as now on fire I am to work them to their good,
So will I melt into a bath to wash them in My blood:
With this He vanished out of sight, and swiftly shrank away,
And straight I callèd unto mind that it was Christmas-day.


# HENRY CONSTABLE/1562–1613

### *Hope, Like the Hyena*

Hope, like the hyena, coming to be old,
Alters his shape, is turned into despair.
Pity my hoary hopes, maid of clear mould;
Think not that frowns can ever make thee fair.
What harm is it to kiss, to laugh, to play?
Beauty's no blossom, if it be not used.
Sweet dalliance keepeth wrinkles long away;
Repentance follows them that have refused.
To bring you to the knowledge of your good,
I seek, I sue. O! try and then believe!
Each image can be chaste that's carved of wood;
You show you live, when men you do relieve.
Iron with wearing shines; rust wasteth treasure;
On earth but love, there is no other pleasure.


### *Miracle of the World*

Miracle of the world! I never will deny
That former poets praise the beauty of their days;
But all those beauties were but figures of thy praise,
And all those poets did of thee but prophesy.
Thy coming to the world hath taught us to descry

What Petrarch's Laura meant, for truth the lip bewrays.
Lo! why th' Italians, yet which never saw thy rays,
To find out Petrarch's sense such forgèd glosses try.
The beauties, which he in a veil enclosed beheld,
But revelations were within his secret heart,
By which in parables thy coming he foretold;
His songs were hymns of thee, which only now before
Thy image should be sung; for thou that goddess art,
Which only we without idolatry adore.


# SAMUEL DANIEL/1563–1619


### Time, Cruel Time

Time, cruel Time, come and subdue that brow,
Which conquers all but thee; and thee too stays,
As if she were exempt from scythe or bow,
From love or years, unsubject to decays.
Or art thou grown in league with those fair eyes,
That they may help thee to consume our days?
Or dost thou spare her for her cruelties,
Being merciless like thee, that no man weighs?
And yet thou see'st thy power she disobeys;
Cares not for thee, but lets thee waste in vain;
And prodigal of hours and years betrays
Beauty and Youth to Opinion and Disdain.
Yet spare her, Time, let her exempted be;
She may become more kind to thee or me.


### Look, Delia, How We Esteem the Half-Blown Rose

Look, Delia, how we esteem the half-blown rose,
The image of thy blush, and summer's honour!
Whilst yet her tender bud doth undisclose
That full of beauty Time bestows upon her.

No sooner spreads her glory in the air
But straight her wide-blown pomp comes to decline;
She then is scorned that late adorned the fair;
So fade the roses of those cheeks of thine.
No April can revive thy withered flowers,
Whose springing grace adorns thy glory now;
Swift, speedy Time, feathered with flying hours,
Dissolves the beauty of the fairest brow.
Then do not thou such treasure waste in vain,
But love now, whilst thou mayst be loved again.

## When Men Shall Find Thy Flower

When men shall find thy flower, thy glory, pass,
And thou with careful brow sitting alone
Receivèd hast this message from thy glass,
That tells the truth and says that all is gone,
Fresh shalt thou see in me the wounds thou madest,
Though spent thy flame, in me the heat remaining;
I that have loved thee thus before thou fadest,
My faith shall wax, when thou art in thy waning.
The world shall find this miracle in me,
That fire can burn when all the matter's spent;
Then what my faith hath been thyself shalt see,
And that thou wast unkind thou mayst repent.
Thou mayst repent that thou hast scorned my tears,
When winter snows upon thy sable hairs.

## Care-Charmer Sleep

Care-charmer Sleep, son of the sable Night,
Brother to Death, in silent darkness born,
Relieve my languish, and restore the light,
With dark forgetting of my cares return.
And let the day be time enough to mourn
The shipwreck of my ill-adventured youth;
Let waking eyes suffice to wail their scorn,

Without the torment of the night's untruth.
Cease, dreams, the images of day-desires,
To model forth the passions of the morrow;
Never let rising sun approve you liars,
To add more grief to aggravate my sorrow.
Still let me sleep, embracing clouds in vain;
And never wake to feel the day's disdain.

### Let Others Sing of Knights

Let others sing of knights and paladins
In agèd accents and untimely words;
Paint shadows in imaginary lines,
Which well the reach of their high wits records:
But I must sing of thee, and those fair eyes
Authentic shall my verse in time to come;
When yet th' unborn shall say, "Lo where she lies,
Whose beauty made him speak that else was dumb."
These are the arks, the trophies I erect,
That fortify thy name against old age;
And these thy sacred virtues must protect
Against the dark, and Time's consuming rage.
Though th' error of my youth in them appear,
Suffice they shew I lived and loved thee dear.

# BARTHOLOMEW GRIFFIN/?-1602

### Care-Charmer Sleep

Care-charmer sleep, sweet ease in restless misery,
The captive's liberty, and his freedom's song,
Balm of the bruisèd heart, man's chief felicity,
Brother of quiet death, when life is too, too long!
A comedy it is, and now an history.

What is not sleep unto the feeble mind?
It easeth him that toils and him that's sorry,
It makes the deaf to hear, to see the blind.
Ungentle sleep, thou helpest all but me,
For when I sleep my soul is vexèd most.
It is Fidessa that doth master thee;
If she approach, alas, thy power is lost.
But here she is. See, how he runs amain!
I fear at night he will not come again.


## MICHAEL DRAYTON/1563–1631


### *To Nothing Fitter*

To nothing fitter can I thee compare
Than to the son of some rich pennyfather,
Who having now brought on his end with care,
Leaves to his son all he had heaped together;
This new-rich novice, lavish of his chest,
To one man gives, doth on another spend,
Then here he riots, yet amongst the rest
Haps to lend some to one true honest friend.
Thy gifts thou in obscurity dost waste,
False friends thy kindness, born but to deceive thee,
Thy love, that is on the unworthy placed,
Time hath thy beauty, which with age will leave thee;
Only that little which to me was lent
I give thee back, when all the rest is spent.


### *Why Should Your Fair Eyes*

Why should your fair eyes with such sovereign grace
Disperse their rays on every vulgar spirit,
Whilst I in darkness in the self-same place

Get not one glance to recompense my merit?
So doth the ploughman gaze the wandering star,
And only rest contented with the light,
That never learned what constellations are,
Beyond the bent of his unknowing sight.
O! why should beauty, custom to obey,
To their gross sense apply herself so ill?
Would God I were as ignorant as they,
When I am made unhappy by my skill;
Only compelled on this poor good to boast,
Heavens are not kind to them that know them most.


### Calling to Mind Since First My Love Begun

Calling to mind since first my love begun,
Th' incertain times oft varying in their course,
How things still unexpectedly have run,
As 't please the Fates, by their resistless force:
Lastly, mine eyes amazedly have seen
Essex's great fall, Tyrone his peace to gain,
The quiet end of that long-living queen,
This king's fair entrance, and our peace with Spain,
We and the Dutch at length ourselves to sever;
Thus the world doth, and evermore, shall reel:
Yet to my goddess I am constant ever,
Howe'er blind Fortune turn her giddy wheel:
Though heaven and earth both prove to me untrue,
Yet am I still inviolate to you.


### How Many Paltry, Foolish, Painted Things

How many paltry, foolish, painted things,
That now in coaches trouble every street,
Shall be forgotten, whom no poet sings,
Ere they be well wrapt in their winding-sheet!
Where I to thee eternity shall give,

When nothing else remaineth of these days,
And queens hereafter shall be glad to live
Upon the alms of thy superfluous praise.
Virgins and matrons, reading these my rimes,
Shall be so much delighted with thy story
That they shall grieve they lived not in these times,
To have seen thee, their sex's only glory.
So shalt thou fly above the vulgar throng,
Still to survive in my immortal song.

### Cupid, I Hate Thee

Cupid, I hate thee, which I'd have thee know,
A naked starveling ever may'st thou be,
Poor rogue, go pawn thy fascia and thy bow,
For some few rags wherewith to cover thee;
Or if thou'lt not, thy archery forbear,
To some base rustic do thyself prefer,
And when corn's sown, or grown into the ear,
Practice thy quiver and turn crow-keeper;
Or being blind (as fittest for the trade),
Go hire thyself some bungling harper's boy;
They that are blind are minstrels often made,
So may'st thou live, to thy fair mother's joy:
That whilst with Mars she holdeth her old way,
Thou, her blind son, may'st sit by them, and play.

### Since There's No Help

Since there's no help, come let us kiss and part.
Nay, I have done; you get no more of me,
And I am glad, yea, glad with all my heart,
That thus so cleanly I myself can free;
Shake hands for ever, cancel all our vows,
And when we meet at any time again,
Be it not seen in either of our brows
That we one jot of former love retain.

Now at the last gasp of Love's latest breath,
When, his pulse failing, Passion speechless lies,
When Faith is kneeling by his bed of death,
And Innocence is closing up his eyes,
Now if thou wouldst, when all have given him over,
From death to life thou mightst him yet recover.


### To the Virginian Voyage

You brave, heroic minds
Worthy your country's name,
   That honour still pursue,
   Go, and subdue,
Whilst loit'ring hinds
Lurk here at home, with shame.

Britons, you stay too long;
Quickly aboard bestow you,
   And with a merry gale
   Swell your stretchèd sail,
With vows as strong
As the winds that blow you.

Your course securely steer,
West and by south forth keep.
   Rocks, lee-shores, nor shoals,
   When Aeolus scowls,
You need not fear,
So absolute the deep.

And cheerfully at sea,
Success you still entice,
   To get the pearl and gold,
   And ours to hold,
Virginia,
Earth's only paradise,

Where Nature hath in store
Fowl, venison, and fish,
    And the fruitful'st soil,
    Without your toil,
Three harvests more,
All greater than your wish.

And the ambitious vine
Crowns with his purple mass
    The cedar reaching high
    To kiss the sky,
The cypress, pine,
And useful sassafras.

To whom, the Golden Age
Still nature's laws doth give,
    No other cares that tend
    But them to defend
From winter's age,
That long there doth not live.

When as the luscious smell
Of that delicious land,
    Above the sea that flows,
    The clear wind throws,
Your hearts to swell,
Approaching the dear strand.

In kenning of the shore
(Thanks to God first given),
    O you, the happiest men,
    Be frolic then;
Let cannons roar,
Frighting the wide heaven.

And in the regions far,
Such heroes bring you forth
    As those from whom we came,
    And plant our name

Under that star
Not known unto our north.

And as there plenty grows
Of laurel everywhere,
   Apollo's sacred tree,
   You it may see
A poet's brows
To crown, that may sing there.

Thy voyages attend,
Industrious Hakluyt,
   Whose reading shall inflame
   Men to seek fame,
And much commend
To after-times thy wit.


### The Cryer

Good folk, for gold or hire,
But help me to a cryer;
For my poor heart is run astray
After two eyes that passed this way.
O yes, O yes, O yes,
If there be any man,
In town or country, can
Bring me my heart again,
I'll please him for his pain;
And by these marks I will you show,
That only I this heart do owe.
It is a wounded heart,
Wherein yet sticks the dart,
Every piece sore hurt throughout it,
Faith and Troth writ round about it:
It was a tame heart, and a dear,
And never used to roam;

But having got this haunt, I fear
'Twill hardly stay at home.
For God's sake, walking by the way,
If you my heart do see,
Either impound it for a stray,
Or send it back to me.


# CHRISTOPHER MARLOWE/1564–1593

### The Passionate Shepherd to His Love

Come live with me and be my love,
And we will all the pleasures prove,
That hills and valleys, dales and fields,
And all the craggy mountains yields.

There we will sit upon the rocks,
And see the shepherds feed their flocks,
By shallow rivers to whose falls
Melodious birds sing madrigals.

And I will make thee beds of roses
With a thousand fragrant posies,
A cap of flowers, and a kirtle
Embroidered all with leaves of myrtle;

A gown made of the finest wool
Which from our pretty lambs we pull;
Fair lined slippers for the cold,
With buckles of the purest gold;

A belt of straw and ivy buds,
With coral clasps and amber studs:
And if these pleasures may thee move,
Come live with me and be my love.

The shepherds' swains shall dance and sing
For thy delight each May morning:
If these delights thy mind may move,
Then live with me and be my love.

# WILLIAM SHAKESPEARE/1564–1616

### Sonnet 2

When forty winters shall besiege thy brow,
And dig deep trenches in thy beauty's field,
Thy youth's proud livery, so gazed on now,
Will be a tattered weed, of small worth held:
Then being asked where all thy beauty lies,
Where all the treasure of thy lusty days,
To say, within thine own deep-sunken eyes,
Were an all-eating shame and thriftless praise.
How much more praise deserved thy beauty's use,
If thou couldst answer, "This fair child of mine
Shall sum my count, and make my old excuse,"
Proving his beauty by succession thine!
This were to be new made when thou art old,
And see thy blood warm when thou feel'st it cold.

### Sonnet 3

Look in thy glass, and tell the face thou viewest
Now is the time that face should form another;
Whose fresh repair if now thou not renewest,
Thou dost beguile the world, unbless some mother.
For where is she so fair whose uneared womb
Disdains the tillage of thy husbandry?
Or who is he so fond will be the tomb
Of his self-love, to stop posterity?
Thou art thy mother's glass, and she in thee

Calls back the lovely April of her prime;
So thou through windows of thine age shalt see,
Despite of wrinkles, this thy golden time.
But if thou live, remembered not to be,
Die single, and thine image dies with thee.

## Sonnet 12

When I do count the clock that tells the time,
And see the brave day sunk in hideous night;
When I behold the violet past prime,
And sable curls, all silvered o'er with white;
When lofty trees I see barren of leaves,
Which erst from heat did canopy the herd,
And summer's green all girded up in sheaves,
Borne on the bier with white and bristly beard,
Then of thy beauty do I question make,
That thou among the wastes of time must go,
Since sweets and beauties do themselves forsake
And die as fast as they see others grow;
And nothing 'gainst Time's scythe can make defence
Save breed, to brave him when he takes thee hence.

## Sonnet 15

When I consider every thing that grows
Holds in perfection but a little moment,
That this huge stage presenteth nought but shows
Whereon the stars in secret influence comment;
When I perceive that men as plants increase,
Cheerèd and checked even by the self-same sky,
Vaunt in their youthful sap, at height decrease,
And wear their brave state out of memory;
Then the conceit of this inconstant stay
Sets you most rich in youth before my sight,
Where wasteful Time debateth with Decay,
To change your day of youth to sullied night;

And, all in war with Time for love of you,
As he takes from you, I engraft you new.


### Sonnet 18

Shall I compare thee to a summer's day?
Thou art more lovely and more temperate:
Rough winds do shake the darling buds of May,
And summer's lease hath all too short a date:
Sometime too hot the eye of heaven shines,
And often is his gold complexion dimmed;
And every fair from fair sometime declines,
By chance, or nature's changing course untrimmed;
But thy eternal summer shall not fade,
Nor lose possession of that fair thou owest,
Nor shall Death brag thou wander'st in his shade,
When in eternal lines to time thou growest;
So long as men can breathe, or eyes can see,
So long lives this, and this gives life to thee.


### Sonnet 19

Devouring Time, blunt thou the lion's paws,
And make the earth devour her own sweet brood;
Pluck the keen teeth from the fierce tiger's jaws,
And burn the long-lived phoenix in her blood;
Make glad and sorry seasons as thou fleets,
And do whate'er thou wilt, swift-footed Time,
To the wide world and all her fading sweets;
But I forbid thee one most heinous crime:
O! carve not with thy hours my love's fair brow,
Nor draw no lines there with thine antique pen;
Him in thy course untainted do allow
For beauty's pattern to succeeding men.
Yet, do thy worst, old Time: despite thy wrong,
My love shall in my verse ever live young.

## Sonnet 25

Let those who are in favour with their stars
Of public honour and proud titles boast,
Whilst I, whom fortune of such triumph bars,
Unlooked for, joy in that I honour most.
Great princes' favourites their fair leaves spread
But as the marigold at the sun's eye,
And in themselves their pride lies burièd,
For at a frown they in their glory die.
The painful warrior famousèd for fight,
After a thousand victories once foiled,
Is from the book of honour razèd quite,
And all the rest forgot for which he toiled:
Then happy I, that love and am beloved,
Where I may not remove nor be removed.

## Sonnet 27

Weary with toil, I haste me to my bed,
The dear repose for limbs with travel tired;
But then begins a journey in my head
To work my mind, when body's work's expired:
For then my thoughts, from far where I abide,
Intend a zealous pilgrimage to thee,
And keep my drooping eyelids open wide,
Looking on darkness which the blind do see:
Save that my soul's imaginary sight
Presents thy shadow to my sightless view,
Which, like a jewel hung in ghastly night,
Makes black night beauteous and her old face new.
Lo! thus, by day my limbs, by night my mind,
For thee and for myself no quiet find.

### Sonnet 29

When in disgrace with fortune and men's eyes
I all alone beweep my outcast state,
And trouble deaf heaven with my bootless cries,
And look upon myself, and curse my fate,
Wishing me like to one more rich in hope,
Featured like him, like him with friends possessed,
Desiring this man's art, and that man's scope,
With what I most enjoy contented least;
Yet in these thoughts myself almost despising,
Haply I think on thee, and then my state,
Like to the lark at break of day arising
From sullen earth, sings hymns at heaven's gate;
For thy sweet love remembered such wealth brings
That then I scorn to change my state with kings.

### Sonnet 30

When to the sessions of sweet silent thought
I summon up remembrance of things past,
I sigh the lack of many a thing I sought,
And with old woes new wail my dear time's waste:
Then can I drown an eye, unused to flow,
For precious friends hid in death's dateless night,
And weep afresh love's long since cancelled woe,
And moan the expense of many a vanished sight:
Then can I grieve at grievances foregone,
And heavily from woe to woe tell o'er
The sad account of fore-bemoanèd moan,
Which I new pay as if not paid before.
But if the while I think on thee, dear friend,
All losses are restored and sorrows end.

*Sonnet 33*

Full many a glorious morning have I seen
Flatter the mountain-tops with sovereign eye,
Kissing with golden face the meadows green,
Gilding pale streams with heavenly alchemy;
Anon permit the basest clouds to ride
With ugly rack on his celestial face,
And from the forlorn world his visage hide,
Stealing unseen to west with this disgrace:
Even so my sun one early morn did shine,
With all-triumphant splendour on my brow;
But out! alack! he was but one hour mine,
The region cloud hath masked him from me now.
Yet him for this my love no whit disdaineth;
Suns of the world may stain when heaven's sun staineth.

*Sonnet 35*

No more be grieved at that which thou hast done,
Roses have thorns, and silver fountains mud,
Clouds and eclipses stain both moon and sun,
And loathsome canker lives in sweetest bud.
All men make faults, and even I in this,
Authorizing thy trespass with compare,
My self corrupting salving thy amiss,
Excusing thy sins more than thy sins are:
For to thy sensual fault I bring in sense,
Thy adverse party is thy advocate,
And 'gainst myself a lawful plea commence,
Such civil war is in my love and hate,
That I an accessory needs must be,
To that sweet thief which sourly robs from me.

## Sonnet 40

Take all my loves, my love, yea, take them all;
What hast thou then more than thou hadst before?
No love, my love, that thou mayst true love call;
All mine was thine before thou hadst this more.
Then, if for my love thou my love receivest,
I cannot blame thee for my love thou usest;
But yet be blamed, if thou thyself deceivest
By wilful taste of what thyself refusest.
I do forgive thy robbery, gentle thief,
Although thou steal thee all my poverty;
And yet love knows it is a greater grief
To bear love's wrong than hate's known injury.
Lascivious grace, in whom all ill well shows,
Kill me with spites; yet we must not be foes.

## Sonnet 53

What is your substance, whereof are you made,
That millions of strange shadows on you tend?
Since every one hath, every one, one shade,
And you, but one, can every shadow lend.
Describe Adonis, and the counterfeit
Is poorly imitated after you;
On Helen's cheek all art of beauty set,
And you in Grecian tires are painted new;
Speak of the spring and foison of the year,
The one doth shadow of your beauty show,
The other as your bounty doth appear;
And you in every blessèd shape we know.
In all external grace you have some part,
But you like none, none you, for constant heart.

## Sonnet 54

O! how much more doth beauty beauteous seem
By that sweet ornament which truth doth give.
The rose looks fair, but fairer we it deem
For that sweet odour which doth in it live.
The canker-blooms have full as deep a dye
As the perfumèd tincture of the roses.
Hang on such thorns, and play as wantonly
When summer's breath their maskèd buds discloses:
But, for their virtue only is their show,
They live unwooed, and unrespected fade,
Die to themselves. Sweet roses do not so;
Of their sweet deaths are sweetest odours made:
And so of you, beauteous and lovely youth,
When that shall vade,[1] my verse distils your truth.

## Sonnet 55

Not marble, nor the gilded monuments
Of princes, shall outlive this powerful rhyme;
But you shall shine more bright in these contents
Than unswept stone, besmeared with sluttish time.
When wasteful war shall statues overturn,
And broils root out the work of masonry,
Nor Mars his sword nor war's quick fire shall burn
The living record of your memory.
'Gainst death and all oblivious enmity
Shall you pace forth; your praise shall still find room
Even in the eyes of all posterity
That wear this world out to the ending doom.
So, till the judgment that yourself arise,
You live in this, and dwell in lovers' eyes.

[1] fade

## Sonnet 56

Sweet love, renew thy force; be it not said
Thy edge should blunter be than appetite,
Which but to-day by feeding is allayed,
To-morrow sharpened in his former might:
So, love, be thou; although to-day thou fill
Thy hungry eyes, even till they wink with fullness,
To-morrow see again, and do not kill
The spirit of love with a perpetual dullness.
Let this sad interim like the ocean be
Which parts the shore, where two contracted new
Come daily to the banks, that, when they see
Return of love, more blest may be the view;
Or call it winter, which, being full of care,
Makes summer's welcome thrice more wished,
        more rare.

## Sonnet 60

Like as the waves make towards the pebbled shore,
So do our minutes hasten to their end,
Each changing place with that which goes before,
In sequent toil all forwards do contend.
Nativity, once in the main of light,
Crawls to maturity, wherewith being crowned,
Crookèd eclipses 'gainst his glory fight,
And Time that gave doth now his gift confound.
Time doth transfix the flourish set on youth,
And delves the parallels in beauty's brow,
Feeds on the rarities of nature's truth,
And nothing stands but for his scythe to mow.
And yet to times in hope my verse shall stand,
Praising thy worth, despite his cruel hand.

## Sonnet 64

When I have seen by Time's fell hand defaced
The rich proud cost of outworn buried age;
When sometime lofty towers I see down razed,
And brass eternal slave to mortal rage;
When I have seen the hungry ocean gain
Advantage on the kingdom of the shore,
And the firm soil win of the watery main,
Increasing store with loss, and loss with store;
When I have seen such interchange of state,
Or state itself confounded to decay,
Ruin hath taught me thus to ruminate,
That Time will come and take my love away.
This thought is as a death, which cannot choose
But weep to have that which it fears to lose.

## Sonnet 65

Since brass, nor stone, nor earth, nor boundless sea,
But sad mortality o'ersways their power,
How with this rage shall beauty hold a plea,
Whose action is no stronger than a flower?
O! how shall summer's honey breath hold out
Against the wrackful siege of battering days,
When rocks impregnable are not so stout,
Nor gates of steel so strong, but Time decays?
O fearful meditation! where, alack,
Shall Time's best jewel from Time's chest lie hid?
Or what strong hand can hold his swift foot back?
Or who his spoil of beauty can forbid?
O! none, unless this miracle have might,
That in black ink my love may still shine bright.

## Sonnet 66

Tired with all these, for restful death I cry,
As to behold desert a beggar born,
And needy nothing trimmed in jollity,
And purest faith unhappily forsworn,
And gilded honour shamefully misplaced,
And maiden virtue rudely strumpeted,
And right perfection wrongfully disgraced,
And strength by limping sway disablèd,
And art made tongue-tied by authority,
And folly—doctor-like—controlling skill,
And simple truth miscalled simplicity,
And captive good attending captain ill:
Tired with all these, from these would I be gone,
Save that, to die, I leave my love alone.

## Sonnet 67

Ah! wherefore with infection should he live,
And with his presence grace impiety,
That sin by him advantage should achieve,
And lace itself with his society?
Why should false painting imitate his cheek,
And steal dead seeing of his living hue?
Why should poor beauty indirectly seek
Roses of shadow, since his rose is true?
Why should he live, now Nature bankrupt is,
Beggared of blood to blush through lively veins?
For she hath no exchequer now but his,
And, proud of many, lives upon his gains.
O! him she stores, to show what wealth she had
In days long since, before these last so bad.

### Sonnet 68

Thus is his cheek the map of days outworn,
When beauty lived and died as flowers do now,
Before these bastard signs of fair were born,
Or durst inhabit on a living brow;
Before the golden tresses of the dead,
The right of sepulchres, were shorn away,
To live a second life on second head;
Ere beauty's dead fleece made another gay.
In him those holy antique hours are seen,
Without all ornament, itself and true,
Making no summer of another's green,
Robbing no old to dress his beauty new;
And him as for a map doth Nature store,
To show false Art what beauty was of yore.

### Sonnet 70

That thou art blamed shall not be thy defect,
For slander's mark was ever yet the fair;
The ornament of beauty is suspect,
A crow that flies in heaven's sweetest air.
So thou be good, slander doth but approve
Thy worth the greater, being wooed of time;
For canker vice the sweetest buds doth love,
And thou present'st a pure unstainèd prime.
Thou hast passed by the ambush of young days
Either not assailed, or victor being charged;
Yet this thy praise cannot be so thy praise,
To tie up envy evermore enlarged:
If some suspect of ill masked not thy show,
Then thou alone kingdoms of hearts shouldst owe.

### Sonnet 71

No longer mourn for me when I am dead,
Than you shall hear the surly sullen bell
Give warning to the world that I am fled
From this vile world, with vilest worms to dwell:
Nay, if you read this line, remember not
The hand that writ it; for I love you so,
That I in your sweet thoughts would be forgot,
If thinking on me then should make you woe.
O! if, I say, you look upon this verse,
When I perhaps compounded am with clay,
Do not so much as my poor name rehearse,
But let your love even with my life decay;
Lest the wise world should look into your moan,
And mock you with me after I am gone.

### Sonnet 73

That time of year thou mayst in me behold
When yellow leaves, or none, or few, do hang
Upon those boughs which shake against the cold,
Bare ruined choirs, where late the sweet birds sang.
In me thou see'st the twilight of such day
As after sunset fadeth in the west,
Which by and by black night doth take away,
Death's second self that seals up all in rest.
In me thou see'st the glowing of such fire,
That on the ashes of his youth doth lie,
As the death-bed, whereon it must expire
Consumed with that which it was nourished by.
This thou perceiv'st, which makes thy love more strong
To love that well, which thou must leave ere long.

### Sonnet 86

Was it the proud full sail of his great verse,
Bound for the prize of all too precious you,
That did my ripe thoughts in my brain inhearse,
Making their tomb the womb wherein they grew?
Was it his spirit, by spirits taught to write
Above a mortal pitch, that struck me dead?
No, neither he, nor his compeers by night
Giving him aid, my verse astonishèd.
He, nor that affable familiar ghost
Which nightly gulls him with intelligence,
As victors of my silence cannot boast;
I was not sick of any fear from thence:
But when your countenance filled up his line,
Then lacked I matter; that enfeebled mine.

### Sonnet 87

Farewell! thou art too dear for my possessing,
And like enough thou know'st thy estimate:
The charter of thy worth gives thee releasing;
My bonds in thee are all determinate.
For how do I hold thee but by thy granting?
And for that riches where is my deserving?
The cause of this fair gift in me is wanting,
And so my patent back again is swerving.
Thyself thou gavest, thy own worth then not knowing,
Or me, to whom thou gavest it, else mistaking;
So thy great gift, upon misprision growing,
Comes home again, on better judgement making.
Thus have I had thee, as a dream doth flatter,
In sleep a king, but, waking, no such matter.

### Sonnet 94

They that have power to hurt and will do none,
That do not do the thing they most do show,
Who, moving others, are themselves as stone,
Unmovèd, cold, and to temptation slow;
They rightly do inherit heaven's graces,
And husband nature's riches from expense;
They are the lords and owners of their faces,
Others but stewards of their excellence.
The summer's flower is to the summer sweet,
Though to itself it only live and die,
But if that flower with base infection meet,
The basest weed outbraves his dignity:
For sweetest things turn sourest by their deeds;
Lilies that fester smell far worse than weeds.

### Sonnet 95

How sweet and lovely dost thou make the shame
Which, like a canker in the fragrant rose,
Doth spot the beauty of thy budding name!
O! in what sweets dost thou thy sins enclose.
That tongue that tells the story of thy days,
Making lascivious comments on thy sport,
Cannot dispraise but in a kind of praise;
Naming thy name blesses an ill report.
O! what a mansion have those vices got
Which for their habitation chose out thee,
Where beauty's veil doth cover every blot
And all things turn to fair that eyes can see!
Take heed, dear heart, of this large privilege;
The hardest knife ill-used doth lose his edge.

## Sonnet 97

How like a winter hath my absence been
From thee, the pleasure of the fleeting year!
What freezings have I felt, what dark days seen!
What old December's bareness everywhere!
And yet this time removed was summer's time,
The teeming autumn, big with rich increase,
Bearing the wanton burden of the prime,
Like widowed wombs after their lords' decease:
Yet this abundant issue seemed to me
But hope of orphans and unfathered fruit;
For summer and his pleasures wait on thee,
And, thou away, the very birds are mute.
Or, if they sing, 'tis with so dull a cheer,
That leaves look pale, dreading the winter's near.

## Sonnet 104

To me, fair friend, you never can be old,
For as you were when first your eye I eyed,
Such seems your beauty still. Three winters cold
Have from the forests shook three summers' pride;
Three beauteous springs to yellow autumn turned
In process of the seasons have I seen,
Three April perfumes in three hot Junes burned,
Since first I saw you fresh, which yet are green.
Ah! yet doth beauty, like a dial-hand,
Steal from his figure, and no pace perceived;
So your sweet hue, which methinks still doth stand,
Hath motion, and mine eye may be deceived.
For fear of which, hear this, thou age unbred;
Ere you were born was beauty's summer dead.

## Sonnet 106

When in the chronicle of wasted time
I see descriptions of the fairest wights,
And beauty making beautiful old rhyme,
In praise of ladies dead and lovely knights,
Then, in the blazon of sweet beauty's best,
Of hand, of foot, of lip, of eye, of brow,
I see their antique pen would have expressed
Even such a beauty as you master now.
So all their praises are but prophecies
Of this our time, all you prefiguring;
And, for they looked but with divining eyes,
They had not skill enough your worth to sing:
For we, which now behold these present days,
Have eyes to wonder, but lack tongues to praise.

## Sonnet 107

Not mine own fears, nor the prophetic soul
Of the wide world dreaming on things to come,
Can yet the lease of my true love control,
Supposed as forfeit to a confined doom.
The mortal moon hath her eclipse endured,
And the sad augurs mock their own presage;
Incertainties now crown themselves assured,
And peace proclaims olives of endless age.
Now with the drops of this most balmy time
My love looks fresh, and Death to me subscribes,
Since, spite of him, I'll live in this poor rhyme,
While he insults o'er dull and speechless tribes.
And thou in this shalt find thy monument,
When tyrants' crests and tombs of brass are spent.

## Sonnet 109

O! never say that I was false of heart,
Though absence seemed my flame to qualify.
As easy might I from myself depart
As from my soul, which in thy breast doth lie:
That is my home of love; if I have ranged,
Like him that travels, I return again,
Just to the time, not with the time exchanged,
So that myself bring water for my stain.
Never believe, though in my nature reigned
All frailties that besiege all kinds of blood,
That it could so preposterously be stained,
To leave for nothing all thy sum of good;
For nothing this wide universe I call,
Save thou, my rose; in it thou art my all.

## Sonnet 113

Since I left you, mine eye is in my mind;
And that which governs me to go about
Doth part his function and is partly blind,
Seems seeing, but effectually is out;
For it no form delivers to the heart
Of bird, of flower, or shape, which it doth latch:
Of his quick objects hath the mind no part,
Nor his own vision holds what it doth catch;
For if it see the rud'st or gentlest sight,
The most sweet favour or deformed'st creature,
The mountain or the sea, the day or night,
The crow or dove, it shapes them to your feature.
Incapable of more, replete with you,
My most true mind thus maketh mine untrue.

## Sonnet 114

Or whether doth my mind, being crowned with you,
Drink up the monarch's plague, this flattery?
Or whether shall I say, mine eye saith true,
And that your love taught it this alchemy,
To make of monsters and things indigest
Such cherubins as your sweet self resemble,
Creating every bad a perfect best,
As fast as objects to his beams assemble?
O! 'tis the first, 'tis flattery in my seeing,
And my great mind most kingly drinks it up:
Mine eye well knows what with his gust is 'greeing,
And to his palate doth prepare the cup:
If it be poisoned, 'tis the lesser sin
That mine eye loves it and doth first begin.

## Sonnet 116

Let me not to the marriage of true minds
Admit impediments. Love is not love
Which alters when it alteration finds,
Or bends with the remover to remove:
Or, no! it is an ever-fixèd mark
That looks on tempests and is never shaken;
It is the star to every wandering bark,
Whose worth's unknown, although his height be taken.
Love's not Time's fool, though rosy lips and cheeks
Within his bending sickle's compass come;
Love alters not with his brief hours and weeks,
But bears it out even to the edge of doom.
If this be error and upon me proved,
I never writ, nor no man ever loved.

## Sonnet 118

Like as, to make our appetites more keen,
With eager compounds we our palate urge;
As, to prevent our maladies unseen,
We sicken to shun sickness when we purge;
Even so, being full of your ne'er-cloying sweetness,
To bitter sauces did I frame my feeding;
And, sick of welfare, found a kind of meetness
To be diseased, ere that there was true needing.
Thus policy in love, to anticipate
The ills that were not, grew to faults assured,
And brought to medicine a healthful state,
Which, rank of goodness, would by ill be cured;
But thence I learn, and find the lesson true,
Drugs poison him that so fell sick of you.

## Sonnet 121

'Tis better to be vile than vile esteemed,
When not to be receives reproach of being;
And the just pleasure lost, which is so deemed
Not by our feeling, but by others' seeing:
For why should others' false adulterate eyes
Give salutation to my sportive blood?
Or on my frailties why are frailer spies,
Which in their wills count bad what I think good?
No, I am that I am, and they that level
At my abuses reckon up their own:
I may be straight though they themselves be bevel;
By their rank thoughts my deeds must not be shown;
Unless this general evil they maintain,
All men are bad and in their badness reign.

### Sonnet 129

The expense of spirit in a waste of shame
Is lust in action; and till action, lust
Is perjured, murderous, bloody, full of blame,
Savage, extreme, rude, cruel, not to trust;
Enjoyed no sooner but despisèd straight;
Past reason hunted; and no sooner had,
Past reason hated, as a swallowed bait,
On purpose laid to make the taker mad:
Mad in pursuit, and in possession so;
Had, having, and in quest to have, extreme;
A bliss in proof, and proved, a very woe;
Before, a joy proposed; behind, a dream.
All this the world well knows; yet none knows well
To shun the heaven that leads men to this hell.

### Sonnet 143

Lo, as a careful housewife runs to catch
One of her feathered creatures broke away,
Sets down her babe, and makes all swift dispatch
In pursuit of the thing she would have stay;
Whilst her neglected child holds her in chase,
Cries to catch her whose busy care is bent
To follow that which flies before her face,
Not prizing her poor infant's discontent:
So runn'st thou after that which flies from thee,
Whilst I thy babe chase thee afar behind;
But if thou catch thy hope, turn back to me,
And play the mother's part, kiss me, be kind;
So will I pray that thou mayst have thy "Will,"
If thou turn back and my loud crying still.

## Sonnet 146

Poor soul, the centre of my sinful earth,
Thrall to these rebel powers that thee array,
Why dost thou pine within and suffer dearth,
Painting thy outward walls so costly gay?
Why so large cost, having so short a lease,
Dost thou upon thy fading mansion spend?
Shall worms, inheritors of this excess,
Eat up thy charge? Is this thy body's end?
Then, soul, live thou upon thy servant's loss,
And let that pine to aggravate thy store;
Buy terms divine in selling hours of dross;
Within be fed, without be rich no more:
So shalt thou feed on Death, that feeds on men,
And Death once dead, there's no more dying then.

## Sonnet 150

O! from what power hast thou this powerful might,
With insufficiency my heart to sway?
To make me give the lie to my true sight,
And swear that brightness doth not grace the day?
Whence hast thou this becoming of things ill,
That in the very refuse of thy deeds
There is such strength and warrantise of skill,
That, in my mind, thy worst all best exceeds?
Who taught thee how to make me love thee more,
The more I hear and see just cause of hate?
O! though I love what others do abhor,
With others thou shouldst not abhor my state:
If thy unworthiness raised love in me,
More worthy I to be beloved of thee.

## Who Is Silvia?

Who is Silvia? what is she,
  That all our swains commend her?
Holy, fair, and wise is she;
  The heaven such grace did lend her,
That she might admirèd be.

Is she kind as she is fair?
  For beauty lives with kindness.
Love doth to her eyes repair,
  To help him of his blindness;
And, being helped, inhabits there.

Then to Silvia let us sing,
  That Silvia is excelling;
She excels each mortal thing
  Upon the dull earth dwelling;
To her let us garlands bring.

## Spring

When daisies pied and violets blue
  And lady-smocks all silver-white
And cuckoo-buds of yellow hue
  Do paint the meadows with delight,
The cuckoo then, on every tree,
Mocks married men; for thus sings he,
        Cuckoo!
Cuckoo, cuckoo! O, word of fear,
Unpleasing to a married ear!

When shepherds pipe on oaten straws,
  And merry larks are ploughmen's clocks,
When turtles tread, and rooks, and daws,
  And maidens bleach their summer smocks,
The cuckoo then, on every tree,

Mocks married men; for thus sings he,
　　　Cuckoo!
Cuckoo, cuckoo! O, word of fear,
Unpleasing to a married ear!


### Winter

When icicles hang by the wall,
　　And Dick the shepherd blows his nail,
And Tom bears logs into the hall,
　　And milk comes frozen home in pail;
When blood is nipped, and ways be foul,
Then nightly sings the staring owl.
Tu-whit, tu-who! a merry note,
While greasy Joan doth keel[1] the pot.

When all aloud the wind doth blow,
　　And coughing drowns the parson's saw,
And birds sit brooding in the snow,
　　And Marian's nose looks red and raw,
When roasted crabs hiss in the bowl,
Then nightly sings the staring owl,
Tu-whit, tu-who! a merry note,
While greasy Joan doth keel the pot.


### You Spotted Snakes

You spotted snakes with double tongue,
　　Thorny hedgehogs, be not seen;
Newts and blind-worms, do no wrong;
　　Come not near our fairy queen.

　　Philomel, with melody,
　　　Sing in our sweet lullaby;
Lulla, lulla, lullaby; lulla, lulla, lullaby!

[1] cool

Never harm,
Nor spell nor charm,
Come our lovely lady nigh.
So, good night, with lullaby.
Weaving spiders, come not here;
Hence, you long-legged spinners, hence!
Beetles black, approach not near;
Worm nor snail, do no offence.

Philomel, with melody,
Sing in our sweet lullaby;
Lulla, lulla, lullaby; lulla, lulla, lullaby!
Never harm,
Nor spell nor charm,
Come our lovely lady nigh.
So, good night, with lullaby.


### Tell Me Where Is Fancy Bred

Tell me where is fancy bred,
Or in the heart or in the head?
How begot, how nourishèd?
Reply, reply.

It is engendered in the eyes,
With gazing fed; and fancy dies
In the cradle where it lies.
Let us all ring fancy's knell.
I'll begin it. Ding, dong, bell.
*Chorus.* Ding, dong, bell.


### Under the Greenwood Tree

Under the greenwood tree
Who loves to lie with me,
And turn his merry note
Unto the sweet bird's throat,

Come hither, come hither, come hither:
    Here shall he see
    No enemy
But winter and rough weather.

Who doth ambition shun,
  And loves to live i' the sun,
  Seeking the food he eats,
  And pleased with what he gets,
Come hither, come hither, come hither:
    Here shall he see
    No enemy
But winter and rough weather.


### Blow, Blow, Thou Winter Wind

Blow, blow, thou winter wind,
Thou art not so unkind
  As man's ingratitude;
Thy tooth is not so keen,
Because thou art not seen,
  Although thy breath be rude.
Heigh-ho! sing, heigh-ho! unto the green holly:
Most friendship is feigning, most loving mere folly.
    Then heigh-ho! the holly!
    This life is most jolly.

Freeze, freeze, thou bitter sky,
That dost not bite so nigh
  As benefits forgot:
Though thou the waters warp,
Thy sting is not so sharp
  As friend remembered not.
Heigh-ho! sing, heigh-ho! unto the green holly:
Most friendship is feigning, most loving mere folly.
    Then heigh-ho! the holly!
    This life is most jolly.

## *It Was a Lover and His Lass*

It was a lover and his lass,
   With a hey, and a ho, and a hey nonino,
That o'er the green corn-field did pass,
   In spring time, the only pretty ring time,
When birds do sing, hey ding a ding, ding;
Sweet lovers love the spring.

Between the acres of the rye,
   With a hey, and a ho, and a hey nonino,
Those pretty country folks would lie,
   In spring time, the only pretty ring time,
When birds do sing, hey ding a ding, ding;
Sweet lovers love the spring.

This carol they began that hour,
   With a hey, and a ho, and a hey nonino,
How that a life was but a flower
   In spring time, the only pretty ring time,
When birds do sing, hey ding a ding, ding;
Sweet lovers love the spring.

And therefore take the present time,
   With a hey, and a ho, and a hey nonino,
For love is crownèd with the prime
   In spring time, the only pretty ring time,
When birds do sing, hey ding a ding, ding;
Sweet lovers love the spring.

## *O Mistress Mine*

O mistress mine, where are you roaming?
O! stay and hear; your true love's coming,
   That can sing both high and low.
Trip no further, pretty sweeting;
Journeys end in lovers meeting,
   Every wise man's son doth know.

What is love? 'Tis not hereafter;
Present mirth hath present laughter;
    What's to come is still unsure.
In delay there lies no plenty;
Then come kiss me, sweet and twenty;
    Youth's a stuff will not endure.


### When That I Was and a Little Tiny Boy

When that I was and a little tiny boy,
    With hey, ho, the wind and the rain;
A foolish thing was but a toy,
    For the rain it raineth every day.

But when I came to man's estate,
    With hey, ho, the wind and the rain;
'Gainst knaves and thieves men shut their gate,
    For the rain it raineth every day.

But when I came, alas! to wive,
    With hey, ho, the wind and the rain;
By swaggering could I never thrive,
    For the rain it raineth every day.

But when I came unto my beds,
    With hey, ho, the wind and the rain;
With toss-pots still had drunken heads,
    For the rain it raineth every day.

A great while ago the world begun,
    With hey, ho, the wind and the rain;
But that's all one, our play is done,
    And we'll strive to please you every day.

## Ophelia's Song

How should I your true love know
    From another one?
By his cockle hat and staff,
    And his sandal shoon.

He is dead and gone, lady,
    He is dead and gone;
At his head a grass-green turf,
    At his heels a stone.

White his shroud as the mountain snow,
    Larded with sweet flowers;
Which bewept to the grave did not go
    With true-love showers.

## Take, O! Take Those Lips Away

Take, O! take those lips away,
    That so sweetly were forsworn,
And those eyes, the break of day,
    Lights that do mislead the morn;
But my kisses bring again,
        Bring again,
Seals of love, but sealed in vain,
        Sealed in vain.

## Fear No More the Heat o' the Sun

Fear no more the heat o' the sun,
    Nor the furious winter's rages;
Thou thy worldly task hast done,
    Home art gone, and ta'en thy wages;
Golden lads and girls all must,
As chimney-sweepers, come to dust.

Fear no more the frown o' the great,
   Thou art past the tyrant's stroke:
Care no more to clothe and eat;
   To thee the reed is as the oak:
The sceptre, learning, physic, must
All follow this, and come to dust.

Fear no more the lightning-flash,
   Nor the all-dreaded thunder-stone;
Fear not slander, censure rash;
   Thou hast finished joy and moan;
All lovers young, all lovers must
Consign to thee, and come to dust.

No exorciser harm thee!
   Nor no witchcraft charm thee!
Ghost unlaid forbear thee!
   Nothing ill come near thee!
Quiet consummation have;
And renownèd be thy grave!

### When Daffodils Begin to Peer

When daffodils begin to peer,
   With heigh! the doxy, over the dale,
Why, then comes in the sweet o' the year;
   For the red blood reigns in the winter's pale.

The white sheet bleaching on the hedge,
   With heigh! the sweet birds, O, how they sing!
Doth set my pugging tooth on edge,
   For a quart of ale is a dish for a king.

The lark, that tirra-lirra chants,
   With heigh! with heigh! the thrush and the jay,
Are summer songs for me and my aunts,
   While we lie tumbling in the hay.

### Come unto These Yellow Sands

Come unto these yellow sands,
   And then take hands:
Curtsied when you have, and kissed
   The wild waves whist,
Foot it featly here and there;
And, sweet sprites, the burden bear.
   Hark, hark!
     Bow, wow
   The watch-dogs bark,
     Bow, wow,
   Hark, hark! I hear
The strain of strutting Chanticleer
Cry, Cock-a-diddle-dow.

### Full Fathom Five

Full fathom five thy father lies;
   Of his bones are coral made;
Those are pearls that were his eyes:
   Nothing of him that doth fade,
But doth suffer a sea-change
Into something rich and strange:
Sea nymphs hourly ring his knell.
         Ding-dong!
   Hark! now I hear them,
         Ding-dong, bell!

### Where the Bee Sucks

Where the bee sucks, there suck I,
In a cowslip's bell I lie,
There I couch when owls do cry,
On the bat's back I do fly
After summer merrily.

Merrily, merrily, shall I live now
Under the blossom that hangs on the bough.


### The Phoenix and the Turtle

Let the bird of loudest lay,
   On the sole Arabian tree,
   Herald sad and trumpet be,
To whose sound chaste wings obey.

But thou shrieking harbinger,
   Foul precurrer of the fiend,
   Augur of the fever's end,
To this troop come thou not near.

From this cession interdict
   Every fowl of tyrant wing,
   Save the eagle, feathered king;
Keep the obsequy so strict.

Let the priest in surplice white
   That defunctive music can,[1]
   Be the death-divining swan,
Lest the requiem lack his right.

And thou treble-dated crow,
   That thy sable gender makest
   With the breath thou givest and takest,
'Mongst our mourners shalt thou go.

Here the anthem doth commence:
   Love and constancy is dead;
   Phoenix and the turtle fled
In a mutual flame from hence.

[1] knows

So they loved, as love in twain
   Had the essence but in one;
   Two distincts, division none;
Number there in love was slain.

Hearts remote, yet not asunder;
   Distance, and no space was seen
   'Twixt the turtle and his queen;
But in them it were a wonder.

So between them love did shine,
   That the turtle saw his right
   Flaming in the phoenix' sight;
Either was the other's mine.

Property was thus appalled,
   That the self was not the same;
   Single nature's double name
Neither two nor one was called.

Reason, in itself confounded,
   Saw division grow together,
   To themselves yet either neither,
Simple were so well compounded:

That it cried, "How true a twain
   Seemeth this concordant one!
   Love hath reason, reason none,
If what parts can so remain."

Whereupon it made this threne[1]
   To the phoenix and the dove,
   Co-supremes and stars of love,
As chorus to their tragic scene.

[1] lament

### THRENOS

Beauty, truth, and rarity,
Grace in all simplicity,
Here enclosed in cinders lie.

Death is now the phoenix' nest;
And the turtle's loyal breast
To eternity doth rest,

Leaving no posterity:
'Twas not their infirmity,
It was married chastity.

Truth may seem, but cannot be;
Beauty brag, but 'tis not she;
Truth and beauty buried be.

To this urn let those repair
That are either true or fair;
For these dead birds sigh a prayer.


# RICHARD VERSTEGAN/1565–1620


## *Lullaby*

Upon my lap my sovereign sits
    And sucks upon my breast.
Meanwhile his love sustains my life,
    And gives my body rest.
        Sing lullaby, my little boy,
        Sing lullaby, my only joy.

When thou hast taken thy repast,
    Repose, my babe, on me;

So may thy mother and thy nurse
   Thy cradle also be.
      Sing lullaby, my little boy,
      Sing lullaby, my only joy.

I grieve that duty doth not work
   All what my wishing would,
Because I would not be to thee
   But in the best I should.
      Sing lullaby, my little boy,
      Sing lullaby, my only joy.

Yet as I am, and as I may,
   I must and will be thine,
Though all too little for thyself,
   Vouchsafing to be mine.
      Sing lullaby, my little boy,
      Sing lullaby, my only joy.

# JOHN HOSKINS/1566–1638

## *Ode**

Absence, hear thou my protestation
    Against thy strength,
    Distance and length:
Do what thou canst for alteration,
    For hearts of truest mettle
    Absence doth join, and time doth settle.

Who loves a mistress of such quality,
    He soon hath found
    Affection's ground

* Also attributed to John Donne.

Beyond time, place, and all mortality.
    To hearts that cannot vary
    Absence is present, time doth tarry.

My senses want their outward motions
      Which now within
      Reason doth win,
Redoubled in her secret notions:
    Like rich men that take pleasure
    In hiding more than handling treasure.

By absence this good means I gain,
    That I can catch her,
    Where none can watch her,
In some close corner of my brain:
    There I embrace and kiss her,
    And so I both enjoy and miss her.


# THOMAS NASHE/1567–1601


### Adieu, Farewell Earth's Bliss

Adieu, farewell earth's bliss,
This world uncertain is;
Fond are life's lustful joys,
Death proves them all but toys,
None from his darts can fly.
I am sick, I must die.
      Lord, have mercy on us!

Rich men, trust not in wealth,
Gold cannot buy you health;
Physic himself must fade,
All things to end are made.
The plague full swift goes by.

I am sick, I must die.
>Lord, have mercy on us!

Beauty is but a flower
Which wrinkles will devour;
Brightness falls from the air,
Queens have died young and fair,
Dust hath closed Helen's eye.
I am sick, I must die.
>Lord, have mercy on us!

Strength stoops unto the grave,
Worms feed on Hector brave,
Swords may not fight with fate,
Earth still holds ope her gate.
Come! come! the bells do cry.
I am sick, I must die.
>Lord, have mercy on us!

Wit with his wantonness
Tasteth death's bitterness;
Hell's executioner
Hath no ears for to hear
What vain art can reply.
I am sick, I must die.
>Lord, have mercy on us!

Haste, therefore, each degree,
To welcome destiny.
Heaven is our heritage,
Earth but a player's stage;
Mount we unto the sky.
I am sick, I must die.
>Lord, have mercy on us!

## Spring

Spring, the sweet spring, is the year's pleasant king;
Then blooms each thing, then maids dance in a ring,
Cold doth not sting, the pretty birds do sing:
    Cuckoo, jug-jug, pu-we, to-witta-woo!

The palm and may make country houses gay,
Lambs frisk and play, the shepherds pipe all day,
And we hear aye birds tune this merry lay:
    Cuckoo, jug-jug, pu-we, to-witta-woo!

The fields breathe sweet, the daisies kiss our feet,
Young lovers meet, old wives a-sunning sit;
In every street these tunes our ears do greet:
    Cuckoo, jug-jug, pu-we, to-witta-woo!
      Spring, the sweet spring!

## Fair Summer Droops

Fair summer droops, droop men and beasts therefore;
So fair a summer look for never more!
All good things vanish less than in a day,
Peace, plenty, pleasure, suddenly decay.
    Go not yet away, bright soul of the sad year,
    The earth is hell when thou leav'st to appear.

What, shall those flowers that decked thy garland erst,
Upon thy grave be wastefully dispersed?
O trees, consume your sap in sorrow's source;
Streams, turn to tears your tributary course.
    Go not yet hence, bright soul of the sad year,
    The earth is hell when thou leav'st to appear.

*Autumn*

Autumn hath all the summer's fruitful treasure;
Gone is our sport, fled is poor Croydon's pleasure.
Short days, sharp days, long nights come on apace,
Ah! who shall hide us from the winter's face?
Cold doth increase, the sickness will not cease,
And here we lie, God knows, with little ease.
　　From winter, plague, and pestilence, good Lord,
　　　　deliver us!

London doth mourn, Lambeth is quite forlorn;
Trades cry, woe worth that ever they were born.
The want of term is town and city's harm;
Close chambers we do want, to keep us warm.
Long banished must we live from our friends;
This low-built house will bring us to our ends.
　　From winter, plague, and pestilence, good Lord,
　　　　deliver us!


WILLIAM   BASSE/?


*A Memento for Mortality*

Taken from the view of Sepulchres
of so many Kings and Nobles, as lie
interred in the Abbey of Westminster.

Mortality, behold and fear!
What a change of flesh is here!
Think how many royal bones
Sleep within this heap of stones,
Hence removed from beds of ease,
Dainty fare, and what might please,
Fretted roofs, and costly shows,
To a roof that flats the nose,
Which proclaims all flesh is grass,

How the world's fair glories pass;
That here is no trust in health,
In youth, in age, in greatness, wealth,
For if such could have reprieved,
Those had been immortal lived.
Know from this the world a snare,
How that greatness is but care,
How all pleasures are but pain,
And how short they do remain:
For here they lie had realms and lands,
That now want strength to stir their hands;
Where from their pulpits seeled[1] with dust
They preach, "In greatness is no trust."
Here's an acre sown indeed
With the richest, royal'st seed
That the earth did e'er suck in
Since the first man died for sin;
Here the bones of birth have cried,
"Though Gods they were, as men they died."
Here are sands, ignoble things,
Dropped from the ruined sides of Kings;
With whom the poor man's earth being shown,
The difference is not easily known.
Here's a world of pomp and state
Forgotten, dead, disconsolate.
Think then, this scythe that mows down kings,
Exempts no meaner mortal things.
Then bid the wanton lady tread
Amid these mazes of the dead;
And these, truly understood,
More shall cool and quench the blood
Than her many sports a-day,
And her nightly wanton play:
Bid her paint till day of doom,
To this favour she must come.
Bid the merchant gather wealth,

[1] closed, like eyelid of hawk sewed up for training

The usurer exact by stealth,
The proud man beat it from his thought—
Yet to this shape all must be brought.


# THOMAS CAMPION/1567–1620


*What Fair Pomp*


What fair pomp have I spied of glittering ladies,
  With locks sparkled abroad, and rosy coronet
On their ivory brows, tracked to the dainty thighs
  With robes like Amazons, blue as violet,
    With gold aglets adorned, some in a changeable
    Pale, with spangs wavering taught to be moveable?


Then those knights, that afar off with dolorous viewing
  Cast their eyes hitherward, lo! in an agony,
All unbraced, cry aloud, their heavy state rueing:
  Moist cheeks with blubbering, painted as ebony
    Black; their feltered[1] hair torn with wrathful hand;
    And whiles astonied stark in a maze they stand.


But hark! what merry sound, what sudden harmony.
  Look, look near the grove, where the ladies do tread
With their knights the measures wayed by the melody.
  Wantons! whose traversing make men enamoured;
    Now they feign an honour,[2] now by the slender waist
    He must lift her aloft, and seal a kiss in haste.


Straight down under a shadow for weariness they lie
  With pleasant dalliance, hand knit with arm in arm;

---

[1] matted   [2] bow

Now close, now set aloof, they gaze with an equal eye,
  Changing kisses alike; straight with a false alarm,
    Mocking kisses alike, pout with a lovely lip.
    Thus drowned with jollities their merry days do slip.

But stay! now I discern they go on a pilgrimage
  Towards Love's holy land, fair Paphos or Cyprus.
Such devotion is meet for a blithesome age;
  With sweet youth it agrees well to be amorous.
    Let old angry fathers lurk in an hermitage;
    Come! we'll associate this jolly pilgrimage.

### *My Sweetest Lesbia, Let Us Live and Love*

My sweetest Lesbia, let us live and love,
And though the sager sort our deeds reprove,
Let us not weigh them. Heaven's great lamps do dive
Into their west, and straight again revive;
But, soon as once set is our little light,
Then must we sleep one ever-during night.

If all would lead their lives in love like me,
Then bloody swords and armour should not be;
No drum nor trumpet peaceful sleeps should move,
Unless alarm came from the camp of love.
But fools do live and waste their little light,
And seek with pain their ever-during night.

When timely death my life and fortune ends,
Let not my hearse be vexed with mourning friends;
But let all lovers, rich in triumph, come
And with sweet pastimes grace my happy tomb:
And, Lesbia, close up thou my little light,
And crown with love my ever-during night.

## *I Care Not for These Ladies*

I care not for these ladies
That must be wooed and prayed;
Give me kind Amaryllis,
The wanton country maid.
Nature art disdaineth;
Her beauty is her own.
Her when we court and kiss,
She cries: forsooth, let go!
But when we come where comfort is,
She never will say no.

If I love Amaryllis,
She gives me fruit and flowers;
But if we love these ladies,
We must give golden showers.
Give them gold that sell love,
Give me the nut-brown lass,
Who when we court and kiss,
She cries: forsooth, let go!
But when we come where comfort is,
She never will say no.

These ladies must have pillows
And beds by strangers wrought.
Give me a bower of willows,
Of moss and leaves unbought,
And fresh Amaryllis
With milk and honey fed,
Who when we court and kiss,
She cries: forsooth, let go!
But when we come where comfort is,
She never will say no.

### Follow Thy Fair Sun, Unhappy Shadow

Follow thy fair sun, unhappy shadow,
Though thou be black as night,
And she made all of light,
Yet follow thy fair sun, unhappy shadow.

Follow her whose light thy light depriveth,
Though here thou liv'st disgraced,
And she in heaven is placed,
Yet follow her whose light the world reviveth.

Follow those pure beams whose beauty burneth,
That so have scorchèd thee,
As thou still black must be,
Till her kind beams thy black to brightness turneth.

Follow her while yet her glory shineth:
There comes a luckless night,
That will dim all her light;
And this the black unhappy shade divineth.

Follow still since so thy fates ordainèd;
The sun must have his shade,
Till both at once do fade,
The sun still proud, the shadow still disdainèd.

### Blame Not My Cheeks

Blame not my cheeks, though pale with love they be;
The kindly heat unto my heart is flown,
To cherish it that is dismayed by thee,
Who art so cruel and unsteadfast grown:
For nature, called for by distressèd hearts,
Neglects and quite forsakes the outward parts.

But they whose cheeks with careless blood are stained,
Nurse not one spark of love within their hearts,

And, when they woo, they speak with passion feigned,
For their fat love lies in their outward parts:
But in their breasts, where love his court should hold,
Poor Cupid sits and blows his nails for cold.


### When Thou Must Home

When thou must home to shades of underground
And there arrived, a new-admirèd guest,
The beauteous spirits do ingirt thee round,
White Iope, blithe Helen, and the rest,
To hear the stories of thy finished love
From that smooth tongue whose music hell can move;

Then wilt thou speak of banqueting delights,
Of masks and revels which sweet youth did make,
Of tourneys and great challenges of knights,
And all these triumphs for thy beauty's sake:
When thou hast told these honours done to thee,
Then tell, O tell, how thou didst murder me.


### Thrice Toss These Oaken Ashes

Thrice toss these oaken ashes in the air;
Thrice sit thou mute in this enchanted chair;
Then thrice three times tie up this true love's knot,
And murmur soft: "She will, or she will not."

Go burn these poisonous weeds in yon blue fire,
These screech-owl's feathers and this prickling briar,
This cypress gathered at a dead man's grave,
That all thy fears and cares an end may have.

Then come, you fairies, dance with me a round;
Melt her hard heart with your melodious sound.
In vain are all the charms I can devise;
She hath an art to break them with her eyes.

### There Is a Garden in Her Face

There is a garden in her face,
  Where roses and white lilies grow,
A heavenly paradise is that place,
  Wherein all pleasant fruits do flow.
There cherries grow, which none may buy
Till "Cherry-ripe" themselves do cry.

Those cherries fairly do enclose
  Of orient pearl a double row,
Which when her lovely laughter shows,
  They look like rosebuds filled with snow.
Yet them nor peer nor prince can buy,
Till "Cherry-ripe" themselves do cry.

Her eyes like angels watch them still;
  Her brows like bended bows do stand,
Threatening with piercing frowns to kill
  All that attempt with eye or hand
Those sacred cherries to come nigh,
Till "Cherry-ripe" themselves do cry.


## SIR HENRY WOTTON/1568–1639


### On His Mistress, the Queen of Bohemia

You meaner beauties of the night,
  That poorly satisfy our eyes
More by your number than your light,
  You common people of the skies;
  What are you when the moon shall rise?

You curious chanters of the wood,
  That warble forth Dame Nature's lays,

Thinking your passions understood
  By your weak accents; what's your praise,
  When Philomel her voice shall raise?

You violets that first appear,
  By your pure purple mantles known
Like the proud virgins of the year,
  As if the spring were all your own;
  What are you when the rose is blown?

So, when my mistress shall be seen
  In form and beauty of her mind,
By virtue first, then choice, a queen,
  Tell me if she were not designed
  Th' eclipse and glory of her kind?


# THOMAS DEKKER/1570?–1632


### Art Thou Poor, yet Hast Thou Golden Slumbers?

Art thou poor, yet hast thou golden slumbers?
    O sweet content!
Art thou rich, yet is thy mind perplexed?
    O punishment!
Dost thou laugh to see how fools are vexed
To add to golden numbers, golden numbers?
O sweet content! O sweet, O sweet content!
  Work apace, apace, apace, apace;
  Honest labour bears a lovely face;
Then hey nonny nonny, hey nonny nonny!

Canst drink the waters of the crispèd spring?
    O sweet content!
Swimm'st thou in wealth, yet sink'st in thine own tears?
    O punishment!
Then he that patiently want's burden bears

No burden bears, but is a king, a king!
O sweet content! O sweet, O sweet content!
   Work apace, apace, apace, apace;
   Honest labour bears a lovely face;
Then hey nonny nonny, hey nonny nonny!


### Golden Slumbers Kiss Your Eyes

      Golden slumbers kiss your eyes,
      Smiles awake you when you rise.
      Sleep, pretty wantons, do not cry,
      And I will sing a lullaby;
      Rock them, rock them, lullaby.

      Care is heavy, therefore sleep you;
      You are care, and care must keep you.
      Sleep, pretty wantons, do not cry,
      And I will sing a lullaby:
      Rock them, rock them, lullaby.


## JOHN DONNE/1573–1631


### The Canonization

For God's sake hold your tongue, and let me love,
   Or chide my palsy, or my gout,
My five gray hairs, or ruined fortune flout,
   With wealth your state, your mind with arts improve,
      Take you a course, get you a place,
      Observe his honour, or his grace,
Or the king's real, or his stampèd face.
   Contemplate, what you will approve,
   So you will let me love.

Alas, alas, who's injured by my love?
　　What merchant's ships have my sighs drowned?
Who says my tears have overflowed his ground?
　　When did my colds a forward spring remove?
　　　　When did the heats which my veins fill
　　　　Add one more to the plaguey bill?
Soldiers find wars, and lawyers find out still
　　Litigious men, which quarrels move,
　　Though she and I do love.

Call us what you will, we are made such by love;
　　Call her one, me another fly,
We are tapers too, and at our own cost die,
　　And we in us find the eagle and the dove.
　　　　The phoenix riddle hath more wit
　　　　By us, we two being one, are it.
So to one neutral thing both sexes fit,
　　We die and rise the same, and prove
　　Mysterious by this love.

We can die by it, if not live by love,
　　And if unfit for tombs and hearse
Our legend be, it will be fit for verse;
　　And if no piece of chronicle we prove,
　　　　We'll build in sonnets pretty rooms;
　　　　As well a well-wrought urn becomes
The greatest ashes, as half-acre tombs,
　　And by these hymns, all shall approve
　　Us *canonized* for love;

And thus invoke us; you whom reverend love
　　Made one another's hermitage;
You to whom love was peace, that now is rage;
　　Who did the whole world's soul contract, and drove
　　　　Into the glasses of your eyes
　　　　(So made such mirrors, and such spies,
That they did all to you epitomize),
　　Countries, towns, courts: beg from above
　　A pattern of your love!

*The Anniversary*

All kings, and all their favourites,
    All glory of honours, beauties, wits,
The sun itself, which makes times, as they pass,
Is elder by a year, now, than it was
When thou and I first one another saw:
All other things to their destruction draw,
    Only our love hath no decay;
This, no tomorrow hath, nor yesterday;
Running, it never runs from us away,
But truly keeps his first, last, everlasting day.

Two graves must hide thine and my corse,
    If one might, death were no divorce.
Alas, as well as other princes, we
(Who prince enough in one another be)
Must leave at last in death, these eyes, and ears,
Oft fed with true oaths, and with sweet salt tears;
    But souls where nothing dwells but love
(All other thoughts being inmates[1]) then shall prove
This, or a love increasèd there above,
When bodies to their graves, souls from their graves
        remove.

And then we shall be throughly blest,
    But we no more than all the rest;
Here upon earth, we are kings, and none but we
Can be such kings, nor of such subjects be.
Who is so safe as we? where none can do
Treason to us, except one of us two.
    True and false fears let us refrain,
Let us love nobly, and live, and add again
Years and years unto years, till we attain
To write threescore: this is the second of our reign.

[1] lodgers

## Twickham Garden

Blasted with sighs, and surrounded with tears,
  Hither I come to seek the spring,
  And at mine eyes, and at mine ears,
Receive such balms, as else cure every thing;
  But O, self-traitor, I do bring
The spider love, which transubstantiates all,
  And can convert manna to gall,
And that this place may thoroughly be thought
  True paradise, I have the serpent brought.

'Twere wholesomer for me, that winter did
  Benight the glory of this place,
  And that a grave frost did forbid
These trees to laugh, and mock me to my face;
  But that I may not this disgrace
Endure, nor yet leave loving, Love, let me
  Some senseless piece of this place be;
Make me a mandrake, so I may groan here,
  Or a stone fountain weeping out my year.

Hither with crystal vials, lovers, come,
  And take my tears, which are love's wine,
  And try your mistress' tears at home,
For all are false that taste not just like mine;
  Alas, hearts do not in eyes shine,
Nor can you more judge woman's thoughts by tears,
  Than by her shadow, what she wears.
O perverse sex, where none is true but she,
  Who's therefore true, because her truth kills me.


## A Valediction: of Weeping

  Let me pour forth
My tears before thy face, whil'st I stay here,
For thy face coins them, and thy stamp they bear,

And by this mintage they are something worth,
    For thus they be
    Pregnant of thee;
Fruits of much grief they are, emblems of more:
When a tear falls, that thou fall'st which it bore,
So thou and I are nothing then, when on a diverse
      shore.

    On a round ball
A workman that hath copies by, can lay
An Europe, Afrique, and an Asia,
And quickly make that, which was nothing, *All*,
    So doth each tear,
    Which thee doth wear,
A globe, yea world by that impression grow,
Till thy tears mixt with mine do overflow
This world, by waters sent from thee, my heaven
      dissolvèd so.

    O more than Moon,
Draw not up seas to drown me in thy sphere,
Weep me not dead, in thine arms, but forbear
To teach the sea, what it may do too soon;
    Let not the wind
    Example find,
To do me more harm than it purposeth:
Since thou and I sigh one another's breath,
Whoe'er sighs most, is cruellest, and hastes the
      other's death.


*A Nocturnal upon St. Lucie's Day,*

*Being the Shortest Day*

'Tis the year's midnight, and it is the day's,
*Lucie's*, who scarce seven hours herself unmasks,
    The sun is spent, and now his flasks
    Send forth light squibs, no constant rays;
      The world's whole sap is sunk:

The general balm th'hydroptic earth hath drunk,
Whither, as to the bed's-feet, life is shrunk,
Dead and interred; yet all these seem to laugh,
Compared with me, who am their epitaph.

Study me then, you who shall lovers be
At the next world, that is, at the next spring:
   For I am every dead thing,
   In whom love wrought new alchemy.
     For his art did express
A quintessence even from nothingness,
From dull privations, and lean emptiness:
He ruined me, and I am re-begot
Of absence, darkness, death; things which are not.

All others, from all things, draw all that's good,
Life, soul, form, spirit, whence they being have;
   I, by love's limbeck, am the grave
   Of all that's nothing. Oft a flood
     Have we two wept, and so
Drowned the whole world, us two; oft did we grow
To be two Chaosses, when we did show
Care to ought else; and often absences
Withdrew our souls, and made us carcasses.

But I am by her death (which word wrongs her),
Of the first nothing, the elixir grown;
   Were I a man, that I were one,
   I needs must know; I should prefer,
     If I were any beast,
Some ends, some means; yea plants, yea stones detest,
And love; all, all some properties invest;
If I an ordinary nothing were,
As shadow, a light and body must be here.

But I am none; nor will my sun renew.
You lovers, for whose sake, the lesser sun
   At this time to the Goat is run
   To fetch new lust, and give it you,
     Enjoy your summer all;

Since she enjoys her long night's festival,
Let me prepare towards her, and let me call
This hour her Vigil, and her Eve, since this
Both the year's, and the day's, deep midnight is.

## The Apparition

When by thy scorn, O murd'ress, I am dead,
And that thou think'st thee free
From all solicitation from me,
Then shall my ghost come to thy bed,
And thee, feigned vestal, in worse arms shall see:
Then thy sick taper will begin to wink,
And he, whose thou art then, being tired before,
Will, if thou stir, or pinch to wake him, think
    Thou call'st for more,
And in false sleep, will from thee shrink:
And then, poor aspen wretch, neglected thou
Bathed in a cold quicksilver sweat wilt lie
    A verier ghost than I.
What I will say, I will not tell thee now,
Lest that preserve thee; and since my love is spent,
I'd rather thou shouldst painfully repent,
Than by my threatenings rest still innocent.

## A Valediction: Forbidding Mourning

As virtuous men pass mildly away,
    And whisper to their souls, to go,
Whilst some of their sad friends do say,
    The breath goes now, and some say, no:

So let us melt, and make no noise,
    No tear-floods, nor sigh-tempests move,
T'were profanation of our joys
    To tell the laity our love.

Moving of th'earth brings harms and fears,
   Men reckon what it did and meant,
But trepidation of the spheres,
   Though greater far, is innocent.

Dull sublunary lovers' love
   (Whose soul is sense) cannot admit
Absence, because it doth remove
   Those things which elemented it.

But we by a love, so much refined
   That our selves know not what it is,
Inter-assurèd of the mind,
   Care less, eyes, lips, and hands to miss.

Our two souls therefore, which are one,
   Though I must go, endure not yet
A breach, but an expansion,
   Like gold to airy thinness beat.

If they be two, they are two so
   As stiff twin compasses are two,
Thy soul, the fixt foot, makes no show
   To move, but doth, if th' other do.

And though it in the center sit,
   Yet when the other far doth roam,
It leans, and hearkens after it,
   And grows erect, as that comes home.

Such wilt thou be to me, who must
   Like th' other foot, obliquely run;
Thy firmness makes my circle just,
   And makes me end, where I begun.

### The Funeral

Whoever comes to shroud me, do not harm
    Nor question much
That subtle wreath of hair which crowns my arm,
The mystery, the sign you must not touch,
    For 'tis my outward soul,
Viceroy to that, which then to heaven being gone,
    Will leave this to control,
And keep these limbs, her provinces, from dissolution.
For if the sinewy thread my brain lets fall
    Through every part
Can tie those parts, and make me one of all;
These hairs which upward grew, and strength and art
    Have from a better brain,
Can better do it; except she meant that I
    By this should know my pain,
As prisoners then are manacled, when they're condemned
    to die.

Whate'er she meant by it, bury it with me,
    For since I am
Love's martyr, it might breed idolatry,
If into others' hands these relics came;
    As 'twas humility
To afford to it all that a soul can do,
    So, 'tis some bravery,
That since you would save none of me, I bury some of you.

### The Blossom

    Little think'st thou, poor flower,
      Whom I have watched six or seven days,
  And seen thy birth, and seen what every hour
  Gave to thy growth, thee to this height to raise,
  And now dost laugh and triumph on this bough,
      Little think'st thou

That it will freeze anon, and that I shall
Tomorrow find thee fallen, or not at all.

    Little think'st thou, poor heart,
      That labor'st yet to nestle thee,
And think'st by hovering here to get a part
In a forbidden or forbidding tree,
And hop'st her stiffness by long siege to bow:
      Little think'st thou,
That thou tomorrow, ere that sun doth wake,
Must with this sun, and me, a journey take.

    But thou, which lov'st to be
      Subtle to plague thyself, wilt say,
Alas, if you must go, what's that to me?
Here lies my business, and here I will stay:
You go to friends, whose love and means present
      Various content
To your eyes, ears, and tongue, and every part.
If then your body go, what need you a heart?

    Well then, stay here; but know,
      When thou hast stayed and done thy most,
A naked thinking heart, that makes no show,
Is to a woman but a kind of ghost;
How shall she know my heart; or having none,
      Know thee for one?
Practise may make her know some other part,
But take my word, she doth not know a heart.

    Meet me at London, then,
      Twenty days hence, and thou shalt see
Me fresher, and more fat, by being with men,
Than if I had stayed still with her and thee.
For God's sake, if you can, be you so too:
      I would give you
There, to another friend, whom we shall find
As glad to have my body, as my mind.

## The Relique

When my grave is broke up again
Some second guest to entertain
(For graves have learned that woman-head
To be to more than one a bed),
      And he that digs it, spies
A bracelet of bright hair about the bone,
      Will he not let'us alone,
And think thát there a loving couple lies,
Who thought that this device might be some way
To make their souls, at the last busy day,
Meet at this grave, and make a little stay?

If this fall in a time, or land,
Where mis-devotion doth command,
Then, he that digs us up, will bring
Us to the bishop, and the king,
      To make us reliques; then
Thou shalt be a Mary Magdalen, and I
      A something else thereby;
All women shall adore us, and some men;
And since at such time, miracles are sought,
I would have that age by this paper taught
What miracles we harmless lovers wrought.

First, we loved well and faithfully,
Yet knew not what we loved, nor why,
Difference of sex no more we knew,
Than our Guardian Angels do;
      Coming and going, we
Perchance might kiss, but not between those meals;
      Our hands ne'er touched the seals,
Which nature, injured by late law, sets free:
These miracles we did; but now alas,
All measure, and all language, I should pass,
Should I tell what a miracle she was.

### *A Lecture upon the Shadow*

Stand still, and I will read to thee
A lecture, Love, in love's philosophy.
    These three hours that we have spent,
    Walking here, two shadows went
Along with us, which we ourselves produced;
But, now the sun is just above our head,
    We do those shadows tread;
    And to brave clearness all things are reduced.
So whilst our infant loves did grow,
Disguises did, and shadows, flow,
From us, and our cares; but, now 'tis not so.

That love hath not attained the high'st degree,
Which is still diligent lest others see.

Except our love at this noon stay,
We shall new shadows make the other way.
    As the first were made to blind
    Others; these which come behind
Will work upon our selves, and blind our eyes.
If our love faint, and westwardly decline;
    To me thou, falsely, thine,
    And I to thee mine actions shall disguise.
The morning shadows wear away,
But these grow longer all the day,
But O, love's day is short, if love decay.

Love is a growing, or full constant light;
And his first minute, after noon, is night.

### *Elegy on His Mistress*

By our first strange and fatal interview,
By all desires which thereof did ensue,
By our long starving hopes, by that remorse
Which my words' masculine persuasive force

Begot in thee, and by the memory
Of hurts, which spies and rivals threatened me,
I calmly beg. But by thy father's wrath,
By all pains, which want and divorcement hath,
I conjure thee, and all the oaths which I
And thou have sworn to seal joint constancy,
Here I unswear, and overswear them thus:
Thou shalt not love by ways so dangerous.
Temper, O fair love, love's impetuous rage;
Be my true mistress still, not my feigned page.
I'll go, and, by thy kind leave, leave behind
Thee, only worthy to nurse in my mind,
Thirst to come back; O! if thou die before,
My soul from other lands to thee shall soar.
Thy (else almighty) beauty cannot move
Rage from the seas, nor thy love teach them love,
Nor tame wild Boreas' harshness; thou hast read
How roughly he in pieces shiverèd
Fair Orithea, whom he swore he loved.
Fall ill or good, 'tis madness to have proved
Dangers unurged; feed on this flattery,
That absent lovers one in th' other be.
Dissemble nothing, not a boy, nor change
Thy body's habit, nor mind; be not strange
To thyself only. All will spy in thy face
A blushing womanly discovering grace;
Richly clothed apes are callèd apes, and as soon
Eclipsed as bright, we call the moon the moon.
Men of France, changeable cameleons,
Spitals of diseases, shops of fashions,
Love's fuellers, and the rightest company
Of players, which upon the world's stage be,
Will quickly know thee, and no less, alas!
Th' indifferent Italian, as we pass
His warm land, well content to think thee page,
Will hunt thee with such lust, and hideous rage,
As Lot's fair guests were vexed. But none of these,
Nor spongy hydroptic Dutch shall thee displease,
If thou stay here. O stay here, for, for thee,

England is only a worthy gallery,
To walk in expectation, till from thence
Our greatest king call thee to his presence.
When I am gone, dream me some happiness;
Nor let thy looks our long-hid love confess;
Nor praise, nor dispraise me, nor bless nor curse
Openly love's force, nor in bed fright thy nurse
With midnight's startings, crying out, O! O!
Nurse, O! my love is slain; I saw him go
O'er the white Alps alone; I saw him, I,
Assailed, fight, taken, stabbed, bleed, fall, and die.
Augur me better chance, except dread Jove
Think it enough for me to have had thy love.

## Thou Hast Made Me

Thou hast made me, and shall Thy work decay?
Repair me now, for now mine end doth haste,
I run to death, and death meets me as fast,
And all my pleasures are like yesterday;
I dare not move my dim eyes any way,
Despair behind, and death before doth cast
Such terror, and my feeble flesh doth waste
By sin in it, which it t'wards hell doth weigh;
Only Thou art above, and when towards Thee
By Thy leave I can look, I rise again;
But our old subtle foe so tempteth me,
That not one hour my self I can sustain;
Thy Grace may wing me to prevent his art,
And Thou like adamant draw mine iron heart.

## At the Round Earth's Imagined Corners

At the round earth's imagined corners blow
Your trumpets, angels, and arise, arise
From death, you numberless infinities
Of souls, and to your scattered bodies go,

All whom the flood did, and fire shall o'erthrow,
All whom war, dearth, age, agues, tyrannies,
Despair, law, chance, hath slain, and you whose eyes
Shall behold God, and never taste death's woe.
But let them sleep, Lord, and me mourn a space;
For, if above all these my sins abound,
'Tis late to ask abundance of Thy grace,
When we are there. Here on this lowly ground,
Teach me how to repent, for that's as good
As if Thou hadst sealed my pardon with Thy blood.


### If Poisonous Minerals

If poisonous minerals, and if that tree
Whose fruit threw death on else immortal us,
If lecherous goats, if serpents envious
Cannot be damned, alas! why should I be?
Why should intent or reason, born in me,
Make sins, else equal, in me more heinous?
And mercy being easy, and glorious
To God, in His stern wrath why threatens He?
But who am I, that dare dispute with Thee,
O God? O! of Thine only worthy blood,
And my tears, make a heavenly Lethean flood,
And drown in it my sin's black memory;
That Thou remember them, some claim as debt,
I think it mercy, if Thou wilt forget.


### Death, Be Not Proud

Death, be not proud, though some have callèd thee
Mighty and dreadful, for thou art not so,
For those whom thou think'st thou dost overthrow
Die not, poor Death, nor yet canst thou kill me.
From rest and sleep, which but thy picture be,
Much pleasure, then from thee much more must flow;
And soonest our best men with thee do go—

Rest of their bones and souls' delivery!
Thou'rt slave to fate, chance, kings and desperate men,
And dost with poison, war, and sickness dwell,
And poppy or charms can make us sleep as well,
And better than thy stroke; why swell'st thou then?
One short sleep past, we wake eternally,
And death shall be no more: Death, thou shalt die!

### A Hymn to God the Father

Wilt Thou forgive that sin where I begun,
   Which was my sin, though it were done before?
Wilt Thou forgive that sin, through which I run,
   And do run still, though still I do deplore?
      When Thou hast done, Thou hast not done,
       For I have more.

Wilt Thou forgive that sin which I have won
   Others to sin, and made my sin their door?
Wilt Thou forgive that sin which I did shun
   A year, or two: but wallowed in, a score?
      When Thou hast done, Thou hast not done,
       For I have more.

I have a sin of fear, that when I have spun
   My last thread, I shall perish on the shore;
But swear by Thy self, that at my death Thy Son
   Shall shine as he shines now, and heretofore;
      And, having done that, Thou hast done;
       I fear no more.

# BEN JONSON/1573-1637

## Hymn to Cynthia

Queen and huntress, chaste and fair,
Now the sun is laid to sleep,
Seated in thy silver chair,
State in wonted manner keep:
    Hesperus entreats thy light,
    Goddess, excellently bright.

Earth, let not thy envious shade
Dare itself to interpose;
Cynthia's shining orb was made
Heaven to clear, when day did close:
    Bless us then with wishèd sight,
    Goddess, excellently bright.

Lay thy bow of pearl apart,
And thy crystal-shining quiver;
Give unto the flying hart
Space to breathe, how short soever:
    Thou that mak'st a day of night,
    Goddess, excellently bright.

## Slow, Slow, Fresh Fount

Slow, slow, fresh fount, keep time with my salt tears;
  Yet slower, yet, O, faintly gentle springs:
List to the heavy part the music bears,
  Woe weeps out her division, when she sings.
    Droop herbs, and flowers;
    Fall grief in showers;
    Our beauties are not ours:
      O, I could still
(Like melting snow upon some craggy hill)

Since nature's pride is, now, a withered daffodil.
    Drop, drop, drop, drop.


### On Something That Walks Somewhere

At court I met it, in clothes brave enough
To be a courtier; and looks grave enough
To seem a statesman: as I near it came,
It made a great face, I asked the name.
A lord, it cried, buried in flesh and blood,
And such from whom let no man hope least good,
For I will do none, and as little ill,
For I will dare none. Good Lord, walk dead still.


### On My First Son

Farewell, thou child of my right hand, and joy;
My sin was too much hope of thee, loved boy.
Seven years thou wert lent to me, and I thee pay,
Exacted by thy fate, on the just day.
O, I could lose all father now. For why
Will man lament the state he should envy?
To have so soon 'scaped world's, and flesh's, rage,
And if no other misery, yet age?
Rest in soft peace, and, asked, say here doth lie
Ben Jonson, his best piece of poetry.
For whose sake, henceforth, all his vows be such,
As what he loves may never like too much.


### Epitaph on S. P.

#### A Child of Queen Elizabeth's Chapel

Weep with me, all you that read
    This little story;

And know, for whom a tear you shed
   Death's self is sorry.
'Twas a child that so did thrive
   In grace and feature,
As Heaven and Nature seemed to strive
   Which owned the creature.

Years he numbered scarce thirteen,
   When Fates turned cruel;
Yet three filled zodiacs had he been
   The stage's jewel;
And did act, what now we moan,
   Old men so duly,
As sooth the Parcae thought him one,
   He played so truly.

So, by error, to his fate
   They all consented;
But, viewing him since—alas, too late!—
   They have repented;
And have sought, to give new birth,
   In baths to steep him;
But, being so much too good for earth,
   Heaven vows to keep him.

### Epitaph on Elizabeth, L. H.

Would'st thou hear what man can say
In a little? Reader, stay.
Underneath this stone doth lie
As much beauty as could die:
Which in life did harbor give
To more virtue than doth live.
If, at all, she had a fault,
Leave it buried in this vault.
One name was Elizabeth,
Th' other, let it sleep with death:

Fitter, where it died, to tell,
Than that it lived at all. Farewell.


### Drink to Me Only with Thine Eyes

Drink to me only with thine eyes,
    And I will pledge with mine;
Or leave a kiss but in the cup
    And I'll not look for wine.
The thirst that from the soul doth rise
    Doth ask a drink divine;
But might I of Jove's nectar sup,
    I would not change for thine.

I sent thee late a rosy wreath,
    Not so much honoring thee
As giving it a hope that there
    It could not withered be;
But thou thereon didst only breathe,
    And sent'st it back to me;
Since when it grows, and smells, I swear,
    Not of itself, but thee!


### To Heaven

Good and great God! can I not think of Thee,
But it must straight my melancholy be?
Is it interpreted in me disease,
That, laden with my sins, I seek for ease?
O, be Thou witness, that the reins dost know
And hearts of all, if I be sad for show;
And judge me after, if I dare pretend
To aught but grace, or aim at other end.
As Thou art all, so be Thou all to me,
First, midst, and last, converted One and Three!
My faith, my hope, my love; and, in this state,
My judge, my witness, and my advocate!

Where have I been this while exiled from Thee,
And whither rapt, now Thou but stoop'st to me?
Dwell, dwell here still! O, being everywhere,
How can I doubt to find Thee ever here?
I know my state, both full of shame and scorn,
Conceived in sin, and unto labor born,
Standing with fear, and must with horror fall,
And destined unto judgment, after all.
I feel my griefs too, and there scarce is ground
Upon my flesh t' inflict another wound;
Yet dare I not complain or wish for death
With holy Paul, lest it be thought the breath
Of discontent; or that these prayers be
For weariness of life, not love of Thee.


### Hymn to Comus

Room! room! make room for the bouncing belly,
First father of sauce and deviser of jelly;
Prime master of arts, and the giver of wit,
That found out the excellent engine the spit,
The plough and the flail, the mill and the hopper,
The hutch and the bolter, the furnace and copper,
The oven, the bavin,[1] the mawkin,[2] the peel,[3]
The hearth and the range, the dog and the wheel:
He, he first invented the hogshead and tun,
The gimlet and vice too, and taught 'em to run;
And since with the funnel and hippocras bag[4]
He has made of himself, that he now cries swag!
Which shows, though the pleasure be but of four inches,
Yet he is a weasel, the gullet that pinches
Of any delight, and not spares from his back
Whatever to make of the belly a sack!
Hail, hail, plump paunch! O, the founder of taste,
For fresh meats, or powdered, or pickle, or paste;

---

[1] bundle of brushwood as fuel for oven   [2] oven mop   [3] baker's shovel
[4] conical bag used as filter

Devourer of broiled, baked, roasted, or sod,[1]
And emptier of cups be they even or odd:
All which have now made thee so wide i' the waist,
As scarce with no pudding thou art to be laced;
But eating and drinking until thou dost nod,
Thou break'st all thy girdles, and break'st forth a god.

### An Ode to Himself

Where dost thou careless lie
  Buried in ease and sloth?
Knowledge that sleeps doth die;
And this security,
  It is the common moth
That eats on wits, and arts, and destroys them both.

Are all th' Aonian springs
  Dried up? lies Thespia waste?
Doth Clarius' harp want strings,
  That not a nymph now sings!
  Or droop they as disgraced,
To see their seats and bowers by chattering pies
        defaced?

If hence thy silence be,
  As 'tis too just a cause;
Let this thought quicken thee,
Minds that are great and free,
  Should not on fortune pause:
'Tis crown enough to virtue still, her own applause.

What though the greedy fry
  Be taken with false baits
Of worded balladry,

[1] seethed

And think it poesy?
 They die with their conceits,
And only piteous scorn upon their folly waits.

Then take in hand thy lyre,
 Strike in thy proper strain,
With Japhet's line, aspire
Sol's chariot for new fire,
 To give the world again:
Who aided him, will thee, the issue of Jove's brain.

And since our dainty age
 Cannot endure reproof,
Make not thyself a page
To that strumpet the stage,
 But sing high and aloof,
Safe from the wolf's black jaw, and the dull ass's
  hoof.

# JOHN MARSTON/1575?–1634

### *To Everlasting Oblivion*

Thou mighty gulf, insatiate cormorant,
Deride me not, though I seem petulant
To fall into thy chops. Let others pray
For ever their fair poems flourish may.
But as for me, hungry *Oblivion*
Devour me quick, accept my orison:
 My earnest prayers, which do importune thee,
 With gloomy shade of thy still empery,
 To vail both me and my rude poesy.
Far worthier lines in silence of thy state
Do sleep securely free from love or hate,
From which this living ne'er can be exempt,
But whilst it breathes will hate and fury tempt.

Then close his eyes with thy all-dimming hand,
Which not right glorious actions can withstand.
Peace, hateful tongues, I now in silence pace.
Unless some hound do wake me from my place,
   I with this sharp, yet well meant poesy,
   Will sleep secure, right free from injury
   Of cankered hate, or rankest villainy.

## JOHN FLETCHER/1579–1625

### Do Not Fear to Put Thy Feet

Do not fear to put thy feet
Naked in the river sweet;
Think not leech, or newt or toad
Will bite thy foot, when thou hast troad;
Nor let the water rising high,
As thou wad'st in, make thee cry
And sob, but ever live with me,
And not a wave shall trouble thee.

### See, the Day Begins to Break

See, the day begins to break,
And the light shoots like a streak
Of subtile fire, the wind blows cold,
Whilst the morning doth unfold;
Now the birds begin to rouse,
And the squirrel from the boughs
Leaps to get him nuts and fruit;
The early lark that erst was mute,
Carols to the rising day
Many a note and many a lay.

### Lay a Garland on My Hearse

Lay a garland on my hearse
  Of the dismal yew;
Maidens, willow-branches bear,
  Say I dièd true.

My love was false, but I was firm
  From my hour of birth;
Upon my buried body lie
  Lightly, gentle earth.

### Care-Charming Sleep

Care-charming sleep, thou easer of all woes,
Brother to death, sweetly thy self dispose
On this afflicted prince, fall like a cloud
In gentle show'rs, give nothing that is loud,
Or painful to his slumbers; easy, sweet,
And as a purling stream, thou son of night,
Pass by his troubled senses; sing his pain
Like hollow murmuring wind, or silver rain,
Into this prince gently, oh gently slide,
And kiss him into slumbers like a bride.

### Let the Bells Ring

Let the bells ring, and let the boys sing,
  The young lasses skip and play,
Let the cups go round, till round goes the ground,
  Our learned old vicar will stay.

Let the pig turn merrily, merrily ah,
  And let the fat goose swim,
For verily, verily, verily ah,
  Our vicar this day shall be trim.

The stewed cock shall crow, cock-a-loodle-loo,
    A loud cock-a-loodle shall he crow;
The duck and the drake, shall swim in a lake
    Of onions and claret below.

Our wives shall be neat, to bring in our meat;
    To thee our most noble adviser,
Our pains shall be great, and bottles shall sweat,
    And we our selves will be wiser.

We'll labour and swink, we'll kiss and we'll drink,
    And tithes shall come thicker and thicker;
We'll fall to our plow, and get children enough,
    And thou shalt be learned old vicar.


## ANONYMOUS


### *The Bellman's Song*

Maids to bed and cover coal;
Let the mouse out of her hole;
Crickets in the chimney sing
Whilst the little bell doth ring:
If fast asleep, who can tell
When the clapper hits the bell?


## JOHN WEBSTER/1580?–1625?


### *Call for the Robin-Redbreast*

Call for the robin-redbreast and the wren,
Since o'er shady groves they hover,
And with leaves and flowers do cover

JOHN WEBSTER 197

The friendless bodies of unburied men.
  Call unto his funeral dole
  The ant, the field-mouse, and the mole,
To rear him hillocks that shall keep him warm,
And, when gay tombs are robbed, sustain no harm;
But keep the wolf far thence, that's foe to men,
For with his nails he'll dig them up again.


### Hark, Now Everything Is Still

  Hark, now everything is still,
  The screech-owl and the whistler shrill,
  Call upon our dame aloud,
  And bid her quickly don her shroud!
  Much you had of land and rent;
  Your length in clay's now competent:
  A long war disturbed your mind;
  Here your perfect peace is signed.
  Of what is 't fools make such vain keeping?
  Sin their conception, their birth weeping,
  Their life a general mist of error,
  Their death a hideous storm of terror.
  Strew your hair with powders sweet,
  Don clean linen, bathe your feet,
  And (the foul fiend more to check)
  A crucifix let bless your neck:
  'Tis now full tide 'tween night and day;
  End your groan, and come away.


### All the Flowers

  All the flowers of the spring
  Meet to perfume our burying;
  These have but their growing prime,
  And man does flourish but his time.
  Survey our progress from our birth—
  We are set, we grow, we turn to earth.

Courts adieu, and all delights,
All bewitching appetites!
Sweetest breath and clearest eye,
Like perfumes go out and die;
And consequently this is done
As shadows wait upon the sun.
Vain the ambition of kings
Who seek by trophies and dead things
To leave a living name behind,
And weave but nets to catch the wind.

## RICHARD CORBET/1582–1635

### The Fairies' Farewell

"Farewell rewards and fairies,"
　Good housewives now may say,
For now foul sluts in dairies
　Do fare as well as they.
And though they sweep their hearths no less
　Than maids were wont to do,
Yet who of late for cleanliness,
　Finds sixpence in her shoe?

Lament, lament, old abbeys,
　The fairies lost command;
They did but change priests' babies,
　But some have changed your land;
And all your children sprung from thence
　Are now grown Puritanes;
Who live as changelings ever since
　For love of your domains.

At morning and at evening both
　You merry were and glad,

So little care of sleep or sloth
   These pretty ladies had;
When Tom came home from labor,
   Or Cisse to milking rose,
Then merrily, merrily went their tabor,
   And nimbly went their toes.

Witness those rings and roundelays
   Of theirs, which yet remain,
Were footed in Queen Mary's days
   On many a grassy plain;
But since of late, Elizabeth,
   And later, James came in,
They never danced on any heath
   As when the time hath been.

By which we note the fairies
   Were of the old profession;
Their songs were Ave-Marys,
   Their dances were procession:
But now, alas! they all are dead
   Or gone beyond the seas,
Or farther for religion fled,
   Or else they take their ease.

A tell-tale in their company
   They never could endure,
And who so kept not secretly
   Their mirth was punished sure.
It was a just and Christian deed
   To pinch such black and blue.
Oh how the commonwealth doth want
   Such justices as you!

Now they have left our quarters,
   A register they have,
Who looketh to their charters,
   A man both wise and grave.

An hundred of their merry pranks
   By one that I could name
Are kept in store; con twenty thanks
   To William for the same.

I marvel who his cloak would turn
   When Puck had led him round;
Or where those walking fires would burn,
   Where Cureton would be found;
How Broker would appear to be
   For whom this age doth mourn
But that their spirits live in thee,
   In thee, old William Churne.

To William Churne of Staffordshire
   Give laud and praises due,
Who every meal can mend your cheer
   With tales both old and true;
To William all give audience
   And pray ye for his noddle,
For all the fairies' evidence
   Were lost, if that were addle.


# WILLIAM DRUMMOND/1585–1649


### Like the Idalian Queen

Like the Idalian Queen
Her hair about her eyne,
With neck and breasts ripe apples to be seen,
At first glance of the morn
In Cyprus gardens gathering those fair flowers
Which of her blood were born,
I saw, but fainting saw, my paramours.
The Graces naked danced about the place,
The winds and trees amazed

With silence on her gazed,
The flowers did smile, like those upon her face,
And as their aspen stalks those fingers band
(That she might read my case)
A hyacinth I wished me in her hand.


### My Lute, Be as Thou Wast

My lute, be as thou wast when thou didst grow
With thy green mother in some shady grove,
When immelodious winds but made thee move,
And birds on thee their ramage did bestow.
Sith that dear voice which did thy sounds approve,
Which used in such harmonious strains to flow,
Is reft from earth to tune those spheres above,
What art thou but a harbinger of woe?
Thy pleasing notes be pleasing notes no more,
But orphan wailings to the fainting ear;
Each stop a sigh, each sound draws forth a tear,
Be therefore silent as in woods before,
Or if that any hand to touch thee deign,
Like widowed turtle, still her loss complain.


### For the Baptist

The last and greatest herald of heaven's King,
Girt with rough skins, hies to the deserts wild,
Among that savage brood the woods forth bring,
Which he than man more harmless found and mild:
His food was locusts, and what young doth spring,
With honey that from virgin hives distilled;
Parched body, hollow eyes, some uncouth thing
Made him appear, long since from earth exiled.
There burst he forth: "All ye, whose hopes rely
On God, with me amidst these deserts mourn;
Repent, repent, and from old errors turn."

Who listened to his voice, obeyed his cry?
Only the echoes, which he made relent,
Rung from their marble caves, "Repent, repent!"

# GEORGE WITHER/1588–1677

### Shall I Wasting in Despair

Shall I wasting in despair,
Die because a woman's fair?
Or make pale my cheeks with care,
Cause another's rosy are?
Be she fairer than the day,
Or the flowery meads in May,
    If she be not so to me,
    What care I how fair she be?

Should my heart be grieved or pined,
Cause I see a woman kind?
Or a well disposèd nature,
Joinèd with a lovely feature?
Be she meeker, kinder, than
Turtle-dove, or pelican,
    If she be not so to me,
    What care I how kind she be?

Shall a woman's virtues move
Me to perish for her love?
Or, her well-deserving known,
Make me quite forget mine own?
Be she with that goodness blest,
Which may gain her, name of Best,
    If she be not such to me,
    What care I how good she be?

Cause her fortune seems too high,
Shall I play the fool, and die?
Those that bear a noble mind,
Where they want of riches find,
Think what with them, they would do,
That without them, dare to woo.
  And, unless that mind I see,
  What care I, though great she be?

Great, or good, or kind, or fair,
I will ne'er the more despair,
If she love me, this believe,
I will die, ere she shall grieve.
If she slight me when I woo,
I can scorn, and let her go.
  For, if she be not for me,
  What care I for whom she be?

# ROBERT HERRICK/1591–1674

### When He Would Have His Verses Read

In sober mornings, do not thou rehearse
The holy incantation of a verse;
But when that men have both well drunk, and fed,
Let my enchantments then be sung, or read.
When laurel spirts i' th' fire, and when the hearth
Smiles to itself, and gilds the roof with mirth;
When up the thyrse is raised, and when the sound
Of sacred orgies flies, around, around;
When the rose reigns, and locks with ointments shine,
Let rigid Cato read these lines of mine.

## To Perilla

Ah, my Perilla! dost thou grieve to see
Me, day by day, to steal away from thee?
Age calls me hence, and my gray hairs bid come,
And haste away to mine eternal home:
'Twill not be long (Perilla) after this,
That I must give thee the supremest kiss.
Dead when I am, first cast in salt, and bring
Part of the cream from the religious spring,
With which (Perilla) wash my hands and feet;
That done, then wind me in that very sheet
Which wrapt thy smooth limbs (when thou didst
    implore
The gods' protection, but the night before);
Follow me weeping to my turf, and there
Let fall a primrose, and with it a tear;
Then lastly, let some weekly strewings be
Devoted to the memory of me:
Then shall my ghost not walk about, but keep
Still in the cool and silent shades of sleep.


## Delight in Disorder

A sweet disorder in the dress
Kindles in clothes a wantonness:
A lawn about the shoulders thrown
Into a fine distraction,
An erring lace, which here and there
Enthralls the crimson stomacher,
A cuff neglectful, and thereby
Ribbands to flow confusedly,
A winning wave (deserving note)
In the tempestuous petticoat,
A careless shoe-string, in whose tie
I see a wild civility,
Do more bewitch me, than when art
Is too precise in every part.

## The Vision

Sitting alone (as one forsook)
Close by a silver-shedding brook;
With hands held up to love, I wept;
And after sorrows spent, I slept.
Then in a vision I did see
A glorious form appear to me:
A virgin's face she had; her dress
Was like a sprightly Spartaness.
A silver bow with green silk strung
Down from her comely shoulders hung;
And as she stood, the wanton air
Dangled the ringlets of her hair.
Her legs were such Diana shows,
When tucked up she a-hunting goes;
With buskins shortened to descry
The happy dawning of her thigh:
Which when I saw, I made access
To kiss that tempting nakedness.
But she forbade me, with a wand
Of myrtle she had in her hand;
And chiding me, said, hence, remove,
Herrick, thou art too coarse to love.

## Corinna's Going A-Maying

Get up, get up for shame, the blooming morn
Upon her wings presents the god unshorn.
　　See how Aurora throws her fair
　　Fresh-quilted colors through the air:
　　Get up, sweet slug-a-bed, and see
　　The dew bespangling herb and tree.
Each flower has wept and bowed toward the east
Above an hour since: yet you not dressed;
　　Nay; not so much as out of bed?

When all the birds have matins said
And sung their thankful hymns, 'tis sin,
Nay, profanation, to keep in,
Whenas a thousand virgins on this day
Spring, sooner than the lark, to fetch in May.

Rise, and put on your foliage, and be seen
To come forth, like the spring-time, fresh and green,
    And sweet as Flora. Take no care
    For jewels for your gown or hair:
    Fear not; the leaves will strew
    Gems in abundance upon you:
Besides, the childhood of the day has kept,
Against you come, some orient pearls unwept;
    Come and receive them while the light
    Hangs on the dew-locks of the night:
    And Titan on the eastern hill
    Retires himself, or else stands still
Till you come forth. Wash, dress, be brief in praying:
Few beads are best when once we go a-Maying.

Come, my Corinna, come; and, coming, mark
How each field turns a street, each street a park
    Made green and trimmed with trees; see how
    Devotion gives each house a bough
    Or branch: each porch, each door ere this
    An ark, a tabernacle is,
Made up of white-thorn, neatly interwove;
As if here were those cooler shades of love.
    Can such delights be in the street
    And open fields and we not see't?
    Come, we'll abroad; and let's obey
    The proclamation made for May:
And sin no more, as we have done, by staying;
But, my Corinna, come, let's go a-Maying.

There's not a budding boy or girl this day
But is got up, and gone to bring in May.
    A deal of youth, ere this, is come

Back, and with white-thorn laden home.
Some have despatched their cakes and cream
Before that we have left to dream:
And some have wept, and wooed, and plighted troth,
And chose their priest, ere we can cast off sloth:
    Many a green-gown has been given;
    Many a kiss, both odd and even:
    Many a glance too has been sent
    From out the eye, love's firmament;
Many a jest told of the keys betraying
This night, and locks picked, yet we're not a-Maying.

Come, let us go while we are in our prime;
And take the harmless folly of the time.
    We shall grow old apace, and die
    Before we know our liberty.
    Our life is short, and our days run
    As fast away as does the sun;
And, as a vapor or a drop of rain,
Once lost, can ne'er be found again,
    So when or you or I are made
    A fable, song, or fleeting shade,
    All love, all liking, all delight
    Lies drowned with us in endless night.
Then while time serves, and we are but decaying,
Come, my Corinna, come, let's go a-Maying.


### The Lily in a Crystal

    You have beheld a smiling rose
        When virgins' hands have drawn
        O'er it a cobweb-lawn:
    And here, you see, this lily shows,
        Tombed in a crystal stone,
    More fair in this transparent case,
        Than when it grew alone;
        And had but single grace.

You see how cream but naked is;
  Nor dances in the eye
  Without a strawberry:
Or some fine tincture, like to this,
  Which draws the sight thereto,
More by that wantoning with it,
  Than when the paler hue
  No mixture did admit.

You see how amber through the streams
  More gently strokes the sight,
  With some concealed delight;
Than when he darts his radiant beams
  Into the boundless air:
Where either too much light, his worth
  Doth all at once impair,
  Or set it little forth.

Put purple grapes, or cherries in-
  To glass, and they will send
  More beauty to commend
Them, from that clean and subtle skin,
  Than if they naked stood,
And had no other pride at all,
  But their own flesh and blood,
  And tinctures natural.

Thus, lily, rose, grape, cherry, cream,
  And strawberry do stir
  More love, when they transfer
A weak, a soft, a broken beam,
  Than if they should discover
At full their proper excellence;
  Without some scene cast over,
  To juggle with the sense.

Thus let this crystalled lily be
  A rule, how far to teach
  Your nakedness must reach:

And that, no further than we see
   Those glaring colors laid
By art's wise hand, but to this end
   They should obey a shade;
   ·Lest they too far extend.

So though y'are white as swan, or snow,
   And have the power to move
   A world of men to love:
Yet, when your lawns and silks shall flow;
   And that white cloud divide
Into a doubtful twilight; then,
   Then will your hidden pride
   Raise greater fires in men.

### *To the Virgins to Make Much of Time*

Gather ye rose-buds while ye may,
   Old Time is still a-flying:
And this same flower that smiles today,
   Tomorrow will be dying.

The glorious lamp of heaven, the Sun,
   The higher he's a-getting
The sooner will his race be run,
   And nearer he's to setting.

That age is best which is the first,
   When youth and blood are warmer;
But being spent, the worse, and worst
   Times, still succeed the former.

Then be not coy, but use your time;
   And while ye may, go marry:
For having lost but once your prime,
   You may for ever tarry.

*To the Willow-Tree*

Thou art to all lost love the best,
    The only true plant found,
Wherewith young men and maids distressed,
    And left of love, are crowned.

When once the lover's rose is dead,
    Or laid aside forlorn;
Then willow-garlands, 'bout the head,
    Bedewed with tears, are worn.

When with neglect, (the lover's bane)
    Poor maids rewarded be,
For their love lost; their only gain
    Is but a wreath from thee.

And underneath thy cooling shade,
    (When weary of the light)
The love-spent youth, and love-sick maid,
    Come to weep out the night.

*To Daffodils*

Fair daffodils, we weep to see
    You haste away so soon;
As yet the early-rising sun
    Has not attained his noon.
        Stay, stay,
    Until the hasting day
        Has run
    But to the evensong;
And, having prayed together, we
    Will go with you along.

We have short time to stay, as you,
    We have as short a spring;

As quick a growth to meet decay,
 As you, or anything.
  We die,
 As hours do, and dry
  Away,
 Like to the summer's rain;
Or as the pearls of morning's dew,
 Ne'er to be found again.


*To Blossoms*

Fair pledges of a fruitful tree,
 Why do ye fall so fast?
 Your date is not so past;
But you may stay yet here a while,
 To blush and gently smile;
  And go at last.

What! were ye born to be
 An hour or half's delight;
 And so to bid good-night?
'Twas pity Nature brought ye forth
 Merely to show your worth,
  And lose you quite.

But you are lovely leaves, where we
 May read how soon things have
 Their end, though ne'er so brave:
And after they have shown their pride,
 Like you a while: they glide
  Into the grave.


*The Bad Season Makes the Poet Sad*

Dull to myself, and almost dead to these,
My many fresh and fragrant mistresses:
Lost to all music now; since every thing

Puts on the semblance here of sorrowing.
Sick is the land to'th'heart; and doth endure
More dangerous faintings by her desp'rate cure.
But if that golden age would come again,
And Charles here rule, as he before did reign;
If smooth and unperplext the seasons were,
As when the sweet Maria livèd here:
I should delight to have my curls half drowned
In Tyrian dews, and head with roses crowned.
And once more yet (ere I am laid out dead)
*Knock at a star with my exalted head.*


### The Night-Piece, to Julia

Her eyes the glow-worm lend thee,
The shooting stars attend thee;
   And the elves also,
   Whose little eyes glow
Like the sparks of fire, befriend thee.

No will-o'-th'-wisp mislight thee;
Nor snake, or slow-worm bite thee:
   But on, on thy way,
   Not making a stay,
Since ghost there's none to affright thee.

Let not the dark thee cumber;
What though the moon does slumber:
   The stars of the night
   Will lend thee their light,
Like tapers clear without number.

Then, Julia, let me woo thee,
Thus, thus to come unto me:
   And when I shall meet
   Thy silv'ry feet,
My soul I'll pour into thee.

### Proof to No Purpose

You see this gentle stream, that glides,
Shoved on, by quick-succeeding tides:
Try if this sober stream you can
Follow to th' wilder ocean,
And see, if there it keeps unspent
In that congesting element.
Next, from that world of waters, then
By pores and caverns back again
Induct that inadultrate same
Stream to the spring from whence it came.
This with a wonder when ye do,
As easy, and else easier too:
Then may ye recollect the grains
Of my particular remains,
After a thousand lusters hurled,
By ruffling winds, about the world.

### Upon Julia's Clothes

Whenas in silks my Julia goes
Then, then (methinks) how sweetly flows
That liquefaction of her clothes.

Next, when I cast mine eyes and see
That brave vibration each way free;
O how that glittering taketh me!

### An Ode for Ben Jonson

Ah, Ben!
Say how or when
Shall we, thy guests,
Meet at those lyric feasts,
Made at the Sun,
The Dog, the Triple Tun;

Where we such clusters had,
As made us nobly wild, not mad?
And yet each verse of thine
Out-did the meat, out-did the frolic wine.

My Ben!
Or come again,
Or send to us
Thy wit's great overplus;
But teach us yet
Wisely to husband it,
Lest we that talent spend;
And having once brought to an end
That precious stock, the store
Of such a wit the world should have no more.


### Another Grace for a Child

Here a little child I stand,
Heaving up my either hand;
Cold as paddocks though they be,
Here I lift them up to Thee,
For a benison to fall
On our meat, and on us all.
            Amen.


# WILLIAM BROWNE/1592–1643?


### Epitaph on the Countess Dowager of Pembroke[1]

Underneath this sable hearse
Lies the subject of all verse:
Sydney's sister, Pembroke's mother:

[1] Sometimes attributed to Ben Jonson

Death, ere thou hast slain another,
Fair, and learn'd, and good as she,
Time shall throw a dart at thee.

# HENRY KING/1592–1669

## The Exequy

*To His Matchless Never-to-Be-Forgotten Friend*

Accept, thou shrine of my dead Saint,
Instead of dirges this complaint;
And for sweet flowers to crown thy hearse,
Receive a strew of weeping verse
From thy grieved friend, whom thou might'st see
Quite melted into tears for thee.

   Dear loss! since thy untimely fate
My task hath been to meditate
On thee, on thee: thou art the book,
The library whereon I look
Though almost blind. For thee (loved clay)
I languish out, not live the day,
Using no other exercise
But what I practise with mine eyes:
By which wet glasses I found out
How lazily time creeps about
To one that mourns: this, only this,
My exercise and bus'ness is:
So I compute the weary hours
With sighs dissolvèd into showers.

   Nor wonder if my time go thus
Backward and most preposterous;
Thou hast benighted me, thy set
This Eve of blackness did beget,

Who wast my day (though overcast
Before thou had'st thy noontide past)
And I remember must in tears,
Thou scarce had'st seen so many years
As day tells hours. By thy clear sun
My life and fortune first did run;
But thou wilt never more appear
Folded within my hemisphere,
Since both thy light and motion
Like a fled star is fallen and gone,
And 'twixt me and my soul's dear wish
An earth now interposèd is,
Which such a strange eclipse doth make
As ne'er was read in almanake.

   I could allow thee for a time
To darken me and my sad clime,
Were it a month, a year, or ten,
I would thy exile live till then;
And all that space my mirth adjourn,
So thou would'st promise to return;
And putting off thy ashy shroud
At length disperse this sorrow's cloud.

   But woe is me! the longest date
Too narrow is to calculate
These empty hopes: never shall I
Be so much blest as to descry
A glimpse of thee, till that day come
Which shall the earth to cinders doom,
And a fierce fever must calcine
The body of this world like thine,
(My little world!). That fit of fire
Once off, our bodies shall aspire
To our soul's bliss: then we shall rise,
And view our selves with clearer eyes
In that calm region, where no night
Can hide us from each other's sight.

Meantime, thou hast her, earth: much good
May my harm do thee. Since it stood
With Heaven's will I might not call
Her longer mine, I give thee all
My short-lived right and interest
In her, whom living I loved best:
With a most free and bounteous grief,
I give thee what I could not keep.
Be kind to her, and prithee look
Thou write into thy Doomsday book
Each parcel of this rarity
Which in thy casket shrined doth lie:
See that thou make thy reck'ning straight,
And yield her back again by weight;
For thou must audit on thy trust
Each grain and atom of this dust,
As thou wilt answer Him that lent,
Not gave thee, my dear monument.

So close the ground, and 'bout her shade
Black curtains draw, my Bride is laid.

Sleep on, my Love, in thy cold bed,
Never to be disquieted!
My last good night! Thou wilt not wake
Till I thy fate shall overtake:
Till age, or grief, or sickness must
Marry my body to that dust
It so much loves; and fill the room
My heart keeps empty in thy tomb.
Stay for me there; I will not fail
To meet thee in that hollow vale.
And think not much of my delay;
I am already on the way,
And follow thee with all the speed
Desire can make, or sorrows breed.
Each minute is a short degree,

And ev'ry hour a step towards thee.
At night when I betake to rest,
Next morn I rise nearer my West
Of life, almost by eight hours' sail,
Than when sleep breathed his drowsy gale.

   Thus from the sun my bottom steers,
And my day's compass downward bears:
Nor labour I to stem the tide
Through which to thee I swiftly glide.

   'Tis true, with shame and grief I yield,
Thou like the van first took'st the field,
And gotten hast the victory
In thus adventuring to die
Before me, whose more years might crave
A just precedence in the grave.
But hark! My pulse like a soft drum
Beats my approach, tells thee I come;
And slow howe'er my marches be,
I shall at last sit down by thee.

   The thought of this bids me go on,
And wait my dissolution
With hope and comfort. Dear (forgive
The crime) I am content to live
Divided, with but half a heart,
Till we shall meet and never part.


## Sic Vita

   Like to the falling of a star;
   Or as the flights of eagles are;
   Or like the fresh spring's gaudy hue;
   Or silver drops of morning dew;
   Or like a wind that chafes the flood;
   Or bubbles which on water stood;

Even such is man, whose borrowed light
Is straight called in, and paid to night.

*The wind blows out; the bubble dies;*
*The spring entombed in autumn lies;*
*The dew dries up; the star is shot;*
*The flight is past; and man forgot.*


### A Contemplation upon Flowers

Brave flowers, that I could gallant it like you
And be as little vain;
You come abroad, and make a harmless shew,
And to your beds of earth again;
You are not proud, you know your birth,
For your embroidered garments are from earth.

You do obey your months, and times, but I
Would have it ever spring;
My fate would know no winter, never die
Nor think of such a thing;
Oh, that I could my bed of earth but view
And smile, and look as cheerfully as you.

Oh, teach me to see death, and not to fear,
But rather to take truce;
How often have I seen you at a bier,
And there look fresh and spruce;
You fragrant flowers, then teach me that my breath
Like yours may sweeten, and perfume my death.

# GEORGE HERBERT/1593–1633

### Redemption

Having been tenant long to a rich lord,
    Not thriving, I resolvèd to be bold,
    And make a suit unto him, to afford
A new small-rented lease, and cancel th' old.

In heaven at his manor I him sought:
    They told me there, that he was lately gone
    About some land, which he had dearly bought
Long since on earth, to take possession.

I straight returned, and knowing his great birth,
    Sought him accordingly in great resorts;
    In cities, theatres, gardens, parks, and courts:
At length I heard a ragged noise and mirth

    Of thieves and murderers: there I him espied,
    Who straight, *Your suit is granted,* said, and died.

### Matins

    I cannot ope mine eyes,
    But Thou art ready there to catch
    My morning-soul and sacrifice:
Then we must needs for that day make a match.

    My God, what is a heart?
    Silver, or gold, or precious stone,
    Or star, or rainbow, or a part
Of all these things, or all of them in one?

My God, what is a heart,
   That Thou shouldst it so eye, and woo,
   Pouring upon it all Thy art,
As if that Thou hadst nothing else to do?

   Indeed, man's whole estate
   Amounts (and richly) to serve Thee:
   He did not heaven and earth create,
Yet studies them, not Him by whom they be.

   Teach me Thy love to know:
   That this new light, which now I see,
   May both the work and workman show:
Then by a sunbeam I will climb to Thee.


*Virtue*

   Sweet day, so cool, so calm, so bright,
   The bridal of the earth and sky:
   The dew shall weep thy fall to-night;
         For thou must die.

   Sweet rose, whose hue angry and brave
   Bids the rash gazer wipe his eye:
   Thy root is ever in its grave,
         And thou must die.

   Sweet spring, full of sweet days and roses,
   A box where sweets compacted lie;
   My music shows ye have your closes,
         And all must die.

   Only a sweet and virtuous soul,
   Like seasoned timber, never gives;
   But though the whole world turn to coal,
         Then chiefly lives.

## Decay

Sweet were the days, when Thou didst lodge with
    Lot,
Struggle with Jacob, sit with Gideon,
Advise with Abraham, when Thy power could not
Encounter Moses' strong complaints and moan:
      Thy words were then, *Let me alone.*

One might have sought and found Thee presently
At some fair oak, or bush, or cave, or well:
Is my God this way? No, they would reply;
He is to Sinai gone, as we heard tell:
      List, ye may hear great Aaron's bell.

But now Thou dost Thyself immure and close
In some one corner of a feeble heart:
Where yet both Sin and Satan, Thy old foes,
Do pinch and straiten Thee, and use much art
      To gain Thy thirds and little part.

I see the world grows old, when as the heat
Of Thy great love once spread, as in an urn
Doth closet up itself, and still retreat,
Cold sin still forcing it, till it return
      And calling Justice, all things burn.

## The Collar

I struck the board, and cried, No more.
      I will abroad.
What? shall I ever sigh and pine?
My lines and life are free; free as the road,
    Loose as the wind, as large as store.
      Shall I be still in suit?
Have I no harvest but a thorn

To let me blood, and not restore
What I have lost with cordial fruit?
Sure there was wine
Before my sighs did dry it: there was corn
Before my tears did drown it.
Is the year only lost to me?
Have I no bays to crown it?
No flowers, no garlands gay? all blasted?
All wasted?
Not so, my heart: but there is fruit,
And thou hast hands.
Recover all thy sigh-blown age
On double pleasures: leave thy cold dispute
Of what is fit, and not. Forsake thy cage,
Thy rope of sands,
Which petty thoughts have made, and made to thee
Good cable, to enforce and draw,
And be thy law,
While thou didst wink and wouldst not see.
Away; take heed:
I will abroad.
Call in thy death's head there: tie up thy fears.
He that forbears
To suit and serve his need,
Deserves his load.
But as I raved and grew more fierce and wild
At every word,
Methought I heard one calling, *Child*.
And I replied, *My Lord*.


### The Pulley


When God at first made man,
Having a glass of blessings standing by,
Let us (said He) pour on him all we can.
Let the world's riches, which dispersèd lie,
Contract into a span.

So strength first made a way,
Then beauty flowed, then wisdom, honour, pleasure.
   When almost all was out, God made a stay,
Perceiving that alone of all His treasure
   Rest in the bottom lay.

   For if I should (said He)
Bestow this jewel also on My creature,
   He would adore My gifts instead of Me,
And rest in Nature, not the God of Nature.
   So both should losers be.

   Yet let him keep the rest,
But keep them with repining restlessness.
   Let him be rich and weary, that at least,
If goodness lead him not, yet weariness
   May toss him to My breast.


THOMAS CAREW/1595?–1639?


*The Inscription on the Tomb of the Lady Mary Wentworth*

MARIA WENTWORTH, *Thomas Comitis Cleveland, filia prae-
mortua prima virginiam animam exhaluit. An. Dom. 1632
Æt. suae 18.*

And here the precious dust is laid;
Whose purely-tempered clay was made
So fine, that it the guest betrayed.

Else the soul grew so fast within,
It broke the outward shell of sin,
And so was hatched a cherubin.

In height, it soared to God above;
In depth, it did to knowledge move,
And spread in breadth to general love.

Before, a pious duty shined
To parents, courtesy behind,
On either side an equal mind.

Good to the poor, to kindred dear,
To servants kind, to friendship clear,
To nothing but her self severe.

So though a virgin, yet a bride
To every grace, she justified
A chaste polygamy, and died.

Learn from hence (Reader) what small trust
We owe this world, where virtue must
Frail as our flesh crumble to dust.

### To a Lady That Desired I Would Love Her

Now you have freely given me leave to love,
      What will you do?
   Shall I your mirth, or passion move,
      When I begin to woo;
Will you torment, or scorn, or love me too?

Each petty beauty can disdain, and I
      Spite of your hate
   Without your leave can see, and die;
      Dispense a nobler fate!
'Tis easy to destroy, you may create.

Then give me leave to love, and love me too
      Not with design
   To raise, as Love's cursed rebels do,
      When puling poets whine,
Fame to their beauty, from their blubbered eyne.

Grief is a puddle, and reflects not clear
            Your beauty's rays;
        Joys are pure streams, your eyes appear
            Sullen in sadder lays;
In cheerful numbers they shine bright with praise,

Which shall not mention to express you fair,
            Wounds, flames, and darts,
        Storms in your brow, nets in your hair,
            Suborning all your parts,
Or to betray, or torture captive hearts.

I'll make your eyes like morning suns appear,
            As mild, and fair;
        Your brow as crystal smooth, and clear,
            And your dishevelled hair
Shall flow like a calm region of the air.

Rich nature's store (which is the poet's treasure)
            I'll spend, to dress
        Your beauties, if your mine of pleasure
            In equal thankfulness
You but unlock, so we each other bless.


### A Song

Ask me no more where Jove bestows,
When June is past, the fading rose:
For in your beauty's orient deep,
These flowers as in their causes sleep.

Ask me no more whither do stray
The golden atoms of the day:
For in pure love heaven did prepare
Those powders to enrich your hair.

Ask me no more whither doth haste
The nightingale, when May is past:

For in your sweet dividing throat
She winters, and keeps warm her note.

Ask me no more where those stars light,
That downwards fall in dead of night:
For in your eyes they sit, and there,
Fixed, become as in their sphere.

Ask me no more if east or west,
The phoenix builds her spicy nest:
For unto you at last she flies,
And in your fragrant bosom dies.


# JAMES SHIRLEY/1596–1666


### The Glories of Our Blood and State

The glories of our blood and state
  Are shadows, not substantial things;
There is no armour against fate;
  Death lays his icy hand on kings:
    Sceptre and crown
    Must tumble down,
And in the dust be equal made
With the poor crooked scythe and spade.

Some men with swords may reap the field,
  And plant fresh laurels where they kill:
But their strong nerves at last must yield;
  They tame but one another still:
    Early or late
    They stoop to fate,
And must give up their murmuring breath
When they, pale captives, creep to death.

The garlands wither on your brow;
  Then boast no more your mighty deeds;
Upon Death's purple altar now
  See, where the victor-victim bleeds.
    Your heads must come
    To the cold tomb:
Only the actions of the just
Smell sweet, and blossom in their dust.


# WILLIAM HABINGTON/1605–1654


### To Roses in the Bosom of Castara

Ye blushing virgins happy are
In the chaste nunn'ry of her breasts,
For he'd profane so chaste a fair
Whoe'er should call them Cupid's nests.

Transplanted thus, how bright ye grow,
How rich a perfume do ye yield!
In some close garden, cowslips so
Are sweeter than i' th' open field.

In those white cloisters live secure
From the rude blasts of wanton breath,
Each hour more innocent and pure,
Till you shall wither into death.

Then that which living gave you room,
Your glorious sepulcher shall be.
There wants no marble for a tomb,
Whose breast hath marble been to me.

*Nox Nocti Indicat Scientiam (David)*

When I survey the bright
　　Celestial sphere,
So rich with jewels hung, that night
Doth like an Æthiop bride appear,

My soul her wings doth spread
　　And heavenward flies,
Th' Almighty's Mysteries to read
In the large volumes of the skies.

For the bright firmament
　　Shoots forth no flame
So silent, but is eloquent
In speaking the Creator's name.

No unregarded star
　　Contracts its light
Into so small a character,
Removed far from our human sight,

But if we steadfast look,
　　We shall discern
In it as in some holy book,
How man may heavenly knowledge learn.

It tells the conqueror,
　　That far-stretched power
Which his proud dangers traffic for,
Is but the triumph of an hour;

That from the farthest north,
　　Some nation may
Yet undiscovered issue forth,
And o'er his new got conquest sway.

Some nation yet shut in
　　With hills of ice

May be let out to scourge his sin
'Till they shall equal him in vice.

And then they likewise shall
    Their ruin have,
For as your selves your empires fall,
And every kingdom hath a grave.

Thus those celestial fires,
    Though seeming mute,
The fallacy of our desires
And all the pride of life confute.

For they have watched since first
    The world had birth:
And found sin in itself accursed,
And nothing permanent on earth.


# SIR WILLIAM DAVENANT/1606–1668


### Song

The lark now leaves his watery nest
    And climbing, shakes his dewy wings;
He takes this window for the East;
    And to implore your light, he sings,
Awake, awake, the morn will never rise,
Till she can dress her beauty at your eyes.

The merchant bows unto the seaman's star,
    The ploughman from the sun his season takes;
But still the lover wonders what they are,
    Who look for day before his mistress wakes.
Awake, awake, break through your veils of lawn!
Then draw your curtains, and begin the dawn

### *Wake All the Dead!*

Wake all the dead! What ho! What ho!
How soundly they sleep whose pillows lie low;
They mind not poor lovers who walk above
On the decks of the world in storms of love.
    No whisper now nor glance can pass
      Through wickets or through panes of glass;
For our windows and doors are shut and barred,
Lie close in the church, and in the churchyard.
    In every grave make room, make room!
The world's at an end, and we come, we come.

The State is now Love's foe, Love's foe;
'T has seized on his arms, his quiver and bow;
Has pinioned his wings, and fettered his feet,
Because he made way for lovers to meet,
    But O sad chance, his judge was old;
      Hearts cruel grow, when blood grows cold.
No man being young his process would draw.
Oh heavens, that love should be subject to law!
    Lovers go woo the dead, the dead!
Lie two in a grave, and to bed, to bed!

# EDMUND WALLER/1606–1687

### *Song*

    Go lovely rose,
  Tell her that wastes her time and me,
    That now she knows,
  When I resemble her to thee,
    How sweet and fair she seems to be.

    Tell her that's young,
  And shuns to have her graces spied,
    That hadst thou sprung

In deserts where no men abide,
    Thou must have uncommended died.

    Small is the worth
Of beauty from the light retired:
    Bid her come forth,
Suffer her self to be desired,
    And not blush so to be admired.

    Then die, that she
The common fate of all things rare
    May read in thee,
How small a part of time they share,
    That are so wondrous sweet and fair.


### *On a Girdle*

That which her slender waist confined,
Shall now my joyful temples bind;
No monarch but would give his crown
His arms might do what this has done.

It is my Heaven's extremest sphere,
The pale which held the lovely dear,
My joy, my grief, my hope, my love,
Do all within this circle move.

A narrow compass, and yet there
Dwells all that's good, and all that's fair:
Give me but what this ribbon tied,
Take all the sun goes round beside.

## To a Very Young Lady

Why came I so untimely forth
Into a world which, wanting thee,
Could entertain us with no worth
Or shadow of felicity?
    That time should me so far remove
    From that which I was born to love.

Yet, fairest blossom, do not slight
That age which you may know so soon;
The rosy morn resigns her light,
And milder glory to the noon:
    And then what wonder shall you do,
    Whose dawning beauty warns us so?

Hope waits upon the flowery prime,
And summer, though it be less gay,
Yet is not looked on as a time
Of declination and decay.
    For with a full hand that does bring
    All that was promised by the spring.

## Of the Last Verses in the Book

When we for age could neither read nor write,
The subject made us able to indite.
The soul with nobler resolutions decked,
The body stooping, does herself erect:
No mortal parts are requisite to raise
Her, that unbodied can her maker praise.

The seas are quiet when the winds give o'er,
So calm are we, when passions are no more:
For then we know how vain it was to boast
Of fleeting things, so certain to be lost.
Clouds of affection from our younger eyes
Conceal that emptiness, which age descries.

The soul's dark cottage, battered and decayed,
Lets in new light through chinks that time has made.
Stronger by weakness, wiser men become
As they draw near to their eternal home:
Leaving the old, both worlds at once they view,
That stand upon the threshold of the new.

# JOHN MILTON/1608–1674

### *On the Morning of Christ's Nativity*

This is the month, and this the happy morn,
Wherein the Son of Heaven's eternal King,
Of wedded maid and virgin mother born,
Our great redemption from above did bring;
For so the holy sages once did sing,
   That He our deadly forfeit should release,
And with His Father work us a perpetual peace.

That glorious form, that light unsufferable,
And that far-beaming blaze of majesty,
Wherewith He wont at Heaven's high council-table
To sit the midst of Trinal Unity,
He laid aside, and, here with us to be,
   Forsook the courts of everlasting day,
And chose with us a darksome house of mortal clay.

Say, Heavenly Muse, shall not thy sacred vein
Afford a present to the Infant God?
Hast thou no verse, no hymn, or solemn strain,
To welcome Him to this His new abode,
Now while the heaven, by the Sun's team untrod,
   Hath took no print of the approaching light,
And all the spangled host keep watch in squadrons
      bright?

See how from far upon the eastern road
The star-led wizards haste with odors sweet!
Oh! run; prevent them with thy humble ode,
And lay it lowly at His blessèd feet;
Have thou the honor first thy Lord to greet,
    And join thy voice unto the Angel Quire,
From out His secret altar touched with hallowed fire.


### THE HYMN


    It was the winter wild,
    While the Heaven-born Child
All meanly wrapt in the rude manger lies;
    Nature, in awe to Him,
    Had doffed her gaudy trim,
With her great Master so to sympathize:
It was no season then for her
To wanton with the Sun, her lusty paramour.


    Only with speeches fair
    She woos the gentle air
To hide her guilty front with innocent snow,
    And on her naked shame,
    Pollute with sinful blame,
The saintly veil of maiden white to throw;
Confounded, that her Maker's eyes
Should look so near upon her foul deformities.


    But He, her fears to cease,
    Sent down the meek-eyed Peace:
She, crowned with olive green, came softly sliding
    Down through the turning sphere,
    His ready harbinger,
With turtle wing the amorous clouds dividing;
And, waving wide her myrtle wand,
She strikes a universal peace through sea and land.

No war, or battle's sound,
  Was heard the world around;
The idle spear and shield were high uphung;
  The hookèd chariot stood,
  Unstained with hostile blood;
The trumpet spake not to the armèd throng;
And kings sat still with awful eye,
As if they surely knew their sovran Lord was by.

  But peaceful was the night
  Wherein the Prince of Light
His reign of peace upon the earth began.
  The winds, with wonder whist,
  Smoothly the waters kissed,
Whispering new joys to the mild Ocean,
Who now hath quite forgot to rave,
While birds of calm sit brooding on the charmèd wave.

  The stars, with deep amaze,
  Stand fixed in steadfast gaze,
Bending one way their precious influence,
  And will not take their flight,
  For all the morning light,
Or Lucifer that often warned them thence;
But in their glimmering orbs did glow,
Until their Lord Himself bespake, and bid them go.

  And, though the shady gloom
  Had given day her room,
The Sun himself withheld his wonted speed,
  And hid his head for shame,
  As his inferior flame
The new-enlightened world no more should need:
He saw a greater Sun appear
Than his bright throne or burning axletree could bear.

  The shepherds on the lawn,
  Or ere the point of dawn,
Sat simply chatting in a rustic row;

Full little thought they than
    That the mighty Pan
  Was kindly come to live with them below:
Perhaps their loves, or else their sheep,
Was all that did their silly thoughts so busy keep.

    When such music sweet
    Their hearts and ears did greet
  As never was by mortal finger struck,
    Divinely-warbled voice
    Answering the stringèd noise,
  As all their souls in blissful rapture took:
The air, such pleasure loth to lose,
With thousand echoes still prolongs each heavenly close.

    Nature, that heard such sound
    Beneath the hollow round
  Of Cynthia's seat the airy region thrilling,
    Now was almost won
    To think her part was done,
  And that her reign had here its last fulfilling:
She knew such harmony alone
Could hold all Heaven and Earth in happier union.

    At last surrounds their sight
    A globe of circular light,
  That with long beams the shamefaced Night arrayed;
    The helmèd cherubim
    And sworded seraphim
  Are seen in glittering ranks with wings displayed,
Harping in loud and solemn quire,
With unexpressive notes, to Heaven's new-born Heir.

    Such music (as 'tis said)
    Before was never made,
  But when of old the Sons of Morning sung,
    While the Creator great
    His constellations set,
  And the well-balanced World on hinges hung,

And cast the dark foundations deep,
And bid the weltering waves their oozy channel keep.

    Ring out, ye crystal spheres!
    Once bless our human ears,
If ye have power to touch our senses so;
    And let your silver chime
    Move in melodious time;
    And let the bass of heaven's deep organ blow;
And with your ninefold harmony
Make up full consort to th' angelic symphony.

    For, if such holy song
    Enwrap our fancy long,
Time will run back and fetch the Age of Gold;
    And speckled Vanity
    Will sicken soon and die,
And leprous Sin will melt from earthly mould;
And Hell itself will pass away,
And leave her dolorous mansions to the peering day.

    Yea, Truth and Justice then
    Will down return to men,
Orbed in a rainbow; and, like glories wearing,
    Mercy will sit between,
    Throned in celestial sheen,
With radiant feet the tissued clouds down steering;
And Heaven, as at some festival,
Will open wide the gates of her high palace-hall.

    But wisest Fate says No,
    This must not yet be so;
The Babe lies yet in smiling infancy
    That on the bitter cross
    Must redeem our loss,
So both Himself and us to glorify:
Yet first, to those ychained in sleep,
The wakeful trump of doom must thunder through the
        deep,

With such a horrid clang
  As on Mount Sinai rang,
While the red fire and smouldering clouds outbrake:
  The aged Earth, aghast
  With terror of that blast,
Shall from the surface to the center shake,
When, at the world's last session,
The dreadful Judge in middle air shall spread his
      throne.

And then at last our bliss
  Full and perfect is,
But now begins; for from this happy day
  Th' old Dragon under ground,
  In straiter limits bound,
Not half so far casts his usurpèd sway;
And, wroth to see his Kingdom fail,
Swinges the scaly horror of his folded tail.

The Oracles are dumb;
  No voice or hideous hum
Runs through the archèd roof in words deceiving.
  Apollo from his shrine
  Can no more divine,
With hollow shriek the steep of Delphos leaving.
No nightly trance, or breathèd spell,
Inspires the pale-eyed priest from the prophetic cell.

The lonely mountains o'er,
  And the resounding shore,
A voice of weeping heard, and loud lament;
  From haunted spring, and dale
  Edged with poplar pale,
The parting genius is with sighing sent,
With flower-inwov'n tresses torn
The nymphs in twilight shade of tangled thickets
      mourn.

In consecrated earth,
And on the holy hearth,
The Lars and Lemurs moan with midnight plaint,
In urns and altars round,
A drear and dying sound
Affrights the flamens at their service quaint;
And the chill marble seems to sweat,
While each peculiar power forgoes his wonted seat.

Peor and Baalim
Forsake their temples dim,
With that twice-battered god of Palestine,
And moonèd Ashtaroth,
Heav'n's queen and mother both,
Now sits not girt with tapers' holy shine,
The Lybic Hammon shrinks his horn;
In vain the Tyrian maids their wounded Thammuz
        mourn.

And sullen Moloch, fled,
Hath left in shadows dread
His burning idol all of blackest hue;
In vain with cymbals' ring
They call the grisly king,
In dismal dance about the furnace blue;
The brutish gods of Nile, as fast,
Isis and Orus and the dog Anubis, haste.

Nor is Osiris seen
In Memphian grove or green,
Trampling the unshowered grass with lowings loud;
Nor can he be at rest
Within his sacred chest;
Naught but profoundest Hell can be his shroud;
In vain, with timbrelled anthems dark,
The sable-stolèd sorcerers bear his worshipped ark.

He feels from Juda's land
The dreaded infant's hand;
The rays of Bethlehem blind his dusky eyn;

Nor all the gods beside
    Longer dare abide,
  Not Typhon huge ending in snaky twine:
Our Babe, to show his Godhead true,
Can in his swaddling bands control the damnèd crew.

    So when the sun in bed,
    Curtained with cloudy red,
  Pillows his chin upon an orient wave,
    The flocking shadows pale
    Troop to th' infernal jail,
  Each fettered ghost slips to his several grave,
And the yellow-skirted fays
Fly after the night-steeds, leaving their moon-loved
        maze.

    But see! the Virgin blest
    Hath laid her Babe to rest.
  Time is our tedious song should here have ending:
    Heav'n's youngest-teemèd star
    Hath fixed her polished car,
  Her sleeping Lord with handmaid lamp attending;
And all about the courtly stable
Bright-harnessed angels sit in order serviceable.

## On Time

Fly envious Time, till thou run out thy race,
Call on the lazy leaden-stepping hours,
Whose speed is but the heavy plummet's pace;
And glut thy self with what thy womb devours,
Which is no more than what is false and vain,
And merely mortal dross;
So little is our loss,
So little is thy gain.
For when as each thing bad thou hast entombed,
And last of all, thy greedy self consumed,
Then long Eternity shall greet our bliss

With an individual kiss;
And Joy shall overtake us as a flood,
When every thing that is sincerely good
And perfectly divine,
With Truth, and Peace, and Love shall ever shine
About the supreme Throne
Of him, t' whose happy-making sight alone,
When once our heav'nly-guided soul shall climb,
Then all this earthy grossness quit,
Attired with stars, we shall for ever sit,
Triumphing over Death, and Chance, and thee, O Time.


### At a Solemn Music

Blest pair of sirens, pledges of Heav'n's joy,
Sphere-born harmonious sisters, Voice and Verse,
Wed your divine sounds, and mixed power employ,
Dead things with inbreathed sense able to pierce;
And to our high-raised phantasy present
That undisturbèd song of pure concent,
Ay sung before the sapphire-coloured throne
To him that sits thereon
With saintly shout and solemn jubilee;
Where the bright Seraphim in burning row
Their loud uplifted angel trumpets blow,
And the Cherubic host in thousand quires
Touch their immortal harps of golden wires,
With those just Spirits that wear victorious palms,
Hymns devout and holy psalms
Singing everlastingly:
That we on Earth, with undiscording voice,
May rightly answer that melodious noise;
As once we did, till disproportioned sin
Jarred against nature's chime, and with harsh din
Broke the fair music that all creatures made
To their great Lord, whose love their motion swayed
In perfect diapason, whilst they stood
In first obedience, and their state of good.

O may we soon again renew that song,
And keep in tune with Heaven, till God ere long
To His celestial consort us unite,
To live with Him, and sing in endless morn of light.


## On Shakespeare

What needs my Shakespeare for his honoured bones
The labour of an age in pilèd stones,
Or that his hallowed reliques should be hid
Under a star-ypointing pyramid?
Dear son of memory, great heir of fame,
What need'st thou such weak witness of thy name!
Thou in our wonder and astonishment
Hast built thy self a live-long monument.
For whilst, to th' shame of slow-endeavouring art,
Thy easy numbers flow, and that each heart
Hath from the leaves of thy unvalued book
Those delphic lines with deep impression took,
Then thou our fancy of itself bereaving,
Dost make us marble with too much conceiving;
And so sepulchered in such pomp dost lie,
That kings for such a tomb would wish to die.


## O Nightingale, That on Yon Bloomy Spray

O nightingale, that on yon bloomy spray
Warbl'st at eve, when all the woods are still,
Thou with fresh hope the lover's heart dost fill,
While the jolly hours lead on propitious May,
Thy liquid notes that close the eye of day,
First heard before the shallow cuckoo's bill,
Portend success in love; O if Jove's will
Have linked that amorous power to thy soft lay,
Now timely sing, ere the rude bird of hate
Foretell my hopeless doom in some grove nigh:
As thou from year to year hast sung too late

For my relief; yet hadst no reason why,
Whether the muse, or love call thee his mate,
Both them I serve, and of their train am I.

## How Soon Hath Time the Subtle Thief of Youth

How soon hath time the subtle thief of youth,
Stol'n on his wing my three-and-twentieth year!
My hasting days fly on with full career,
But my late spring no bud or blossom shew'th.
Perhaps my semblance might deceive the truth
That I to manhood am arriv'd so near;
And inward ripeness doth much less appear,
That some more timely-happy spirits indu'th.
Yet be it less or more, or soon or slow,
It shall be still in strictest measure ev'n
To that same lot, however mean or high,
Toward which Time leads me, and the will of Heav'n
All is, if I have grace to use it so,
As ever in my great task master's eye.

## When the Assault Was Intended to the City

Captain or colonel, or knight in arms,
Whose chance on these defenceless doors may seize,
If deed of honour did thee ever please,
Guard them, and him within protect from harms,
He can requite thee, for he knows the charms
That call fame on such gentle acts as these,
And he can spread thy name o'er lands and seas,
What ever clime the sun's bright circle warms.
Lift not thy spear against the muses' bower,
The great Emathian conqueror bid spare
The house of Pindarus, when temple and tower
Went to the ground: And the repeated air
Of sad Electra's poet had the power
To save th' Athenian walls from ruin bare.

## *Lycidas*

Yet once more, O ye Laurels, and once more,
Ye Myrtles brown, with Ivy never sear,
I come to pluck your berries harsh and crude,
And with forced fingers rude
Shatter your leaves before the mellowing year.
Bitter constraint and sad occasion dear
Compels me to disturb your season due;
For Lycidas is dead, dead ere his prime,
Young Lycidas, and hath not left his peer.
Who would not sing for Lycidas? he knew
Himself to sing, and build the lofty rhyme.
He must not float upon his wat'ry bier
Unwept, and welter to the parching wind,
Without the meed of some melodious tear.
  Begin, then, Sisters of the Sacred Well
That from beneath the seat of Jove doth spring,
Begin, and somewhat loudly sweep the string.
Hence with denial vain and coy excuse:
So may some gentle Muse
With lucky words favor my destined urn,
And, as he passes, turn,
And bid fair peace be to my sable shroud!
For we were nursed upon the self-same hill,
Fed the same flocks, by fountain, shade, and rill;
  Together both, ere the high lawns appeared
Under the opening eyelids of the Morn,
We drove a-field, and both together heard
What time the gray-fly winds her sultry horn,
Battening our flocks with the fresh dews of night,
Oft till the star that rose at evening bright
Towards Heaven's descent had sloped his westering
      wheel.
Meanwhile the rural ditties were not mute,
Tempered to the oaten flute,
Rough Satyrs danced, and Fauns with cloven heel
From the glad sound would not be absent long;
And old Damætas loved to hear our song.

But, O the heavy change, now thou art gone,
Now thou art gone, and never must return!
Thee, Shepherd, thee the woods and desert caves,
With wild thyme and the gadding vine o'ergrown,
And all their echoes mourn.
The willows, and the hazel copses green,
Shall now no more be seen
Fanning their joyous leaves to thy soft lays.
As killing as the canker to the rose,
Or taint-worm to the weanling herds that graze,
Or frost to flowers, that their gay wardrobe wear
When first the white thorn blows;
Such, Lycidas, thy loss to shepherd's ear.

Where were ye, Nymphs, when the remorseless deep
Closed o'er the head of your loved Lycidas?
For neither were ye playing on the steep
Where your old bards, the famous Druids, lie,
Nor yet on the shaggy top of Mona high,
Nor yet where Deva spreads her wizard stream.
Ay me! I fondly dream
"Had ye been there" . . . for what could that have done?
What could the Muse herself that Orpheus bore,
The Muse herself, for her enchanting son,
Whom universal Nature did lament,
When, by the rout that made the hideous roar,
His gory visage down the stream was sent,
Down the swift Hebrus to the Lesbian shore?

Alas! what boots it with uncessant care
To tend the homely, slighted, shepherd's trade,
And strictly meditate the thankless Muse?
Were it not better done, as others use,
To sport with Amaryllis in the shade,
Or with the tangles of Neæra's hair?
Fame is the spur that the clear spirit doth raise
(That last infirmity of noble mind)
To scorn delights and live laborious days;
But the fair guerdon when we hope to find,
And think to burst out into sudden blaze,
Comes the blind Fury with the abhorrèd shears,

And slits the thin-spun life. "But not the praise,"
Phœbus replied, and touched my trembling ears:
"Fame is no plant that grows on mortal soil,
Nor in the glistering foil
Set off to the world, nor in broad Rumor lies,
But lives and spreads aloft by those pure eyes
And perfect witness of all-judging Jove;
As he pronounces lastly on each deed,
Of so much fame in Heav'n expect thy meed."
    O fountain Arethuse, and thou honored flood,
Smooth-sliding Mincius, crowned with vocal reeds,
That strain I heard was of a higher mood:
But now my oat proceeds,
And listens to the Herald of the Sea,
That came in Neptune's plea.
He asked the waves, and asked the felon winds,
What hard mishap hath doomed this gentle swain?
And questioned every gust of rugged wings
That blows from off each beakèd promontory:
They knew not of his story;
And sage Hippotadés their answer brings,
That not a blast was from his dungeon strayed:
The air was calm, and on the level brine
Sleek Panopé with all her sisters played.
It was that fatal and perfidious bark,
Built in the eclipse, and rigged with curses dark,
That sunk so low that sacred head of thine.
    Next, Camus, reverend sire, went footing slow,
His mantle hairy, and his bonnet sedge,
Inwrought with figures dim, and on the edge
Like to that sanguine flower inscribed with woe.
"Ah! who hath reft," quoth he, "my dearest pledge?"
Last came, and last did go,
The pilot of the Galilean lake;
Two massy keys he bore of metals twain
(The golden opes, the iron shuts amain).
He shook his mitered locks, and stern bespake:—
"How well could I have spared for thee, young Swain,
Enow of such, as for their bellies' sake,

Creep, and intrude, and climb into the fold!
Of other care they little reckoning make
Than how to scramble at the shearers' feast,
And shove away the worthy bidden guest.
Blind mouths! that scarce themselves know how to hold
A sheep-hook, or have learned aught else the least
That to the faithful herdsman's art belongs!
What recks it them? What need they? they are sped;
And, when they list, their lean and flashy songs
Grate on their scrannel pipes of wretched straw;
The hungry sheep look up, and are not fed,
But, swollen with wind and the rank mist they draw,
Rot inwardly, and foul contagion spread;
Besides what the grim wolf with privy paw
Daily devours apace, and nothing said;
But that two-handed engine at the door
Stands ready to smite once, and smite no more."
　　Return, Alphéus; the dread voice is past
That shrunk thy streams; return, Sicilian Muse,
And call the vales, and bid them hither cast
Their bells and flowerets of a thousand hues.
Ye valleys low, where the mild whispers use
Of shades, and wanton winds, and gushing brooks,
On whose fresh lap the swart star sparely looks,
Throw hither all your quaint enameled eyes,
That on the green turf suck the honied showers,
And purple all the ground with vernal flowers.
Bring the rathe primrose that forsaken dies,
The tufted crow-toe, and pale jessamine,
The white pink, and the pansy freaked with jet,
The glowing violet,
The musk-rose, and the well-attired woodbine,
With cowslips wan that hang the pensive head,
And every flower that sad embroidery wears;
Bid Amaranthus all his beauty shed,
And daffadillies fill their cups with tears,
To strew the laureate hearse where Lycid lies.
For so, to interpose a little ease,
Let our frail thoughts dally with false surmise,

Ay me! whilst thee the shores and sounding seas
Wash far away, where'er thy bones are hurled;
Whether beyond the stormy Hebrides,
Where thou, perhaps, under the whelming tide
Visit'st the bottom of the monstrous world;
Or whether thou, to our moist vows denied,
Sleep'st by the fable of Bellerus old,
Where the great Vision of the guarded mount
Looks toward Namancos and Bayona's hold:
Look homeward, angel, now, and melt with ruth;
And, O ye Dolphins, waft the hapless youth.
   Weep no more, woeful shepherds, weep no more,
For Lycidas, your sorrow, is not dead,
Sunk though he be beneath the watery floor:
So sinks the day-star in the ocean bed,
And yet anon repairs his drooping head,
And tricks his beams, and with new-spangled ore
Flames in the forehead of the morning sky:
So Lycidas sunk low, but mounted high,
Through the dear might of Him that walked the waves,
Where, other groves and other streams along,
With nectar pure his oozy locks he laves,
And hears the unexpressive nuptial song,
In the blest kingdoms meek of Joy and Love.
There entertain him all the Saints above,
In solemn troops, and sweet societies,
That sing, and singing in their glory move,
And wipe the tears forever from his eyes.
Now, Lycidas, the shepherds weep no more;
Henceforth thou art the Genius of the shore,
In thy large recompense, and shalt be good
To all that wander in that perilous flood.

   Thus sang the uncouth swain to the oaks and rills,
While the still Morn went out with sandals grey;
He touched the tender stops of various quills,
With eager thought warbling his Doric lay:
And now the sun had stretched out all the hills,
And now was dropped into the western bay.

At last he rose, and twitched his mantle blue:
Tomorrow to fresh woods and pastures new.


### On the Late Massacre in Piedmont

Avenge, O Lord, thy slaughtered saints, whose bones
Lie scattered on the Alpine mountains cold;
Ev'n them who kept thy truth so pure of old,
When all our fathers worshipped stocks and stones,
Forget not: in thy book record their groans
Who were thy sheep, and in their ancient fold
Slain by the bloody Piedmontese, that rolled
Mother with infant down the rocks. Their moans
The vales redoubled to the hills, and they
To heav'n. Their martyred blood and ashes sow
O'er all th' Italian fields, where still doth sway
The triple Tyrant that from these may grow
A hundredfold, who, having learnt thy way,
Early may fly the Babylonian woe.


### When I Consider How My Light Is Spent

When I consider how my light is spent
Ere half my days in this dark world and wide,
And that one talent which is death to hide
Lodged with me useless, though my soul more bent
To serve therewith my Maker, and present
My true account, lest He returning chide,
"Doth God exact day-labor, light denied?"
I fondly ask. But Patience, to prevent
That murmur, soon replies, "God doth not need
Either man's work or his own gifts. Who best
Bear His mild yoke, they serve Him best. His state
Is kingly: thousands at His bidding speed,
And post o'er land and ocean without rest;
They also serve who only stand and wait."

*Methought I Saw My Late Espousèd Saint*

Methought I saw my late espousèd Saint
Brought to me like Alcestis from the grave,
Whom Jove's great son to her glad husband gave,
Rescued from death by force though pale and faint.
Mine as whom washt from spot of child-bed taint,
Purification in the old Law did save,
And such, as yet once more I trust to have
Full sight of her in Heaven without restraint,
Came vested all in white, pure as her mind:
Her face was veiled; yet to my fancied sight,
Love, sweetness, goodness, in her person shined
So clear, as in no face with more delight.
But O as to embrace me she enclined
I waked, she fled, and day brought back my night.


*To the Lord General Cromwell, May, 1652*

*On the Proposals of Certain Ministers at the Committee for
Propagation of the Gospel.*

Cromwell, our chief of men, who through a cloud
Not of war only, but detractions rude,
Guided by faith and matchless fortitude,
To peace and truth thy glorious way hast ploughed,
And on the neck of crownèd fortune proud
Hast reared God's trophies, and His work pursued,
While Darwen stream with blood of Scots imbrued,
And Dunbar field resounds thy praises loud,
And Worster's laureat wreath; yet much remains
To conquer still; peace hath her victories
No less renowned than war, new foes arise
Threat'ning to bind our souls with secular chains:
Help us to save free conscience from the paw
Of hireling wolves whose Gospel is their maw.

# RICHARD LOVELACE/1618–1658

### Going to the Wars

Tell me not (Sweet) I am unkind,
   That from the nunnery
Of thy chaste breast, and quiet mind,
   To war and arms I fly.

True; a new mistress now I chase,
   The first foe in the field;
And with a stronger faith embrace
   A sword, a horse, a shield.

Yet this inconstancy is such,
   As you too shall adore;
I could not love thee (Dear) so much,
   Loved I not honour more.

### The Grasshopper

#### To My Noble Friend, Mr. Charles Cotton

Oh, thou that swing'st upon the waving ear
   Of some well-fillèd oaten beard,
Drunk ev'ry night with a delicious tear
   Dropt thee from heav'n, where now th'art reared.

The joys of earth and air are thine entire,
   That with thy feet and wings dost hop and fly;
And when thy poppy works thou dost retire
   To thy carved acron-bed to lie.

Up with the day, the sun thou welcom'st then,
   Sport'st in the gilt-plats of his beams,
And all these merry days mak'st merry men,
   Thy self, and melancholy streams.

But ah, the sickle! golden ears are cropped;
   Ceres and Bacchus bid goodnight;
Sharp frosty fingers all your flow'rs have topped,
   And what scythes spared, winds shave off quite.

Poor verdant fool! and now green ice! thy joys
   Large and as lasting as thy perch of grass,
Bid us lay in 'gainst winter rain, and poise
   Their floods, with an o'erflowing glass.

Thou best of men and friends! we will create
   A genuine summer in each other's breast;
And spite of this cold time and frozen fate
   Thaw us a warm seat to our rest.

Our sacred hearths shall burn eternally
   As vestal flames; the north-wind, he
Shall strike his frost stretched wings, dissolve and fly
   This Ætna in epitome.

Dropping December shall come weeping in,
   Bewail th' usurping of his reign;
But when in show'rs of old Greek we begin,
   Shall cry, he hath his crown again!

Night as clear Hesper shall our tapers whip
   From the light casements where we play,
And the dark Hag from her black mantle strip,
   And stick there everlasting day.

Thus richer than untempted kings are we,
   That asking nothing, nothing need:
Though lord of all what seas embrace, yet he
   That wants himself, is poor indeed.

## To Althea from Prison

When Love with unconfinèd wings
   Hovers within my gates;
And my divine Althea brings
   To whisper at the grates:
When I lie tangled in her hair,
   And fettered to her eye;
The birds, that wanton in the air,
   Know no such liberty.

When flowing cups run swiftly round
   With no allaying Thames,
Our careless heads with roses bound,
   Our hearts with loyal flames;
When thirsty grief in wine we steep,
   When healths and draughts go free,
Fishes that tipple in the deep,
   Know no such liberty.

When (like committed linnets) I
   With shriller throat shall sing
The sweetness, mercy, majesty,
   And glories of my King;
When I shall voice aloud, how good
   He is, how great should be;
Enlargèd winds that curl the flood,
   Know no such liberty.

Stone walls do not a prison make,
   Nor iron bars a cage;
Minds innocent and quiet take
   That for an hermitage;
If I have freedom in my Love,
   And in my soul am free;
Angels alone that soar above,
   Enjoy such liberty.

# ANDREW MARVELL/1621–1678

## *On a Drop of Dew*

See how the orient dew,
   Shed from the bosom of the morn
   Into the blowing roses,
Yet careless of its mansion new;
For the clear region where 'twas born
   Round in itself encloses:
   And in its little globe's extent,
Frames as it can its native element.
   How it the purple flower does slight,
      Scarce touching where it lies,
   But gazing back upon the skies,
      Shines with a mournful light;
        Like its own tear,
Because so long divided from the sphere.
      Restless it rolls and unsecure,
        Trembling lest it grow impure:
      Till the warm sun pity its pain,
And to the skies exhale it back again.
      So the soul, that drop, that ray
Of the clear fountain of eternal day,
Could it within the human flower be seen,
      Rememb'ring still its former height,
      Shuns the sweet leaves and blossoms green;
      And, recollecting its own light,
Does, in its pure and circling thoughts, express
The greater heaven in a heaven less.
      In how coy a figure wound,
      Every way it turns away:
      So the world excluding round,
      Yet receiving in the day.
      Dark beneath, but bright above:
      Here disdaining, there in love.
      How loose and easy hence to go:

How girt and ready to ascend.
Moving but on a point below,
It all about does upwards bend.
Such did the manna's sacred dew distill;
White, and entire, though congealed and chill.
Congealed on earth: but does, dissolving, run
Into the glories of the almighty sun.


### The Coronet

When for the thorns with which I long, too long,
      With many a piercing wound,
      My Saviour's head have crowned,
I seek with garlands to redress that wrong:
      Through every garden, every mead,
I gather flowers (my fruits are only flowers)
      Dismantling all the fragrant towers
That once adorned my shepherdess's head.
And now when I have summed up all my store,
      Thinking (so I myself deceive)
      So rich a chaplet thence to weave
As never yet the King of Glory wore:
      Alas I find the serpent old
      That, twining in his speckled breast,
      About the flowers disguised does fold,
      With wreaths of fame and interest.
Ah, foolish Man, that would'st debase with them,
And mortal glory, Heaven's diadem!
But Thou who only could'st the serpent tame,
Either his slipp'ry knots at once untie,
And disentangle all his winding snare:
Or shatter too with him my curious frame:
And let these wither, so that he may die,
Though set with skill and chosen out with care.
That they, while Thou on both their spoils dost tread,
May crown Thy feet, that could not crown Thy head.

## Bermudas

Where the remote Bermudas ride
In th' ocean's bosom unespied,
From a small boat, that rowed along,
The list'ning winds received this song.
    What should we do but sing His praise
That led us through the wat'ry maze,
Unto an isle so long unknown,
And yet far kinder than our own?
Where He the huge sea-monsters wracks,
That lift the deep upon their backs.
He lands us on a grassy stage;
Safe from the storms, and prelate's rage.
He gave us this eternal spring,
Which here enamels everything;
And sends the fowls to us in care,
On daily visits through the air.
He hangs in shades the orange bright,
Like golden lamps in a green night.
And does in the pomegranates close
Jewels more rich than Ormus shows.
He makes the figs our mouths to meet;
And throws the melons at our feet.
But apples plants of such a price,
No tree could ever bear them twice.
With cedars, chosen by His hand,
From Lebanon, He stores the land.
And makes the hollow seas, that roar,
Proclaim the ambergris on shore,
He cast (of which we rather boast)
The gospel's pearl upon our coast.
And in these rocks for us did frame
A temple, where to sound His name.
Oh let our voice His praise exalt,
Till it arrive at Heaven's vault:
Which thence (perhaps) rebounding, may
Echo beyond the Mexique Bay.
Thus sung they, in the English boat,

An holy and a cheerful note,
And all the way, to guide their chime,
With falling oars they kept the time.

### To His Coy Mistress

Had we but world enough, and time,
This coyness, Lady, were no crime.
We would sit down, and think which way
To walk, and pass our long love's day.
Thou by the Indian Ganges' side
Should'st rubies find: I by the tide
Of Humber would complain. I would
Love you ten years before the Flood:
And you should if you please refuse
Till the conversion of the Jews.
My vegetable love should grow
Vaster than empires, and more slow.
An hundred years should go to praise
Thine eyes, and on thy forehead gaze.
Two hundred to adore each breast:
But thirty thousand to the rest.
An age at least to every part,
And the last age should show your heart.
For, Lady, you deserve this state;
Nor would I love at lower rate.
    But at my back I always hear
Time's wingèd chariot hurrying near:
And yonder all before us lie
Deserts of vast eternity.
Thy beauty shall no more be found,
Nor, in thy marble vault, shall sound
My echoing song: then worms shall try
That long preserved virginity:
And your quaint honour turn to dust;
And into ashes all my lust.
The grave's a fine and private place,
But none, I think, do there embrace.

Now therefore, while the youthful hue
Sits on thy skin like morning dew,
And while thy willing soul transpires
At every pore with instant fires,
Now let us sport us while we may;
And now, like am'rous birds of prey,
Rather at once our time devour,
Than languish in his slow-chapt pow'r.
Let us roll all our strength, and all
Our sweetness, up into one ball:
And tear our pleasures with rough strife,
Thorough the iron gates of life.
Thus, though we cannot make our sun
Stand still, yet we will make him run.


### The Fair Singer


To make a final conquest of all me,
Love did compose so sweet an enemy,
In whom both beauties to my death agree,
Joining themselves in fatal harmony;
That while she with her eyes my heart doth bind,
She with her voice might captivate my mind.

I could have fled from one but singly fair;
My disentangled soul itself might save,
Breaking the curlèd trammels of her hair;
But how could I avoid to be her slave,
Whose subtile art invisibly can wreathe
My fetters of the very air I breathe?

It had been easy fighting in some plain
Where victory might hang in equal choice;
But all resistance against her is vain
Who has th' advantage both of eyes and voice;
And all my forces needs must be undone,
She having gainèd both the wind and sun.

## The Definition of Love

My love is of a birth as rare
As 'tis for object strange and high:
It was begotten by Despair
Upon Impossibility.

Magnanimous Despair alone
Could show me so divine a thing,
Where feeble Hope could ne'er have flown
But vainly flapped its tinsel wing.

And yet I quickly might arrive
Where my extended soul is fixed,
But Fate does iron wedges drive,
And always crowds itself betwixt.

For Fate with jealous eye does see
Two perfect loves, nor lets them close:
Their union would her ruin be,
And her tyrannic power depose.

And therefore her decrees of steel
Us as the distant poles have placed,
(Though love's whole world on us doth wheel)
Not by themselves to be embraced,

Unless the giddy heaven fall,
And earth some new convulsion tear,
And, us to join, the world should all
Be cramped into a planisphere.

As lines, so loves oblique may well
Themselves in every angle greet;
But ours, so truly parallel,
Though infinite, can never meet.

Therefore the love which us doth bind,
But fate so enviously debars,

Is the conjunction of the mind,
And opposition of the stars.


*The Picture of Little T. C. in a Prospect of Flowers*

See with what simplicity
This nymph begins her golden days!
In the green grass she loves to lie,
And there with her fair aspect tames
The wilder flowers, and gives them names:
But only with the roses plays;
       And then does tell
What colour best becomes them, and what smell.

Who can foretell for what high cause
This darling of the gods was born!
Yet this is she whose chaster laws
The wanton Love shall one day fear,
And, under her command severe,
See his bow broke and ensigns torn.
       Happy, who can
Appease this virtuous enemy of man!

O, then let me in time compound,
And parley with those conquering eyes,
Ere they have tried their force to wound,
Ere, with their glancing wheels, they drive
In triumph over hearts that strive,
And them that yield but more despise.
       Let me be laid,
Where I may see thy glories from some shade.

Meantime, whilst every verdant thing
Itself does at thy beauty charm,
Reform the errors of the spring;
Make that the tulips may have share
Of sweetness, seeing they are fair;
And roses of their thorns disarm:

      But most procure
That violets may a longer age endure.

But O, young beauty of the woods,
Whom nature courts with fruits and flowers,
Gather the flowers, but spare the buds;
Lest Flora, angry at thy crime,
To kill her infants in their prime,
Do quickly make th' example yours;
        And, ere we see,
Nip in the blossom all our hopes and thee.

### The Mower to the Glowworms

Ye living lamps, by whose dear light
The nightingale doth sit so late,
And studying all the summer-night,
Her matchless songs does meditate;

Ye country comets that portend
No war, nor prince's funeral,
Shining unto no higher end
Than to presage the grass's fall;

Ye glowworms, whose officious flame
To wandering mowers shows the way,
That in the night have lost their aim,
And after foolish fires do stray;

Your courteous lights in vain you waste,
Since Juliana here is come;
For she my mind hath so displaced,
That I shall never find my home.

## The Garden

How vainly men themselves amaze,
To win the palm, the oak, or bays,
And their uncessant labors see
Crowned from some single herb or tree
Whose short and narrow-vergèd shade
Does prudently their toils upbraid,
While all the flowers and trees do close
To weave the garlands of repose!

Fair Quiet, have I found thee here,
And Innocence, thy sister dear?
Mistaken long, I sought you then
In busy companies of men.
Your sacred plants, if here below,
Only among the plants will grow;
Society is all but rude
To this delicious solitude.

No white nor red was ever seen
So amorous as this lovely green.
Fond lovers, cruel as their flame,
Cut in these trees their mistress' name.
Little, alas! they know or heed,
How far these beauties hers exceed!
Fair trees! wheres'e'r your barks I wound
No name shall but your own be found.

When we have run our passion's heat,
Love hither makes his best retreat.
The gods, that mortal beauty chase,
Still in a tree did end their race;
Apollo hunted Daphne so,
Only that she might laurel grow;
And Pan did after Syrinx speed,
Not as a nymph, but for a reed.

What wondrous life is this I lead!
Ripe apples drop about my head;
The luscious clusters of the vine
Upon my mouth do crush their wine;
The nectarine, and curious peach,
Into my hands themselves do reach;
Stumbling on melons, as I pass,
Ensnared with flowers, I fall on grass.

Meanwhile the mind, from pleasure less,
Withdraws into its happiness:
The mind, that ocean where each kind
Does straight its own resemblance find;
Yet it creates, transcending these,
Far other worlds, and other seas,
Annihilating all that's made
To a green thought in a green shade.

Here at the fountain's sliding foot,
Or at some fruit-tree's mossy root,
Casting the body's vest aside,
My soul into the boughs does glide:
There, like a bird, it sits and sings,
Then whets and combs its silver wings,
And, till prepared for longer flight,
Waves in its plumes the various light.

Such was that happy garden-state,
While man there walked without a mate
After a place so pure and sweet.
What other help could yet be meet!
But 'twas beyond a mortal's share
To wander solitary there:
Two paradises 'twere in one,
To live in paradise alone.

How well the skilful gardener drew
Of flowers, and herbs, this dial new;

Where, from above, the milder sun
Does through a fragrant zodiac run,
And, as it works, th' industrious bee
Computes its time as well as we!
How could such sweet and wholesome hours
Be reckoned but with herbs and flowers?


### An Horatian Ode upon Cromwell's Return
### from Ireland

The forward youth that would appear
Must now forsake his muses dear,
   Nor in the shadows sing
   His numbers languishing:

'Tis time to leave the books in dust,
And oil the unused armor's rust,
   Removing from the wall
   The corselet of the hall.

So restless Cromwell could not cease
In the inglorious arts of peace,
   But through adventurous war
   Urgèd his active star;

And, like the three-forked lightning, first
Breaking the clouds where it was nursed,
   Did thorough his own side
   His fiery way divide;

For 'tis all one to courage high,
The emulous, or enemy,
   And with such to inclose,
   Is more than to oppose.

Then burning through the air he went,
And palaces and temples rent;

And Caesar's head at last
Did through his laurels blast.

'Tis madness to resist or blame
The face of angry heaven's flame;
    And if we would speak true,
    Much to the man is due,

Who from his private gardens, where
He lived reservèd and austere,
    As if his highest plot
    To plant the bergamot,

Could by industrious valor climb
To ruin the great work of Time,
    And cast the kingdoms old,
    Into another mould;

Though Justice against Fate complain,
And plead the ancient rights in vain;
    But those do hold or break,
    As men are strong or weak.

Nature, that hateth emptiness,
Allows of penetration less,
    And therefore must make room
    Where greater spirits come.

What field of all the civil war,
Where his were not the deepest scar?
    And Hampton shows what part
    He had of wiser art;

Where, twining subtle fears with hope,
He wove a net of such a scope
    That Charles himself might chase
    To Carisbrooke's narrow case.

That thence the royal actor borne
The tragic scaffold might adorn:
   While round the armèd bands
   Did clap their bloody hands.

He nothing common did or mean
Upon that memorable scene:
   But with his keener eye
   The ax's edge did try:

Nor called the gods with vulgar spite
To vindicate his helpless right,
   But bowed his comely head,
   Down as upon a bed.

This was that memorable hour
Which first assured the forcèd power.
   So when they did design
   The Capitol's first line,

A bleeding head where they begun,
Did fright the architects to run;
   And yet in that the state
   Foresaw its happy fate.

And now the Irish are ashamed
To see themselves in one year tamed:
   So much one man can do,
   That does both act and know.

They can affirm his praises best,
And have, though overcome, confessed
   How good he is, how just,
   And fit for highest trust:

Nor yet grown stiffer with command,
But still in the Republic's hand:
   How fit he is to sway
   That can so well obey.

He to the Commons' feet presents
A kingdom, for his first year's rents;
 And what he may, forbears
 His fame to make it theirs:

And has his sword and spoils ungirt,
To lay them at the public's skirt.
 So when the falcon high
 Falls heavy from the sky,

She, having killed, no more does search,
But on the next green bough to perch;
 Where, when he first does lure,
 The falconer has her sure.

What may not then our isle presume
While victory his crest does plume!
 What may not others fear
 If thus he crowns each year!

A Caesar he ere long to Gaul,
To Italy a Hannibal,
 And to all states not free
 Shall climacteric be.

The Pict no shelter now shall find
Within his parti-colored mind;
 But from this valor sad
 Shrink underneath the plaid:

Happy if in the tufted brake
The English hunter him mistake;
 Nor lay his hounds in near
 The Caledonian deer.

But thou, the War's and Fortune's son
March indefatigably on;

And for the last effect
Still keep thy sword erect:

Besides the force it has to fright
The spirits of the shady night,
The same arts that did gain
A power must it maintain.


PATRICK CAREY/*flourished* 1650


*Nulla Fides*

For God's sake mark that fly:
See what a poor, weak, little thing it is.
When thou hast marked, and scorned it, know that this,
This little, poor, weak fly
Has killed a pope; can make an emp'ror die.

Behold yon spark of fire:
How little hot! how near to nothing 'tis!
When thou hast done despising, know that this,
This contemned spark of fire,
Hast burnt whole towns; can burn a world entire.

That crawling worm there see:
Ponder how ugly, filthy, vile it is.
When thou hast seen and loathed it, know that this,
This base worm thou dost see,
Has quite devoured thy parents; shall eat thee.

Honor, the world, and man,
What trifles are they; since most true it is
That this poor fly, this little spark, this
So much abhorred worm, can
Honor destroy; burn worlds; devour up man.

# HENRY VAUGHAN/1622–1695

## *The Retreat*

Happy those early days! when I
Shined in my angel-infancy:
Before I understood this place
Appointed for my second race,
Or taught my soul to fancy ought
But a white, celestial thought;
When yet I had not walked above
A mile, or two, from my first love,
And looking back (at that short space,)
Could see a glimpse of his bright-face;
When on some gilded cloud, or flower
My gazing soul would dwell an hour,
And in those weaker glories spy
Some shadows of eternity;
Before I taught my tongue to wound
My conscience with a sinful sound,
Or had the black art to dispense
A sev'ral sin to ev'ry sense,
But felt through all this fleshly dress
Bright shoots of everlastingness.
    O how I long to travel back
And tread again that ancient track!
That I might once more reach that plain,
Where first I left my glorious train,
From whence th' enlightned spirit sees
That shady city of palm trees;
But (ah!) my soul with too much stay
Is drunk, and staggers in the way.
Some men a forward motion love,
But I by backward steps would move,
And when this dust falls to the urn
In that state I came return.

## Peace

My soul, there is a country
   Far beyond the stars,
Where stands a wingèd sentry
   All skilful in the wars;
There above noise, and danger
   Sweet peace sits crowned with smiles,
And one born in a manger
   Commands the beauteous files;
He is thy gracious friend,
   And (O, my Soul, awake!)
Did in pure love descend
   To die here for thy sake.
If thou canst get but thither,
   There grows the flower of peace,
The rose that cannot wither,
   Thy fortress, and thy ease;
Leave then thy foolish ranges,
   For none can thee secure,
But one, who never changes,
   Thy God, thy life, thy cure.

## The World

I saw Eternity the other night
Like a great *Ring* of pure and endless light,
   All calm, as it was bright,
And round beneath it, Time in hours, days, years
     Driv'n by the spheres
Like a vast shadow moved, in which the world
   And all her train were hurled;
The doting lover in his quaintest strain
     Did there complain,
Near him, his lute, his fancy, and his flights,
     Wit's sour delights,
With gloves, and knots the silly snares of pleasure;
     Yet his dear treasure

All scattered lay, while he his eyes did pour
　　　Upon a flower.

The darksome statesman, hung with weights and woe,
Like a thick midnight-fog moved there so slow
　　　He did nor stay, nor go;
Condemning thoughts (like sad Eclipses) scowl
　　　Upon his soul,
And clouds of crying witnesses without
　　　Pursued him with one shout.
Yet digged the mole, and lest his ways be found
　　　Worked under ground,
Where he did clutch his prey, but one did see
　　　That policy;
Churches and altars fed him, perjuries
　　　Were gnats and flies,
It rained about him blood and tears, but he
　　　Drank them as free.

The fearful miser on a heap of rust
Sat pining all his life there, did scarce trust
　　　His own hands with the dust,
Yet would not place one piece above, but lives
　　　In fear of thieves.
Thousands there were as frantic as himself
　　　And hugged each one his pelf;
The downright epicure placed heaven in sense
　　　And scorned pretence
While others, slipped into a wide excess,
　　　Said little less;
The weaker sort slight, trivial wares enslave
　　　Who think them brave,
And poor, despisèd Truth sat counting by
　　　Their victory.

Yet some, who all this while did weep and sing,
And sing, and weep, soared up into the *Ring*,
　　　But most would use no wing.

O fools (said I) thus to prefer dark night
    Before true light,
To live in grots, and caves, and hate the day
    Because it shews the way,
The way which from this dead and dark abode
    Leads up to God,
A way where you might tread the Sun, and be
    More bright than he.
But as I did their madness so discuss
    One whispered thus,
*This Ring the Bridegroom did for none provide*
    *But for his bride.*

John Chap. 2. ver. 16, 17.
*All that is in the world, the lust of the flesh, the lust of the Eyes, and the pride of life, is not of the father, but is of the world.*
*And the world passeth away, and the lusts thereof, but he that doth the will of God abideth for ever.*

## Man

    Weighing the stedfastness and state
Of some mean things which here below reside,
Where birds like watchful clocks the noiseless date
    And intercourse of times divide,
Where bees at night get home and hive, and flowers
    Early, as well as late,
Rise with the sun, and set in the same bowers;

    I would (said I) my God would give
The staidness of these things to man! for these
To his divine appointments ever cleave,
    And no new business breaks their peace;
The birds nor sow, nor reap, yet sup and dine,
    The flowers without clothes live,
Yet Solomon was never dressed so fine.

    Man hath still either toys, or care,
He hath no root, nor to one place is tied,

But ever restless and irregular
    About this earth doth run and ride,
He knows he hath a home, but scarce knows where,
      He says it is so far
That he hath quite forgot how to go there.

    He knocks at all doors, strays and roams,
Nay, hath not so much wit as some stones have
Which in the darkest nights point to their homes,
    By some hid sense their Maker gave;
Man is the shuttle, to whose winding quest
      And passage through these looms
God ordered motion, but ordained no rest.

### The Night

    Through that pure virgin-shrine,
  That sacred veil drawn o'er thy glorious noon
That men might look and live as glowworms shine,
    And face the moon:
  Wise Nicodemus saw such light
  As made him know his God by night.

    Most blest believer he!
Who in that land of darkness and blind eyes
Thy long-expected healing wings could see,
    When thou didst rise,
  And what can never more be done,
  Did at midnight speak with the Sun!

    O who will tell me, where
He found thee at that dead and silent hour!
What hallowed solitary ground did bear
    So rare a flower,
  Within whose sacred leaves did lie
  The fullness of the Deity.

No mercy-seat of gold,
No dead and dusty cherub, nor carved stone,
But His own living works did my Lord hold
    And lodge alone;
    Where trees and herbs did watch and peep
    And wonder, while the Jews did sleep.

Dear Night! this world's defeat;
The stop to busy fools; care's check and curb;
The day of spirits; my soul's calm retreat
    Which none disturb!
    Christ's progress, and His prayer time;
    The hours to which high heaven doth chime.

God's silent, searching flight:
When my Lord's head is filled with dew, and all
His locks are wet with the clear drops of night;
    His still, soft call;
    His knocking time; the soul's dumb watch,
    When spirits their fair kindred catch.

Were all my loud, evil days
Calm and unhaunted as is thy dark tent,
Whose peace but by some angel's wing or voice
    Is seldom rent;
    Then I in heaven all the long year
    Would keep, and never wander here.

But living where the sun
Doth all things wake, and where all mix and tire
Themselves and others, I consent and run
    To every mire,
    And by this world's ill-guiding light,
    Err more than I can do by night.

There is in God (some say)
A deep, but dazzling darkness; as men here

Say it is late and dusky, because they
    See not all clear;
      O for that night! where I in Him
      Might live invisible and dim.


*They Are All Gone into the World of Light!*

They are all gone into the world of light!
    And I alone sit ling'ring here;
Their very memory is fair and bright,
      And my sad thoughts doth clear.

It glows and glitters in my cloudy breast
    Like stars upon some gloomy grove,
Or those faint beams in which this hill is dressed,
      After the sun's remove.

I see them walking in an air of glory,
    Whose light doth trample on my days:
My days, which are at best but dull and hoary,
      Mere glimmering and decays.

O holy hope! and high humility,
    High as the heavens above!
These are your walks, and you have shewed them me
      To kindle my cold love,

Dear, beauteous Death! the Jewel of the Just,
    Shining no where, but in the dark;
What mysteries do lie beyond thy dust;
      Could man outlook that mark!

He that hath found some fledged bird's nest, may know
    At first sight, if the bird be flown;
But what fair well, or grove he sings in now,
      That is to him unknown.

And yet, as angels in some brighter dreams
    Call to the soul, when man doth sleep:
So some strange thoughts transcend our wonted themes
    And into glory peep.

If a star were confined into a tomb,
    Her captive flames must needs burn there;
But when the hand that locked her up, gives room,
    She'll shine through all the sphere.

O Father of eternal life, and all
    Created glories under Thee!
Resume Thy spirit from this world of thrall
    Into true liberty.

Either disperse these mists, which blot and fill
    My perspective (still) as they pass,
Or else remove me hence unto that hill,
    Where I shall need no glass.


## CHARLES COTTON/1630–1687


### Evening Quatrains

The day's grown old, the fainting sun
Has but a little way to run,
And yet his steeds, with all his skill,
Scarce lug the chariot down the hill.

With labour spent, and thirst opprest,
Whilst they strain hard to gain the West,
From fetlocks hot drops melted light,
Which turn to meteors in the night.

The shadows now so long do grow,
That brambles like tall cedars show,

Mole-hills seem mountains, and the ant
Appears a monstrous elephant.

A very little, little flock
Shades thrice the ground that it would stock;
Whilst the small stripling following them,
Appears a mighty Polypheme.

These being brought into the fold,
And by the thrifty master told,
He thinks his wages are well paid,
Since none are either lost or strayed.

Now lowing herds are each-where heard,
Chains rattle in the villain's yard,
The cart's on tail set down to rest,
Bearing on high the cuckold's crest.

The hedge is stripped, the clothes brought in,
Nought's left without should be within,
The bees are hived, and hum their charm,
Whilst every house does seem a swarm.

The cock now to the roost is prest;
For he must call up all the rest;
The sow's fast pegged within the sty,
To still her squeaking progeny.

Each one has had his supping mess,
The cheese is put into the press,
The pans and bowls clean scalded all,
Reared up against the milk-house wall.

And now on benches all are sat
In the cool air to sit and chat,
Till Phœbus, dipping in the west,
Shall lead the world the way to rest.

# JOHN DRYDEN/1631–1700

### *To the Memory of Mr. Oldham*

Farewell, too little and too lately known,
Whom I began to think and call my own;
For sure our souls were near allied, and thine
Cast in the same poetic mould with mine.
One common note on either lyre did strike,
And knaves and fools we both abhorred alike.
To the same goal did both our studies drive:
The last set out the soonest did arrive.
Thus Nisus fell upon the slippery place,
Whilst his young friend performed and won the race.
O early ripe! to thy abundant store
What could advancing Age have added more?
It might (what Nature never gives the young)
Have taught the numbers of thy native tongue.
But Satire needs not those, and wit will shine
Through the harsh cadence of a rugged line.
A noble error, and but seldom made,
When poets are by too much force betrayed.
Thy gen'rous fruits, though gathered ere their prime,
Still shewed a quickness; and maturing time
But mellows what we write to the dull sweets of rhyme.
Once more, hail, and farewell! farewell, thou young
But ah! too short, Marcellus of our tongue!
Thy brows with ivy and with laurels bound;
But fate and gloomy night encompass thee around.

### A Song for Saint Cecilia's Day, November 22, 1687

From harmony, from heavenly harmony
　　This universal frame began;
　When Nature underneath a heap
　　Of jarring atoms lay,
　And could not heave her head,
The tuneful voice was heard from high,
　　Arise, ye more than dead.
Then cold and hot and moist and dry
　In order to their stations leap,
　　And Music's power obey.
From harmony, from heavenly harmony
　　This universal frame began;
　　From harmony to harmony
Through all the compass of the notes it ran,
The diapason closing full in Man.


What passion cannot Music raise and quell?
　　When Jubal struck the corded shell,
　His listening brethren stood around,
　　And, wondering, on their faces fell
　To worship that celestial sound.
　Less than a god they thought there could not dwell
　　Within the hollow of that shell,
　　That spoke so sweetly, and so well.
What passion cannot Music raise and quell?


　　The trumpet's loud clangor
　　　Excites us to arms
　　With shrill notes of anger
　　　And mortal alarms.
　　The double, double, double beat
　　　Of the thundering drum
　　　Cries, "Hark! the foes come;
Charge, charge, 'tis too late to retreat!"


　　The soft complaining flute
　　In dying notes discovers

The woes of hopeless lovers,
Whose dirge is whispered by the warbling lute.

Sharp violins proclaim
Their jealous pangs and desperation,
Fury, frantic indignation,
Depth of pains and height of passion,
    For the fair, disdainful dame.

But, oh! what art can teach,
What human voice can reach
    The sacred organ's praise?
    Notes inspiring holy love,
Notes that wing their heavenly ways
    To mend the choirs above.

Orpheus could lead the savage race,
And trees unrooted left their place,
    Sequacious of the lyre;
But bright Cecilia raised the wonder higher;
When to her organ vocal breath was given,
An angel heard, and straight appeared,
    Mistaking earth for heaven.

As from the power of sacred lays
    The spheres began to move,
And sung the great Creator's praise
    To all the blest above;
So when the last and dreadful hour
This crumbling pageant shall devour,
The trumpet shall be heard on high,
The dead shall live, the living die,
And Music shall untune the sky.

JOHN DRYDEN

## The Secular Masque

JANUS:    Chronos, Chronos, mend thy pace,
An hundred times the rolling sun
Around the radiant belt has run
In his revolving race.
Behold, behold, the goal in sight,
Spread thy fans, and wing thy flight.

CHRONOS:    Weary, weary of my weight,
Let me, let me, drop my freight,
And leave the world behind.
I could not bear,
Another year,
The load of human-kind.

MOMUS:    Ha! ha! ha! ha! ha! ha! well hast thou done
To lay down thy pack,
And lighten thy back,
The world was a fool, e'er since it begun,
And since neither Janus, nor Chronos, nor I,
Can hinder the crimes,
Or mend the bad times,
'Tis better to laugh than to cry.

CHORUS OF
ALL THREE:    'Tis better to laugh than to cry.

JANUS:    Since Momus comes to laugh below,
Old Time, begin the show,
That he may see, in every scene,
What changes in this age have been.

CHRONOS:    The goddess of the silver bow begin.

DIANA:    With horns and with hounds, I waken the day;
And hye to the woodland-walks away:
I tuck up my robe, and am buskined soon,
And tie to my forehead a wexing moon.

I course the fleet stag, unkennel the fox,
And chase the wild goats o'er summits of
    rocks,
With shouting and hooting we pierce through
    the sky,
And Echo turns hunter, and doubles the cry.

CHORUS OF
  ALL:   With shouting and hooting we pierce through
    the sky,
And Echo turns hunter, and doubles the cry.

JANUS:   Then our age was in its prime:

CHRONOS:   Free from rage:

DIANA:          —And free from crime:

MOMUS:   A very merry, dancing, drinking,
Laughing, quaffing, and unthinking time.

CHORUS OF
  ALL:   Then our age was in its prime,
Free from rage, and free from crime,
A very merry, dancing, drinking,
Laughing, quaffing, and unthinking time.

MARS:   Inspire the vocal brass, inspire;
The world is past its infant age:
    Arms and honor,
    Arms and honor,
Set the martial mind on fire,
And kindle manly rage;
Mars has looked the sky to red;
And Peace, the lazy good, is fled.
Plenty, peace, and pleasure fly;
    The sprightly green,
In woodland-walks, no more is seen;
The sprightly green has drunk the
    Tyrian dye.

CHORUS OF
   ALL:   Plenty, peace, &c.

  MARS:   Sound the trumpet, beat the drum;
           Through all the world around,
           Sound a reveillé, sound, sound,
           The warrior god is come.

CHORUS OF
   ALL:   Sound the trumpet, &c.

 MOMUS:   Thy sword within the scabbard keep,
             And let mankind agree;
           Better the world were fast asleep,
           Than kept awake by thee.
           The fools are only thinner,
             With all our cost and care;
           But neither side a winner,
             For things are as they were.

CHORUS OF
   ALL:   The fools are only, &c.

 VENUS:   Calms appear, when storms are past;
           Love will have his hour at last:
           Nature is my kindly care;
           Mars destroys, and I repair;
           Take me, take me, while you may,
           Venus comes not every day.

CHORUS OF
   ALL:   Take her, take her, &c.

CHRONOS:   The world was then so light,
           I scarcely felt the weight;
           Joy ruled the day, and Love the night.
           But since the queen of pleasure left the ground,
            I faint, I lag,
             And feebly drag
           The pondrous orb around.

 MOMUS:   All, all of a piece throughout:

TO DIANA. Thy chase had a beast in view.

TO MARS. Thy wars brought nothing about;

TO VENUS. Thy lovers were all untrue.

JANUS: 'Tis well an old age is out.

CHRONOS: And time to begin a new.

CHORUS OF
ALL: All, all of a piece throughout;
Thy chase had a beast in view:
Thy wars brought nothing about;
Thy lovers were all untrue.
'Tis well an old age is out,
And time to begin a new.


# THOMAS TRAHERNE/1637?–1674

### Shadows in the Water

In unexperienced infancy
Many a sweet mistake doth lie:
Mistake though false, intending true;
A seeming somewhat more than view,
    That doth instruct the mind
    In things that lie behind,
And many secrets to us show
Which afterwards we come to know.

Thus did I by the water's brink
Another world beneath me think;
And while the lofty spacious skies
Reversèd there abused mine eyes,
    I fancied other feet

Came mine to touch or meet;
As by some puddle I did play
Another world within it lay.

Beneath the water people drowned,
Yet with another heaven crowned,
In spacious regions seemed to go
As freely moving to and fro:
   In bright and open space
   I saw their very face;
Eyes, hands, and feet they had like mine;
Another sun did with them shine.

'Twas strange that people there should walk,
And yet I could not hear them talk:
That through a little wat'ry chink,
Which one dry ox or horse might drink,
   We other worlds should see,
   Yet not admitted be;
And other confines there behold
Of light and darkness, heat and cold.

I called them oft, but called in vain;
No speeches we could entertain:
Yet did I there expect to find
Some other world, to please my mind.
   I plainly saw by these
   A new Antipodes,
Whom, though they were so plainly seen,
A film kept off that stood between.

By walking men's reversèd feet
I chanced another world to meet;
Though it did not to view exceed
A phantasm, 'tis a world indeed,
   Where skies beneath us shine,
   And earth by art divine

Another face presents below,
Where people's feet against ours go.

Within the regions of the air,
Compassed about with heavens fair,
Great tracts of land there may be found
Enriched with fields and fertile ground;
   Where many numerous hosts,
    In those far distant coasts,
For other great and glorious ends,
Inhabit, my yet unknown friends.

O ye that stand upon the brink,
Whom I so near me, through the chink,
With wonder see: what faces there,
Whose feet, whose bodies, do ye wear?
   I my companions see
    In you, another me.
They seemed others, but are we;
Our second selves those shadows be.

Look how far off those lower skies
Extend themselves! scarce with mine eyes
I can them reach, O ye my friends,
What secret borders on those ends?
   Are lofty heavens hurled
    'Bout your inferior world?
Are ye the representatives
Of other people's distant lives?

Of all the playmates which I knew
That here I do the image view
In other selves; what can it mean
But that below the purling stream
   Some unknown joys there be
    Laid up in store for me;
To which I shall, when that thin skin
Is broken, be admitted in.

# JOHN WILMOT, EARL OF ROCHESTER
## 1647-1680

### *The Maimed Debauchee*

As some brave Admiral, in former war
  Deprived of force, but pressed with courage still,
Two rival fleets appearing from afar,
  Crawls to the top of an adjacent hill;

From whence (with thoughts full of concern) he views
  The wise and daring conduct of the fight:
And each bold action to his mind renews
  His present glory, and his past delight.

From his fierce eyes flashes of rage he throws,
  As from black clouds when lightning breaks away,
Transported thinks himself amidst his foes,
  And absent, yet enjoys the bloody day.

So when my days of impotence approach,
  And I'm by love and wine's unlucky chance
Driven from the pleasing billows of debauch,
  On the dull shore of lazy temperance;

My pains at last some respite shall afford,
  While I behold the battles you maintain:
When fleets of glasses sail around the board,
  From whose broadsides volleys of wit shall rain.

Nor shall the sight of honorable scars,
  Which my too forward valor did procure,
Frighten new-listed soldiers from the wars;
  Past joys have more than paid what I endure.

Should some brave youth (worth being drunk) prove
    nice
  And from his fair inviter meanly shrink,
'Twould please the ghost of my departed vice,
  If, at my counsel, he repent and drink.


Or should some cold-complexioned sot forbid,
  With his dull morals, our night's brisk alarms,
I'll fire his blood, by telling what I did
  When I was strong, and able to bear arms.


I'll tell of whores attacked, their lords at home,
  Bawd's quarters beaten up, and fortress won,
Windows demolished, watches overcome,
  And handsome ills by my contrivance done.


With tales like these I will such heat inspire
  As to important mischief shall incline;
I'll make him long some ancient church to fire,
  And fear no lewdness they're called to by wine.


Thus statesmanlike I'll saucily impose,
  And safe from danger, valiantly advise;
Sheltered in impotence, urge you to blows,
  And being good for nothing else, be wise.


### Upon Nothing


*Nothing!* thou elder brother ev'n to shade,
Thou hadst a being ere the world was made,
And (well fixt) art alone, of ending not afraid.


Ere time and place were, time and place were not,
When primitive *Nothing* something straight begot,
Then all proceeded from the great united—What.

Something, the gen'ral attribute of all,
Severed from thee, its sole original,
Into thy boundless self must undistinguished fall.

Yet something did thy mighty power command,
And from thy fruitful emptiness's hand,
Snatched men, beasts, birds, fire, air, and land.

Matter, the wickedest offspring of thy race,
By form assisted, flew from thy embrace,
And rebel light obscured thy reverend dusky face.

With form and matter, time and place did join;
Body, thy foe, with three did leagues combine,
To spoil thy peaceful realm, and ruin all thy line.

But turncoat time assists the foe in vain,
And, bribed by thee, assists thy short-lived reign,
And to thy hungry womb drives back thy slaves again.

Though mysteries are barred from laic eyes,
And the divine alone, with warrant, pries
Into thy bosom, where the truth in private lies:

Yet this of thee the wise may freely say,
Thou from the virtuous nothing tak'st away,
And to be part with thee the wicked wisely pray.

Great Negative, how vainly would the wise
Enquire, define, distinguish, teach, devise?
Didst thou not stand to point their dull philosophies.

*Is,* or *is not,* the two great ends of fate,
And, true or false, the subject of debate,
That perfect, or destroy, the vast designs of fate;

When they have racked the politician's breast,
Within thy bosom most securely rest,
And, when reduced to thee, are least unsafe and best.

But, *Nothing,* why does *Something* still permit,
That sacred monarchs should at council sit,
With persons highly thought at best for nothing fit.

Whilst weighty *Something* modestly abstains,
From princes' coffers, and from statesmen's brains,
And nothing there like stately *Nothing* reigns.

*Nothing,* who dwell'st with fools in grave disguise,
For whom they reverend shapes, and forms devise
Lawn sleeves, and furs, and gowns, when they like thee
    look wise.

French truth, Dutch prowess, British policy,
Hibernian learning, Scotch civility,
Spaniards' dispatch, Danes' wit, are mainly seen in thee.

The great man's gratitude to his best friend,
Kings' promises, whores' vows, towards thee they bend,
Flow swiftly into thee, and in thee ever end.


### *Epitaph on Charles II*

Here lies our Sovereign Lord the King,
    Whose word no man relies on;
Who never said a foolish thing,
    Nor ever did a wise one.

# JONATHAN SWIFT/1667–1745

## A City Shower

### In Imitation of Virgil's Georgics

Careful observers may foretell the hour
(By sure prognostics) when to dread a shower.
While rain depends, the pensive cat gives o'er
Her frolics, and pursues her tail no more;
Returning home at night, you'll find the sink
Strike your offended sense with double stink.
If you be wise, then, go not far to dine:
You'll spend in coach-hire more than save in wine.
A coming shower your shooting corns presage,
Old aches will throb, your hollow tooth will rage.
Sauntering in coffee-house is Dulman seen;
He damns the climate, and complains of spleen.

    Meanwhile, the south, rising with dabbled wings,
A sable cloud athwart the welkin flings,
That swilled more liquor than it could contain,
And, like a drunkard, gives it up again.
Brisk Susan whips her linen from the rope,
While the first drizzling shower is borne aslope:
Such is that sprinkling which some careless quean
Flirts on you from her mop, but not so clean:
You fly, invoke the gods; then, turning, stop
To rail; she, singing, still whirls on her mop.
Not yet the dust had shunned th' unequal strife,
But aided by the wind, fought still for life;
And, wafted with its foe by violent gust,
'Twas doubtful which was rain and which was dust.
Ah! where must needy poet seek for aid,
When dust and rain at once his coat invade?
Sole coat! where dust cemented by the rain
Erects the nap, and leaves a cloudy stain!

    Now in contiguous drops the rain comes down,
Threatening with deluge this devoted town.

To shops in crowds the daggled females fly,
Pretend to cheapen goods but nothing buy.
The templar spruce, while every spout's abroach,
Stays till 'tis fair, yet seems to call a coach.
The tucked up seamstress walks with hasty strides,
While streams run down her oiled umbrella's sides.
Here various kinds, by various fortunes led,
Commence acquaintance underneath a shed.
Triumphant Tories and desponding Whigs
Forget their feuds, and join to save their wigs.
Boxed in a chair, the beau impatient sits,
While spouts run clattering o'er the roof by fits,
And ever and anon with frightful din
The leather sounds; he trembles from within.
So when Troy chairmen bore the wooden steed,
Pregnant with Greeks impatient to be freed
(Those bully Greeks, who, as the moderns do,
Instead of paying chairmen, ran them through),
Laocoön struck the outside with his spear,
And each imprisoned hero quaked for fear.

Now from all parts the swelling kennels flow,
And bear their trophies with them as they go:
Filths of all hues and odour seem to tell
What street they sailed from by their sight and smell.
They, as each torrent drives with rapid force,
From Smithfield or St. 'Pulchre's shape their course,
And in huge confluence joined at Snowhill ridge,
Fall from the conduit prone to Holborn bridge.
Sweepings from butchers' stalls, dung, guts, and blood,
Drowned puppies, stinking sprats, all drenched in mud,
Dead cats, and turnip tops, come tumbling down the
    flood.

## Stella's Birthday

March 13, 1726–7

This day, whate'er the Fates decree,
Shall still be kept with joy by me:
This day then, let us not be told,
That you are sick, and I grown old,
Nor think on our approaching ills,
And talk of spectacles and pills;
Tomorrow will be time enough
To hear such mortifying stuff.
Yet, since from reason may be brought
A better and more pleasing thought,
Which can in spite of all decays,
Support a few remaining days:
From not the gravest of divines,
Accept for once some serious lines.

    Although we now can form no more
Long schemes of life, as heretofore;
Yet you, while time is running fast,
Can look with joy on what is past.

    Were future happiness and pain,
A mere contrivance of the brain,
As atheists argue, to entice,
And fit their proselytes for vice;
(The only comfort they propose,
To have companions in their woes).
Grant this the case, yet sure 'tis hard,
That virtue, styled its own reward,
And by all sages understood
To be the chief of human good,
Should acting, die, nor leave behind
Some lasting pleasure in the mind,
Which by remembrance will assuage
Grief, sickness, poverty, and age;

And strongly shoot a radiant dart,
To shine through life's declining part.

    Say, Stella, feel you no content,
Reflecting on a life well spent?
Your skilful hand employed to save
Despairing wretches from the grave;
And then supporting with your store,
Those whom you dragged from death before:
(So Providence on mortals waits,
Preserving what it first creates)
Your gen'rous boldness to defend
An innocent and absent friend;
That courage which can make you just,
To merit humbled in the dust:
The detestation you express
For vice in all its glitt'ring dress:
That patience under tort'ring pain,
Where stubborn stoics would complain.

    Must these like empty shadows pass,
Or forms reflected from a glass?
Or mere chimæras in the mind,
That fly and leave no marks behind?
Does not the body thrive and grow
By food of twenty years ago?
And, had it not been still supplied,
It must a thousand times have died.
Then, who with reason can maintain,
That no effects of food remain?
And, is not virtue in mankind
The nutriment that feeds the mind?
Upheld by each good action past,
And still continued by the last:
Then, who with reason can pretend,
That all effects of virtue end?

    Believe me, Stella, when you show
That true contempt for things below,

Nor prize your life for other ends
Than merely to oblige your friends;
Your former actions claim their part,
And join to fortify your heart.
For virtue in her daily race,
Like Janus, bears a double face;
Looks back with joy where she has gone,
And therefore goes with courage on.
She at your sickly couch will wait,
And guide you to a better state.

O then, whatever heav'n intends,
Take pity on your pitying friends;
Nor let your ills affect your mind,
To fancy they can be unkind.
Me, surely me, you ought to spare,
Who gladly would your suff'rings share;
Or give my scrap of life to you,
And think it far beneath your due;
You, to whose care so oft I owe,
That I'm alive to tell you so.

### The Day of Judgement

With a whirl of thought oppressed,
I sunk from reverie to rest.
An horrid vision seized my head,
I saw the graves give up their dead!
Jove, armed with terrors, burst the skies,
And thunder roars, and lightning flies!
Amazed, confused, its fate unknown,
The world stands trembling at his throne!
While each pale sinner hung his head,
Jove, nodding, shook the heavens, and said:
"Offending race of humankind,
By nature, reason, learning, blind;
You who, through frailty, stepped aside;
And you who never fell, through pride;

You who in different sects were shamed,
And come to see each other damned
(So some folks told you, but they knew
No more of Jove's designs than you);
—The world's mad business now is o'er,
And I resent these pranks no more.
—I to such blockheads set my wit!
I damn such fools!—Go, go, you're bit."

## On a Curate's Complaint of Hard Duty

I marched three miles through scorching sand,
With zeal in heart, and notes in hand;
I rode four more to Great St. Mary,
Using four legs, when two were weary:
To three fair virgins I did tie men,
In the close bands of pleasing Hymen;
I dipped two babes in holy water,
And purified their mother after.
Within an hour and eke a half,
I preached three congregations deaf;
Where, thundering out, with lungs long-winded,
I chopped so fast that few there minded.
My emblem, the laborious sun,
Saw all these mighty labours done
Before one race of his was run.
All this performed by Robert Hewit:
What mortal else could e'er go through it!

# ISAAC WATTS/1674–1748

### *Horace Paraphrased*

There are a number of us creep
Into this world to eat and sleep,
And know no reason why they're born
But merely to consume the corn,
Devour the cattle, fowl and fish,
And leave behind an empty dish.
The crows and ravens do the same,
Unlucky birds of hateful name;
Ravens or crows might fill their place,
And swallow corn and carcases.
Then if their tombstone when they die
Ben't taught to flatter and to lie,
There's nothing better will be said
Than that "They've eat up all their bread,
Drank up their drink and gone to bed."

### *The Day of Judgement*

#### *An Ode, Attempted in English Sapphic*

When the fierce North wind with his airy forces,
Rears up the Baltic to a foaming fury;
And the red lightning, with a storm of hail, comes
                Rushing amain down;

How the poor sailors stand amazed, and tremble!—
While the hoarse thunder, like a bloody trumpet,
Roars a loud onset to the gaping waters,
                Quick to devour them:

Such shall the noise be, and the wild disorder,
(If things eternal may be like these earthly)

Such the dire terror, when the Great Archangel
        Shakes the creation,

Tears the strong pillars of the vault of Heav'n,
Breaks up old marble, the repose of princes;—
See—the graves open,—and the bones arising,
        Flames all around 'em!

Hark, the shrill outcries of the guilty wretches!
Lively bright horror, and amazing anguish
Stare thro' their eyelids, while the living worm lies
        Gnawing within them.

Thoughts, like old vultures, prey upon their heartstrings,
And the smart twinges, when the eye beholds the
Lofty Judge frowning, and a flood of vengeance
        Rolling afore Him.

Hopeless immortals! how they scream and shiver,
While devils push them to the pit wide-yawning
Hideous and gloomy to receive them headlong
        Down to the centre:

Stop here, my fancy: (all away ye horrid
Doleful ideas) come arise to Jesus;
How He sits Godlike! and the saints around Him
        Throned, yet adoring!

O may I sit there when He comes triumphant,
Dooming the nations! then ascend to glory,
While our Hosannas all along the passage,
        Shout the Redeemer.

### A Cradle Hymn

    Hush! my dear, lie still and slumber,
      Holy angels guard thy bed!

Heavenly blessings without number
    Gently falling on thy head.

Sleep, my babe; thy food and raiment,
    House and home, thy friends provide;
All without thy care or payment,
    All thy wants are well supplied.

How much better thou'rt attended
    Than the Son of God could be,
When from Heaven He descended,
    And became a child like thee!

Soft and easy is thy cradle:
    Coarse and hard thy Savior lay:
When His birthplace was a stable,
    And His softest bed was hay.

Blessèd babe! what glorious features,
    Spotless fair, divinely bright!
Must He dwell with brutal creatures!
    How could angels bear the sight?

Was there nothing but a manger
    Cursèd sinners could afford
To receive the heavenly stranger!
    Did they thus affront their Lord?

Soft, my child; I did not chide thee,
    Though my song might sound too hard;
'Tis thy mother[1] sits beside thee,
    And her arms shall be thy guard.

Yet to read the shameful story,
    How the Jews abused their King,
How they served the Lord of Glory,
    Makes me angry while I sing.

[1] Or: nurse that

See the kinder shepherds round Him,
    Telling wonders from the sky!
Where they sought Him, there they found Him,
    With His virgin mother by.

See the lovely babe a-dressing;
    Lovely infant, how He smiled!
When He wept, the mother's blessing
    Soothed and hushed the holy child.

Lo, He slumbers in his manger,
    Where the hornèd oxen fed;
Peace, my darling, here's no danger,
    Here's no ox a-near thy bed.

'Twas to save thee, child, from dying,
    Save my dear from burning flame,
Bitter groans and endless crying,
    That thy blest Redeemer came.

Mayst thou live to know and fear Him,
    Trust and love Him all thy days;
Then go dwell forever near Him,
    See His face, and sing His praise!

I could give thee thousand kisses,
    Hoping what I most desire;
Not a mother's fondest wishes
    Can to greater joys aspire.

# JOHN GAY/1685–1732

## To a Lady

### On Her Passion for Old China

What ecstasies her bosom fire!
How her eyes languish with desire!
How blest, how happy should I be,
Were that fond glance bestowed on me!
New doubts and fears within me war:
What rival's near? a China jar.

China's the passion of her soul;
A cup, a plate, a dish, a bowl
Can kindle wishes in her breast,
Inflame with joy, or break her rest.

Some gems collect; some medals prize,
And view the rust with lovers' eyes;
Some court the stars at midnight hours;
Some dote on Nature's charms in flowers!
But ev'ry beauty I can trace
In Laura's mind, in Laura's face;
My stars are in this brighter sphere,
My lily and my rose is here.

Philosophers more grave than wise
Hunt science down in butterflies;
Or fondly poring on a spider,
Stretch human contemplation wider;
Fossils give joy to Galen's soul,
He digs for knowledge, like a mole;
In shells so learned, that all agree
No fish that swims knows more than he!
In such pursuits if wisdom lies,
Who, Laura, shall thy taste despise?

When I some antique jar behold,
Or white, or blue, or specked with gold,
Vessels so pure, and so refined

Appear the types of woman-kind:
Are they not valued for their beauty,
Too fair, too fine for household duty?
With flowers and gold and azure dyed,
Of ev'ry house the grace and pride?
How white, how polished is their skin,
And valued most when only seen!
She who before was highest prizèd
Is for a crack or flaw despised;
I grant they're frail, yet they're so rare,
The treasure cannot cost too dear!
But man is made of coarser stuff,
And serves convenience well enough;
He's a strong earthen vessel made,
For drudging, labour, toil and trade;
And when wives lose their other self,
With ease they bear the loss of Delf.

   Husbands more covetous than sage
Condemn this China-buying rage;
They count that woman's prudence little,
Who sets her heart on things so brittle.
But are those wise-men's inclinations
Fixed on more strong, more sure foundations?
If all that's frail we must despise,
No human view or scheme is wise.
Are not ambition's hopes as weak?
They swell like bubbles, shine and break.
A courtier's promise is so slight,
'Tis made at noon, and broke at night.
What pleasure's sure? The Miss you keep
Breaks both your fortune and your sleep.
The man who loves a country life,
Breaks all the comforts of his wife;
And if he quit his farm and plough,
His wife in town may break her vow.
Love, Laura, love, while youth is warm,
For each new winter breaks a charm;
And woman's not like China sold,

But cheaper grows in growing old;
Then quickly choose the prudent part,
Or else you break a faithful heart.

# ALLAN RAMSAY/1686–1758

## *The Wawking of the Fauld*

My Peggy is a young thing,
    Just entered in her teens,
Fair as the day, and sweet as May,
Fair as the day, and always gay.
My Peggy is a young thing,
    And I'm not very auld,
Yet well I like to meet her at
    The wawking[1] of the fauld.

My Peggy speaks sae sweetly,
    Whene'er we meet alane,
I wish nae mair to lay my care
I wish nae mair of a' that's rare.
My Peggy speaks sae sweetly,
    To a' the lave[2] I'm cauld;
But she gars a' my spirits glow
    At wawking of the fauld.

My Peggy smiles sae kindly,
    Whene'er I whisper love,
That I look down on a' the town,
That I look down upon a crown.
My Peggy smiles sae kindly,
    It makes me blythe and bauld,
And naething gi'es me sic delight,
    As wawking of the fauld.

[1] keeping watch on   [2] the rest

My Peggy sings sae saftly,
        When on my pipe I play;
By a' the rest it is confest,
By a' the rest that she sings best.
    My Peggy sings sae saftly,
        And in her sangs are tald,
With innocence, the wale[1] of sense,
        At wawking of the fauld.

# ALEXANDER POPE/1688–1744

*Ode on Solitude*

Happy the man, whose wish and care
    A few paternal acres bound,
Content to breathe his native air,
                In his own ground.

Whose herds with milk, whose fields with bread,
    Whose flocks supply him with attire,
Whose trees in summer yield him shade,
                In winter fire.

Blest, who can unconcern'dly find
    Hours, days, and years slide soft away,
In health of body, peace of mind,
                Quiet by day,

Sound sleep by night; study and ease,
    Together mixed; sweet recreation;
And innocence, which most does please
                With meditation.

[1] choice

Thus let me live, unseen, unknown,
   Thus unlamented let me die,
Steal from the world, and not a stone
      Tell where I lie.


*Elegy to the Memory of an Unfortunate Lady*

What beck'ning ghost, along the moon-light shade
Invites my steps, and points to yonder glade?
'Tis she!—but why that bleeding bosom gored,
Why dimly gleams the visionary sword?
Oh ever beauteous, ever friendly! tell,
Is it, in heav'n, a crime to love too well?
To bear too tender, or too firm a heart,
To act a lover's, or a Roman's part?
Is there no bright reversion in the sky,
For those who greatly think, or bravely die?

   Why bade ye else, ye Pow'rs! her soul aspire
Above the vulgar flight of low desire?
Ambition first sprung from your blest abodes;
The glorious fault of angels and of gods;
Thence to their images on earth it flows,
And in the breasts of kings and heroes glows.
Most souls, 'tis true, but peep out once an age,
Dull sullen pris'ners in the body's cage:
Dim lights of life, that burn a length of years
Useless, unseen, as lamps in sepulchres;
Like eastern kings, a lazy state they keep,
And close confined to their own palace, sleep.

   From these perhaps (ere nature bade her die)
Fate snatched her early to the pitying sky.
As into air the purer spirits flow,
And sep'rate from their kindred dregs below;
So flew the soul to its congenial place,
Nor left one virtue to redeem her race.

   But thou, false guardian of a charge too good,
Thou, mean deserter of thy brother's blood!
See on these ruby lips the trembling breath,

These cheeks now fading at the blast of death:
Cold is that breast which warmed the world before,
And those love-darting eyes must roll no more.
Thus, if eternal justice rules the ball,
Thus shall your wives, and thus your children fall;
On all the line a sudden vengeance waits,
And frequent hearses shall besiege your gates.
There passengers shall stand, and pointing say,
(While the long fun'rals blacken all the way)
"Lo these were they, whose souls the Furies steeled,
And cursed with hearts unknowing how to yield."
Thus unlamented pass the proud away,
The gaze of fools, and pageant of a day!
So perish all, whose breast ne'er learned to glow
For others good, or melt at others woe.
　　What can atone (oh ever-injured shade!)
Thy fate unpitied, and thy rites unpaid?
No friend's complaint, no kind domestic tear
Pleased thy pale ghost, or graced thy mournful bier.
By foreign hands thy dying eyes were closed,
By foreign hands thy decent limbs composed,
By foreign hands thy humble grave adorned,
By strangers honoured, and by strangers mourned!
What tho' no friends in sable weeds appear,
Grieve for an hour, perhaps, then mourn a year,
And bear about the mockery of woe
To midnight dances, and the public show?
What tho' no weeping loves thy ashes grace,
Nor polished marble emulate thy face?
What tho' no sacred earth allow thee room,
Nor hallowed dirge be muttered o'er thy tomb?
Yet shall thy grave with rising flow'rs be drest,
And the green turf lie lightly on thy breast:
There shall the morn her earliest tears bestow,
There the first roses of the year shall blow;
While angels with their silver wings o'ershade
The ground, now sacred by thy relics made.
　　So peaceful rests, without a stone, a name,
What once had beauty, titles, wealth, and fame.

How loved, how honoured once, avails thee not,
To whom related, or by whom begot;
A heap of dust alone remains of thee,
'Tis all thou art, and all the proud shall be!
    Poets themselves must fall, like those they sung,
Deaf the praised ear, and mute the tuneful tongue.
Ev'n he, whose soul now melts in mournful lays,
Shall shortly want the gen'rous tear he pays;
Then from his closing eyes thy form shall part,
And the last pang shall tear thee from his heart,
Life's idle business at one gasp be o'er,
The Muse forgot, and thou be loved no more!

# WILLIAM OLDYS/1696-1761

## The Fly

### An Anacreontic

Busy, curious, thirsty fly,
Gently drink, and drink as I;
Freely welcome to my cup,
Could'st thou sip, and sip it up;
Make the most of life you may,
Life is short and wears away.

Just alike, both mine and thine,
Hasten quick to their decline;
Thine's a summer, mine's no more,
Though repeated to threescore;
Threescore summers when they're gone,
Will appear as short as one.

# JAMES THOMSON/1700–1748

## Verses Occasioned by the Death of Dr. Aikman

### A Particular Friend of the Author's

As those we love decay, we die in part,
String after string is severed from the heart;
Till loosened life, at last, but breathing clay,
Without one pang is glad to fall away.
Unhappy he, who latest feels the blow,
Whose eyes have wept o'er every friend laid low,
Dragged ling'ring on from partial death to death,
Till, dying, all he can resign is breath.


# SAMUEL JOHNSON/1709–1784

## To a Young Heir

Long-expected one-and-twenty,
   Ling'ring year, at length is flown:
Pride and pleasure, pomp and plenty,
   Great * * *   * * * *, are now your own.

Loosened from the minor's tether,
   Free to mortgage or to sell,
Wild as wind, and light as feather,
   Bid the sons of thrift farewell.

Call the Betsies, Kates, and Jennies,
   All the names that banish care;
Lavish of your grandsire's guineas,
   Show the spirit of an heir.

All that prey on vice and folly
   Joy to see their quarry fly:
There the gamester, light and jolly,
   There the lender, grave and sly.

Wealth, my lad, was made to wander,
   Let it wander as it will;
Call the jockey, call the pander,
   Bid them come and take their fill.

When the bonny blade carouses,
   Pockets full, and spirits high—
What are acres? What are houses?
   Only dirt, or wet or dry.

Should the guardian friend or mother
   Tell the woes of wilful waste,
Scorn their counsel, scorn their pother;—
   You can hang or drown at last!


### Lines Written in Ridicule of Certain Poems

Wheresoe'er I turn my view,
All is strange, yet nothing new;
Endless labor all along,
Endless labor to be wrong;
Phrase that time has flung away,
Uncouth words in disarray,
Tricked in antique ruff and bonnet,
Ode, and elegy, and sonnet.

## On the Death of Mr. Robert Levett,

### A Practiser in Physic

Condemned to hope's delusive mine,
As on we toil from day to day,
By sudden blasts, or slow decline,
Our social comforts drop away.

Well tried through many a varying year,
See Levett to the grave descend,
Officious, innocent, sincere,
Of ev'ry friendless name the friend.

Yet still he fills affection's eye,
Obscurely wise and coarsely kind;
Nor lettered arrogance deny
Thy praise to merit unrefined.

When fainting nature called for aid,
And hov'ring death prepared the blow,
His vigorous remedy displayed
The power of art without the show.

In mis'ry's darkest cavern known,
His useful care was ever nigh,
Where hopeless anguish poured his groan,
And lonely want retired to die.

No summons mocked by chill delay,
No petty gain disdained by pride;
The modest wants of ev'ry day
The toil of ev'ry day supplied.

His virtues walked their narrow round,
Nor made a pause, nor left a void;
And sure the Eternal Master found
The single talent well employed.

The busy day—the peaceful night,
Unfelt, unclouded, glided by;
His frame was firm—his powers were bright,
Though now his eightieth year was nigh.

Then with no fiery throbbing pain,
No cold gradations of decay,
Death broke at once the vital chain,
And freed his soul the nearest way.


# THOMAS GRAY/1716–1771


## Ode

### On a Distant Prospect of Eton College

Ye distant spires, ye antique towers,
That crown the wat'ry glade,
Where grateful Science still adores
Her Henry's holy shade;
And ye, that from the stately brow
Of Windsor's heights th' expanse below
Of grove, of lawn, of mead survey,
Whose turf, whose shade, whose flowers among
Wanders the hoary Thames along
His silver-winding way.

Ah happy hills, ah pleasing shade,
Ah fields beloved in vain,
Where once my careless childhood strayed,
A stranger yet to pain!
I feel the gales, that from ye blow,
A momentary bliss bestow,
As waving fresh their gladsome wing,
My weary soul they seem to soothe,

And, redolent of joy and youth,
To breathe a second spring.

    Say, Father Thames, for thou hast seen
Full many a sprightly race
Disporting on thy margent green
The paths of pleasure trace,
Who foremost now delight to cleave
With pliant arm thy glassy wave?
The captive linnet which enthrall?
What idle progeny succeed
To chase the rolling circle's speed,
Or urge the flying ball?

    While some on earnest business bent
Their murm'ring labours ply
'Gainst graver hours, that bring constraint
To sweeten liberty:
Some bold adventurers disdain
The limits of their little reign,
And unknown regions dare descry:
Still as they run they look behind,
They hear a voice in every wind,
And snatch a fearful joy.

    Gay hope is theirs by fancy fed,
Less pleasing when possessed;
The tear forgot as soon as shed,
The sunshine of the breast:
Theirs buxom health of rosy hue,
Wild wit, invention ever-new,
And lively cheer of vigour born;
The thoughtless day, the easy night,
The spirits pure, the slumbers light,
That fly th' approach of morn.

    Alas, regardless of their doom,
The little victims play!
No sense have they of ills to come,

Nor care beyond to-day:
Yet see how all around 'em wait
The Ministers of human fate,
And black Misfortune's baleful train!
Ah, shew them where in ambush stand
To seize their prey the murth'rous band
Ah, tell them, they are men!

These shall the fury Passions tear,
The vultures of the mind,
Disdainful Anger, pallid Fear,
And Shame that sculks behind;
Or pining Love shall waste their youth,
Or Jealousy with rankling tooth,
That inly gnaws the secret heart,
And Envy wan, and faded Care,
Grim-visaged comfortless Despair,
And Sorrow's piercing dart.

Ambition this shall tempt to rise,
Then whirl the wretch from high,
To bitter Scorn a sacrifice,
And grinning Infamy.
The stings of Falsehood those shall try
And hard Unkindness' altered eye,
That mocks the tear it forced to flow;
And keen Remorse with blood defiled,
And moody Madness laughing wild
Amid severest woe.

Lo, in the vale of years beneath
A grisly troop are seen,
The painful family of Death,
More hideous than their Queen:
This racks the joints, this fires the veins,
That every labouring sinew strains,

Those in the deeper vitals rage:
Lo, Poverty, to fill the band,
That numbs the soul with icy hand,
And slow-consuming Age.

    To each his suff'rings: all are men,
Condemned alike to groan;
The tender for another's pain,
Th' unfeeling for his own.
Yet ah! why should they know their fate?
Since sorrow never comes too late,
And happiness too swiftly flies.
Thought would destroy their paradise.
No more; where ignorance is bliss,
'Tis folly to be wise.


*Elegy*

### Written in a Country Churchyard

The curfew tolls the knell of parting day,
The lowing herd wind slowly o'er the lea,
The plowman homeward plods his weary way,
And leaves the world to darkness and to me.

Now fades the glimmering landscape on the sight,
And all the air a solemn stillness holds,
Save where the beetle wheels his droning flight,
And drowsy tinklings lull the distant folds;

Save that from yonder ivy-mantled tow'r
The moping owl does to the moon complain
Of such, as wand'ring near her secret bow'r,
Molest her ancient solitary reign.

Beneath those rugged elms, that yew-tree's shade,
Where heaves the turf in many a mould'ring heap,

Each in his narrow cell for ever laid,
The rude forefathers of the hamlet sleep.

The breezy call of incense-breathing morn,
The swallow twitt'ring from the straw-built shed,
The cock's shrill clarion, or the echoing horn,
No more shall rouse them from their lowly bed.

For them no more the blazing hearth shall burn,
Or busy housewife ply her evening care:
No children run to lisp their sire's return,
Or climb his knees the envied kiss to share.

Oft did the harvest to their sickle yield,
Their furrow oft the stubborn glebe has broke;
How jocund did they drive their team afield!
How bowed the woods beneath their sturdy stroke!

Let not Ambition mock their useful toil,
Their homely joys, and destiny obscure;
Nor Grandeur hear with a disdainful smile,
The short and simple annals of the poor.

The boast of heraldry, the pomp of pow'r,
And all that beauty, all that wealth e'er gave,
Awaits alike th' inevitable hour.
The paths of glory lead but to the grave.

Nor you, ye Proud, impute to these the fault,
If Mem'ry o'er their tomb no trophies raise,
Where thro' the long-drawn aisle and fretted vault
The pealing anthem swells the note of praise.

Can storied urn or animated bust
Back to its mansion call the fleeting breath?
Can Honour's voice provoke the silent dust,
Or Flatt'ry soothe the dull cold ear of Death?

Perhaps in this neglected spot is laid
Some heart once pregnant with celestial fire;
Hands that the rod of empire might have swayed,
Or waked to ecstasy the living lyre.

But Knowledge to their eyes her ample page
Rich with the spoils of time did ne'er unroll:
Chill Penury repressed their noble rage,
And froze the genial current of the soul.

Full many a gem of purest ray serene,
The dark unfathomed caves of ocean bear:
Full many a flower is born to blush unseen,
And waste its sweetness on the desert air.

Some village-Hampden, that with dauntless breast
The little tyrant of his fields withstood;
Some mute inglorious Milton here may rest,
Some Cromwell guiltless of his country's blood.

Th' applause of list'ning senates to command,
The threats of pain and ruin to despise,
To scatter plenty o'er a smiling land,
And read their hist'ry in a nation's eyes,

Their lot forbad: nor circumscribed alone
Their growing virtues, but their crimes confined;
Forbad to wade through slaughter to a throne,
And shut the gates of mercy on mankind,

The struggling pangs of conscious truth to hide,
To quench the blushes of ingenuous shame,
Or heap the shrine of Luxury and Pride
With incense kindled at the Muse's flame.

Far from the madding crowd's ignoble strife,
Their sober wishes never learned to stray;
Along the cool sequestered vale of life
They kept the noiseless tenor of their way.

Yet ev'n these bones from insult to protect
Some frail memorial still erected nigh,
With uncouth rhymes and shapeless sculpture
    decked,
Implores the passing tribute of a sigh.

Their name, their years, spelt by th' unlettered muse,
The place of fame and elegy supply:
And many a holy text around she strews,
That teach the rustic moralist to die.

For who to dumb forgetfulness a prey,
This pleasing anxious being e'er resigned,
Left the warm precincts of the cheerful day,
Nor cast one longing ling'ring look behind?

On some fond breast the parting soul relies,
Some pious drops the closing eye requires;
Ev'n from the tomb the voice of Nature cries,
Ev'n in our ashes live their wonted fires.

For thee, who mindful of th' unhonoured dead
Dost in these lines their artless tale relate;
If chance, by lonely contemplation led,
Some kindred spirit shall inquire thy fate,

Haply some hoary-headed swain may say,
"Oft have we seen him at the peep of dawn
Brushing with hasty steps the dews away
To meet the sun upon the upland lawn.

"There at the foot of yonder nodding beech
That wreathes its old fantastic roots so high,
His listless length at noontide would he stretch,
And pore upon the brook that babbles by.

"Hard by yon wood, now smiling as in scorn,
Mutt'ring his wayward fancies he would rove,

Now drooping, woeful wan, like one forlorn,
Or crazed with care, or crossed in hopeless love.

"One morn I missed him on the customed hill,
Along the heath and near his fav'rite tree;
Another came; nor yet beside the rill,
Nor up the lawn, nor at the wood was he;

"The next with dirges due in sad array
Slow thro' the church-way path we saw him borne.
Approach and read (for thou canst read) the lay,
Graved on the stone beneath yon agèd thorn.

"(There scattered oft, the earliest of the year,
By hands unseen, are show'rs of violets found;
The red-breast loves to build and warble there,
And little footsteps lightly print the ground.)"[1]


## THE EPITAPH

*Here rests his head upon the lap of Earth*
*A Youth to Fortune and to Fame unknown.*
*Fair Science frowned not on his humble birth,*
*And Melancholy marked him for her own.*

*Large was his bounty, and his soul sincere,*
*Heav'n did a recompence as largely send:*
*He gave to Mis'ry all he had, a tear,*
*He gained from Heav'n ('twas all he wished) a friend.*

*No farther seek his merits to disclose,*
*Or draw his frailties from their dread abode,*
*(There they alike in trembling hope repose,)*
*The bosom of his Father and his God.*

[1] This stanza was added by the author in the third edition of the poem and later deleted.

# WILLIAM COLLINS/1721–1759

### *Dirge in Cymbeline*

To fair Fidele's grassy tomb
    Soft maids, and village hinds shall bring
Each op'ning sweet, of earliest bloom,
    And rifle all the breathing spring.

No wailing ghost shall dare appear
    To vex with shrieks this quiet grove:
But shepherd lads assemble here,
    And melting virgins own their love.

No withered witch shall here be seen,
    No goblins lead their nightly crew:
The female fays shall haunt the green,
    And dress thy grave with pearly dew!

The redbreast oft at ev'ning hours
    Shall kindly lend his little aid,
With hoary moss, and gathered flow'rs,
    To deck the ground where thou are laid.

When howling winds, and beating rain,
    In tempests shake the sylvan cell:
Or midst the chase on ev'ry plain,
    The tender thought on thee shall dwell.

Each lonely scene shall thee restore,
    For thee the tear be duly shed:
Beloved, till life could charm no more;
    And mourned, till pity's self be dead.

*Ode to Fear*

Thou, to whom the world unknown
With all its shadowy shapes is shown;
Who seest appalled th' unreal scene,
While Fancy lifts the veil between:
    Ah, Fear! ah, frantic Fear!
    I see, I see thee near.
I know thy hurried steps, thy haggard eye!
Like thee, I start, like thee disordered fly,
For, lo, what monsters in thy train appear!
Danger, whose limbs of giant mould
What mortal eye can fixt behold?
Who stalks his round, a hideous form,
Howling amidst the midnight storm,
Or throws him on the ridgy steep
Of some loose-hanging rock to sleep;
And with him thousand phantoms joined,
Who prompt to deeds accursed the mind;
And those, the fiends, who, near allied,
O'er Nature's wounds and wrecks preside;
While Vengeance, in the lurid air,
Lifts her red arm, exposed and bare;
On whom that ravening brood of Fate,
Who lap the blood of Sorrow, wait;
Who, Fear, this ghastly train can see,
And look not madly wild, like thee?


EPODE

In earliest Greece, to thee, with partial choice,
    The grief-full Muse addressed her infant tongue;
The maids and matrons, on her awful voice,
    Silent and pale, in wild amazement hung.

Yet he, the bard who first invoked thy name,
    Disdained in Marathon its power to feel:

For not alone he nursed the poet's flame,
    But reached from Virtue's hand the patriot's steel.

But who is he, whom later garlands grace,
    Who left a while o'er Hybla's dews to rove,
With trembling eyes thy dreary steps to trace,
    Where thou and furies shared the baleful grove?

Wrapt in thy cloudy veil th' incestuous queen
    Sighed the sad call her son and husband heard,
When once alone it broke the silent scene,
    And he, the wretch of Thebes, no more appeared.

O Fear! I know thee by my throbbing heart,
    Thy withering power inspired each mournful line;
Though gentle Pity claim her mingled part,
    Yet all the thunders of the scene are thine.


ANTISTROPHE

    Thou who such weary lengths hast past,
Where wilt thou rest, mad Nymph, at last?
Say, wilt thou shroud in haunted cell,
Where gloomy Rape and Murder dwell?
Or in some hollowed seat,
'Gainst which the big waves beat,
Hear drowning seamen's cries in tempests brought!
Dark power, with shuddering, meek, submitted
    thought,
Be mine, to read the visions old,
Which thy awakening bards have told.
    And, lest thou meet my blasted view,
Hold each strange tale devoutly true;
Ne'er be I found, by thee o'er-awed,
In that thrice-hallowed eve abroad,
When ghosts, as cottage maids believe,
Their pebbled beds permitted leave,
And goblins haunt from fire, or fen,

Or mine, or flood, the walks of men!
O thou, whose spirit most possessed
The sacred seat of Shakespeare's breast!
By all that from thy prophet broke,
In thy divine emotions spoke!
Hither again thy fury deal,
Teach me but once like him to feel:
His cypress wreath my meed decree,
And I, O Fear, will dwell with thee!


*Ode to Evening*


If ought of oaten stop, or pastoral song,
May hope, chaste Eve, to sooth thy modest ear,
Like thy own solemn springs,
Thy springs, and dying gales,
O Nymph reserved, while now the bright-haired sun
Sits in yon western tent, whose cloudy skirts,
With brede ethereal wove,
O'erhang his wavy bed:
Now air is hushed, save where the weak-eyed bat,
With short shrill shriek flits by on leathern wing,
Or where the beetle winds
His small but sullen horn,
As oft he rises 'midst the twilight path,
Against the pilgrim born in heedless hum:
Now teach me, maid composed,
To breathe some softened strain,
Whose numbers stealing thro' thy dark'ning vale,
May not unseemly with its stillness suit,
As musing slow, I hail
Thy genial loved return!
For when thy folding star arising shews
His paly circlet, at his warning lamp
The fragrant hours, and elves
Who slept in flow'rs the day,
And many a nymph who wreaths her brows with sedge,

And sheds the fresh'ning dew, and lovelier still,
    The Pensive Pleasures sweet
    Prepare thy shadowy car.
Then lead, calm vot'ress, where some sheety lake
Cheers the lone heath, or some time-hallowed pile,
    Or up-land fallows grey
    Reflect its last cool gleam.
But when chill blust'ring winds, or driving rain,
Forbid my willing feet, be mine the hut,
    That from the mountain's side,
    Views wilds, and swelling floods,
And hamlets brown, and dim-discovered spires,
And hears their simple bell, and marks o'er all
    Thy dewy fingers draw
    The gradual dusky veil.
While Spring shall pour his show'rs, as oft he wont,
And bathe thy breathing tresses, meekest Eve!
    While Summer loves to sport
    Beneath thy ling'ring light;
While sallow Autumn fills thy lap with leaves;
Or Winter yelling thro' the troublous air,
    Affrights thy shrinking train,
    And rudely rends thy robes;
So long, sure-found beneath the sylvan shed,
Shall Fancy, Friendship, Science, rose-lipped Health,
    Thy gentlest influence own,
    And hymn thy fav'rite name!

### Ode

How sleep the brave, who sink to rest,
By all their country's wishes blest!
When Spring, with dewy fingers cold,
Returns to deck their hallowed mold,
She there shall dress a sweeter sod,
Than Fancy's feet have ever trod.

By fairy hands their knell is rung,
By forms unseen their dirge is sung;
There Honour comes, a pilgrim grey,
To bless the turf that wraps their clay,
And Freedom shall awhile repair,
To dwell a weeping hermit there!


# CHRISTOPHER SMART/1722–1771


### The Nativity of Our Lord

Where is this stupendous stranger,
    Swains of Solyma, advise,
Lead me to my Master's manger,
    Shew me where my Saviour lies?

O Most Mighty! O Most Holy!
    Far beyond the seraph's thought,
Art thou then so mean and lowly
    As unheeded prophets taught?

O the magnitude of meekness!
    Worth from worth immortal sprung;
O the strength of infant weakness,
    If eternal is so young!

If so young and thus eternal,
    Michael tune the shepherd's reed,
Where the scenes are ever vernal,
    And the loves be love indeed!

See the God blasphemed and doubted
    In the schools of Greece and Rome;
See the pow'rs of darkness routed,
    Taken at their utmost gloom.

Nature's decorations glisten
    Far above their usual trim;
Birds on box and laurel listen,
    As so near the cherubs hymn.

Boreas now no longer winters
    On the desolated coast;
Oaks no more are riv'n in splinters
    By the whirlwind and his host.

Spinks and ouzels sing sublimely,
    "We too have a Saviour born";
Whiter blossoms burst untimely
    On the blest Mosaic thorn.

God all-bounteous, all-creative,
    Whom no ills from good dissuade,
Is incarnate, and a native
    Of the very world he made.

## JEAN ELLIOT/1727–1805

### *The Flowers of the Forest*

I've heard them lilting, at the ewe milking,
    Lasses a' lilting, before dawn of day;
But now they are moaning, on ilka green loaning;
    The flowers of the forest are a' wede[1] away.

At bughts,[2] in the morning, nae blithe lads are scorning;
    Lasses are lonely, and dowie, and wae;
Nae daffing,[3] nae gabbing, but sighing and sabbing;
    Ilk ane lifts her leglin,[4] and hies her away.

[1] weeded    [2] sheep-folds    [3] making merry    [4] milk-pail

At har'st, at the shearing, nae youths now are jearing;
  Bandsters[1] are runkled, and lyart[2] or gray;
At fair, or at preaching, nae wooing, nae fleeching:[3]
  The flowers of the forest are a' wede away.

At e'en, in the gloaming, nae younkers are roaming
  'Bout stacks, with the lasses at bogle to play;
But ilk maid sits dreary, lamenting her deary—
  The flowers of the forest are weded away.

Dool and wae for the order, sent our lads to the Border!
  The English, for ance, by guile wan the day;
The flowers of the forest, that fought aye the foremost,
  The prime of our land, are cauld in the clay.

We'll hear nae mair lilting, at the ewe milking;
  Women and bairns are heartless and wae:
Sighing and moaning, on ilka green loaning—
  The flowers of the forest are a' wede away.

## OLIVER GOLDSMITH/1728–1774

### When Lovely Woman Stoops to Folly

When lovely woman stoops to folly,
  And finds too late that men betray,
What charm can sooth her melancholy,
  What art can wash her guilt away?

The only art her guilt to cover,
  To hide her shame from every eye,
To give repentance to her lover,
  And wring his bosom—is to die.

[1] binders  [2] grizzled  [3] beseeching

# WILLIAM COWPER/1731–1800

### Oh! For a Closer Walk With God

Oh! for a closer walk with God,
    A calm and heav'nly frame;
A light to shine upon the road
    That leads me to the Lamb!

Where is the blessedness I knew
    When first I saw the Lord?
Where is the soul-refreshing view
    Of Jesus, and his word?

What peaceful hours I once enjoyed!
    How sweet their mem'ry still!
But they have left an aching void,
    The world can never fill.

Return, O holy Dove, return,
    Sweet messenger of rest;
I hate the sins that made thee mourn,
    And drove thee from my breast.

The dearest idol I have known,
    Whate'er that idol be;
Help me to tear it from thy throne,
    And worship only thee.

So shall my walk be close with God,
    Calm and serene my frame;
So purer light shall mark the road
    That leads me to the Lamb!

### Light Shining Out of Darkness

God moves in a mysterious way,
His wonders to perform;
He plants His footsteps in the sea,
And rides upon the storm.

Deep in unfathomable mines
Of never failing skill,
He treasures up His bright designs,
And works His sovereign will.

Ye fearful saints fresh courage take,
The clouds ye so much dread
Are big with mercy, and shall break
In blessings on your head.

Judge not the Lord by feeble sense,
But trust Him for His grace;
Behind a frowning providence,
He hides a smiling face.

His purposes will ripen fast,
Unfolding ev'ry hour;
The bud may have a bitter taste,
But sweet will be the flow'r.

Blind unbelief is sure to err,
And scan His work in vain;
God is His own interpreter,
And He will make it plain.

# AUGUSTUS MONTAGUE TOPLADY
## 1740–1778

### *Rock of Ages*

Rock of Ages, cleft for me,
Let me hide myself in Thee!
Let the Water and the Blood,
From thy riven Side which flowed,
Be of sin the double cure;
Cleanse me from its guilt and pow'r.

Not the labours of my hands
Can fulfill thy Law's demands:
Could my zeal no respite know,
Could my tears for ever flow,
All for sin could not atone:
Thou must save, and Thou alone.

Nothing in my hand I bring;
Simply to thy Cross I cling;
Naked, come to Thee for dress;
Helpless, look to Thee for grace;
Foul, I to the Fountain fly:
Wash me, Savior, or I die!

While I draw this fleeting breath—
When my eye-strings break in death—
When I soar to worlds unknown—
See Thee on thy judgment-throne—
Rock of Ages, cleft for me,
Let me hide myself in Thee.

# JOHN LOGAN/1748–1788

## *The Braes of Yarrow*

"Thy braes were bonny, Yarrow stream!
   When first on them I met my lover;
Thy braes how dreary, Yarrow stream!
   When now thy waves his body cover!
For ever now, O Yarrow stream!
   Thou art to me a stream of sorrow;
For never on thy banks shall I
   Behold my love, the flower of Yarrow.

"He promised me a milk-white steed,
   To bear me to his father's bowers;
He promised me a little page,
   To squire me to his father's towers;
He promised me a wedding-ring,—
   The wedding-day was fixed to-morrow;—
Now he is wedded to his grave,
   Alas, his watery grave, in Yarrow!

"Sweet were his words when last we met;
   My passion I as freely told him!
Clasped in his arms, I little thought
   That I should never more behold him!
Scarce was he gone, I saw his ghost;
   It vanished with a shriek of sorrow;
Thrice did the water-wraith ascend,
   And gave a doleful groan thro' Yarrow.

"His mother from the window looked,
   With all the longing of a mother;
His little sister weeping walked
   The green-wood path to meet her brother:
They sought him east, they sought him west,
   They sought him all the forest thorough;

They only saw the cloud of night,
  They only heard the roar of Yarrow!

"No longer from thy window look,
  Thou hast no son, thou tender mother!
No longer walk, thou lovely maid!
  Alas, thou hast no more a brother!
No longer seek him east or west,
  And search no more the forest thorough;
For, wandering in the night so dark,
  He fell a lifeless corse in Yarrow.

"The tear shall never leave my cheek,
  No other youth shall be my marrow;
I'll seek thy body in the stream,
  And then with thee I'll sleep in Yarrow."
The tear did never leave her cheek,
  No other youth became her marrow;
She found his body in the stream,
  And now with him she sleeps in Yarrow.


# THOMAS CHATTERTON/1752–1770

### The Minstrel's Song

Oh! sing unto my roundelay;
  Oh! drop the briny tear with me;
Dance no more at holiday;
  Like a running river be.
    My love is dead,
    Gone to his death-bed,
    All under the willow-tree.

Black his crine as the winter night,
  White his rode[1] as the summer snow,

---

[1] complexion

Red his face as the morning light;
   Cold he lies in the grave below.
     My love is dead,
      Gone to his death-bed,
     All under the willow-tree.

Sweet his tongue as the throstle's note,
   Quick in dance as thought can be,
Deft his tabour, cudgel stout;
   Oh! he lies by the willow-tree.
     My love is dead,
      Gone to his death-bed,
     All under the willow-tree.

Hark! the raven flaps his wing,
   In the briarèd dell below;
Hark! the death-owl loud doth sing
   To the night-mares, as they go.
     My love is dead,
      Gone to his death-bed,
     All under the willow-tree.

See! the white moon shines on high,
   Whiter is my true love's shroud,
Whiter than the morning sky,
   Whiter than the evening cloud.
     My love is dead,
      Gone to his death-bed,
     All under the willow-tree.

Here, upon my true love's grave,
   Shall the barren flowers be laid;
Not one holy saint to save
   All the celness[1] of a maid.
     My love is dead,
      Gone to his death-bed,
     All under the willow-tree.

[1] coldness

With my hands I'll dente[1] the briars,
   Round his holy corse to gre,[2]
Elfin fairy, light your fires,
   Here, my body still shall be.
     My love is dead,
     Gone to his death-bed,
     All under the willow-tree.

Come, with acorn-cup and thorn,
   Drain my hartys blood away;
Life and all its good I scorn,
   Dance by night, or feast by day.
     My love is dead,
     Gone to his death-bed,
     All under the willow-tree.

Water-witches, crowned with reytes,[3]
   Bear me to your lethal tide.
I die; I come; my true love waits.
   Thus the damsel spake and died.

# WILLIAM BLAKE/1757–1827

### To Spring

O, thou with dewy locks, who lookest down
Thro' the clear windows of the morning, turn
Thine angel eyes upon our western isle,
Which in full choir hails thy approach, O Spring!

The hills tell each other, and the list'ning
Valleys hear; all our longing eyes are turned
Up to thy bright pavillions: issue forth,
And let thy holy feet visit our clime.

[1] fasten   [2] grow   [3] water-flags

Come o'er the eastern hills, and let our winds
Kiss thy perfumed garments; let us taste
Thy morn and evening breath; scatter thy pearls
Upon our love-sick land that mourns for thee.

O, deck her forth with thy fair fingers; pour
Thy soft kisses on her bosom; and put
Thy golden crown upon her languished head,
Whose modest tresses were bound up for thee!


## Song

My silks and fine array,
　　My smiles and languished air,
By love are driv'n away;
　　And mournful lean Despair
Brings me yew to deck my grave:
Such end true lovers have.

His face is fair as heav'n,
　　When springing buds unfold;
O why to him was't giv'n,
　　Whose heart is wintry cold?
His breast is love's all worshipped tomb,
Where all love's pilgrims come.

Bring me an axe and spade,
　　Bring me a winding sheet;
When I my grave have made,
　　Let winds and tempests beat:
Then down I'll lie, as cold as clay.
True love doth pass away!


## To the Muses

Whether on Ida's shady brow,
　　Or in the chambers of the East,

The chambers of the sun, that now
   From antient melody have ceased;

Whether in Heav'n ye wander fair,
   Or the green corners of the earth,
Or the blue regions of the air,
   Where the melodious winds have birth;

Whether on chrystal rocks ye rove,
   Beneath the bosom of the sea
Wand'ring in many a coral grove,
   Fair Nine, forsaking Poetry!

How have you left the antient love
   That bards of old enjoyed in you!
The languid strings do scarcely move!
   The sound is forced, the notes are few!

### The Lamb

   Little Lamb, who made thee?
     Dost thou know who made thee?
Gave thee life, and bid thee feed
By the stream and o'er the mead;
Gave thee clothing of delight,
Softest clothing, wooly, bright;
Gave thee such a tender voice,
Making all the vales rejoice?
   Little Lamb, who made thee?
     Dost thou know who made thee?

   Little Lamb, I'll tell thee,
   Little Lamb, I'll tell thee:
He is callèd by thy name,
For he calls himself a Lamb.
He is meek, and he is mild;
He became a little child.
I a child, and thou a lamb,

We are callèd by his name.
   Little Lamb, God bless thee!
   Little Lamb, God bless thee!


### The Little Black Boy

My mother bore me in the southern wild,
And I am black, but O! my soul is white;
White as an angel is the English child,
But I am black, as if bereaved of light.

My mother taught me underneath a tree,
And sitting down before the heat of day,
She took me on her lap and kissèd me,
And pointing to the east, began to say:

"Look on the rising sun: there God does live,
And gives His light, and gives His heat away;
And flowers and trees and beasts and men receive
Comfort in morning, joy in the noonday.

"And we are put on earth a little space,
That we may learn to bear the beams of love;
And these black bodies and this sunburnt face
Is but a cloud, and like a shady grove.

"For when our souls have learned the heat to bear,
The cloud will vanish; we shall hear His voice,
Saying: 'Come out from the grove, my love and care,
And round my golden tent like lambs rejoice.'"

Thus did my mother say, and kissèd me;
And thus I say to little English boy:
When I from black and he from white cloud free,
And round the tent of God like lambs we joy,

I'll shade him from the heat, till he can bear
To lean in joy upon our Father's knee;

And then I'll stand and stroke his silver hair,
And be like him, and he will then love me.


### The Chimney Sweeper


When my mother died I was very young,
And my father sold me while yet my tongue
Could scarcely cry "'weep! 'weep! 'weep! 'weep!"
So your chimneys I sweep, and in soot I sleep.

There's little Tom Dacre, who cried when his head,
That curled like a lamb's back, was shaved: so I said
"Hush, Tom! never mind it, for when your head's bare
You know that the soot cannot spoil your white hair."

And so he was quiet, and that very night,
As Tom was a-sleeping, he had such a sight!
That thousands of sweepers, Dick, Joe, Ned, and Jack,
Were all of them locked up in coffins of black.

And by came an Angel who had a bright key,
And he opened the coffins and set them all free;
Then down a green plain leaping, laughing, they run,
And wash in a river, and shine in the Sun.

Then naked and white, all their bags left behind,
They rise upon clouds and sport in the wind;
And the Angel told Tom, if he'd be a good boy,
He'd have God for his father, and never want joy.

And so Tom awoke; and we rose in the dark,
And got with our bags and our brushes to work.
Tho' the morning was cold, Tom was happy and warm;
So if all do their duty they need not fear harm.

## Nurse's Song

When the voices of children are heard on the green
And laughing is heard on the hill,
My heart is at rest within my breast
    And everything else is still.

"Then come home, my children, the sun is gone down
And the dews of night arise;
Come, come, leave off play, and let us away
Till the morning appears in the skies."

"No, no, let us play, for it is yet day
And we cannot go to sleep;
Besides, in the sky the little birds fly
And the hills are all covered with sheep."

"Well, well, go and play till the light fades away
And then go home to bed."
The little ones leaped and shouted and laughed
    And all the hills echoèd.

## The Clod and the Pebble

    "Love seeketh not itself to please,
      Nor for itself hath any care,
    But for another gives its ease,
    And builds a Heaven in Hell's despair."

    So sung a little Clod of Clay
    Trodden with the cattle's feet,
    But a Pebble of the brook
    Warbled out these metres meet:

    "Love seeketh only self to please,
    To bind another to its delight,
    Joys in another's loss of ease,
    And builds a Hell in Heaven's despite."

## Nurse's Song

When the voices of children are heard on the green
And whisp'rings are in the dale,
The days of my youth rise fresh in my mind,
My face turns green and pale.

Then come home, my children, the sun is gone down,
And the dews of night arise;
Your spring and your day are wasted in play,
And your winter and night in disguise.

## The Sick Rose

O rose, thou art sick!
The invisible worm
That flies in the night,
In the howling storm,

Has found out thy bed
Of crimson joy,
And his dark secret love
Does thy life destroy.

## The Tyger

Tyger! Tyger! burning bright
In the forests of the night,
What immortal hand or eye
Could frame thy fearful symmetry?

In what distant deeps or skies
Burnt the fire of thine eyes?
On what wings dare he aspire?
What the hand dare seize the fire?

And what shoulder, and what art,
Could twist the sinews of thy heart?
And when thy heart began to beat,
What dread hand? and what dread feet?

What the hammer? what the chain?
In what furnace was thy brain?
What the anvil? what dread grasp
Dare its deadly terrors clasp?

When the stars threw down their spears,
And watered heaven with their tears,
Did he smile his work to see?
Did he who made the Lamb make thee?

Tyger! Tyger! burning bright
In the forests of the night,
What immortal hand or eye,
Dare frame thy fearful symmetry?


*Ah, Sunflower*

Ah, Sunflower, weary of time,
    Who countest the steps of the sun;
Seeking after that sweet golden clime
    Where the traveller's journey is done;

Where the Youth pined away with desire,
    And the pale Virgin shrouded in snow,
Arise from their graves, and aspire
    Where my Sunflower wishes to go!


*The Garden of Love*

I went to the Garden of Love,
And saw what I never had seen:

A Chapel was built in the midst,
Where I used to play on the green.

And the gates of this Chapel were shut,
And "Thou shalt not" writ over the door;
So I turned to the Garden of Love
That so many sweet flowers bore;

And I saw it filled with graves,
And tomb-stones where flowers should be;
And Priests in black gowns were walking their rounds,
And binding with briars my joys and desires.


## London

I wander thro' each chartered street,
Near where the chartered Thames does flow,
And mark in every face I meet
Marks of weakness, marks of woe.

In every cry of every Man,
In every Infant's cry of fear,
In every voice, in every ban,
The mind-forged manacles I hear.

How the Chimney-sweeper's cry
Every black'ning Church appalls;
And the hapless Soldier's sigh
Runs in blood down Palace walls.

But most thro' midnight streets I hear
How the youthful Harlot's curse
Blasts the new born Infant's tear,
And blights with plagues the Marriage hearse.

### Never Seek to Tell Thy Love

Never seek to tell thy love
Love that never told can be;
For the gentle wind does move
Silently, invisibly.

I told my love, I told my love,
I told her all my heart,
Trembling, cold, in ghastly fears—
Ah, she doth depart.

Soon as she was gone from me
A traveller came by
Silently, invisibly—
O, was no deny.

### Eternity

He who binds to himself a joy
Does the wingèd life destroy;
But he who kisses the joy as it flies
Lives in eternity's sun rise.

### Mock on, Mock on, Voltaire, Rousseau

Mock on, mock on, Voltaire, Rousseau:
Mock on, mock on: 'tis all in vain!
You throw the sand against the wind,
And the wind blows it back again.

And every sand becomes a Gem
Reflected in the beams divine;

Blown back they blind the mocking Eye,
But still in Israel's paths they shine.

The Atoms of Democritus
And Newton's Particles of light
Are sands upon the Red Sea shore,
Where Israel's tents do shine so bright.

### The Caverns of the Grave

The Caverns of the Grave I've seen,
And these I shewed to England's Queen.
But now the Caves of Hell I view:
Who shall I dare to shew them to?
What mighty Soul in Beauty's form
Shall dauntless view the Infernal Storm?
Egremont's Countess can control
The flames of Hell that round me roll.
If she refuse, I still go on
Till the Heavens and Earth are gone,
Still admired by noble minds,
Followed by Envy on the winds,
Re-engraved time after time,
Ever in their youthful prime,
My designs unchanged remain.
Time may rage but rage in vain.
Far above Time's troubled Fountains
On the Great Atlantic Mountains,
In my Golden House on high,
There they shine eternally.

### And Did Those Feet in Ancient Time

And did those feet in ancient time
Walk upon England's mountains green?
And was the holy Lamb of God
On England's pleasant pastures seen?

And did the Countenance Divine
Shine forth upon our clouded hills?
And was Jerusalem builded here
Among these dark Satanic Mills?

Bring me my Bow of burning gold:
Bring me my Arrows of desire:
Bring me my Spear: O clouds unfold!
Bring me my Chariot of fire.

I will not cease from Mental Fight,
Nor shall my Sword sleep in my hand
Till we have built Jerusalem
In England's green and pleasant Land.


*To the Accuser Who Is the God of This World*

Truly, my Satan, thou art but a Dunce,
And dost not know the Garment from the Man.
Every Harlot was a Virgin once,
Nor can'st thou ever change Kate into Nan.

Tho' thou art worshipped by the Names Divine
Of Jesus and Jehovah, thou art still
The Son of Morn in weary Night's decline,
The lost Traveller's Dream under the hill.


# ROBERT BURNS/1759-1796

*Green Grow the Rashes O*

Green grow the rashes O,
   Green grow the rashes O;
The sweetest hours that e'er I spend,
   Are spent amang the lasses O!

There 's nought but care on ev'ry han',
    In ev'ry hour that passes O;
What signifies the life o' man,
    An' 'twere na for the lasses O.

The warly[1] race may riches chase,
    An' riches still may fly them O;
An' tho' at last they catch them fast,
    Their hearts can ne'er enjoy them O.

But gie me a canny hour at e'en,
    My arms about my dearie O;
An' warly cares, an' warly men,
    May a' gae tapsalteerie[2] O!

For you sae douce, ye sneer at this,
    Ye're nought but senseless asses O:
The wisest man the warl' saw,
    He dearly lov'd the lasses O.

Auld nature swears, the lovely dears
    Her noblest work she classes O;
Her prentice han' she tried on man,
    An' then she made the lasses O.

## To a Mouse

*On turning her up in her nest with the plough, November, 1785*

Wee, sleekit, cowrin, tim'rous beastie,
O, what a panic's in thy breastie!
Thou need na start awa sae hasty,
                Wi' bickering brattle![3]

---

[1] worldly    [2] topsy-turvy    [3] scamper

I wad be laith to rin an' chase thee,
        Wi' murd'ring pattle![1]

I'm truly sorry Man's dominion
Has broken Nature's social union,
An' justifies that ill opinion
        Which makes thee startle
At me, thy poor, earth-born companion,
        An' fellow-mortal!

I doubt na, whyles, but thou may thieve
What then? poor beastie, thou maun live!
A daimen[2] icker[3] in a thrave[4]
        'S a sma' request.
I'll get a blessin wi' the lave,
        And never miss't!

Thy wee bit housie, too, in ruin!
Its silly wa's the win's are strewin!
An' naething, now, to big[5] a new ane,
        O' foggage[6] green!
An' bleak December's winds ensuin,
        Baith snell[7] and keen!

Thou saw the fields laid bare an' waste,
An' weary Winter comin fast,
An' cozie here, beneath the blast,
        Thou thought to dwell,
Till crash! the cruel coulter past
        Out thro' thy cell.

That wee bit heap o' leaves an' stibble,
Has cost thee mony a weary nibble!
Now thou's turned out, for a' thy trouble,
        But[8] house or hald,

[1] plough-staff   [2] odd   [3] ear of corn   [4] twenty-four sheaves   [5] build   [6] coarse grass
[7] biting   [8] without

To thole[1] the Winter's sleety dribble,
          An' cranreuch[2] cauld!

But, Mousie, thou are no thy lane,[3]
In proving foresight may be vain:
The best-laid schemes o' Mice an' Men,
          Gang aft a-gley,[4]
An' lea'e us nought but grief and pain,
          For promised joy.

Still thou art blest, compared wi' me!
The present only toucheth thee;
But, Och! I backward cast my e'e,
          On prospects drear!
An' forward, tho' I canna see,
          I guess an' fear!

### Auld Lang Syne

Should auld acquaintance be forgot,
   And never brought to min'?
Should auld acquaintance be forgot,
   And auld lang syne?

     For auld lang syne, my dear.
       For auld lang syne,
     We'll tak a cup o' kindness yet,
       For auld lang syne.

We twa hae run about the braes,
   And pu'd the gowans[5] fine;
But we've wandered mony a weary foot
   Sin' auld lang syne.

We twa hae paidled[6] i' the burn,
   From morning sun till dine;

---

[1] endure   [2] hoar-frost   [3] by thyself   [4] askew   [5] daisies   [6] paddled

But seas between us braid hae roared
  Sin' auld lang syne.

And there's a hand, my trusty fiere,[1]
  And gie 's a hand o' thine:
And we'll tak a right guid-willie waught,[2]
  For auld lang syne.

And surely ye'll be[3] your pint-stowp,
  And surely I'll be mine;
And we'll tak a cup o' kindness yet
  For auld lang syne.

### A Red, Red Rose

O, my luve is like a red red rose
That's newly sprung in June:
O, my luve is like the melodie
  That's sweetly played in tune.

As fair art thou, my bonie lass,
  So deep in luve am I;
And I will luve thee still, my dear,
  Till a' the seas gang dry.

Till a' the seas gang dry, my dear,
  And the rocks melt wi' the sun;
And I will luve thee still, my dear,
  While the sands o' life shall run.

And fare thee weel, my only luve!
  And fare thee weel a while!
And I will come again, my luve,
  Tho' it were ten thousand mile.

[1] friend   [2] good draught   [3] be good for

### Ye Flowery Banks o' Bonie Doon

Ye flowery banks o' bonie Doon,
  How can ye blume sae fair?
How can ye chant, ye little birds,
  And I sae fu' o' care?

Thou'll break my heart, thou bonie bird,
  That sings upon the bough:
Thou minds me o' the happy days
  When my fause Luve was true.

Thou'll break my heart, thou bonie bird,
  That sings beside thy mate:
For sae I sat, and sae I sang,
  And wist na o' my fate.

Aft hae I rov'd by bonie Doon
  To see the woodbine twine,
And ilka bird sang o' its luve,
  And sae did I o' mine.

Wi' lightsome heart I pu'd a rose
  Frae aff its thorny tree,
And my fause luver staw my rose,
  But left the thorn wi' me.

### O, Wert Thou in the Cauld Blast

O, wert thou in the cauld blast,
  On yonder lea, on yonder lea,
My plaidie to the angry airt,[1]
  I'd shelter thee, I'd shelter thee.
Or did Misfortune's bitter storms
  Around thee blaw, around thee blaw,

---

[1] quarter of the wind

Thy bield[1] should be my bosom,
   To share it a', to share it a'.


Or were I in the wildest waste,
   Sae black and bare, sae black and bare,
The desert were a paradise,
   If thou wert there, if thou wert there.
Or were I monarch o' the globe,
   Wi' thee to reign, wi' thee to reign,
The brightest jewel in my crown
   Wad be my queen, wad be my queen.


### Oh, Open the Door to Me, Oh!

Oh, open the door, some pity to shew,
   Oh, open the door to me, oh!
Tho' thou hast been false, I'll ever prove true,
   Oh, open the door to me, oh!


Cauld is the blast upon my pale cheek,
   But caulder thy love for me, oh!
The frost that freezes the life at my heart
   Is naught to my pains fra thee, oh!


The wan moon is setting behind the white wave,
   And time is setting with me, oh!
False friends, false love, farewell! for mair
   I'll ne'er trouble them, nor thee, oh!


She has open'd the door, she has open'd it wide;
   She sees his pale corse on the plain, oh!
My true love! she cried, and sank down by his side,
   Never to rise again, oh!

[1] shelter

### *My Heart Leaps Up When I Behold*

My heart leaps up when I behold
    A rainbow in the sky:
So was it when my life began;
So is it now I am a man;
So be it when I shall grow old,
    Or let me die!
The Child is father of the Man;
And I could wish my days to be
Bound each to each by natural piety.

### *Strange Fits of Passion Have I Known*

Strange fits of passion have I known:
And I will dare to tell,
But in the lover's ear alone,
What once to me befell.

When she I loved looked every day
Fresh as a rose in June,
I to her cottage bent my way,
Beneath an evening-moon.

Upon the moon I fixed my eye,
All over the wide lea;
With quickening pace my horse drew nigh
Those paths so dear to me.

And now we reached the orchard-plot;
And, as we climbed the hill,
The sinking moon to Lucy's cot
Came near, and nearer still.

In one of those sweet dreams I slept,
Kind Nature's gentlest boon!
And all the while my eyes I kept
On the descending moon.

My horse moved on; hoof after hoof
He raised, and never stopped:
When down behind the cottage roof,
At once, the bright moon dropped.

What fond and wayward thoughts will slide
Into a lover's head!
"O mercy!" to myself I cried,
"If Lucy should be dead!"

### She Dwelt among the Untrodden Ways

She dwelt among the untrodden ways
    Beside the springs of Dove,
A maid whom there were none to praise
    And very few to love:

A violet by a mossy stone
    Half hidden from the eye!
—Fair as a star, when only one
    Is shining in the sky.

She lived unknown, and few could know
    When Lucy ceased to be;
But she is in her grave, and, oh,
    The difference to me!

### I Travelled among Unknown Men

I travelled among unknown men,
    In lands beyond the sea;

Nor, England! did I know till then
    What love I bore to thee.

'T is past, that melancholy dream!
    Nor will I quit thy shore
A second time; for still I seem
    To love thee more and more.

Among thy mountains did I feel
    The joy of my desire;
And she I cherished turned her wheel
    Beside an English fire.

### She Was a Phantom of Delight

She was a phantom of delight
When first she gleamed upon my sight;
A lovely apparition, sent
To be a moment's ornament;
Her eyes as stars of twilight fair;
Like twilight's, too, her dusky hair;
But all things else about her drawn
From May-time and the cheerful dawn;
A dancing shape, an image gay,
To haunt, to startle, and waylay.

I saw her upon nearer view,
A spirit, yet a woman too!
Her household motions light and free,
And steps of virgin-liberty;
A countenance in which did meet
Sweet records, promises as sweet;
A creature not too bright or good
For human nature's daily food;
For transient sorrows, simple wiles,
Praise, blame, love, kisses, tears, and smiles.

And now I see with eye serene
The very pulse of the machine;
A being breathing thoughtful breath,
A traveller between life and death;
The reason firm, the temperate will,
Endurance, foresight, strength, and skill;
A perfect woman, nobly planned,
To warn, to comfort, and command;
And yet a spirit still, and bright
With something of angelic light.

### Three Years She Grew in Sun and Shower

Three years she grew in sun and shower,
Then Nature said, "A lovelier flower
On earth was never sown;
This child I to myself will take;
She shall be mine, and I will make
A lady of my own.

"Myself will to my darling be
Both law and impulse: and with me
The girl, in rock and plain,
In earth and heaven, in glade and bower,
Shall feel an overseeing power
To kindle or restrain.

"She shall be sportive as the fawn
That wild with glee across the lawn,
Or up the mountain springs;
And hers shall be the breathing balm,
And hers the silence and the calm
Of mute insensate things.

"The floating clouds their state shall lend
To her; for her the willow bend;
Nor shall she fail to see
Even in the motions of the storm

Grace that shall mould the maiden's form
By silent sympathy.

"The stars of midnight shall be dear
To her; and she shall lean her ear
In many a secret place
Where rivulets dance their wayward round,
And beauty born of murmuring sound
Shall pass into her face.

"And vital feelings of delight
Shall rear her form to stately height,
Her virgin bosom swell;
Such thoughts to Lucy I will give
While she and I together live
Here in this happy dell."

Thus Nature spake—the work was done—
How soon my Lucy's race was run!
She died, and left to me
This heath, this calm, and quiet scene;
The memory of what has been,
And never more will be.

### A Slumber Did My Spirit Seal

A slumber did my spirit seal;
    I had no human fears:
She seemed a thing that could not feel
    The touch of earthly years.

No motion has she now, no force;
    She neither hears nor sees;
Rolled round in earth's diurnal course,
    With rocks, and stones, and trees.

*I Wandered Lonely as a Cloud*

I wandered lonely as a cloud
That floats on high o'er vales and hills,
When all at once I saw a crowd,
A host, of golden daffodils;
Beside the lake, beneath the trees,
Fluttering and dancing in the breeze.

Continuous as the stars that shine
And twinkle on the milky way,
They stretched in never-ending line
Along the margin of a bay:
Ten thousand saw I at a glance,
Tossing their heads in sprightly dance.

The waves beside them danced; but they
Out-did the sparkling waves in glee:
A poet could not but be gay,
In such a jocund company:
I gazed—and gazed—but little thought
What wealth the show to me had brought:

For oft, when on my couch I lie,
In vacant or in pensive mood,
They flash upon that inward eye
Which is the bliss of solitude;
And then my heart with pleasure fills,
And dances with the daffodils.

*Written in March*

While Resting on the Bridge at the Foot of Brother's Water

The cock is crowing,
The stream is flowing,
The small birds twitter,
The lake doth glitter,

The green field sleeps in the sun;
 The oldest and youngest
 Are at work with the strongest;
 The cattle are grazing,
 Their heads never raising;
There are forty feeding like one!

 Like an army defeated
 The snow hath retreated,
 And now doth fare ill
 On the top of the bare hill;
The ploughboy is whooping—anon—anon:
 There's joy in the mountains;
 There's life in the fountains;
 Small clouds are sailing,
 Blue sky prevailing;
The rain is over and gone!

## Lines

*Composed a Few Miles above Tintern Abbey, on
Revisiting the Banks of the Wye During a Tour.
July 13, 1798*

Five years have past; five summers, with the length
Of five long winters! and again I hear
These waters, rolling from their mountain-springs
With a soft inland murmur.—Once again
Do I behold these steep and lofty cliffs,
That on a wild secluded scene impress
Thoughts of more deep seclusion; and connect
The landscape with the quiet of the sky.
The day is come when I again repose
Here, under this dark sycamore, and view
These plots of cottage-ground, these orchard-tufts,
Which at this season, with their unripe fruits,
Are clad in one green hue, and lose themselves
'Mid groves and copses. Once again I see
These hedge-rows, hardly hedge-rows, little lines

Of sportive wood run wild: these pastoral farms,
Green to the very door; and wreaths of smoke
Sent up, in silence, from among the trees!
With some uncertain notice, as might seem
Of vagrant dwellers in the houseless woods,
Or of some hermit's cave, where by his fire
The hermit sits alone.

           These beauteous forms,
Through a long absence, have not been to me
As is a landscape to a blind man's eye:
But oft, in lonely rooms, and 'mid the din
Of towns and cities, I have owed to them
In hours of weariness, sensations sweet,
Felt in the blood, and felt along the heart;
And passing even into my purer mind,
With tranquil restoration:—feelings too
Of unremembered pleasure: such, perhaps,
As have no slight or trivial influence
On that best portion of a good man's life,
His little, nameless, unremembered, acts
Of kindness and of love. Nor less, I trust,
To them I may have owed another gift,
Of aspect more sublime; that blessèd mood,
In which the burthen of the mystery,
In which the heavy and the weary weight
Of all this unintelligible world,
Is lightened:—that serene and blessèd mood,
In which the affections gently lead us on,—
Until, the breath of this corporeal frame
And even the motion of our human blood
Almost suspended, we are laid asleep
In body, and become a living soul:
While with an eye made quiet by the power
Of harmony, and the deep power of joy,
We see into the life of things.

                If this
Be but a vain belief, yet, oh! how oft—
In darkness and amid the many shapes
Of joyless daylight; when the fretful stir

Unprofitable, and the fever of the world,
Have hung upon the beatings of my heart—
How oft, in spirit, have I turned to thee,
O sylvan Wye! thou wanderer thro' the woods,
How often has my spirit turned to thee!
   And now, with gleams of half-extinguished thought,
With many recognitions dim and faint,
And somewhat of a sad perplexity,
The picture of the mind revives again:
While here I stand, not only with the sense
Of present pleasure, but with pleasing thoughts
That in this moment there is life and food
For future years. And so I dare to hope,
Though changed, no doubt, from what I was when first
I came among these hills; when like a roe
I bounded o'er the mountains, by the sides
Of the deep rivers, and the lonely streams,
Wherever nature led: more like a man
Flying from something that he dreads, than one
Who sought the thing he loved. For nature then
(The coarser pleasures of my boyish days,
And their glad animal movements all gone by)
To me was all in all. I cannot paint
What then I was. The sounding cataract
Haunted me like a passion: the tall rock,
The mountain, and the deep and gloomy wood,
Their colors and their forms, were then to me
An appetite; a feeling and a love,
That had no need of a remoter charm,
By thought supplied, nor any interest
Unborrowed from the eye.—That time is past,
And all its aching joys are now no more,
And all its dizzy raptures. Not for this
Faint I, nor mourn nor murmur; other gifts
Have followed; for such loss, I would believe,
Abundant recompense. For I have learned
To look on nature, not as in the hour
Of thoughtless youth; but hearing oftentimes
The still, sad music of humanity,

Nor harsh nor grating, though of ample power
To chasten and subdue. And I have felt
A presence that disturbs me with the joy
Of elevated thoughts; a sense sublime
Of something far more deeply interfused,
Whose dwelling is the light of setting suns,
And the round ocean and the living air,
And the blue sky, and in the mind of man;
A motion and a spirit, that impels
All thinking things, all objects of all thought,
And rolls through all things. Therefore am I still
A lover of the meadows and the woods,
And mountains; and of all that we behold
From this green earth; of all the mighty world
Of eye, and ear,—both what they half create,
And what perceive; well pleased to recognise
In nature and the language of the sense,
The anchor of my purest thoughts, the nurse,
The guide, the guardian of my heart, and soul
Of all my moral being.

              Nor perchance,
If I were not thus taught, should I the more
Suffer my genial spirits to decay:
For thou art with me here upon the banks
Of this fair river; thou my dearest friend,
My dear, dear friend; and in thy voice I catch
The language of my former heart, and read
My former pleasures in the shooting lights
Of thy wild eyes. Oh! yet a little while
May I behold in thee what I was once,
My dear, dear Sister! and this prayer I make,
Knowing that Nature never did betray
The heart that loved her; 't is her privilege,
Through all the years of this our life, to lead
From joy to joy: for she can so inform
The mind that is within us, so impress
With quietness and beauty, and so feed
With lofty thoughts, that neither evil tongues,
Rash judgments, nor the sneers of selfish men,

Nor greetings where no kindness is, nor all
The dreary intercourse of daily life,
Shall e'er prevail against us, or disturb
Our cheerful faith, that all which we behold
Is full of blessings. Therefore let the moon
Shine on thee in thy solitary walk;
And let the misty mountain-winds be free
To blow against thee: and, in after years,
When these wild ecstasies shall be matured
Into a sober pleasure; when thy mind
Shall be a mansion for all lovely forms,
Thy memory be as a dwelling-place
For all sweet sounds and harmonies; oh! then,
If solitude, or fear, or pain, or grief,
Should be thy portion, with what healing thoughts
Of tender joy wilt thou remember me,
And these my exhortations! Nor, perchance—
If I should be where I no more can hear
Thy voice, nor catch from thy wild eyes these gleams
Of past existence—wilt thou then forget
That on the banks of this delightful stream
We stood together; and that I, so long
A worshipper of Nature, hither came
Unwearied in that service; rather say
With warmer love—oh! with far deeper zeal
Of holier love. Nor wilt thou then forget,
That after many wanderings, many years
Of absence, these steep woods and lofty cliffs,
And this green pastoral landscape, were to me
More dear, both for themselves and for thy sake!


### Surprised by Joy—Impatient as the Wind

Surprised by joy—impatient as the wind
I turned to share the transport—Oh! with whom
But Thee, deep buried in the silent tomb,
That spot which no vicissitude can find?
Love, faithful love, recalled thee to my mind—

But how could I forget thee? Through what power,
Even for the least division of an hour,
Have I been so beguiled as to be blind
To my most grievous loss?—That thought's return
Was the worst pang that sorrow ever bore,
Save one, one only, when I stood forlorn,
Knowing my heart's best treasure was no more;
That neither present time, nor years unborn
Could to my sight that heavenly face restore.

### It Is a Beauteous Evening, Calm and Free

It is a beauteous evening, calm and free,
The holy time is quiet as a nun
Breathless with adoration; the broad sun
Is sinking down in its tranquillity;
The gentleness of heaven broods o'er the sea:
Listen! the mighty being is awake,
And doth with his eternal motion make
A sound like thunder—everlastingly.
Dear child! dear girl! that walkest with me here,
If thou appear untouched by solemn thought,
Thy nature is not therefore less divine:
Thou liest in Abraham's bosom all the year;
And worship'st at the temple's inner shrine,
God being with thee when we know it not.

### With Ships the Sea Was Sprinkled Far and Nigh

With ships the sea was sprinkled far and nigh,
Like stars in heaven, and joyously it showed;
Some lying fast at anchor in the road,
Some veering up and down, one knew not why.
A goodly vessel did I then espy
Come like a giant from a haven broad;
And lustily along the bay she strode,
Her tackling rich, and of apparel high.

This ship was nought to me, nor I to her,
Yet I pursued her with a lover's look;
This ship to all the rest did I prefer:
When will she turn, and whither? She will brook
No tarrying; where she comes the winds must stir:
On went she, and due north her journey took.


### The World Is Too Much with Us; Late and Soon

The world is too much with us; late and soon,
Getting and spending, we lay waste our powers:
Little we see in Nature that is ours;
We have given our hearts away, a sordid boon!
The sea that bares her bosom to the moon;
The winds that will be howling at all hours,
And are up-gathered now like sleeping flowers;
For this, for everything, we are out of tune;
It moves us not.—Great God! I'd rather be
A pagan suckled in a creed outworn;
So might I, standing on this pleasant lea,
Have glimpses that would make me less forlorn;
Have sight of Proteus rising from the sea;
Or hear old Triton blow his wreathèd horn.


### Composed upon Westminster Bridge

#### Sept. 3, 1802

Earth has not anything to show more fair:
Dull would he be of soul who could pass by
A sight so touching in its majesty:
This city now doth, like a garment, wear
The beauty of the morning; silent, bare,
Ships, towers, domes, theatres, and temples lie
Open unto the fields, and to the sky;
All bright and glittering in the smokeless air.
Never did sun more beautifully steep

In his first splendour, valley, rock, or hill;
Ne'er saw I, never felt, a calm so deep!
The river glideth at his own sweet will:
Dear God! the very houses seem asleep;
And all that mighty heart is lying still!

### Stepping Westward

"*What, you are stepping westward?*"—"*Yea.*"
—'T would be a *wildish* destiny,
If we, who thus together roam
In a strange land, and far from home,
Were in this place the guests of Chance:
Yet who would stop, or fear to advance,
Though home or shelter he had none,
With such a sky to lead him on?

The dewy ground was dark and cold;
Behind, all gloomy to behold;
And stepping westward seemed to be
A kind of *heavenly* destiny:
I liked the greeting; 't was a sound
Of something without place or bound;
And seemed to give me spiritual right
To travel through that region bright.

The voice was soft, and she who spake
Was walking by her native lake:
The salutation had to me
The very sound of courtesy:
Its power was felt; and while my eye
Was fixed upon the glowing sky,
The echo of the voice enwrought
A human sweetness with the thought
Of travelling through the world that lay
Before me in my endless way.

## *The Solitary Reaper*

Behold her, single in the field,
Yon solitary Highland Lass!
Reaping and singing by herself;
Stop here, or gently pass!
Alone she cuts and binds the grain,
And sings a melancholy strain;
O listen! for the vale profound
Is overflowing with the sound.

No nightingale did ever chaunt
More welcome notes to weary bands
Of travellers in some shady haunt,
Among Arabian sands:
A voice so thrilling ne'er was heard
In spring-time from the cuckoo-bird,
Breaking the silence of the seas
Among the farthest Hebrides.

Will no one tell me what she sings?—
Perhaps the plaintive numbers flow
For old, unhappy, far-off things,
And battles long ago:
Or is it some more humble lay,
Familiar matter of to-day?
Some natural sorrow, loss, or pain,
That has been, and may be again?

Whate'er the theme, the maiden sang
As if her song could have no ending;
I saw her singing at her work,
And o'er the sickle bending;—
I listened, motionless and still;
And, as I mounted up the hill,
The music in my heart I bore,
Long after it was heard no more.

### London, 1802

Milton! thou should'st be living at this hour:
England hath need of thee: she is a fen
Of stagnant waters: altar, sword, and pen,
Fireside, the heroic wealth of hall and bower,
Have forfeited their ancient English dower
Of inward happiness. We are selfish men;
Oh! raise us up, return to us again;
And give us manners, virtue, freedom, power.
Thy soul was like a star, and dwelt apart:
Thou hadst a voice whose sound was like the sea:
Pure as the naked heavens, majestic, free,
So didst thou travel on life's common way,
In cheerful godliness; and yet thy heart
The lowliest duties on herself did lay.

### Ode
### Intimations of Immortality from
### Recollections of Early Childhood

There was a time when meadow, grove, and stream,
The earth, and every common sight,
    To me did seem
   Apparelled in celestial light,
The glory and the freshness of a dream.
It is not now as it hath been of yore;—
    Turn wheresoe'er I may,
      By night or day,
The things which I have seen I now can see no more.

    The rainbow comes and goes,
    And lovely is the rose,
    The moon doth with delight
Look round her when the heavens are bare,

Waters on a starry night
Are beautiful and fair;
The sunshine is a glorious birth;
But yet I know, where'er I go,
That there hath past away a glory from the earth.

Now, while the birds thus sing a joyous song,
And while the young lambs bound
As to the tabor's sound,
To me alone there came a thought of grief:
A timely utterance gave that thought relief,
And I again am strong:
The cataracts blow their trumpets from the steep;
No more shall grief of mine the season wrong;
I hear the echoes through the mountains throng,
The winds come to me from the fields of sleep,
And all the earth is gay;
Land and sea
Give themselves up to jollity,
And with the heart of May
Doth every beast keep holiday;—
Thou child of joy,
Shout round me, let me hear thy shouts, thou happy
Shepherd-boy!

Ye blessèd creatures, I have heard the call
Ye to each other make; I see
The heavens laugh with you in your jubilee;
My heart is at your festival,
My head hath its coronal,
The fulness of your bliss, I feel—I feel it all.
Oh evil day! if I were sullen
While earth herself is adorning,
This sweet May-morning,
And the children are culling
On every side,
In a thousand valleys far and wide,
Fresh flowers; while the sun shines warm,

And the babe leaps up on his mother's arm:—
   I hear, I hear, with joy I hear!
   —But there's a tree, of many, one,
A single field which I have looked upon,
Both of them speak of something that is gone:
   The pansy at my feet
   Doth the same tale repeat:
Whither is fled the visionary gleam?
Where is it now, the glory and the dream?

Our birth is but a sleep and a forgetting;
The soul that rises with us, our life's star,
   Hath had elsewhere its setting,
     And cometh from afar:
   Not in entire forgetfulness,
   And not in utter nakedness,
But trailing clouds of glory do we come
   From God, who is our home:
Heaven lies about us in our infancy!
Shades of the prison-house begin to close
   Upon the growing boy,
But he beholds the light, and whence it flows,
   He sees it in his joy;
The youth, who daily farther from the east
   Must travel, still is Nature's priest,
   And by the vision splendid
   Is on his way attended;
At length the man perceives it die away,
And fade into the light of common day.

Earth fills her lap with pleasures of her own;
Yearnings she hath in her own natural kind,
And, even with something of a mother's mind,
   And no unworthy aim,
   The homely nurse doth all she can
To make her foster-child, her inmate man,
   Forget the glories he hath known,
And that imperial palace whence he came.

Behold the child among his new-born blisses,
A six years' darling of a pigmy size!
See, where 'mid work of his own hand he lies,
Fretted by sallies of his mother's kisses,
With light upon him from his father's eyes!
See, at his feet, some little plan or chart,
Some fragment from his dream of human life,
Shaped by himself with newly-learnèd art;
    A wedding or a festival,
    A mourning or a funeral;
       And this hath now his heart,
    And unto this he frames his song:
       Then will he fit his tongue
To dialogues of business, love, or strife;
    But it will not be long
    Ere this be thrown aside,
    And with new joy and pride
The little actor cons another part;
Filling from time to time his "humorous stage"
With all the persons, down to palsied Age,
That life brings with her in her equipage;
    As if his whole vocation
    Were endless imitation.


Thou, whose exterior semblance doth belie
    Thy soul's immensity;
Thou best philosopher, who yet dost keep
Thy heritage, thou eye among the blind,
That, deaf and silent, read'st the eternal deep,
Haunted for ever by the eternal mind,—
    Mighty prophet! Seer blest!
    On whom those truths do rest,
Which we are toiling all our lives to find,
In darkness lost, the darkness of the grave;
Thou, over whom thy immortality
Broods like the day, a master o'er a slave,
A presence which is not to be put by;
Thou little child, yet glorious in the might
Of heaven-born freedom on thy being's height,

Why with such earnest pains dost thou provoke
The years to bring the inevitable yoke,
Thus blindly with thy blessedness at strife?
Full soon thy soul shall have her earthly freight,
And custom lie upon thee with a weight,
Heavy as frost, and deep almost as life!

O joy! that in our embers
Is something that doth live,
That nature yet remembers
What was so fugitive!
The thought of our past years in me doth breed
Perpetual benediction: not indeed
For that which is most worthy to be blest—
Delight and liberty, the simple creed
Of childhood, whether busy or at rest,
With new-fledged hope still fluttering in his breast:—
Not for these I raise
The song of thanks and praise;
But for those obstinate questionings
Of sense and outward things,
Fallings from us, vanishings;
Blank misgivings of a creature
Moving about in worlds not realised,
High instincts before which our mortal nature
Did tremble like a guilty thing surprised:
But for those first affections,
Those shadowy recollections,
Which, be they what they may,
Are yet the fountain light of all our day,
Are yet a master light of all our seeing;
Uphold us, cherish, and have power to make
Our noisy years seem moments in the being
Of the eternal silence: truths that wake,
To perish never;
Which neither listlessness, nor mad endeavour,
Nor man nor boy,
Nor all that is at enmity with joy,
Can utterly abolish or destroy!

Hence in a season of calm weather
    Though inland far we be,
Our souls have sight of that immortal sea
    Which brought us hither,
    Can in a moment travel thither,
And see the children sport upon the shore,
And hear the mighty waters rolling evermore.

Then sing, ye birds, sing, sing a joyous song!
    And let the young lambs bound
    As to the tabor's sound!
We in thought will join your throng,
    Ye that pipe and ye that play,
    Ye that through your hearts to-day
    Feel the gladness of the May!
What though the radiance which was once so bright
Be now forever taken from my sight,
    Though nothing can bring back the hour
Of splendour in the grass, of glory in the flower;
    We will grieve not, rather find
    Strength in what remains behind;
    In the primal sympathy
    Which having been must ever be;
    In the soothing thoughts that spring
    Out of human suffering;
    In the faith that looks through death,
In years that bring the philosophic mind.

And O, ye fountains, meadows, hills, and groves,
Forebode not any severing of our loves!
Yet in my heart of hearts I feel your might;
I only have relinquished one delight
To live beneath your more habitual sway.
I love the brooks which down their channels fret,
Even more than when I tripped lightly as they;
The innocent brightness of a new-born day
        Is lovely yet;
The clouds that gather round the setting sun
Do take a sober colouring from an eye

That hath kept watch o'er man's mortality;
Another race hath been, and other palms are won.
Thanks to the human heart by which we live,
Thanks to its tenderness, its joys, and fears,
To me the meanest flower that blows can give
Thoughts that do often lie too deep for tears.

# SIR WALTER SCOTT/1771–1832

### Hunting Song

Waken, lords and ladies gay,
On the mountain dawns the day,
All the jolly chase is here,
With hawk and horse and hunting-spear!
Hounds are in their couples yelling,
Hawks are whistling, horns are knelling,
Merrily, merrily, mingle they,
"Waken, lords and ladies gay."

Waken, lords and ladies gay,
The mist has left the mountain gray,
Springlets in the dawn are steaming,
Diamonds on the brake are gleaming:
And foresters have busy been
To track the buck in thicket green;
Now we come to chant our lay,
"Waken, lords and ladies gay."

Waken, lords and ladies gay,
To the green-wood haste away;
We can show you where he lies,
Fleet of foot and tall of size;
We can show the marks he made,
When 'gainst the oak his antlers frayed;

You shall see him brought to bay,
"Waken, lords and ladies gay."

Louder, louder chant the lay,
Waken, lords and ladies gay!
Tell them youth and mirth and glee
Run a course as well as we;
Time, stern huntsman, who can balk,
Stanch as hound and fleet as hawk?
Think of this and rise with day,
Gentle lords and ladies gay.


### *Coronach*[1]

He is gone on the mountain,
    He is lost to the forest,
Like a summer-dried fountain,
    When our need was sorest.
The font, reappearing,
    From the rain-drops shall borrow,
But to us comes no cheering,
    To Duncan no morrow!

The hand of the reaper
    Takes the ears that are hoary,
But the voice of the weeper
    Wails manhood in glory.
The autumn winds rushing
    Waft the leaves that are serest,
But our flower was in flushing,
    When blighting was nearest.

Fleet foot on the correi,[2]
    Sage counsel in cumber,[3]
Red hand in the foray,
    How sound is thy slumber!

---

[1] lament    [2] hillside for hunting    [3] trouble

Like dew on the mountain,
    Like foam on the river,
Like the bubble on the fountain,
    Thou art gone, and forever!


*Proud Maisie*

Proud Maisie is in the wood,
    Walking so early;
Sweet Robin sits on the bush,
    Singing so rarely.

"Tell me, thou bonny bird,
    When shall I marry me?"
"When six braw[1] gentlemen,
    Kirkward shall carry ye."

"Who makes the bridal bed,
    Birdie, say truly?"—
"The gray-headed sexton
    That delves the grave duly.

"The glow-worm o'er grave and stone
    Shall light thee steady;
The owl from the steeple sing,
    'Welcome, proud lady.'"

[1] brave

# SAMUEL TAYLOR COLERIDGE
## 1772–1834

### *Kubla Khan*

In Xanadu did Kubla Khan
   A stately pleasure-dome decree:
Where Alph, the sacred river, ran
Through caverns measureless to man
   Down to a sunless sea.
So twïce five miles of fertile ground
With walls and towers were girdled round:
And here were gardens bright with sinuous rills,
Where blossomed many an incense-bearing tree,
And here were forests ancient as the hills,
Enfolding sunny spots of greenery.

But oh! that deep romantic chasm which slanted
Down the green hill athwart a cedarn cover!
A savage place! as holy and enchanted
As e'er beneath a waning moon was haunted
By woman wailing for her demon-lover!
And from this chasm, with ceaseless turmoil seething,
As if this earth in fast thick pants were breathing,
A mighty fountain momently was forced,
Amid whose swift half-intermitted burst
Huge fragments vaulted like rebounding hail,
Or chaffy grain beneath the thresher's flail:
And 'mid these dancing rocks at once and ever
It flung up momently the sacred river.
Five miles meandering with a mazy motion
Through wood and dale the sacred river ran,
Then reached the caverns measureless to man,
And sank in tumult to a lifeless ocean:
And 'mid this tumult Kubla heard from far
Ancestral voices prophesying war!

    The shadow of the dome of pleasure
    Floated midway on the waves;

Where was heard the mingled measure
From the fountain and the caves.
It was a miracle of rare device,
A sunny pleasure-dome with caves of ice!
    A damsel with a dulcimer
    In a vision once I saw:
    It was an Abyssinian maid,
    And on her dulcimer she played,
    Singing of Mount Abora.
    Could I revive within me
    Her symphony and song,
    To such a deep delight 'twould win me,
That with music loud and long,
I would build that dome in air,
That sunny dome! those caves of ice!
And all who heard should see them there,
And all should cry, Beware! Beware!
His flashing eyes, his floating hair!
Weave a circle round him thrice,
And close your eyes with holy dread,
For he on honey-dew hath fed,
And drunk the milk of Paradise.

*The Rime of the Ancient Mariner*

PART I

An ancient Mariner
meeteth three Gallants
bidden to a wedding-
feast, and detaineth
one.

It is an ancient Mariner,
And he stoppeth one of three.
"By thy long gray beard and glittering eye,
Now wherefore stopp'st thou me?

The Bridegroom's doors are opened wide,
And I am next of kin;
The guests are met, the feast is set:
May'st hear the merry din."

He holds him with his skinny hand,
"There was a ship," quoth he.
"Hold off! unhand me, gray-beard loon!"
Eftsoons his hand dropt he.

The Wedding-Guest is
spellbound by the eye
of the old seafaring
man, and constrained
to hear his tale.

He holds him with his glittering eye—
The Wedding-Guest stood still,
And listens like a three years' child:
The Mariner hath his will.

The Wedding-Guest sat on a stone:
He cannot choose but hear;
And thus spake on that ancient man,
The bright-eyed Mariner.

"The ship was cheered, the harbor cleared,
Merrily did we drop
Below the kirk, below the hill,
Below the lighthouse top.

The Mariner tells how
the ship sailed
southward with a good
wind and fair weather,
till it reached the Line.

The sun came up upon the left,
Out of the sea came he!
And he shone bright, and on the right
Went down into the sea.

Higher and higher every day,
Till over the mast at noon—"
The Wedding-Guest here beat his breast,
For he heard the loud bassoon.

The Wedding-Guest
heareth the bridal
music; but the Mariner
continueth his tale.

The bride hath paced into the hall,
Red as a rose is she;
Nodding their heads before her goes
The merry minstrelsy.

The Wedding-Guest he beat his breast,
Yet he cannot choose but hear;
And thus spake on that ancient man,
The bright-eyed Mariner.

The ship driven by a
storm toward the south
pole.

"And now the storm-blast came, and he
Was tyrannous and strong:
He struck with his o'ertaking wings,
And chased us south along.

With sloping masts and dipping prow,
As who pursued with yell and blow
Still treads the shadow of his foe,
And forward bends his head,
The ship drove fast, loud roared the blast,
And southward aye we fled.

And now there came both mist and snow,
And it grew wondrous cold:
And ice, mast-high, came floating by,
As green as emerald.

The land of ice, and of
fearful sounds where
no living thing was to
be seen.

And through the drifts the snowy clifts
Did send a dismal sheen:
Nor shapes of men nor beasts we ken—
The ice was all between.

The ice was here, the ice was there,
The ice was all around:
It cracked and growled, and roared and
    howled,
Like noises in a swound!

Till a great sea-bird,
called the Albatross,
came through the
snow-fog, and was
received with great joy
and hospitality.

At length did cross an Albatross,
Thorough the fog it came;
As if it had been a Christian soul,
We hailed it in God's name.

It ate the food it ne'er had eat,
And round and round it flew.
The ice did split with a thunder-fit;
The helmsman steered us through!

And lo! the Albatross
proveth a bird of good
omen, and followeth

And a good south wind sprung up behind;
The Albatross did follow,

the ship as it returned
northward through fog
and floating ice.

And every day, for food or play,
Came to the mariners' hollo!

In mist or cloud, on mast or shroud,
It perched for vespers nine;
Whiles all the night, through fog-smoke
    white,
Glimmered the white moon-shine."

The ancient Mariner
inhospitably killeth the
pious bird of good
omen.

"God save thee, ancient Mariner!
From the fiends, that plague thee thus!—
Why look'st thou so?"—"With my cross-
    bow
I shot the Albatross."

PART II

"The Sun now rose upon the right:
Out of the sea came he,
Still hid in mist, and on the left
Went down into the sea.

And the good south wind still blew
    behind,
But no sweet bird did follow,
Nor any day for food or play
Came to the mariners' hollo!

His shipmates cry out
against the ancient
Mariner, for killing the
bird of good luck.

And I had done a hellish thing,
And it would work 'em woe:
For all averred, I had killed the bird
That made the breeze to blow.
'Ah wretch!' said they, 'the bird to slay,
That made the breeze to blow!'

But when the fog
cleared off, they justify
the same, and thus
make themselves
accomplices in the
crime.

Nor dim nor red, like God's own head,
The glorious Sun uprist:
Then all averred, I had killed the bird
That brought the fog and mist.

' 'Twas right,' said they, 'such birds to
    slay,
That bring the fog and mist.'

The fair breeze
continues; the ship
enters the Pacific
Ocean, and sails
northward, even till it
reaches the Line.

The fair breeze blew, the white foam flew,
The furrow followed free;
We were the first that ever burst
Into that silent sea.

The ship hath been
suddenly becalmed.

Down dropt the breeze, the sails dropt
    down,
'Twas sad as sad could be;
And we did speak only to break
The silence of the sea!

All in a hot and copper sky,
The bloody Sun, at noon,
Right up above the mast did stand,
No bigger than the Moon.

Day after day, day after day,
We stuck, nor breath nor motion;
As idle as a painted ship
Upon a painted ocean.

And the Albatross
begins to be avenged.

Water, water, everywhere,
And all the boards did shrink;
Water, water, everywhere
Nor any drop to drink.

The very deep did rot: O Christ!
That ever this should be!
Yea, slimy things did crawl with legs
Upon the slimy sea.

About, about, in reel and rout
The death-fires danced at night;
The water, like a witch's oils,
Burnt green, and blue, and white.

A Spirit had followed
them; one of the
invisible inhabitants of

And some in dreams assured were
Of the Spirit that plagued us so:

this planet, neither
departed souls nor
angels; concerning
whom the learned Jew,
Josephus, and the
Platonic
Constantinopolitan,
Michael Psellus, may
be consulted. They are
very numerous, and
there is no climate or
element without one or
more.

Nine fathom deep he had followed us
From the land of mist and snow.

And every tongue, through utter drought,
Was withered at the root;
We could not speak, no more than if
We had been choked with soot.

The ship-mates, in
their sore distress,
would fain throw the
whole guilt on the
ancient Mariner; in
sign whereof they hang
the dead sea-bird
round his neck.

Ah! well a-day! what evil looks
Had I from old and young!
Instead of the cross, the Albatross
About my neck was hung."

## PART III

The ancient Mariner
beholdeth a sign in the
element afar off.

"There passed a weary time. Each throat
Was parched, and glazed each eye.
A weary time! a weary time!
How glazed each weary eye,
When looking westward, I beheld
A something in the sky.

At first it seemed a little speck,
And then it seemed a mist;
It moved and moved, and took at last
A certain shape, I wist.

A speck, a mist, a shape, I wist!
And still it neared and neared:
As if it dodged a water-sprite,
It plunged and tacked and veered.

At its nearer approach,
it seemeth him to be a
ship; and at a dear
ransom he freeth his
speech from the bonds
of thirst.

With throats unslaked, with black lips
    baked,
We could nor laugh nor wail;
Through utter drought all dumb we
    stood!
I bit my arm, I sucked the blood,
And cried, 'A sail! a sail!'

With throats unslaked, with black lips
   baked,
Agape they heard me call;
*A flash of joy;* Gramercy! they for joy did grin,
And all at once their breath drew in,
As they were drinking all.

*And horror follows. For
can it be a ship that
comes onward without
wind or tide?*
'See,! see! (I cried) she tacks no more!
Hither to work us weal;
Without a breeze, without a tide,
She steadies with upright keel!'

The western wave was all a-flame;
The day was well nigh done!
Almost upon the western wave
Rested the broad bright Sun;
When that strange shape drove suddenly
Betwixt us and the Sun.

*It seemeth him but the
skeleton of a ship.*
And straight the Sun was flecked with bars
(Heaven's Mother send us grace!)
As if through a dungeon-grate he peered
With broad and burning face.

Alas! (thought I, and my heart beat loud)
How fast she nears and nears!
Are those her sails that glance in the Sun,
Like restless gossameres?

*And its ribs are seen as
bars on the face of the
setting Sun. The
Spectre-Woman and
her Death-mate, and
no other on board the
skeleton-ship. Like
vessel, like crew!*
Are those her ribs through which the Sun
Did peer, as through a grate?
And is that Woman all her crew?
Is that a Death? and are there two?
Is Death that woman's mate?

Her lips were red, her looks were free,
Her locks were yellow as gold:
Her skin was as white as leprosy,
The nightmare Life-in-Death was she,
Who thicks man's blood with cold.

Death and Life-in-
Death have diced for
the ship's crew, and
she (the latter) winneth
the ancient Mariner.

The naked hulk alongside came,
And the twain were casting dice;
'The game is done! I've won! I've won!'
Quoth she, and whistles thrice.

No twilight within the
courts of the Sun.

The Sun's rim dips; the stars rush out:
At one stride comes the dark;
With far-heard whisper, o'er the sea,
Off shot the spectre-bark.

At the rising of the
Moon,

We listened and looked sideways up!
Fear at my heart, as at a cup,
My life-blood seemed to sip!
The stars were dim, and thick the night,
The steersman's face by his lamp gleamed
      white;
From the sails the dew did drip—
Till clomb above the eastern bar
The hornèd Moon, with one bright star
Within the nether tip.

One after another,

One after one, by the star-dogged Moon,
Too quick for groan or sigh,
Each turned his face with a ghastly pang,
And cursed me with his eye.

His ship-mates drop
down dead.

Four times fifty living men
(And I heard nor sigh nor groan)
With heavy thump, a lifeless lump,
They dropped down one by one.

But Life-in-Death
begins her work on the
ancient Mariner.

The souls did from their bodies fly—
They fled to bliss or woe!
And every soul, it passed me by,
Like the whizz of my cross-bow!"

PART IV

The Wedding-Guest
feareth that a Spirit is
talking to him;

"I fear thee, ancient Mariner!
I fear thy skinny hand!

And thou art long, and lank, and brown,
As is the ribbed sea-sand.

*But the ancient Mariner assureth him of his bodily life, and proceedeth to relate his horrible penance.*

I fear thee and thy glittering eye,
And thy skinny hand, so brown."—
"Fear not, fear not, thou Wedding-Guest!
This body dropt not down.

Alone, alone, all, all alone,
Alone on a wide, wide sea!
And never a saint took pity on
My soul in agony.

*He despiseth the creatures of the calm.*

The many men, so beautiful!
And they all dead did lie:
And a thousand thousand slimy things
Lived on; and so did I.

*And envieth that they should live, and so many lie dead.*

I looked upon the rotting sea,
And drew my eyes away;
I looked upon the rotting deck,
And there the dead men lay.

I looked to heaven, and tried to pray;
But or ever a prayer had gusht,
A wicked whisper came, and made
My heart as dry as dust.

I closed my lids, and kept them close,
And the balls like pulses beat;
For the sky and the sea, and the sea and
    the sky
Lay like a load on my weary eye,
And the dead were at my feet.

*But the curse liveth for him in the eye of the dead men.*

The cold sweat melted from their limbs,
Nor rot nor reek did they:
The look with which they looked on me
Had never passed away.

An orphan's curse would drag to hell
A spirit from on high;

But oh! more horrible than that
Is the curse in a dead man's eye!
Seven days, seven nights, I saw that curse,
And yet I could not die.

*In his loneliness and fixedness he yearneth toward the journeying Moon, and the stars that still sojourn, yet still move onward; and everywhere the blue sky belongs to them, and is their appointed rest, and their native country and their own natural homes, which they enter unannounced, as lords that are certainly expected and yet there is a silent joy at their arrival.*

The moving Moon went up the sky,
And nowhere did abide:
Softly she was going up,
And a star or two beside—

Her beams bemocked the sultry main,
Like April hoar-frost spread;
But where the ship's huge shadow lay,
The charmèd water burnt alway
A still and awful red.

*By the light of the Moon he beholdeth God's creatures of the great calm.*

Beyond the shadow of the ship,
I watched the water-snakes:
They moved in tracks of shining white,
And when they reared, the elfish light
Fell off in hoary flakes.

Within the shadow of the ship
I watched their rich attire:
Blue, glossy green, and velvet black,
They coiled and swam; and every track
Was a flash of golden fire.

*Their beauty and their happiness.*

*He blesseth them in his heart.*

O happy living things! no tongue
Their beauty might declare:
A spring of love gushed from my heart,
And I blessed them unaware:
Sure my kind saint took pity on me,
And I blessed them unaware.

*The spell begins to break.*

The selfsame moment I could pray;
And from my neck so free
The Albatross fell off, and sank
Like lead into the sea."

PART V

"Oh, sleep! it is a gentle thing,
Beloved from pole to pole!
To Mary Queen the praise be given!
She sent the gentle sleep from Heaven,
That slid into my soul.

*By grace of the holy Mother, the ancient Mariner is refreshed with rain.*

The silly buckets on the deck,
That had so long remained,
I dreamt that they were filled with dew;
And when I awoke, it rained.

My lips were wet, my throat was cold,
My garments all were dank;
Sure I had drunken in my dreams,
And still my body drank.

I moved, and could not feel my limbs;
I was so light—almost
I thought that I had died in sleep,
And was a blessèd ghost.

*He heareth sounds and seeth strange sights and commotions in the sky and the element.*

And soon I heard a roaring wind:
It did not come anear;
But with its sound it shook the sails,
That were so thin and sere.

The upper air burst into life!
And a hundred fire-flags sheen,
To and fro they were hurried about!
And to and fro, and in and out,
The wan stars danced between.

And the coming wind did roar more loud,
And the sails did sigh like sedge;
And the rain poured down from one black
    cloud;
The Moon was at its edge.

The thick black cloud was cleft, and still
The Moon was at its side:
Like waters shot from some high crag,
The lightning fell with never a jag,
A river steep and wide.

The loud wind never reached the ship,
Yet now the ship moved on!
Beneath the lightning and the Moon
The dead men gave a groan.

*The bodies of the ship's crew are inspired, and the ship moves on;*

They groaned, they stirred, they all
    uprose,
Nor spake, nor moved their eyes;
It had been strange, even in a dream,
To have seen those dead men rise.

The helmsman steered, the ship moved on;
Yet never a breeze up blew;
The mariners all 'gan work the ropes,
Where they were wont to do;
They raised their limbs like lifeless tools—
We were a ghastly crew.

The body of my brother's son
Stood by me, knee to knee:
The body and I pulled at one rope
But he said nought to me."

*But not by the souls of the men, nor by daemons of earth or middle air, but by a blessed troop of angelic spirits, sent down by the invocation of the guardian saint.*

"I fear thee, ancient Mariner!"
"Be calm, thou Wedding-Guest!
'Twas not those souls that fled in pain,
Which to their corses came again,
But a troop of spirits blest:

For when it dawned—they dropped their
    arms,
And clustered round the mast;

Sweet sounds rose slowly through their
    mouths,
And from their bodies passed.

Around, around, flew each sweet sound,
Then darted to the Sun;
Slowly the sounds came back again,
Now mixed, now one by one.

Sometimes a-dropping from the sky
I heard the sky-lark sing;
Sometimes all little birds that are,
How they seemed to fill the sea and air
With their sweet jargoning!

And now 'twas like all instruments,
Now like a lonely flute;
And now it is an angel's song,
That makes the heavens be mute.

It ceased; yet still the sails made on
A pleasant noise till noon,
A noise like of a hidden brook
In the leafy month of June,
That to the sleeping woods all night
Singeth a quiet tune.

Till noon we quietly sailed on,
Yet never a breeze did breathe:
Slowly and smoothly went the ship,
Moved onward from beneath.

The lonesome Spirit from the south pole carries on the ship as far as the Line, in obedience to the angelic troop, but still requireth vengeance.

Under the keel nine fathom deep,
From the land of mist and snow,
The Spirit slid: and it was he
That made the ship to go.
The sails at noon left off their tune,
And the ship stood still also.

The Sun, right up above the mast,
Had fixed her to the ocean:
But in a minute she 'gan stir,

With a short uneasy motion—
Backwards and forwards half her length
With a short uneasy motion.

Then like a pawing horse let go,
She made a sudden bound:
It flung the blood into my head,
And I fell down in a swound.

The Polar Spirit's
fellow-daemons, the
invisible inhabitants of
the element, take part
in his wrong; and two
of them relate, one to
the other, that penance
long and heavy for the
ancient Mariner hath
been accorded to the
Polar Spirit, who
returneth southward.

How long in that same fit I lay,
I have not to declare;
But ere my living life returned,
I heard and in my soul discerned
Two voices in the air.

'Is it he?' quoth one, 'Is this the man?
By Him who died on cross,
With his cruel bow he laid full low
The harmless Albatross.

The Spirit who bideth by himself
In the land of mist and snow,
He loved the bird that loved the man
Who shot him with his bow.'

The other was a softer voice,
As soft as honey-dew:
Quoth he, 'The man hath penance done,
And penance more will do.' "

PART VI

*First Voice*
" 'But tell me, tell me! speak again,
Thy soft response renewing—
What makes that ship drive on so fast?
What is the ocean doing?'

*Second Voice*

'Still as a slave before his lord,
The ocean hath no blast;
His great bright eye most silently
Up to the Moon is cast—

If he may know which way to go;
For she guides him smooth or grim.
See, brother, see! how graciously
She looketh down on him.'

*First Voice*

The Mariner hath been cast into a trance; for the angelic power causeth the vessel to drive northward faster than human life could endure.

'But why drives on that ship so fast,
Without or wave or wind?'

*Second Voice*

'The air is cut away before,
And closes from behind.

Fly, brother, fly! more high, more high!
Or we shall be belated:
For slow and slow that ship will go,
When the Mariner's trance is abated.'

The supernatural motion is retarded; the Mariner awakes, and his penance begins anew.

I woke, and we were sailing on
As in a gentle weather:
'Twas night, calm night, the Moon was high,
The dead men stood together.

All stood together on the deck,
For a charnel-dungeon fitter:
All fixed on me their stony eyes,
That in the Moon did glitter.

The pang, the curse, with which they died,
Had never passed away:
I could not draw my eyes from theirs,
Nor turn them up to pray.

*The curse is finally expiated.*

And now this spell was snapt: once more
I viewed the ocean green,
And looked far forth, yet little saw
Of what had else been seen—

Like one, that on a lonesome road
Doth walk in fear and dread,
And having once turned round walks on,
And turns no more his head;
Because he knows a frightful fiend
Doth close behind him tread.

But soon there breathed a wind on me,
Nor sound nor motion made:
Its path was not upon the sea,
In ripple or in shade.

It raised my hair, it fanned my cheek
Like a meadow-gale of spring—
It mingled strangely with my fears,
Yet it felt like a welcoming.

Swiftly, swiftly flew the ship,
Yet she sailed softly too:
Sweetly, sweetly blew the breeze—
On me alone it blew.

*And the ancient Mariner beholdeth his native country.*

Oh! dream of joy! is this indeed
The light-house top I see?
Is this the hill? is this the kirk?
Is this mine own countree?

We drifted o'er the harbor-bar,
And I with sobs did pray—
O let me be awake, my God!
Or let me sleep alway.

The harbor-bay was clear as glass,
So smoothly it was strewn!
And on the bay the moonlight lay,
And the shadow of the Moon.

The rock shone bright, the kirk no less,
That stands above the rock:
The moonlight steeped in silentness
The steady weathercock.

And the bay was white with silent light
Till rising from the same,
Full many shapes, that shadows were,
In crimson colors came.

The angelic spirits leave the dead bodies,

A little distance from the prow
Those crimson shadows were:
I turned my eyes upon the deck—
Oh, Christ, what saw I there!

And appear in their own forms of light.

Each corse lay flat, lifeless and flat,
And, by the holy rood!
A man all light, a seraph-man,
On every corse there stood.

This seraph-band, each waved his hand;
It was a heavenly sight!
They stood as signals to the land,
Each one a lovely light;

This seraph-band, each waved his hand,
No voice did they impart—
No voice; but oh! the silence sank
Like music on my heart.

But soon I heard the dash of oars,
I heard the Pilot's cheer;
My head was turned perforce away,
And I saw a boat appear.

The Pilot and the Pilot's boy,
I heard them coming fast:
Dear Lord in Heaven! it was a joy
The dead men could not blast.

I saw a third—I heard his voice:
It is the Hermit good!
He singeth loud his godly hymns
That he makes in the wood.
He'll shrieve my soul; he'll wash away
The Albatross's blood."

### PART VII

The Hermit of the Wood,

"This Hermit good lives in that wood
Which slopes down to the sea.
How loudly his sweet voice he rears!
He loves to talk with marineres
That come from a far countree.

He kneels at morn, and noon, and eve—
He hath a cushion plump:
It is the moss that wholly hides
The rotted old oak-stump.

The skiff-boat neared: I heard them talk,
'Why, this is strange, I trow!
Where are those lights so many and fair,
That signal made but now?'

Approacheth the ship with wonder.

'Strange, by my faith!' the Hermit said—
'And they answered not our cheer!
The planks look warped! and see those
    sails,
How thin they are and sere!
I never saw aught like to them,
Unless perchance it were

Brown skeletons of leaves that lag
My forest-brook along;
When the ivy-tod is heavy with snow,
And the owlet whoops to the wolf below,
That eats the she-wolf's young.'

'Dear Lord! it hath a fiendish look—
(The Pilot made reply)

I am a-feared'—'Push on, push on!'
Said the Hermit cheerily.

The boat came closer to the ship,
But I nor spake nor stirred;
The boat came close beneath the ship,
And straight a sound was heard.

The ship suddenly
sinketh.

Under the water it rumbled on,
Still louder and more dread:
It reached the ship, it split the bay;
The ship went down like lead.

The ancient Mariner is
saved in the Pilot's
boat.

Stunned by that loud and dreadful sound,
Which sky and ocean smote,
Like one that hath been seven days
    drowned
My body lay afloat;
But swift as dreams, myself I found
Within the Pilot's boat.

Upon the whirl, where sank the ship,
The boat spun round and round;
And all was still, save that the hill
Was telling of the sound.

I moved my lips—the Pilot shrieked
And fell down in a fit;
The holy Hermit raised his eyes,
And prayed where he did sit.

I took the oars: the Pilot's boy,
Who now doth crazy go,
Laughed loud and long, and all the while
His eyes went to and fro.
'Ha! ha!' quoth he, 'full plain I see,
The Devil knows how to row.'

And now, all in my own countree,
I stood on the firm land!

The Hermit stepped forth from the boat,
And scarcely he could stand.

'O shrieve me, shrieve me, holy man!'
The Hermit crossed his brow.
'Say quick,' quoth he, 'I bid thee say—
What manner of man art thou?'

Forthwith this frame of mine was
    wrenched
With a woful agony,
Which forced me to begin my tale;
And then it left me free.

Since then, at an uncertain hour,
That agony returns:
And till my ghastly tale is told,
This heart within me burns.

I pass, like night, from land to land;
I have strange power of speech;
That moment that his face I see,
I know the man that must hear me:
To him my tale I teach.

What loud uproar bursts from that door!
The wedding-guests are there:
But in the garden-bower the bride
And bride-maids singing are:
And hark the little vesper bell
Which biddeth me to prayer!

O Wedding-Guest! this soul hath been
Alone on a wide, wide sea;
So lonely 'twas, that God himself
Scarce seemed there to be.

O sweeter than the marriage-feast,
'Tis sweeter far to me,
To walk together to the kirk
With a goodly company!—

To walk together to the kirk,
And all together pray,
While each to his great Father bends,
Old men, and babes, and loving friends,
And youths and maidens gay!

And to teach, by his
own example, love and
reverence to all things
that God made and
loveth.

Farewell, farewell! but this I tell
To thee, thou Wedding-Guest!
He prayeth well, who loveth well
Both man and bird and beast.

He prayeth best, who loveth best
All things both great and small;
For the dear God who loveth us,
He made and loveth all."

The Mariner, whose eye is bright,
Whose beard with age is hoar,
Is gone: and now the Wedding-Guest
Turned from the Bridegroom's door.

He went like one that hath been stunned,
And is of sense forlorn:
A sadder and a wiser man,
He rose the morrow morn.

# WALTER SAVAGE LANDOR/1775–1864

*Rose Aylmer*

Ah, what avails the sceptred race!
    Ah, what the form divine!
What every virtue, every grace!
    Rose Aylmer, all were thine.

Rose Aylmer, whom these wakeful eyes
    May weep, but never see,

A night of memories and sighs
I consecrate to thee.


### Past Ruined Ilion

Past ruined Ilion Helen lives,
   Alcestis rises from the shades;
Verse calls them forth; 'tis verse that gives
   Immortal youth to mortal maids.

Soon shall oblivion's deepening veil
   Hide all the peopled hills you see,
The gay, the proud, while lovers hail
   These many summers you and me.


### Dirce

Stand close around, ye Stygian set,
   With Dirce in one boat conveyed!
Or Charon, seeing, may forget
   That he is old and she a shade.


### On Lucretia Borgia's Hair

Borgia, thou once wert almost too august
And high for adoration; now thou'rt dust;
All that remains of thee these plaits unfold,
Calm hair meandering in pellucid gold.


### Behold, O Aspasia! I Send You Verses

Beauty! thou art a wanderer on the earth,
   And hast no temple in the fairest isle
Or city over-sea, where Wealth and Mirth
   And all the Graces, all the Muses, smile.

Yet these have always nursed thee with such fond,
    Such lasting love, that they have followed up
Thy steps through every land, and placed beyond
    The reach of thirsty Time thy nectar-cup.

Thou art a wanderer, Beauty! like the rays
    That now upon the platan, now upon
The sleepy lake, glance quick or idly gaze,
    And now are manifold and now are none.

I have called, panting, after thee, and thou
    Hast turned and looked and said some pretty word,
Parting the hair, perhaps, upon my brow,
    And telling me none ever was preferred.

In more than one bright form hast thou appeared,
    In more than one sweet dialect hast thou spoken:
Beauty! thy spells the heart within me heard,
    Grieved that they bound it, grieves that they are
        broken.


### On His Seventy-Fifth Birthday

I strove with none, for none was worth my strife.
    Nature I loved and, next to Nature, Art:
I warmed both hands before the fire of life;
    It sinks, and I am ready to depart.


# THOMAS MOORE/1779–1852


### Oft, in the Stilly Night

Oft, in the stilly night,
    Ere Slumber's chain has bound me,
Fond Memory brings the light

Of other days around me;
    The smiles, the tears,
    Of boyhood's years,
The words of love then spoken;
    The eyes that shone,
    Now dimmed and gone,
The cheerful hearts now broken!
Thus, in the stilly night,
    Ere Slumber's chain hath bound me,
Sad Memory brings the light
    Of other days around me.

When I remember all
    The friends, so linked together,
I've seen around me fall,
    Like leaves in wintry weather;
    I feel like one,
    Who treads alone
Some banquet-hall deserted,
    Whose lights are fled,
    Whose garlands dead,
And all but he departed!
Thus, in the stilly night,
    Ere Slumber's chain has bound me,
Sad Memory brings the light
    Of other days around me.


LEIGH HUNT/1784-1859


*To a Fish*


You strange, astonished-looking, angle-faced,
Dreary-mouthed, gaping wretches of the sea,
Gulping salt water everlastingly,
Cold-blooded, though with red your blood be graced,
And mute, though dwellers in the roaring waste;

And you, all shapes beside, that fishy be—
Some round, some flat, some long, all devilry,
Legless, unloving, infamously chaste:

O scaly, slippery, wet, swift, staring wights,
What is't ye do? What life lead? eh, dull goggles?
How do ye vary your vile days and nights?
How pass your Sundays? Are ye still but joggles
In ceaseless wash? Still naught but gapes and bites,
And drinks, and stares, diversified with boggles?

## A Fish Answers

Amazing monster! that for aught I know,
With the first sight of thee didst make our race
For ever stare! O flat and shocking face,
Grimly divided from the breast below!
Thou that on dry land horribly dost go
With a split body and most ridiculous pace,
Prong after prong, disgracer of all grace,
Long-useless-finned, haired, upright, unwet, slow!

O breather of unbreathable, sword-sharp air,
How canst exist? How bear thyself, thou dry
And dreary sloth? What particle canst share
Of the only blessed life, the watery?
I sometimes see of ye an actual *pair*
Go by! linked fin by fin! most odiously.

## Rondeau

Jenny kissed me when we met,
    Jumping from the chair she sat in;
Time, you thief, who love to get
    Sweets into your list, put that in:

Say I'm weary, say I'm sad,
  Say that health and wealth have missed me,
Say I'm growing old, but add,
  Jenny kissed me.


# GEORGE GORDON, LORD BYRON
## 1788–1824

*When We Two Parted*

When we two parted
  In silence and tears,
Half broken-hearted
  To sever for years,
Pale grew thy cheek and cold,
  Colder thy kiss;
Truly that hour foretold
  Sorrow to this.

The dew of the morning
  Sunk chill on my brow—
It felt like the warning
  Of what I feel now.
Thy vows are all broken,
  And light is thy fame:
I hear thy name spoken,
  And share in its shame.

They name thee before me,
  A knell to mine ear;
A shudder comes o'er me—
  Why wert thou so dear?
They know not I knew thee,
  Who knew thee too well:—
Long, long shall I rue thee,
  Too deeply to tell.

In secret me met—
   In silence I grieve,
That thy heart could forget,
   Thy spirit deceive.
If I should meet thee
   After long years,
How should I greet thee?—
   With silence and tears.


## She Walks in Beauty

She walks in Beauty, like the night
   Of cloudless climes and starry skies;
And all that's best of dark and bright
   Meet in her aspect and her eyes:
Thus mellowed to that tender light
   Which Heaven to gaudy day denies.

One shade the more, one ray the less,
   Had half impaired the nameless grace
Which waves in every raven tress,
   Or softly lightens o'er her face;
Where thoughts serenely sweet express,
   How pure, how dear their dwelling-place.

And on that cheek, and o'er that brow,
   So soft, so calm, yet eloquent,
The smiles that win, the tints that glow,
   But tell of days in goodness spent,
A mind at peace with all below,
   A heart whose love is innocent!


## The Destruction of Sennacherib

The Assyrian came down like the wolf on the fold,
And his cohorts were gleaming in purple and gold;

And the sheen of their spears was like stars on the sea,
When the blue wave rolls nightly on deep Galilee.

Like the leaves of the forest when summer is green,
That host with their banners at sunset were seen:
Like the leaves of the forest when autumn hath blown,
That host on the morrow lay withered and strown.

For the angel of Death spread his wings on the blast,
And breathed in the face of the foe as he passed;
And the eyes of the sleepers waxed deadly and chill,
And their hearts but once heaved—and for ever grew still!

And there lay the steed with his nostril all wide,
But through it there rolled not the breath of his pride;
And the foam of his gasping lay white on the turf,
And cold as the spray of the rock-beating surf.

And there lay the rider distorted and pale,
With the dew on his brow, and the rust on his mail:
And the tents were all silent—the banners alone—
The lances unlifted—the trumpet unblown.

And the widows of Ashur are loud in their wail,
And the idols are broke in the temple of Baal;
And the might of the Gentile, unsmote by the sword,
Hath melted like snow in the glance of the Lord!

### So We'll Go No More A-Roving

So we'll go no more a-roving
  So late into the night,
Though the heart be still as loving,
  And the moon be still as bright.

For the sword outwears its sheath,
  And the soul wears out the breast,

And the heart must pause to breathe,
   And Love itself have rest.

Though the night was made for loving,
   And the day returns too soon,
Yet we'll go no more a-roving
   By the light of the moon.

# PERCY BYSSHE SHELLEY/1792–1822

## *Stanzas—April, 1814*

Away! the moor is dark beneath the moon,
   Rapid clouds have drank the last pale beam of even:
Away! the gathering winds will call the darkness soon,
   And profoundest midnight shroud the serene lights of
      heaven.

Pause not! the time is past! Every voice cries, Away!
   Tempt not with one last tear thy friend's ungentle mood:
Thy lover's eye, so glazed and cold, dares not entreat thy stay:
   Duty and dereliction guide thee back to solitude.

Away, away! to thy sad and silent home;
   Pour bitter tears on its desolated hearth;
Watch the dim shades as like ghosts they go and come,
   And complicate strange webs of melancholy mirth.

The leaves of wasted autumn woods shall float around thine
      head;
   The blooms of dewy spring shall gleam beneath thy feet:
But thy soul or this world must fade in the frost that binds
   the dead,
   Ere midnight's frown and morning's smile, ere thou and
      peace may meet.

The cloud shadows of midnight possess their own repose,
    For the weary winds are silent, or the moon is in the deep:
Some respite to its turbulence unresting ocean knows;
    Whatever moves, or toils, or grieves, hath its appointed
      sleep.

Thou in the grave shalt rest—yet till the phantoms flee
    Which that house and heath and garden made dear to thee
      erewhile,
Thy remembrance, and repentance, and deep musings are not
    free
    From the music of two voices and the light of one sweet
      smile.

## Ozymandias

I met a traveller from an antique land
Who said: Two vast and trunkless legs of stone
Stand in the desert . . . Near them, on the sand,
Half sunk, a shattered visage lies, whose frown,
And wrinkled lip, and sneer of cold command,
Tell that its sculptor well those passions read
Which yet survive, stamped on these lifeless things,
The hand that mocked them, and the heart that fed:
And on the pedestal these words appear:
"My name is Ozymandias, king of kings:
Look on my works, ye Mighty, and despair!"
Nothing beside remains. Round the decay
Of that colossal wreck, boundless and bare
The lone and level sands stretch far away.

## Ode to the West Wind

### I

O wild West Wind, thou breath of Autumn's being,
Thou, from whose unseen presence the leaves dead
Are driven, like ghosts from an enchanter fleeing,

Yellow, and black, and pale, and hectic red,
Pestilence-stricken multitudes: O thou,
Who chariotest to their dark wintry bed

The wingèd seeds, where they lie cold and low,
Each like a corpse within its grave, until
Thine azure sister of the Spring shall blow

Her clarion o'er the dreaming earth, and fill
(Driving sweet buds like flocks to feed in air)
With living hues and odours plain and hill:

Wild Spirit, which art moving everywhere;
Destroyer and preserver; hear, oh, hear!

### II

Thou on whose stream, mid the steep sky's
     commotion,
Loose clouds like earth's decaying leaves are shed,
Shook from the tangled boughs of Heaven and
     Ocean,

Angels of rain and lightning: there are spread
On the blue surface of thine aëry surge,
Like the bright hair uplifted from the head

Of some fierce Maenad, even from the dim verge
Of the horizon to the zenith's height,
The locks of the approaching storm. Thou dirge

Of the dying year, to which this closing night
Will be the dome of a vast sepulchre,
Vaulted with all thy congregated might

Of vapours, from whose solid atmosphere
Black rain, and fire, and hail will burst: oh, hear!


III

Thou who didst waken from his summer dreams
The blue Mediterranean, where he lay,
Lulled by the coil of his crystàlline streams,

Beside a pumice isle in Baiae's bay,
And saw in sleep old palaces and towers
Quivering within the wave's intenser day,

All overgrown with azure moss and flowers
So sweet, the sense faints picturing them! Thou
For whose path the Atlantic's level powers

Cleave themselves into chasms, while far below
The sea-blooms and the oozy woods which wear
The sapless foliage of the ocean, know

Thy voice, and suddenly grow gray with fear,
And tremble and despoil themselves: oh, hear!


IV

If I were a dead leaf thou mightest bear;
If I were a swift cloud to fly with thee;
A wave to pant beneath thy power, and share

The impulse of thy strength, only less free
Than thou, O uncontrollable! If even
I were as in my boyhood, and could be

The comrade of thy wanderings over Heaven,
As then, when to outstrip thy skiey speed
Scarce seemed a vision; I would ne'er have striven

As thus with thee in prayer in my sore need.
Oh, lift me as a wave, a leaf, a cloud!
I fall upon the thorns of life! I bleed!

A heavy weight of hours has chained and bowed
One too like thee: tameless, and swift, and proud.

V

Make me thy lyre, even as the forest is:
What if my leaves are falling like its own!
The tumult of thy mighty harmonies

Will take from both a deep, autumnal tone,
Sweet though in sadness. Be thou, Spirit fierce,
My spirit! Be thou me, impetuous one!

Drive my dead thoughts over the universe
Like withered leaves to quicken a new birth!
And, by the incantation of this verse,

Scatter, as from an unextinguished hearth
Ashes and sparks, my words among mankind!
Be through my lips to unawakened earth

The trumpet of a prophecy! O, Wind,
If Winter comes, can Spring be far behind?

## Love's Philosophy

The fountains mingle with the river
    And the rivers with the ocean,
The winds of heaven mix for ever
    With a sweet emotion;
Nothing in the world is single;
    All things by a law divine
In one spirit meet and mingle.
    Why not I with thine?—

See the mountains kiss high heaven
    And the waves clasp one another;
No sister-flower would be forgiven
    If it disdained its brother;
And the sunlight clasps the earth
    And the moonbeams kiss the sea:
What is all this sweet work worth
    If thou kiss not me?

## Fragment: Wake the Serpent Not

Wake the serpent not—lest he
Should not know the way to go,—
Let him crawl which yet lies sleeping
Through the deep grass of the meadow!
Not a bee shall hear him creeping,
Not a may-fly shall awaken
From its cradling blue-bell shaken,
Not the starlight as he's sliding
Through the grass with silent gliding.

## To a Skylark

Hail to thee, blithe Spirit!
    Bird thou never wert,
That from Heaven, or near it,

Pourest thy full heart
In profuse strains of unpremeditated art.

Higher still and higher
From the earth thou springest
Like a cloud of fire;
The blue deep thou wingest,
And singing still dost soar, and soaring ever singest.

In the golden lightning
Of the sunken sun,
O'er which clouds are bright'ning,
Thou dost float and run;
Like an unbodied joy whose race is just begun.

The pale purple even
Melts around thy flight;
Like a star of Heaven,
In the broad daylight
Thou art unseen, but yet I hear thy shrill delight,

Keen as are the arrows
Of that silver sphere,
Whose intense lamp narrows
In the white dawn clear
Until we hardly see—we feel that it is there.

All the earth and air
With thy voice is loud,
As, when night is bare,
From one lonely cloud
The moon rains out her beams, and Heaven is overflowed.

What thou art we know not;
What is most like thee?
From rainbow clouds there flow not
Drops so bright to see
As from thy presence showers a rain of melody.

Like a poet hidden
  In the light of thought,
Singing hymns unbidden,
  Till the world is wrought
To sympathy with hopes and fears it heeded not:

Like a high-born maiden
  In a palace-tower,
Soothing her love-laden
  Soul in secret hour
With music sweet as love, which overflows her bower:

Like a glow-worm golden
  In a dell of dew,
Scattering unbeholden
  Its aëreal hue
Among the flowers and grass, which screen it from the
    view!

Like a rose embowered
  In its own green leaves,
By warm winds deflowered,
  Till the scent it gives
Makes faint with too much sweet those heavy-wingèd
    thieves:

Sound of vernal showers
  On the twinkling grass,
Rain-awakened flowers,
  All that ever was
Joyous, and clear, and fresh, thy music doth surpass:

Teach us, Sprite or Bird,
  What sweet thoughts are thine:
I have never heard
  Praise of love or wine
That panted forth a flood of rapture so divine.

Chorus Hymeneal,
   Or triumphal chant,
Matched with thine would be all
   But an empty vaunt,
A thing wherein we feel there is some hidden want.

   What objects are the fountains
      Of thy happy strain?
What fields, or waves, or mountains?
      What shapes of sky or plain?
What love of thine own kind? what ignorance of pain?

   With thy clear keen joyance
      Languor cannot be:
Shadow of annoyance
      Never came near thee:
Thou lovest—but ne'er knew love's sad satiety.

   Waking or asleep,
      Thou of death must deem
Things more true and deep
      Than we mortals dream,
Or how could thy notes flow in such a crystal stream?

   We look before and after,
      And pine for what is not:
Our sincerest laughter
      With some pain is fraught;
Our sweetest songs are those that tell of saddest thought.

   Yet if we could scorn
      Hate, and pride, and fear;
If we were things born
      Not to shed a tear,
I know not how thy joy we ever should come near.

   Better than all measures
      Of delightful sound,
Better than all treasures

That in books are found,
Thy skill to poet were, thou scorner of the ground!

Teach me half the gladness
    That thy brain must know,
Such harmonious madness
    From my lips would flow
The world should listen then—as I am listening now.


### Summer and Winter

It was a bright and cheerful afternoon,
Towards the end of the sunny month of June,
When the north wind congregates in crowds
The floating mountains of the silver clouds
From the horizon—and the stainless sky
Opens beyond them like eternity.
All things rejoiced beneath the sun; the weeds,
The river, and the corn-fields, and the reeds;
The willow leaves that glanced in the light breeze,
And the firm foliage of the larger trees.

It was a winter such as when birds die
In the deep forests; and the fishes lie
Stiffened in the translucent ice, which makes
Even the mud and slime of the warm lakes
A wrinkled clod as hard as brick; and when,
Among their children, comfortable men
Gather about great fires, and yet feel cold:
Alas, then, for the homeless beggar old!


### Lines: When the Lamp Is Shattered

When the lamp is shattered
The light in the dust lies dead—
    When the cloud is scattered
The rainbow's glory is shed.

When the lute is broken,
Sweet tones are remembered not;
  When the lips have spoken,
Loved accents are soon forgot.

  As music and splendour
Survive not the lamp and the lute,
  The heart's echoes render
No song when the spirit is mute:—
  No song but sad dirges,
Like the wind through a ruined cell,
  Or the mournful surges
That ring the dead seaman's knell.

  When hearts have once mingled
Love first leaves the well-built nest;
  The weak one is singled
To endure what it once possessed.
  O Love! who bewailest
The frailty of all things here,
  Why choose you the frailest
For your cradle, your home, and your bier?

  Its passions will rock thee
As the storms rock the ravens on high;
  Bright season will mock thee,
Like the sun from a wintry sky.
  From thy nest every rafter
Will rot, and thine eagle home
  Leave thee naked to laughter,
When leaves fall and cold winds come.


*A Dirge*


  Rough wind, that moanest loud
    Grief too sad for song;
  Wild wind, when sullen cloud
    Knells all the night long;

Sad storm, whose tears are vain,
   Bare woods, whose branches strain,
Deep caves and dreary main,—
   Wail, for the world's wrong!


# JOHN CLARE/1793–1864


### *Little Trotty Wagtail*

Little trotty wagtail, he went in the rain,
And tittering, tottering sideways he ne'er got straight again.
He stooped to get a worm, and looked up to get a fly,
And then he flew away ere his feathers they were dry.

Little trotty wagtail, he waddled in the mud,
And left his little footmarks, trample where he would.
He waddled in the water-pudge, and waggle went his tail,
And chirrup up his wings to dry upon the garden rail.

Little trotty wagtail, you nimble all about,
And in the dimpling water-pudge you waddle in and out;
Your home is nigh at hand, and in the warm pigsty,
So, little Master Wagtail, I'll bid you a good-bye.


### *The Rawk o' the Autumn*

The rawk[1] o' the autumn hangs over the woodlands
   Like smoke from a city dismembered and pale;
The sun without beams burns dim o'er the floodlands
   Where white cawdy-mawdies[2] slow swiver[3] and sail;
The flood froths away like a fathomless ocean,
   The wind winnows chill like a breeze from the sea,

---

[1] mist   [2] curlews   [3] flutter

And thoughts of my Susan give my heart an emotion
　　To think does she e'er waste a thought upon me.

Full oft I think so on the banks of the meadows,
　　Where the pale cawdy-mawdy flies swopping[1] all day;
I think of our true love where grass and flowers hid us
　　As by the dyke-side of the meadows we lay.
The seasons have changed since I sat wi' my true love;
　　Now the flood roars and raves o'er the bed where we lay;
There the bees kissed the flowers. Has she got a new love?
　　I feel like a wreck of the flood cast away.

The rawk of the autumn hangs o'er the woodland
　　Like smoke from a city sulphurously grey;
The heronshaw lonely hangs over the floodland
　　And cranks[2] its lone story throughout the dull day;
There's no green on the hedges, no leaves on the dark
　　　　wood,
　　No cows on the pasture or sheep on the lea;
The linnets chirp still, and how happy the lark would
　　Sing songs to sweet Susan to remind her of me.


*Married to a Soldier*

　　The pride of all the village,
　　　　The fairest to be seen,
　　The pride of all the village
　　　　That might have been a queen,
　　Has bid goodbye to neighbors
　　　　And left the dance and play
　　And married to a soldier
　　　　And wandered far away.

　　The cottage is neglected,
　　　　Where young men used to go
　　And talk about her beauty

[1] swooping　　[2] croaks

And see her come and go;
The bench agen her cottage
　　Where she used to work at eve
Is vanished with the woodbine;
　　And all are taken leave.

Her cottage is neglected,
　　Her garden gathers green,
The summer comes unnoticed,
　　Her flowers are never seen;
There's none to tie a blossom up
　　Or clean a weed away;
She's married to a soldier
　　And wandered far away.

The neighbors wonder at her,
　　And surely well they may,
To think one so could flatter
　　Her heart to go away.
But the cocked hat and the feather
　　Appeared so very gay,
She bundled clothes together
　　And married far away.


*Secret Love*


I hid my love when young till I
Couldn't bear the buzzing of a fly;
I hid my love to my despite
Till I could not bear to look at light:
I dare not gaze upon her face
But left her memory in each place;
Where'er I saw a wild flower lie
I kissed and bade my love goodbye.

I met her in the greenest dells,
Where dewdrops pearl the wood bluebells;
The lost breeze kissed her bright blue eye,

The bee kissed and went singing by,
A sunbeam found a passage there,
A gold chain round her neck so fair;
As secret as the wild bee's song
She lay there all the summer long.

I hid my love in field and town
Till e'en the breeze would knock me down;
The bees seemed singing ballads o'er,
The fly's bass turned a lion's roar;
And even silence found a tongue,
To haunt me all the summer long;
The riddle nature could not prove
Was nothing else but secret love.


### Meet Me in the Green Glen

Love, meet me in the green glen,
  Beside the tall elm-tree,
Where the sweetbrier smells so sweet agen;
  There come with me.
    Meet me in the green glen.

Meet me at the sunset
  Down in the green glen,
Where we've often met
  By hawthorn-tree and foxes' den,
    Meet me in the green glen.

Meet me in the green glen,
  By sweetbrier bushes there;
Meet me by your own sen,[1]
  Where the wild thyme blossoms fair.
    Meet me in the green glen.

[1] self

Meet me by the sweetbrier,
   By the mole-hill swelling there;
When the west glows like a fire
   God's crimson bed is there.
     Meet me in the green glen.

### Badger

When midnight comes a host of boys and men
Go out and track the badger to his den,
And put a sack within the hole, and lie
Till the old grunting badger passes by.
He comes and hears—they let the strongest loose.
The old fox hears the noise and drops the goose.
The poacher shoots and hurries from the cry,
And the old hare half wounded buzzes by.
They get a forked stick to bear him down
And clap the dogs and take him to the town,
And bait him all the day with many dogs,
And laugh and shout and fright the scampering hogs.
He runs along and bites at all he meets:
They shout and hollo down the noisy streets.

He turns about to face the loud uproar
And drives the rebels to their very door.
The frequent stone is hurled where'er they go;
When badgers fight, then every one's a foe.
The dogs are clapt and urged to join the fray;
The badger turns and drives them all away.
Though scarcely half as big, demure and small,
He fights with dogs for hours and beats them all.
The heavy mastiff, savage in the fray,
Lies down and licks his feet and turns away.
The bulldog knows his match and waxes cold,
The badger grins and never leaves his hold.
He drives the crowd and follows at their heels
And bites them through—the drunkard swears and reels.

The frighted women take the boys away,
The blackguard laughs and hurries on the fray.
He tries to reach the woods, an awkward race,
But sticks and cudgels quickly stop the chase.
He turns agen and drives the noisy crowd
And beats the many dogs in noises loud.
He drives away and beats them every one,
And then they loose them all and set them on.
He falls as dead and kicked by boys and men,
Then starts and grins and drives the crowd agen;
Till kicked and torn and beaten out he lies
And leaves his hold and cackles, groans, and dies.


# JOHN KEATS/1795–1821


*On First Looking into Chapman's Homer*

Much have I travelled in the realms of gold,
And many goodly states and kingdoms seen;
Round many western islands have I been
Which bards in fealty to Apollo hold.
Oft of one wide expanse had I been told
That deep-browed Homer ruled as his demesne;
Yet did I never breathe its pure serene
Till I heard Chapman speak out loud and bold:
Then felt I like some watcher of the skies
When a new planet swims into his ken;
Or like stout Cortez when with eagle eyes
He stared at the Pacific—and all his men
Looked at each other with a wild surmise—
Silent, upon a peak in Darien.

## *Ode to a Nightingale*

My heart aches, and a drowsy numbness pains
   My sense, as though of hemlock I had drunk,
Or emptied some dull opiate to the drains
   One minute past, and Lethe-wards had sunk:
'Tis not through envy of thy happy lot,
   But being too happy in thine happiness,—
      That thou, light-wingèd Dryad of the trees,
        In some melodious plot
   Of beechen green, and shadows numberless,
      Singest of summer in full-throated ease.

O, for a draught of vintage! that hath been
   Cooled a long age in the deep-delvèd earth,
Tasting of Flora and the country green,
   Dance, and Provençal song, and sunburnt mirth!
O for a beaker full of the warm South,
   Full of the true, the blushful Hippocrene,
      With beaded bubbles winking at the brim,
        And purple-stainèd mouth;
   That I might drink, and leave the world unseen,
      And with thee fade away into the forest dim:

Fade far away, dissolve, and quite forget
   What thou among the leaves hast never known,
The weariness, the fever, and the fret
   Here, where men sit and hear each other groan;
Where palsy shakes a few, sad, last gray hairs,
   Where youth grows pale, and spectre-thin, and dies;
      Where but to think is to be full of sorrow
        And leaden-eyed despairs,
   Where Beauty cannot keep her lustrous eyes,
      Or new Love pine at them beyond to-morrow.

Away! away! for I will fly to thee,
   Not charioted by Bacchus and his pards,
But on the viewless wings of Poesy,
   Though the dull brain perplexes and retards:

Already with thee! tender is the night,
   And haply the Queen-Moon is on her throne,
      Clustered around by all her starry Fays;
         But here there is no light,
Save what from heaven is with the breezes blown
   Through verdurous glooms and winding mossy
      ways.

I cannot see what flowers are at my feet,
   Nor what soft incense hangs upon the boughs,
But, in embalmed darkness, guess each sweet
   Wherewith the seasonable month endows
The grass, the thicket, and the fruit-tree wild;
   White hawthorn, and the pastoral eglantine;
      Fast fading violets covered up in leaves;
         And mid-May's eldest child,
   The coming musk-rose, full of dewy wine,
      The murmurous haunt of flies on summer eves.

Darkling I listen; and, for many a time
   I have been half in love with easeful Death,
Called him soft names in many a musèd rhyme,
   To take into the air my quiet breath;
Now more than ever seems it rich to die,
   To cease upon the midnight with no pain,
      While thou art pouring forth thy soul abroad
         In such an ecstasy!
   Still wouldst thou sing, and I have ears in vain—
      To thy high requiem become a sod.

Thou wast not born for death, immortal Bird!
   No hungry generations tread thee down;
The voice I hear this passing night was heard
   In ancient days by emperor and clown:
Perhaps the self-same song that found a path
   Through the sad heart of Ruth, when, sick for home,
      She stood in tears amid the alien corn;
         The same that oft-times hath

Charmed magic casements, opening on the foam
  Of perilous seas, in faery lands forlorn.

Forlorn! the very word is like a bell
  To toll me back from thee to my sole self!
Adieu! the fancy cannot cheat so well
  As she is famed to do, deceiving elf.
Adieu! adieu! thy plaintive anthem fades
  Past the near meadows, over the still stream,
    Up the hill-side; and now 'tis buried deep
      In the next valley-glades:
  Was it a vision, or a waking dream?
    Fled is that music:—Do I wake or sleep?


### Ode on a Grecian Urn

Thou still unravished bride of quietness,
  Thou foster-child of silence and slow time,
Sylvan historian, who canst thus express
  A flowery tale more sweetly than our rhyme:
What leaf-fringed legend haunts about thy shape
  Of deities or mortals, or of both,
    In Tempe or the dales of Arcady?
What men or gods are these? What maidens loth?
  What mad pursuit? What struggle to escape?
    What pipes and timbrels? What wild ecstasy?

Heard melodies are sweet, but those unheard
  Are sweeter; therefore, ye soft pipes, play on;
Not to the sensual ear, but, more endeared,
  Pipe to the spirit ditties of no tone:
Fair youth, beneath the trees, thou canst not leave
  Thy song, nor ever can those trees be bare;
    Bold Lover, never, never canst thou kiss,
Though winning near the goal—yet, do not grieve;
  She cannot fade, though thou hast not thy bliss,
    For ever wilt thou love, and she be fair!

Ah, happy, happy boughs! that cannot shed
    Your leaves, nor ever bid the spring adieu;
And, happy melodist, unwearièd,
    For ever piping songs for ever new;
More happy love! more happy, happy love!
    For ever warm and still to be enjoyed,
        For ever panting, and for ever young;
All breathing human passion far above,
    That leaves a heart high-sorrowful and cloyed,
        A burning forehead, and a parching tongue.

Who are these coming to the sacrifice?
    To what green altar, O mysterious priest,
Lead'st thou that heifer lowing at the skies,
    And all her silken flanks with garlands dressed?
What little town by river or sea shore,
    Or mountain-built with peaceful citadel,
        Is emptied of this folk, this pious morn?
And, little town, thy streets for evermore
    Will silent be; and not a soul to tell
        Why thou art desolate, can e'er return.

O Attic shape! Fair attitude! with brede
    Of marble men and maidens overwrought,
With forest branches and the trodden weed;
    Thou, silent form, dost tease us out of thought
As doth eternity: Cold Pastoral!
    When old age shall this generation waste,
        Thou shalt remain, in midst of other woe
Than ours, a friend to man, to whom thou say'st,
    "Beauty is truth, truth beauty,"—that is all
        Ye know on earth, and all ye need to know.


### Lines on the Mermaid Tavern

Souls of poets dead and gone,
What Elysium have ye known,
Happy field or mossy cavern,

Choicer than the Mermaid Tavern?
Have ye tippled drink more fine
Than mine host's Canary wine?
Or are fruits of paradise
Sweeter than those dainty pies
Of venison? O generous food!
Dressed as though bold Robin Hood
Would, with his maid Marian,
Sup and bowse from horn and can.

I have heard that on a day
Mine host's sign-board flew away,
Nobody knew whither, till
An astrologer's old quill
To a sheepskin gave the story,
Said he saw you in your glory,
Underneath a new old sign
Sipping beverage divine,
And pledging with contented smack
The Mermaid in the Zodiac.
Souls of Poets dead and gone,
What Elysium have ye known,
Happy field or mossy cavern,
Choicer than the Mermaid Tavern?


*Robin Hood*

To a Friend

No! those days are gone away,
And their hours are old and gray,
And their minutes buried all
Under the down-trodden pall
Of the leaves of many years:
Many times have winter's shears,
Frozen North, and chilling East,
Sounded tempests to the feast

Of the forest's whispering fleeces,
Since men knew nor rent nor leases.

   No, the bugle sounds no more,
And the twanging bow no more;
Silent is the ivory shrill
Past the heath and up the hill;
There is no mid-forest laugh,
Where lone Echo gives the half
To some wight, amazed to hear
Jesting, deep in forest drear.

   On the fairest time of June
You may go, with sun or moon,
Or the seven stars to light you,
Or the polar ray to right you;
But you never may behold
Little John, or Robin bold;
Never one, of all the clan,
Thrumming on an empty can
Some old hunting ditty, while
He doth his green way beguile
To fair hostess Merriment,
Down beside the pasture Trent;
For he left the merry tale
Messenger for spicy ale.

   Gone, the merry morris din;
Gone, the song of Gamelyn;
Gone, the tough-belted outlaw
Idling in the "grenè shawe";
All are gone away and past!
And if Robin should be cast
Sudden from his turfèd grave,
And if Marian should have
Once again her forest days,
She would weep, and he would craze:

He would swear, for all his oaks,
Fallen beneath the dockyard strokes,
Have rotted on the briny seas;
She would weep that her wild bees
Sang not to her—strange! that honey
Can't be got without hard money!

So it is: yet let us sing,
Honour to the old bow-string!
Honour to the bugle-horn!
Honour to the woods unshorn!
Honour to the Lincoln green!
Honour to the archer keen!
Honour to tight little John,
And the horse he rode upon!
Honour to bold Robin Hood,
Sleeping in the underwood!
Honour to maid Marian,
And to all the Sherwood-clan!
Though their days have hurried by
Let us two a burden try.


### To Autumn

Season of mists and mellow fruitfulness,
  Close bosom-friend of the maturing sun;
Conspiring with him how to load and bless
  With fruit the vines that round the thatch-eves run;
To bend with apples the mossed cottage-trees,
  And fill all fruit with ripeness to the core;
    To swell the gourd, and plump the hazel shells
  With a sweet kernel; to set budding more,
And still more, later flowers for the bees,
Until they think warm days will never cease,
    For Summer has o'er-brimmed their clammy
      cells.

Who hath not seen thee oft amid thy store?
  Sometimes whoever seeks abroad may find
Thee sitting careless on a granary floor,
  Thy hair soft-lifted by the winnowing wind;
Or on a half-reaped furrow sound asleep,
    Drowsed with the fume of poppies, while thy hook
      Spares the next swath and all its twinèd flowers:
And sometimes like a gleaner thou dost keep
    Steady thy laden head across a brook;
    Or by a cider-press, with patient look,
      Thou watchest the last oozings hours by hours.

Where are the songs of Spring? Ay, where are they?
  Think not of them, thou hast thy music too,—
While barred clouds bloom the soft-dying day,
  And touch the stubble-plains with rosy hue;
Then in a wailful choir the small gnats mourn
    Among the river sallows, borne aloft
      Or sinking as the light wind lives or dies;
And full-grown lambs loud bleat from hilly bourn;
    Hedge-crickets sing; and now with treble soft
    The red-breast whistles from a garden-croft;
      And gathering swallows twitter in the skies.

### Ode on Melancholy

No, no, go not to Lethe, neither twist
  Wolf's bane, tight-rooted, for its poisonous wine;
Nor suffer thy pale forehead to be kissed
  By nightshade, ruby grape of Proserpine;
Make not your rosary of yew-berries,
    Nor let the beetle, nor the death-moth be
      Your mournful Psyche, nor the downy owl
A partner in your sorrow's mysteries;
    For shade to shade will come too drowsily,
      And drown the wakeful anguish of the soul.

But when the melancholy fit shall fall
   Sudden from heaven like a weeping cloud,
That fosters the droop-headed flowers all,
   And hides the green hill in an April shroud;
Then glut thy sorrow on a morning rose,
   Or on the rainbow of the salt sand-wave,
     Or on the wealth of globèd peonies;
Or if thy mistress some rich anger shows,
   Emprison her soft hand, and let her rave,
     And feed deep, deep upon her peerless eyes.

She dwells with Beauty—Beauty that must die;
   And Joy, whose hand is ever at his lips
Bidding adieu; and aching Pleasure nigh,
   Turning to poison while the bee-mouth sips:
Ay, in the very temple of delight
   Veiled Melancholy has her sovran shrine,
     Though seen of none save him whose strenuous
       tongue
Can burst Joy's grape against his palate fine;
   His soul shall taste the sadness of her might,
     And be among her cloudy trophies hung.


*On Oxford*

A Parody

   The Gothic looks solemn,
   The plain Doric column
Supports an old Bishop and Crosier;
   The mouldering arch,
   Shaded o'er by a larch
Stands next door to Wilson the Hosier.

   Vice—that is, by turns,—
   O'er pale faces mourns
The black tasselled trencher and common hat;

The chantry boy sings,
The steeple-bell rings,
And as for the Chancellor—*dominat.*

There are plenty of trees,
And plenty of ease,
And plenty of fat deer for parsons;
And when it is venison,
Short is the benison,—
Then each on a leg or thigh fastens.


### Modern Love

And what is love? It is a doll dressed up
For idleness to cosset, nurse, and dandle;
A thing of soft misnomers, so divine
That silly youth doth think to make itself
Divine by loving, and so goes on
Yawning and doting a whole summer long,
Till Miss's comb is made a pearl tiara,
And common Wellingtons turn Romeo boots;
Then Cleopatra lives at number seven,
And Antony resides in Brunswick Square.
Fools! if some passions high have warmed the world,
If queens and soldiers have played deep for hearts,
It is no reason why such agonies
Should be more common than the growth of weeds.
Fools! make me whole again that weighty pearl
The Queen of Egypt melted, and I'll say
That ye may love in spite of beaver hats.


### When I Have Fears That I May Cease to Be

When I have fears that I may cease to be
Before my pen has gleaned my teeming brain,
Before high-pilèd books, in charactery,
Hold like rich garners the full ripened grain;

When I behold, upon the night's starred face,
Huge cloudy symbols of a high romance,
And think that I may never live to trace
Their shadows, with the magic hand of chance;
And when I feel, fair creature of an hour,
That I shall never look upon thee more,
Never have relish in the faery power
Of unreflecting love;—then on the shore
Of the wide world I stand alone, and think
Till love and fame to nothingness do sink.

### La Belle Dame sans Merci

Ah, what can ail thee, wretched wight,
    Alone and palely loitering;
The sedge is withered from the lake,
    And no birds sing.

Ah, what can ail thee, wretched wight,
    So haggard and so woe-begone?
The squirrel's granary is full,
    And the harvest's done.

I see a lily on thy brow,
    With anguish moist and fever dew;
And on thy cheek a fading rose
    Fast withereth too.

I met a lady in the meads
    Full beautiful, a faery's child;
Her hair was long, her foot was light,
    And her eyes were wild.

I set her on my pacing steed,
    And nothing else saw all day long;
For sideways would she lean, and sing
    A faery's song.

I made a garland for her head,
   And bracelets too, and fragrant zone;
She looked at me as she did love,
   And made sweet moan.

She found me roots of relish sweet,
   And honey wild, and manna dew;
And sure in language strange she said,
   I love thee true.

She took me to her elfin grot,
   And there she gazed and sighèd deep,
And there I shut her wild sad eyes—
   So kissed to sleep.

And there we slumbered on the moss,
   And there I dreamed, ah woe betide,
The latest dream I ever dreamed
   On the cold hill side.

I saw pale kings, and princes too,
   Pale warriors, death-pale were they all;
Who cried—"La belle Dame sans merci
   Hath thee in thrall!"

I saw their starved lips in the gloam
   With horrid warning gapèd wide,
And I awoke, and found me here
   On the cold hill side.

And this is why I sojourn here
   Alone and palely loitering,
Though the sedge is withered from the lake,
   And no birds sing.

# THOMAS CARLYLE/1795–1881

### *The Sower's Song*

Now hands to seedsheet, boys!
We step and we cast; old Time's on wing,
And would ye partake of harvest's joys,
The corn must be sown in spring.
    *Fall gently and still, good corn,*
    *Lie warm in thy earthy bed;*
    *And stand so yellow some morn,*
    *For beast and man must be fed.*

Old earth is a pleasure to see
In sunshiny cloak of red and green;
The furrow lies fresh; this year will be
As years that are past have been.
    *Fall gently and still, good corn,*
    *Lie warm in thy earthy bed;*
    *And stand so yellow some morn,*
    *For beast and man must be fed.*

Old Mother, receive this corn,
The son of six thousand golden sires:
All these on thy kindly breast were born;
One more thy poor child requires.
    *Fall gently and still, good corn,*
    *Lie warm in thy earthy bed;*
    *And stand so yellow some morn,*
    *For beast and man must be fed.*

Now steady and sure again,
And measure of stroke and step we keep;
Thus up and thus down we cast our grain:
Sow well, and you gladly reap.

*Fall gently and still, good corn,*
*Lie warm in thy earthy bed;*
*And stand so yellow some morn,*
*For beast and man must be fed.*

# WILLIAM BARNES/1801–1886

## The Wife A-Lost

Since I noo mwore do zee your feäce,
  Up steärs or down below,
I'll zit me in the lwonesome pleäce,
  Where flat-boughed beech do grow;

Below the beeches' bough, my love,
  Where you did never come,
An' I don't look to meet ye now,
  As I do look at hwome.

Since you noo mwore be at my zide,
  In walks in zummer het,
I'll goo alwone where mist do ride,
  Droo trees a-drippèn wet;
Below the raïn-wet bough, my love,
  Where you did never come,
An' I don't grieve to miss ye now,
  As I do grieve at hwome.

Since now bezide my dinner-bwoard
  Your vaïce do never sound,
I'll eat the bit I can avword
  A-vield upon the ground;
Below the darksome bough, my love,
  Where you did never dine,
An' I don't grieve to miss ye now,
  As I at hwome do pine.

Since I do miss your vaïce an' feäce
    In prayer at eventide,
I'll pray wi' woone sad vaïce vor greäce
    To goo where you do bide;
Above the tree an' bough, my love,
    Where you be gone avore,
An' be a-waïtèn vor me now,
    To come vor evermwore.


### The Echo

About the tow'r an' churchyard wall,
    Out nearly overright our door,
A tongue ov wind did always call
    Whatever we did call avore.
The vaïce did mock our neämes, our cheers,
    Our merry laughs, our hands' loud claps,
An' mother's call "Come, come my dears"
                        —*my dears;*
    Or "Do as I do bid, bad chaps"
                        —*bad chaps.*


An' when o' Zundays on the green,
    In frocks an' cwoats as gäy as new,
We walked wi' shoes a-meäde to sheen
    So black an' bright's a vull-ripe slooe
We then did hear the tongue ov air
    A-Mockèn mother's vaïce so thin,
"Come, now the bell do goo vor praÿ'r"
                        —*vor praÿ'r;*
    "'Tis time to goo to church; come in"
                        —*come in.*


The night when little Anne, that died,
    Begun to zickèn, back in Maÿ,
An' she at dusk ov evenèn-tide,
    Wer out wi' others at their play,

Within the churchyard that do keep
　　Her little bed, the vaïce o' thin
Dark aïr, mock'd mother's call "To sleep"
　　　　　　　　—*to sleep;*
" 'Tis bed time now, my love, come in"
　　　　　　　　—*come in.*


### Jenny out from Hwome

O wild-reävèn west winds, as you do roar on,
　　The elems do rock an' the poplars do ply,
An' weäve do dreve weäve in the dark-watered pon'—
　　Oh, where do ye rise vrom, an' where do ye die?

O wild-reävèn winds, I do wish I could vlee
　　Wi' you, lik' a bird o' the clouds, up above
The rudge o' the hill an' the top o' the tree,
　　To where I do long vor, an' vo'kes I do love.

Or else that in under theäse rocks I could hear,
　　In the soft-zwellèn sounds you do leäve in your road,
Zome words you mid bring me, vrom tongues that be dear,
　　Vrom friends that do love me, all scattered abrode.

O wild-reävèn winds! If you ever do roar
　　By the house an' the elems vrom where I'm a-come,
Breathe up at the window, or call at the door,
　　An' tell you've a-voun' me a-thinkèn o' hwome.


### A Brisk Wind

The burdock leaves beside the ledge,
The leaves upon the poplar's height,
Were blown by windblasts up on edge,

And showed their undersides of white;
And willow trees beside the rocks,
All bent gray leaves, and swung gray boughs,
As there, on wagging heads, dark locks
Bespread red cheeks, behung white brows.

### Lullaby

The rook's nest do rock on the tree-top
Where vew foes can stand;
The martin's is high, an' is deep
In the steep cliff o' zand.
But thou, love, a-sleepen where vootsteps
Mid come to thy bed,
Hast father an' mother to watch thee
An' shelter thy head.
      Lullaby, Lilybrow. Lie asleep;
      Blest be thy rest.

An' zome birds do keep under ruffen
Their young vrom the storm,
An' zome wi' nesthoodèns o' moss
And o' wool, do lie warm.
An' we wull look well to the houseruf
That o'er thee mid leäk,
An' the blast that mid beät on thy winder
Shall not smite thy cheäk.
      Lullaby, Lilybrow. Lie asleep;
      Blest be thy rest.

### Sing Again Together

Since now, once more beside this mound,
We friends are here below the limes,
Come, let us try if we can sound
A song we sang in early times.

When out among the hay in mead,
Or o'er the fields, or down the lane,
Our Jenny's voice would gaily lead
The others, chiming strain by strain.

When roses' buds are all outblown,
The lilies' cups will open white,
When lilies' cups, at last, are flown,
The later pinks unfold to sight.

We learnt good songs that came out new,
But now are old among the young,
And, after we are gone, but few
Will know the songs that we have sung.

So let us sing another rhyme
On this old mound in summer time.


# ALFRED, LORD TENNYSON/1809–1892

## *Mariana*

*"Mariana in the moated grange."* Measure for Measure

With blackest moss the flower-pots
   Were thickly crusted, one and all;
The rusted nails fell from the knots
   That held the pear to the gable-wall.
The broken sheds looked sad and strange:
   Unlifted was the clinking latch;
   Weeded and worn the ancient thatch
Upon the lonely moated grange.
     She only said, "My life is dreary,
      He cometh not," she said;
     She said, "I am aweary, aweary,
      I would that I were dead!"

Her tears fell with the dews at even;
    Her tears fell ere the dews were dried;
She could not look on the sweet heaven,
    Either at morn or eventide.
After the flitting of the bats,
    When thickest dark did trance the sky,
    She drew her casement-curtain by,
And glanced athwart the glooming flats.
      She only said, "The night is dreary,
        He cometh not," she said;
      She said, "I am aweary, aweary,
        I would that I were dead!"

Upon the middle of the night,
    Waking she heard the night-fowl crow;
The cock sung out an hour ere light;
    From the dark fen the oxen's low
Came to her; without hope of change,
    In sleep she seemed to walk forlorn,
    Till cold winds woke the gray-eyed morn
About the lonely moated grange.
      She only said, "The day is dreary,
        He cometh not," she said;
      She said, "I am aweary, aweary,
        I would that I were dead!"

About a stone-cast from the wall
    A sluice with blackened waters slept,
And o'er it many, round and small,
    The clustered marish-mosses crept.
Hard by a poplar shook alway,
    All silver-green with gnarlèd bark:
    For leagues no other tree did mark
The level waste, the rounding gray.
      She only said, "My life is dreary,
        He cometh not," she said;
      She said, "I am aweary, aweary,
        I would that I were dead!"

And ever when the moon was low,
   And the shrill winds were up and away,
In the white curtain, to and fro,
   She saw the gusty shadow sway.
But when the moon was very low,
   And wild winds bound within their cell,
   The shadow of the poplar fell
Upon her bed, across her brow.
      She only said, "The night is dreary,
        He cometh not," she said;
      She said, "I am aweary, aweary,
        I would that I were dead!"

All day within the dreamy house,
   The doors upon their hinges creaked;
The blue fly sung in the pane; the mouse
   Behind the mouldering wainscot shrieked,
Or from the crevice peered about.
   Old faces glimmered thro' the doors,
   Old footsteps trod the upper floors,
Old voices called her from without.
      She only said, "My life is dreary,
        He cometh not," she said;
      She said, "I am aweary, aweary,
        I would that I were dead!"

The sparrow's chirrup on the roof,
   The slow clock ticking, and the sound
Which to the wooing wind aloof
   The poplar made, did all confound
Her sense; but most she loathed the hour
   When the thick-moted sunbeam lay
   Athwart the chambers, and the day
Was sloping toward his western bower.
      Then said she, "I am very dreary,
        He will not come," she said;
      She wept, "I am aweary, aweary,
        O God, that I were dead!"

## The Lotos-Eaters

"Courage!" he said, and pointed toward the land,
"This mounting wave will roll us shoreward soon."
In the afternoon they came unto a land
In which it seemèd always afternoon.
All round the coast the languid air did swoon,
Breathing like one that hath a weary dream.
Full-faced above the valley stood the moon;
And, like a downward smoke, the slender stream
Along the cliff to fall and pause and fall did seem.

A land of streams! some, like a downward smoke,
Slow-dropping veils of thinnest lawn, did go;
And some thro' wavering lights and shadows broke,
Rolling a slumbrous sheet of foam below.
They saw the gleaming river seaward flow
From the inner land; far off, three mountain-tops,
Three silent pinnacles of aged snow,
Stood sunset-flushed; and dewed with showery drops,
Up-clomb the shadowy pine above the woven copse.

The charmèd sunset lingered low adown
In the red West; thro' mountain clefts the dale
Was seen far inland, and the yellow down
Bordered with palm, and many a winding vale
And meadow, set with slender galingale;
A land where all things always seemed the same!
And round about the keel with faces pale,
Dark faces pale against that rosy flame,
The mild-eyed melancholy Lotos-eaters came.

Branches they bore of that enchanted stem,
Laden with flower and fruit, whereof they gave
To each, but whoso did receive of them
And taste, to him the gushing of the wave
Far far away did seem to mourn and rave
On alien shores; and if his fellow spake,
His voice was thin, as voices from the grave;

And deep-asleep he seemed, yet all awake,
And music in his ears his beating heart did make.

They sat them down upon the yellow sand,
Between the sun and the moon upon the shore;
And sweet it was to dream of Fatherland,
Of child, and wife, and slave; but evermore
Most weary seemed the sea, weary the oar,
Weary the wandering fields of barren foam.
Then some one said, "We will return no more;"
And all at once they sang, "Our island home
Is far beyond the wave; we will no longer roam."

## Ulysses

It little profits that an idle king,
By this still hearth, among these barren crags,
Matched with an agèd wife, I mete and dole
Unequal laws unto a savage race,
That hoard, and sleep, and feed, and know not me.
I cannot rest from travel; I will drink
Life to the lees. All times I have enjoyed
Greatly, have suffered greatly, both with those
That loved me, and alone; on shore, and when
Thro' scudding drifts the rainy Hyades
Vext the dim sea. I am become a name;
For always roaming with a hungry heart
Much have I seen and known,—cities of men
And manners, climates, councils, governments,
Myself not least, but honored of them all,—
And drunk delight of battle with my peers,
Far on the ringing plains of windy Troy.
I am a part of all that I have met;
Yet all experience is an arch wherethro'
Gleams that untravelled world whose margin fades
For ever and for ever when I move.
How dull it is to pause, to make an end,
To rust unburnished, not to shine in use!

As tho' to breathe were life! Life piled on life
Were all too little, and of one to me
Little remains; but every hour is saved
From that eternal silence, something more,.
A bringer of new things; and vile it were
For some three suns to store and hoard myself,
And this gray spirit yearning in desire
To follow knowledge like a sinking star,
Beyond the utmost bound of human thought.
     This is my son, mine own Telemachus,
To whom I leave the sceptre and the isle,—
Well-loved of me, discerning to fulfill
This labor, by slow prudence to make mild
A rugged people, and thro' soft degrees
Subdue them to the useful and the good.
Most blameless is he, centred in the sphere
Of common duties, decent not to fail
In offices of tenderness, and pay
Meet adoration to my household gods,
When I am gone. He works his work, I mine.
     There lies the port; the vessel puffs her sail;
There gloom the dark, broad seas. My mariners,
Souls that have toiled, and wrought, and thought with
     me,—
That ever with a frolic welcome took
The thunder and the sunshine, and opposed
Free hearts, free foreheads,—you and I are old;
Old age hath yet his honor and his toil.
Death closes all; but something ere the end,
Some work of noble note, may yet be done,
Not unbecoming men that strove with Gods.
The lights begin to twinkle from the rocks;
The long day wanes; the slow moon climbs; the deep
Moans round with many voices. Come, my friends.
'T is not too late to seek a newer world.
Push off, and sitting well in order smite
The sounding furrows; for my purpose holds
To sail beyond the sunset, and the baths
Of all the western stars, until I die.

It may be that the gulfs will wash us down;
It may be we shall touch the Happy Isles,
And see the great Achilles, whom we knew.
Tho' much is taken, much abides; and tho'
We are not now that strength which in old days
Moved earth and heaven, that which we are, we are,—
One equal temper of heroic hearts,
Made weak by time and fate, but strong in will
To strive, to seek, to find, and not to yield.

## Tithonus

The woods decay, the woods decay and fall,
The vapors weep their burthen to the ground,
Man comes and tills the field and lies beneath,
And after many a summer dies the swan.
Me only cruel immortality
Consumes; I wither slowly in thine arms,
Here at the quiet limit of the world,
A white-haired shadow roaming like a dream
The ever-silent spaces of the East,
Far-folded mists, and gleaming halls of morn.
   Alas! for this gray shadow, once a man—
So glorious in his beauty and thy choice,
Who madest him thy chosen, that he seemed
To his great heart none other than a God!
I asked thee, "Give me immortality."
Then didst thou grant mine asking with a smile,
Like wealthy men who care not how they give.
But thy strong Hours indignant worked their wills,
And beat me down and marred and wasted me,
And tho' they could not end me, left me maimed
To dwell in presence of immortal youth,
Immortal age beside immortal youth,
And all I was in ashes. Can thy love,
Thy beauty, make amends, tho' even now,
Close over us, the silver star, thy guide,
Shines in those tremulous eyes that fill with tears

To hear me? Let me go; take back thy gift.
Why should a man desire in any way
To vary from the kindly race of men,
Or pass beyond the goal of ordinance
Where all should pause, as is most meet for all?

   A soft air fans the cloud apart; there comes
A glimpse of that dark world where I was born.
Once more the old mysterious glimmer steals
From thy pure brows, and from thy shoulders pure,
And bosom beating with a heart renewed.
Thy cheek begins to redden thro' the gloom,
Thy sweet eyes brighten slowly close to mine,
Ere yet they blind the stars, and the wild team
Which love thee, yearning for thy yoke, arise
And shake the darkness from their loosened manes,
And beat the twilight into flakes of fire.

   Lo! ever thus thou growest beautiful
In silence, then before thine answer given
Departest, and thy tears are on my cheek.

   Why wilt thou ever scare me with thy tears,
And make me tremble lest a saying learnt,
In days far-off, on that dark earth, be true?
"The Gods themselves cannot recall their gifts."

   Ay me! ay me! with what another heart
In days far-off, and with what other eyes
I used to watch—if I be he that watched—
The lucid outline forming round thee; saw
The dim curls kindle into sunny rings;
Changed with thy mystic change, and felt my blood
Glow with the glow that slowly crimsoned all
Thy presence and thy portals, while I lay,
Mouth, forehead, eyelids, growing dewy-warm
With kisses balmier than half-opening buds
Of April, and could hear the lips that kissed
Whispering I knew not what of wild and sweet,
Like that strange song I heard Apollo sing,
While Ilion like a mist rose into towers.

   Yet hold me not for ever in thine East;
How can my nature longer mix with thine?

Coldly thy rosy shadows bathe me, cold
Are all thy lights, and cold my wrinkled feet
Upon thy glimmering thresholds, when the steam
Floats up from those dim fields about the homes
Of happy men that have the power to die,
And grassy barrows of the happier dead.
Release me, and restore me to the ground.
Thou seest all things, thou wilt see my grave;
Thou wilt renew thy beauty morn by morn,
I earth in earth forget these empty courts,
And thee returning on thy silver wheels.


### The Eagle

He clasps the crag with crooked hands;
Close to the sun in lonely lands,
Ringed with the azure world, he stands.
The wrinkled sea beneath him crawls;
He watches from his mountain walls,
And like a thunderbolt he falls.


### As Through the Land

As thro' the land at eve we went,
    And plucked the ripened ears,
We fell out, my wife and I,
O, we fell out, I know not why,
    And kissed again with tears.
And blessings on the falling out
    That all the more endears,
When we fall out with those we love
    And kiss again with tears!
For when we came where lies the child
    We lost in other years,
There above the little grave,
O, there above the little grave,
    We kissed again with tears.

## Sweet and Low

Sweet and low, sweet and low,
    Wind of the western sea,
Low, low, breathe and blow,
    Wind of the western sea!
Over the rolling waters go,
Come from the dying moon, and blow,
    Blow him again to me;
While my little one, while my pretty one sleeps.

Sleep and rest, sleep and rest,
    Father will come to thee soon;
Rest, rest, on mother's breast,
    Father will come to thee soon;
Father will come to his babe in the nest,
Silver sails all out of the west
    Under the silver moon;
Sleep, my little one, sleep, my pretty one, sleep.

## Tears, Idle Tears

Tears, idle tears, I know not what they mean,
Tears from the depth of some divine despair
Rise in the heart, and gather to the eyes,
In looking on the happy Autumn-fields,
And thinking of the days that are no more.

Fresh as the first beam glittering on a sail,
That brings our friends up from the underworld,
Sad as the last which reddens over one
That sinks with all we love below the verge;
So sad, so fresh, the days that are no more.

Ah, sad and strange as in dark summer dawns
The earliest pipe of half-awakened birds
To dying ears, when unto dying eyes

The casement slowly grows a glimmering square;
So sad, so strange, the days that are no more.

Dear as remembered kisses after death,
And sweet as those by hopeless fancy feigned
On lips that are for others; deep as love,
Deep as first love, and wild with all regret;
O Death in Life, the days that are no more!

## O Swallow, Swallow

"O Swallow, Swallow, flying, flying south,
Fly to her, and fall upon her gilded eaves,
And tell her, tell her, what I tell to thee.

"O, tell her, Swallow, thou that knowest each,
That bright and fierce and fickle is the South,
And dark and true and tender is the North.

"O Swallow, Swallow, if I could follow, and light
Upon her lattice, I would pipe and trill,
And cheep and twitter twenty million loves.

"O, were I thou that she might take me in,
And lay me on her bosom, and her heart
Would rock the snowy cradle till I died!

"Why lingereth she to clothe her heart with love,
Delaying as the tender ash delays
To clothe herself, when all the woods are green?

"O, tell her, Swallow, that thy brood is flown;
Say to her, I do but wanton in the South,
But in the North long since my nest is made.

"O, tell her, brief is life but love is long,
And brief the sun of summer in the North,
And brief the moon of beauty in the South.

"O Swallow, flying from the golden woods,
Fly to her, and pipe and woo her, and make her mine,
And tell her, tell her, that I follow thee."


### Come Down, O Maid

"Come down, O maid, from yonder mountain height.
What pleasure lives in height (the shepherd sang),
In height and cold, the splendor of the hills?
But cease to move so near the heavens and cease
To glide a sunbeam by the blasted pine,
To sit a star upon the sparkling spire;
And come, for Love is of the valley, come,
For Love is of the valley, come thou down
And find him; by the happy threshold, he,
Or hand in hand with Plenty in the maize,
Or red with spirted purple of the vats,
Or foxlike in the vine; nor cares to walk
With Death and Morning on the Silver Horns,
Nor wilt thou snare him in the white ravine,
Nor find him dropped upon the firths of ice,
That huddling slant in furrow-cloven falls
To roll the torrent out of dusky doors.
But follow; let the torrent dance thee down
To find him in the valley; let the wild
Lean-headed eagles yelp alone, and leave
The monstrous ledges there to slope, and spill
Their thousand wreaths of dangling water-smoke,
That like a broken purpose waste in air.
So waste not thou, but come; for all the vales
Await thee; azure pillars of the hearth
Arise to thee; the children call, and I
Thy shepherd pipe, and sweet is every sound,
Sweeter thy voice, but every sound is sweet;
Myriads of rivulets hurrying thro' the lawn,
The moan of doves in immemorial elms,
And murmuring of innumerable bees."

## Now Sleeps the Crimson Petal

"Now sleeps the crimson petal, now the white;
Nor waves the cypress in the palace walk;
Nor winks the gold fin in the porphyry font.
The fire-fly wakens; waken thou with me.

"Now droops the milk-white peacock like a ghost,
And like a ghost she glimmers on to me.

"Now lies the Earth all Danaë to the stars,
And all thy heart lies open unto me.

"Now slides the silent meteor on, and leaves
A shining furrow, as thy thoughts in me.

"Now folds the lily all her sweetness up,
And slips into the bosom of the lake.
So fold thyself, my dearest, thou, and slip
Into my bosom and be lost in me."

## Dark House

Dark house, by which once more I stand
    Here in the long unlovely street,
    Doors, where my heart was used to beat
So quickly, waiting for a hand,

A hand that can be clasped no more—
    Behold me, for I cannot sleep,
    And like a guilty thing I creep
At earliest morning to the door.

He is not here; but far away
    The noise of life begins again,
    And ghastly thro' the drizzling rain
On the bald street breaks the blank day.

## Be Near Me

Be near me when my light is low,
    When the blood creeps, and the nerves prick
    And tingle; and the heart is sick,
And all the wheels of being slow.

Be near me when the sensuous frame
    Is racked with pangs that conquer trust;
    And Time, a maniac scattering dust,
And Life, a Fury slinging flame.

Be near me when my faith is dry,
    And men the flies of latter spring,
    That lay their eggs, and sting and sing
And weave their petty cells and die.

Be near me when I fade away,
    To point the term of human strife,
    And on the low dark verge of life
The twilight of eternal day.

## When on My Bed

When on my bed the moonlight falls,
    I know that in thy place of rest
    By that broad water of the west,
There comes a glory on the walls:

Thy marble bright in dark appears,
    As slowly steals a silver flame
    Along the letters of thy name,
And o'er the number of thy years.

The mystic glory swims away;
    From off my bed the moonlight dies;
    And closing eaves of wearied eyes
I sleep till dusk is dipt in gray:

And then I know the mist is drawn
   A lucid veil from coast to coast,
   And in the dark church like a ghost
Thy tablet glimmers to the dawn.


## The Sailor Boy

He rose at dawn and, fired with hope,
   Shot o'er the seething harbor-bar,
And reached the ship and caught the rope,
   And whistled to the morning star.

And while he whistled long and loud
   He heard a fierce mermaiden cry,
"O boy, tho' thou art young and proud,
   I see the place where thou wilt lie.

"The sands and yeasty surges mix
   In caves about the dreary bay,
And on thy ribs the limpet sticks,
   And in thy heart the scrawl shall play."

"Fool," he answered, "death is sure
   To those that stay and those that roam,
But I will nevermore endure
   To sit with empty hands at home.

"My mother clings about my neck,
   My sisters crying, 'Stay for shame;'
My father raves of death and wreck,—
   They are all to blame, they are all to blame.

"God help me! save I take my part
   Of danger on the roaring sea,
A devil rises in my heart,
   Far worse than any death to me."

*Frater Ave Atque Vale*

Row us out from Desenzano, to your Sirmione row!
So they rowed, and there we landed—"O venusta Sirmio!"
There to me thro' all the groves of olive in the summer glow,
There beneath the Roman ruin where the purple flowers
    grow,
Came that "Ave atque Vale" of the Poet's hopeless woe,
Tenderest of Roman poets nineteen hundred years ago,
"Frater Ave atque Vale"—as we wandered to and fro
Gazing at the Lydian laughter of the Garda Lake below
Sweet Catullus's all-but-island, olive-silvery Sirmio!


# ROBERT BROWNING/1812–1889


*The Lost Leader*

Just for a handful of silver he left us,
    Just for a riband to stick in his coat—
Found the one gift of which fortune bereft us,
    Lost all the others she lets us devote;
They, with the gold to give, doled him out silver,
    So much was theirs who so little allowed:
How all our copper had gone for his service!
    Rags—were they purple, his heart had been proud!
We that had loved him so, followed him, honoured him,
    Lived in his mild and magnificent eye,
Learned his great language, caught his clear accents,
    Made him our pattern to live and to die!
Shakespeare was of us, Milton was for us,
    Burns, Shelley, were with us,—they watch from their
        graves!
He alone breaks from the van and the freemen,
    He alone sinks to the rear and the slaves!
We shall march prospering,—not thro' his presence;
    Songs may inspirit us,—not from his lyre;

Deeds will be done,—while he boasts his quiescence,
  Still bidding crouch whom the rest bade aspire:
Blot out his name, then, record one lost soul more,
  One task more declined, one more footpath untrod,
One more triumph for devils and sorrow for angels,
  One wrong more to man, one more insult to God!
Life's night begins: let him never come back to us!
  There would be doubt, hesitation and pain,
Forced praise on our part—the glimmer of twilight,
  Never glad confident morning again!
Best fight on well, for we taught him,—strike gallantly,
  Menace our heart ere we master his own;
Then let him receive the new knowledge and wait us,
  Pardoned in Heaven, the first by the throne!

### Meeting at Night

The grey sea and the long black land:
And the yellow half-moon large and low;
And the startled little waves that leap
In fiery ringlets from their sleep,
As I gain the cove with pushing prow,
And quench its speed in the slushy sand.

Then a mile of warm sea-scented beach;
Three fields to cross till a farm appears;
A tap at the pane, the quick sharp scratch
And blue spurt of a lighted match,
And a voice less loud, thro' its joys and fears,
Than the two hearts beating each to each!

### Parting at Morning

Round the cape of a sudden came the sea,
And the sun looked over the mountain's rim:
And straight was a path of gold for him,
And the need of a world of men for me.

### Love among the Ruins

Where the quiet-coloured end of evening smiles
    Miles and miles
On the solitary pastures where our sheep
    Half-asleep
Tinkle homeward thro' the twilight, stray or stop
    As they crop—
Was the site once of a city great and gay,
    (So they say)
Of our country's very capital, its prince
    Ages since
Held his court in, gathered councils, wielding far
    Peace or war.

Now—the country does not even boast a tree,
    As you see,
To distinguish slopes of verdure, certain rills
    From the hills
Intersect and give a name to (else they run
    Into one)
Where the domed and daring palace shot its spires
    Up like fires
O'er the hundred-gated circuit of a wall
    Bounding all,
Made of marble, men might march on nor be pressed
    Twelve abreast.

And such plenty and perfection, see, of grass
    Never was!
Such a carpet as, this summer-time, o'erspreads

And embeds
Every vestige of the city, guessed alone,
    Stock or stone—
Where a multitude of men breathed joy and woe
    Long ago;
Lust of glory pricked their hearts up, dread of shame
    Struck them tame;
And that glory and that shame alike, the gold
    Bought and sold.

Now,—the single little turret that remains
    On the plains,
By the caper overrooted, by the gourd
    Overscored,
While the patching houseleek's head of blossom winks
    Through the chinks—
Marks the basement whence a tower in ancient time
    Sprang sublime,
And a burning ring, all round, the chariots traced
    As they raced,
And the monarch and his minions and his dames
    Viewed the games.

And I know, while thus the quiet-coloured eve
    Smiles to leave
To their folding, all our many-tinkling fleece
    In such peace,
And the slopes and rills in undistinguished grey
    Melt away—
That a girl with eager eyes and yellow hair
    Waits me there
In the turret whence the charioteers caught soul
    For the goal,
When the king looked, where she looks now, breathless,
      dumb
    Till I come.

But he looked upon the city, every side,
    Far and wide,

All the mountains topped with temples, all the glades'
    Colonnades,
All the causeys, bridges, aqueducts,—and then,
    All the men!
When I do come, she will speak not, she will stand,
    Either hand
On my shoulder, give her eyes the first embrace
    Of my face,
Ere we rush, ere we extinguish sight and speech
    Each on each.

In one year they sent a million fighters forth
    South and north,
And they built their gods a brazen pillar high
    As the sky,
Yet reserved a thousand chariots in full force—
    Gold, of course.
Oh, heart! oh, blood that freezes, blood that burns!
    Earth's returns
For whole centuries of folly, noise and sin!
    Shut them in,
With their triumphs and their glories and the rest.
    Love is best!


### De Gustibus—

Your ghost will walk, you lover of trees
    (If our loves remain),
    In an English lane,
By a cornfield-side a-flutter with poppies.
Hark, those two in the hazel coppice—
A boy and a girl, if the good fates please,
    Making love, say,—
    The happier they!
Draw yourself up from the light of the moon,

And let them pass, as they will too soon,
    With the beanflowers' boon,
    And the blackbird's tune,
    And May, and June!

What I love best in all the world,
Is, a castle, precipice-encurled,
In a gash of the wind-grieved Apennine.
Or look for me, old fellow of mine
(If I get my head from out the mouth
O' the grave, and loose my spirit's bands,
And come again to the land of lands),—
In a sea-side house to the farther south,
Where the baked cicalas die of drouth,
And one sharp tree—'tis a cypress—stands,
By the many hundred years red-rusted,
Rough iron-spiked, ripe fruit-o'er-crusted,
My sentinel to guard the sands
To the water's edge. For, what expands
Before the house, but the great opaque
Blue breadth of sea without a break?
While, in the house, for ever crumbles
Some fragment of the frescoed walls,
From blisters where a scorpion sprawls.
A girl bare-footed brings, and tumbles
Down on the pavement, green-flesh melons,
And says there's news to-day—the king
Was shot at, touched in the liver-wing,
Goes with his Bourbon arm in a sling:
—She hopes they have not caught the felons.
    Italy, my Italy!
Queen Mary's saying serves for me
    (When fortune's malice
    Lost her, Calais)—
Open my heart and you will see
Graved inside of it, "Italy."
Such lovers old are I and she;
So it always was, so shall ever be!

## Home-Thoughts, from the Sea

Nobly, nobly Cape Saint Vincent to the north-west died away;
Sunset ran, one glorious blood-red, reeking into Cadiz Bay;
Bluish 'mid the burning water, full in face Trafalgar lay;
In the dimmest north-east distance, dawned Gibraltar grand
    and grey;
"Here and here did England help me: how can I help
    England?"—say,
Whoso turns as I, this evening, turn to God to praise and
    pray,
While Jove's planet rises yonder, silent over Africa.

## Two in the Campagna

I wonder do you feel to-day
   As I have felt, since, hand in hand,
We sat down on the grass, to stray
   In spirit better through the land,
This morn of Rome and May?

For me, I touched a thought, I know,
   Has tantalized me many times
(Like turns of thread the spiders throw
   Mocking across our path), for rhymes
To catch at and let go.

Help me to hold it! First it left
   The yellowing fennel, run to seed
There, branching from the brickwork's cleft,
   Some old tomb's ruin: yonder weed
Took up the floating weft,

Where one small orange cup amassed
   Five beetles,—blind and green they grope
Among the honey-meal: and last,
   Everywhere on the grassy slope
I traced it. Hold it fast!

The champaign with its endless fleece
  Of feathery grasses everywhere!
Silence and passion, joy and peace,
  An everlasting wash of air—
Rome's ghost since her decease.

Such life there, through such lengths of hours,
  Such miracles performed in play,
Such primal naked forms of flowers,
  Such letting Nature have her way
While Heaven looks from its towers!

How say you? Let us, O my dove,
  Let us be unashamed of soul,
As earth lies bare to heaven above!
  How is it under our control
To love or not to love?

I would that you were all to me,
  You that are just so much, no more.
Nor yours, nor mine,—nor slave nor free!
  Where does the fault lie? what the core
Of the wound, since wound must be?

I would I could adopt your will,
  See with your eyes, and set my heart
Beating by yours, and drink my fill
  At your soul's springs,—your part, my part
In life, for good and ill.

No. I yearn upward, touch you close,
  Then stand away. I kiss your cheek,
Catch your soul's warmth,—I pluck the rose
  And love it more than tongue can speak—
Then the good minute goes.

Already how am I so far
  Out of that minute? Must I go

Still like the thistle ball, no bar,
    Onward, whenever light winds blow,
Fixed by no friendly star?

Just when I seemed about to learn!
    Where is the thread now? Off again!
The old trick! Only I discern—
    Infinite passion, and the pain
Of finite hearts that yearn.

## My Last Duchess

### Ferrars

That's my last Duchess painted on the wall,
Looking as if she were alive; I call
That piece a wonder, now: Frà Pandolf's hands
Worked busily a day, and there she stands.
Will't please you sit and look at her? I said
"Frà Pandolf" by design, for never read
Strangers like you that pictured countenance,
The depth and passion of its earnest glance,
But to myself they turned (since none puts by
The curtain I have drawn for you, but I)
And seemed as they would ask me, if they durst,
How such a glance came there; so, not the first
Are you to turn and ask thus. Sir, 'twas not
Her husband's presence only, called that spot
Of joy into the Duchess' cheek: perhaps
Frà Pandolf chanced to say "Her mantle laps
Over my Lady's wrist too much," or "Paint
Must never hope to reproduce the faint
Half-flush that dies along her throat,": such stuff
Was courtesy, she thought, and cause enough
For calling up that spot of joy. She had
A heart—how shall I say?—too soon made glad,
Too easily impressed; she liked whate'er
She looked on, and her looks went everywhere.

Sir, 'twas all one! My favour at her breast,
The dropping of the daylight in the West.
The bough of cherries some officious fool
Broke in the orchard for her, the white mule
She rode with round the terrace—all and each
Would draw from her alike the approving speech,
Or blush, at least. She thanked men,—good; but thanked
Somehow—I know not how—as if she ranked
My gift of a nine-hundred-years-old name
With anybody's gift. Who'd stoop to blame
This sort of trifling? Even had you skill
In speech—(which I have not)—to make your will
Quite clear to such an one, and say, "Just this
Or that in you disgusts me; here you miss,
Or there exceed the mark"—and if she let
Herself be lessoned so, nor plainly set
Her wits to yours, forsooth, and made excuse,
—E'en then would be some stooping, and I choose
Never to stoop. Oh, Sir, she smiled, no doubt,
Whene'er I passed her; but who passed without
Much the same smile? This grew; I gave commands;
Then all smiles stopped together. There she stands
As if alive. Will't please you rise? We'll meet
The company below, then. I repeat,
The Count your Master's known munificence
Is ample warrant that no just pretence
Of mine for dowry will be disallowed;
Though his fair daughter's self, as I avowed
At starting, is my object. Nay, we'll go
Together down, Sir! Notice Neptune, though,
Taming a sea-horse, thought a rarity,
Which Claus of Innsbruck cast in bronze for me.

### The Bishop Orders His Tomb
### at Saint Praxed's Church

*[Rome, 15—.]*

Vanity, saith the preacher, vanity!
Draw round my bed: is Anselm keeping back?
Nephews—sons mine . . . ah God, I know not! Well—
She, men would have to be your mother once,
Old Gandolf envied me, so fair she was!
What's done is done, and she is dead beside,
Dead long ago, and I am Bishop since,
And as she died so must we die ourselves,
And thence ye may perceive the world's a dream.
Life, how and what is it? As here I lie
In this state-chamber, dying by degrees,
Hours and long hours in the dead night, I ask
"Do I live, am I dead?" Peace, peace seems all.
Saint Praxed's ever was the church for peace;
And so, about this tomb of mine. I fought
With tooth and nail to save my niche, ye know:
—Old Gandolf cozened me, despite my care;
Shrewd was that snatch from out the corner South
He graced his carrion with, God curse the same!
Yet still my niche is not so cramped but thence
One sees the pulpit o' the epistle-side,
And somewhat of the choir, those silent seats,
And up into the aery dome where live
The angels, and a sunbeam's sure to lurk:
And I shall fill my slab of basalt there,
And 'neath my tabernacle take my rest,
With those nine columns round me, two and two,
The odd one at my feet where Anselm stands:
Peach-blossom marble all, the rare, the ripe
As fresh-poured red wine of a mighty pulse
—Old Gandolf with his paltry onion-stone,
Put me where I may look at him! True peach,
Rosy and flawless: how I earned the prize!
Draw close: that conflagration of my church

—What then? So much was saved if aught were missed!
My sons, ye would not be my death? Go dig
The white-grape vineyard where the oil-press stood,
Drop water gently till the surface sinks,
And if ye find . . . Ah, God I know not, I! . . .
Bedded in store of rotten figleaves soft,
And corded up in a tight olive-frail,
Some lump, ah God, of lapis lazuli,
Big as a Jew's head cut off at the nape,
Blue as a vein o'er the Madonna's breast . . .
Sons, all have I bequeathed you, villas, all,
That brave Frascati villa with its bath,
So, let the blue lump poise between my knees,
Like God the Father's globe on both His hands
Ye worship in the Jesu Church so gay,
For Gandolf shall not choose but see and burst!
Swift as a weaver's shuttle fleet our years:
Man goeth to the grave, and where is he?
Did I say basalt for my slab, sons? Black—
'Twas ever antique-black I meant! How else
Shall ye contrast my frieze to come beneath?
The bas-relief in bronze ye promised me,
Those Pans and Nymphs ye wot of, and perchance
Some tripod, thyrsus, with a vase or so,
The Saviour at his sermon on the mount,
Saint Praxed in a glory, and one Pan
Ready to twitch the Nymph's last garment off,
And Moses with the tables . . . but I know
Ye mark me not! What do they whisper thee,
Child of my bowels, Anselm? Ah, ye hope
To revel down my villas while I gasp
Bricked o'er with beggar's mouldy travertine
Which Gandolf from his tomb-top chuckles at!
Nay, boys, ye love me—all of jasper, then!
'Tis jasper ye stand pledged to, lest I grieve
My bath must needs be left behind, alas!
One block, pure green as a pistachio-nut,
There's plenty jasper somewhere in the world—
And have I not Saint Praxed's ear to pray

Horses for ye, and brown Greek manuscripts,
And mistresses with great smooth marbly limbs?
—That's if ye carve my epitaph aright,
Choice Latin, picked phrase, Tully's every word,
No gaudy ware like Gandolf's second line—
Tully, my masters? Ulpian serves his need!
And then how I shall lie through centuries,
And hear the blessèd mutter of the mass,
And see God made and eaten all day long,
And feel the steady candle-flame, and taste
Good strong thick stupefying incense-smoke!
For as I lie here, hours of the dead night,
Dying in state and by such slow degrees,
I fold my arms as if they clasped a crook,
And stretch my feet forth straight as stone can point
And let the bedclothes for a mortcloth drop
Into great laps and folds of sculptor's-work:
And as yon tapers dwindle, and strange thoughts
Grow, with a certain humming in my ears,
About the life before I lived this life,
And this life too, popes, cardinals and priests,
Saint Praxed at his sermon on the mount,
Your tall pale mother with her talking eyes,
And new-found agate urns as fresh as day,
And marble's language, Latin pure, discreet,
—Aha, ELUCESCEBAT quoth our friend?
No Tully, said I, Ulpian at the best!
Evil and brief hath been my pilgrimage.
All lapis, all, sons! Else I give the Pope
My villas: will ye ever eat my heart?
Ever your eyes were as a lizard's quick,
They glitter like your mother's for my soul,
Or ye would heighten my impoverished frieze,
Piece out its starved design, and fill my vase
With grapes, and add a vizor and a Term,
And to the tripod ye would tie a lynx
That in his struggle throws the thyrsus down,
To comfort me on my entablature
Whereon I am to lie till I must ask

"Do I live, am I dead?" There, leave me, there!
For ye have stabbed me with ingratitude
To death—ye wish it—God, ye wish it! Stone—
Gritstone, a-crumble! Clammy squares which sweat
As if the corpse they keep were oozing through—
And no more lapis to delight the world!
Well, go! I bless ye. Fewer tapers there,
But in a row: and, going, turn your backs
—Ay, like departing altar-ministrants,
And leave me in my church, the church for peace,
That I may watch at leisure if he leers—
Old Gandolf, at me, from his onion-stone,
As still he envied me, so fair she was!

### In the Doorway

The swallow has set her six young on the rail,
    And looks sea-ward:
The water's in stripes like a snake, olive-pale
    To the leeward,—
On the weather-side, black, spotted white with the wind:
"Good fortune departs, and disaster's behind,"—
Hark, the wind with its wants and its infinite wail!

Our fig-tree, that leaned for the saltness, has furled
    Her five fingers,
Each leaf like a hand opened wide to the world
    Where there lingers
No glint of the gold, summer sent for her sake:
How the vines writhe in rows, each impaled on its stake!
My heart shrivels up, and my spirit shrinks curled.

Yet here are we two; we have love, house enough,
    With the field there,
This house of four rooms, that field red and rough,
    Though it yield there,
For the rabbit that robs, scarce a blade or a bent;

If a magpie alight now, it seems an event;
And they both will be gone at November's rebuff.

But why must cold spread? but wherefore bring change
    To the spirit,
God meant should mate His with an infinite range,
    And inherit
His power to put life in the darkness and cold?
Oh, live and love worthily, bear and be bold!
Whom summer made friends of, let winter estrange!

# EMILY BRONTË/1818–1848

## *Often Rebuked*[1]

Often rebuked, yet always back returning
    To those first feelings that were born with me,
And leaving busy chase of wealth and learning
    For idle dreams of things which cannot be:

Today, I will not seek the shadowy region:
    Its unsustaining vastness waxes drear;
And visions rising, legion after legion,
    Bring the unreal world too strangely near.

I'll walk, but not in old heroic traces,
    And not in paths of high morality,
And not among the half-distinguished faces,
    The clouded forms of long-past history.

I'll walk where my own nature would be leading:
    It vexes me to choose another guide:

[1] Possibly by Charlotte Brontë, though she included it in her edition of Emily Brontë's poems.

Where the gray flocks in ferny glens are feeding;
   Where the wild wind blows on the mountain-side.

What have those lonely mountains worth revealing?
   More glory and more grief than I can tell:
The earth that wakes *one* human heart to feeling
   Can centre both the worlds of Heaven and Hell.

### How Still, How Happy!

How still, how happy! Those are words
That once would scarce agree together;
I loved the plashing of the surge,
The changing heaven, the breezy weather,

More than smooth seas and cloudless skies
And solemn, soothing, softened airs
That in the solemn forest woke no sighs
And from the green spray shook no tears.

How still, how happy! Now I feel
Where silence dwells is sweeter far
Than laughing mirth's most rapturous swell
However pure its raptures are.

Come, sit down on this sunny stone:
'Tis wintry light o'er flowerless moors—
But sit—for we are all alone
And clear expands heaven's breathless shores.

I could think in the withered grass
Spring's budding wreaths we might discern;
The violet's eye might shyly flash
And young leaves shoot among the fern.

It is but thought—full many a night
The snow shall clothe those hills afar

And storms shall add a drearier blight
And winds shall wage a wilder war,

Before the lark may herald in
Fresh foliage twined with blossoms fair
And summer days again begin
Their glory-haloed crown to wear.

Yet my heart loves December's smile
As much as July's golden beam;
Then let us sit and watch the while
The blue ice curdling on the stream.


### Cold in the Earth

Cold in the earth, and the deep snow piled above thee!
Far, far removed, cold in the dreary grave!
Have I forgot, my Only Love, to love thee,
Severed at last by Time's all-wearing wave?

Now, when alone, do my thoughts no longer hover
Over the mountains on Angora's shore;
Resting their wings where heath and fern-leaves cover
That noble heart for ever, ever more?

Cold in the earth, and fifteen wild Decembers
From those brown hills have melted into spring—
Faithful indeed is the spirit that remembers
After such years of change and suffering!

Sweet Love of youth, forgive if I forget thee
While the world's tide is bearing me along:
Sterner desires and darker hopes beset me,
Hopes which obscure but cannot do thee wrong.

No other sun has lightened up my heaven;
No other star has ever shone for me:

All my life's bliss from thy dear life was given—
All my life's bliss is in the grave with thee.

But when the days of golden dreams had perished
And even despair was powerless to destroy,
Then did I learn how existence could be cherished,
Strengthened and fed without the aid of joy;

Then did I check the tears of useless passion,
Weaned my young soul from yearning after thine;
Sternly denied its burning wish to hasten
Down to that tomb already more than mine!

And even yet, I dare not let it languish,
Dare not indulge in memory's rapturous pain;
Once drinking deep of that divinest anguish,
How could I seek the empty world again?

## The Visionary

Silent is the house: all are laid asleep:
One alone looks out o'er the snow-wreaths deep,
Watching every cloud, dreading every breeze
That whirls the 'wildering drift, and bends the groaning
        trees.

Cheerful is the hearth, soft the matted floor;
Not one shivering gust creeps through pane or door;
The little lamp burns straight, its rays shoot strong and far:
I trim it well, to be the wanderer's guiding-star.

Frown, my haughty sire! chide, my angry dame!
Set your slaves to spy; threaten me with shame:
But neither sire nor dame, nor prying serf shall know
What angel nightly tracks that waste of frozen snow.

What I love shall come like visitant of air,
Safe in secret power from lurking human snare;

Who loves me, no word of mine shall e'er betray,
Though for faith unstained my life must forfeit pay.


Burn then, little lamp; glimmer straight and clear—
Hush! a rustling wing stirs, methinks, the air:
He for whom I wait thus ever comes to me;
Strange Power! I trust thy might; trust thou my constancy.


# ARTHUR HUGH CLOUGH/1819–1861

### The Latest Decalogue

Thou shalt have one God only; who
Would be at the expense of two?

No graven images may be
Worshipped, except the currency:

Swear not at all; for, for thy curse
Thine enemy is none the worse:

At church on Sunday to attend
Will serve to keep the world thy friend:

Honour thy parents; that is, all
From whom advancement may befall:

Thou shalt not kill; but need'st not strive
Officiously to keep alive:

Do not adultery commit;
Advantage rarely comes of it:

Thou shalt not steal; an empty feat,
When 'tis so lucrative to cheat:

Bear not false witness; let the lie
Have time on its own wings to fly:

Thou shalt not covet, but tradition
Approves all forms of competition.

### Say Not, the Struggle Nought Availeth

Say not, the struggle nought availeth,
   The labour and the wounds are vain,
The enemy faints not, nor faileth,
   And as things have been they remain.

If hopes were dupes, fears may be liars;
   It may be, in yon smoke concealed,
Your comrades chase e'en now the fliers,
   And, but for you, possess the field.

For while the tired waves, vainly breaking,
   Seem here no painful inch to gain,
Far back, through creeks and inlets making,
   Comes silent, flooding in, the main,

And not by eastern windows only,
   When daylight comes, comes in the light,
In front, the sun climbs slow, how slowly,
   But westward, look, the land is bright.

# MATTHEW ARNOLD/1822-1888

### Shakespeare

Others abide our question. Thou art free.
We ask and ask: Thou smilest and art still,
Out-topping knowledge. For the loftiest hill
That to the stars uncrowns his majesty,
Planting his steadfast footsteps in the sea,
Making the heaven of heavens his dwelling-place,
Spares but the cloudy border of his base
To the foiled searching of mortality;
And thou, who didst the stars and sunbeams know,
Self-schooled, self-scanned, self-honoured, self-secure,
Didst walk on earth unguessed at. Better so!
All pains the immortal spirit must endure,
All weakness that impairs, all griefs that bow,
Find their sole voice in that victorious brow.

### The Scholar-Gipsy

Go, for they call you, Shepherd, from the hill;
  Go, Shepherd, and untie the wattled cotes:
    No longer leave thy wistful flock unfed,
  Nor let thy bawling fellows rack their throats,
    Nor the cropped grasses shoot another head.
      But when the fields are still,
  And the tired men and dogs all gone to rest,
    And only the white sheep are sometimes seen
    Cross and recross the strips of moon-blanched green:
  Come, Shepherd, and again begin the quest.

Here, where the reaper was at work of late,
  In this high field's dark corner, where he leaves
    His coat, his basket, and his earthen cruise,
  And in the sun all morning binds the sheaves,

Then here, at noon, comes back his stores to use;
   Here will I sit and wait,
While to my ear from uplands far away
   The bleating of the folded flocks is borne,
   With distant cries of reapers in the corn—
All the live murmur of a summer's day.


Screened is this nook o'er the high, half-reaped field,
   And here till sundown, Shepherd, will I be.
   Through the thick corn the scarlet poppies peep,
   And round green roots and yellowing stalks I see
   Pale blue convolvulus in tendrils creep:
     And air-swept lindens yield
Their scent, and rustle down their perfumed showers
   Of bloom on the bent grass where I am laid,
   And bower me from the August sun with shade;
And the eye travels down to Oxford's towers:


And near me on the grass lies Glanvil's book—
   Come, let me read the oft-read tale again:
   The story of that Oxford scholar poor,
Of pregnant parts and quick inventive brain,
   Who, tired of knocking at Preferment's door,
     One summer morn forsook
His friends, and went to learn the Gipsy lore,
   And roamed the world with that wild brotherhood,
   And came, as most men deemed, to little good,
But came to Oxford and his friends no more.


But once, years after, in the country lanes,
   Two scholars, whom at college erst he knew,
   Met him, and of his way of life inquired.
Whereat he answered that the Gipsy crew,
   His mates, had arts to rule as they desired
     The workings of men's brains;
And they can bind them to what thoughts they will:
   "And I," he said, "the secret of their art,

When fully learned, will to the world impart:
But it needs Heaven-sent moments for this skill!"

This said, he left them, and returned no more,
    But rumours hung about the country-side,
        That the lost Scholar long was seen to stray,
    Seen by rare glimpses, pensive and tongue-tied,
        In hat of antique shape, and cloak of grey,
            The same the Gipsies wore.
    Shepherds had met him on the Hurst in spring;
        At some lone alehouse in the Berkshire moors,
            On the warm ingle-bench, the smock-frocked boors
    Had found him seated at their entering,

But, 'mid their drink and clatter, he would fly:
    And I myself seem half to know thy looks,
        And put the shepherds, Wanderer, on thy trace;
    And boys who in lone wheatfields scare the rooks
        I ask if thou hast passed their quiet place;
            Or in my boat I lie
    Moored to the cool bank in the summer heats,
        'Mid wide grass meadows which the sunshine fills,
            And watch the warm green-muffled Cumnor hills,
    And wonder if thou haunt'st their shy retreats.

For most, I know, thou lov'st retirèd ground.
    Thee, at the ferry, Oxford riders blithe,
        Returning home on summer nights, have met
    Crossing the stripling Thames at Bablock-hithe,
        Trailing in the cool stream thy fingers wet,
            As the slow punt swings round:
    And leaning backwards in a pensive dream,
        And fostering in thy lap a heap of flowers
            Plucked in shy fields and distant Wychwood bowers,
    And thine eyes resting on the moonlit stream:

And then they land, and thou art seen no more.
    Maidens who from the distant hamlets come
        To dance around the Fyfield elm in May,

Oft through the darkening fields have seen thee roam,
  Or cross a stile into the public way.
    Oft thou hast given them store
Of flowers—the frail-leafed, white anemone—
  Dark bluebells drenched with dews of summer eves,
  And purple orchises with spotted leaves—
But none has words she can report of thee.

And, above Godstow Bridge, when hay-time's here
  In June, and many a scythe in sunshine flames,
    Men who through those wide fields of breezy grass
  Where black-winged swallows haunt the glittering
        Thames,
    To bathe in the abandoned lasher pass,
      Have often passed thee near
Sitting upon the river bank o'ergrown:
  Marked thine outlandish garb, thy figure spare,
  Thy dark vague eyes, and soft abstracted air;
But, when they came from bathing, thou wert gone.

At some lone homestead in the Cumnor hills,
  Where at her open door the housewife darns,
    Thou hast been seen, or hanging on a gate
To watch the threshers in the mossy barns.
    Children, who early range these slopes and late
      For cresses from the rills,
Have known thee watching, all an April day,
  The springing pastures and the feeding kine,
  And marked thee, when the stars come out and shine,
Through the long dewy grass move slow away.

In autumn, on the skirts of Bagley Wood,
  Where most the Gipsies by the turf-edged way
    Pitch their smoked tents, and every bush you see
With scarlet patches tagged and shreds of gray,
    Above the forest-ground called Thessaly—
      The blackbird picking food
Sees thee, nor stops his meal, nor fears at all;
  So often has he known thee past him stray

Rapt, twirling in thy hand a withered spray,
And waiting for the spark from Heaven to fall.

And once, in winter, on the causeway chill
  Where home through flooded fields foot-travellers go,
    Have I not passed thee on the wooden bridge
  Wrapt in thy cloak and battling with the snow,
    Thy face towards Hinksey and its wintry ridge?
      And thou hast climbed the hill
  And gained the white brow of the Cumnor range;
    Turned once to watch, while thick the snowflakes fall,
    The line of festal light in Christ Church hall—
  Then sought thy straw in some sequestered grange.

But what—I dream! Two hundred years are flown
  Since first thy story ran through Oxford halls,
    And the grave Glanvil did the tale inscribe
  That thou wert wandered from the studious walls
    To learn strange arts, and join a Gipsy tribe:
      And thou from earth art gone
  Long since, and in some quiet churchyard laid;
    Some country nook, where o'er thy unknown grave
    Tall grasses and white flowering nettles wave—
  Under a dark red-fruited yew-tree's shade.

—No, no, thou hast not felt the lapse of hours.
  For what wears out the life of mortal men?
    'Tis that from change to change their being rolls:
  'Tis that repeated shocks, again, again,
    Exhaust the energy of strongest souls,
      And numb the elastic powers.
  Till having used our nerves with bliss and teen,
    And tired upon a thousand schemes our wit,
    To the just-pausing Genius we remit
  Our worn-out life, and are—what we have been.

Thou hast not lived, why shouldst thou perish, so?
  Thou hadst *one* aim, *one* business, *one* desire:
    Else wert thou long since numbered with the dead—

Else hadst thou spent, like other men, thy fire.
   The generations of thy peers are fled,
      And we ourselves shall go;
But thou possessed an immortal lot,
     And we imagine thee exempt from age
     And living as thou liv'st on Glanvil's page,
Because thou hadst—what we, alas, have not!

For early didst thou leave the world, with powers
   Fresh, undiverted to the world without,
     Firm to their mark, not spent on other things;
   Free from the sick fatigue, the languid doubt,
     Which much to have tried, in much been baffled,
       brings.
      O Life unlike to ours!
   Who fluctuate idly without term or scope,
     Of whom each strives, nor knows for what he strives,
     And each half lives a hundred different lives;
Who wait like thee, but not, like thee, in hope.

Thou waitest for the spark from Heaven: and we,
   Vague half-believers of our casual creeds,
     Who never deeply felt, nor clearly willed,
   Whose insight never has borne fruit in deeds,
     Whose weak resolves never have been fulfilled;
     For whom each year we see
Breeds new beginnings, disappointments new;
     Who hesitate and falter life away,
     And lose to-morrow the ground won to-day—
Ah, do not we, Wanderer, await it too?

Yes, we await it, but it still delays,
   And then we suffer; and amongst us One,
     Who most has suffered, takes dejectedly
   His seat upon the intellectual throne;
     And all his store of sad experience he
      Lays bare of wretched days;
   Tells us his misery's birth and growth and signs,
     And how the dying spark of hope was fed,

And how the breast was soothed, and how the head,
And all his hourly varied anodynes.

This for our wisest: and we others pine,
   And wish the long unhappy dream would end,
      And waive all claim to bliss, and try to bear,
   With close-lipped Patience for our only friend,
      Sad Patience, too near neighbour to Despair:
         But none has hope like thine.
   Thou thro' the fields and thro' the woods dost stray,
      Roaming the country-side, a truant boy,
      Nursing thy project in unclouded joy,
   And every doubt long blown by time away.

O born in days when wits were fresh and clear,
   And life ran gaily as the sparkling Thames;
      Before this strange disease of modern life,
   With its sick hurry, its divided aims,
      Its heads o'ertaxed, its palsied hearts, was rife—
         Fly hence, our contact fear!
   Still fly, plunge deeper in the bowering wood!
      Averse, as Dido did with gesture stern
      From her false friend's approach in Hades turn,
   Wave us away, and keep thy solitude.

Still nursing the unconquerable hope,
   Still clutching the inviolable shade,
      With a free onward impulse brushing through,
   By night, the silvered branches of the glade—
      Far on the forest-skirts, where none pursue,
         On some mild pastoral slope
   Emerge, and resting on the moonlit pales,
      Freshen thy flowers, as in former years,
      With dew, or listen with enchanted ears,
   From the dark dingles, to the nightingales

But fly our paths, our feverish contact fly!
   For strong the infection of our mental strife,
      Which, though it gives no bliss, yet spoils for rest;

And we should win thee from thy own fair life,
     Like us distracted, and like us unblest.
         Soon, soon thy cheer would die,
Thy hopes grow timorous, and unfixed thy powers,
     And thy clear aims be cross and shifting made:
     And then thy glad perennial youth would fade,
Fade, and grow old at last, and die like ours.

Then fly our greetings, fly our speech and smiles!
     —As some grave Tyrian trader, from the sea,
         Descried at sunrise an emerging prow
Lifting the cool-haired creepers stealthily,
     The fringes of a southward-facing brow
         Among the Ægean isles;
And saw the merry Grecian coaster come,
     Freighted with amber grapes, and Chian wine,
     Green bursting figs, and tunnies steeped in brine;
And knew the intruders on his ancient home,

The young light-hearted masters of the waves;
     And snatched his rudder, and shook out more sail,
         And day and night held on indignantly
O'er the blue Midland waters with the gale,
     Betwixt the Syrtes and soft Sicily,
         To where the Atlantic raves
Outside the Western Straits, and unbent sails
     There, where down cloudy cliffs, through sheets of
         foam,
     Shy traffickers, the dark Iberians come;
And on the beach undid his corded bales.


### East London

'Twas August, and the fierce sun overhead
Smote on the squalid streets of Bethnal Green,
And the pale weaver, through his windows seen
In Spitalfields, looked thrice dispirited;
I met a preacher there I knew, and said:

"Ill and o'erworked, how fare you in this scene?"
"Bravely!" said he; "for I of late have been
Much cheered with thoughts of Christ, *the living
    bread."*
O human soul! as long as thou canst so
Set up a mark of everlasting light,
Above the howling senses' ebb and flow,
To cheer thee, and to right thee if thou roam,
Not with lost toil thou labourest through the night,
Thou mak'st the heaven thou hop'st indeed thy home.


### West London

Crouched on the pavement close by Belgrave Square,
A tramp I saw, ill, moody, and tongue-tied;
A babe was in her arms, and at her side
A girl; their clothes were rags, their feet were bare.
Some labouring men, whose work lay somewhere there,
Passed opposite; she touched her girl, who hied
Across and begged, and came back satisfied.
The rich she had let pass with frozen stare.
Thought I: Above her state this spirit towers;
She will not ask of aliens, but of friends,
Of sharers in a common human fate.
She turns from that cold succor, which attends
The unknown little from the unknowing great,
And points us to a better time than ours.


### Dover Beach

The sea is calm to-night,
The tide is full, the moon lies fair
Upon the Straits;—on the French coast, the light
Gleams, and is gone; the cliffs of England stand,
Glimmering and vast, out in the tranquil bay.
Come to the window, sweet is the night air!
Only, from the long line of spray

Where the ebb meets the moon-blanched sand,
Listen! you hear the grating roar
Of pebbles which the waves suck back, and fling,
At their return, up the high strand,
Begin, and cease, and then again begin,
With tremulous cadence slow, and bring
The eternal note of sadness in.

   Sophocles long ago
Heard it on the Ægean, and it brought
Into his mind the turbid ebb and flow
Of human misery; we
Find also in the sound a thought,
Hearing it by this distant northern sea.

The sea of faith
Was once, too, at the full, and round earth's shore
Lay like the folds of a bright girdle furled;
But now I only hear
Its melancholy, long, withdrawing roar,
Retreating to the breath
Of the night-wind down the vast edges drear
And naked shingles of the world.

Ah, love, let us be true
To one another! for the world, which seems
To lie before us like a land of dreams,
So various, so beautiful, so new,
Hath really neither joy, nor love, nor light,
Nor certitude, nor peace, nor help for pain;
And we are here as on a darkling plain
Swept with confused alarms of struggle and flight,
Where ignorant armies clash by night.

## The Last Word

   Creep into thy narrow bed,
   Creep, and let no more be said!

Vain thy onset! all stands fast;
Thou thyself must break at last.

Let the long contention cease!
Geese are swans, and swans are geese.
Let them have it how they will!
Thou art tired; best be still!

They out-talked thee, hissed thee, tore thee;
Better men fared thus before thee;
Fired their ringing shot and passed,
Hotly charged—and broke at last.

Charge once more, then, and be dumb!
Let the victors, when they come,
When the forts of folly fall,
Find thy body by the wall.

## WILLIAM CORY/1823–1892

### Heraclitus

They told me, Heraclitus, they told me you were
    dead,
They brought me bitter news to hear and bitter
    tears to shed.
I wept as I remembered how often you and I
Had tired the sun with talking and sent him down
    the sky.

And now that thou art lying, my dear old Carian
    guest,
A handful of grey ashes, long, long ago at rest,

Still are thy pleasant voices, thy nightingales,
   awake;
For Death, he taketh all away, but them he
   cannot take.


# DANTE GABRIEL ROSSETTI/1828–1882

### The Woodspurge

The wind flapped loose, the wind was still,
Shaken out dead from tree and hill:
I had walked on at the wind's will,—
I sat now, for the wind was still.

Between my knees my forehead was,—
My lips, drawn in, said not Alas!
My hair was over in the grass,
My naked ears heard the day pass.

My eyes, wide open, had the run
Of some ten weeds to fix upon;
Among those few, out of the sun,
The woodspurge flowered, three cups in one.

From perfect grief there need not be
Wisdom or even memory:
One thing then learnt remains to me,—
The woodspurge has a cup of three.


### On Refusal of Aid Between Nations

Not that the earth is changing, O my God!
Nor that the seasons totter in their walk,—
Not that the virulent ill of act and talk
Seethes ever as a winepress ever trod,—

Not therefore are we certain that the rod
Weighs in thine hand to smite thy world; though now
Beneath thine hand so many nations bow,
So many kings:—not therefore, O my God!—
But because Man is parcelled out in men
To-day; because, for any wrongful blow,
No man not stricken asks, "I would be told
Why thou dost thus?" but his heart whispers then,
"He is he, I am I." By this we know
That our earth falls asunder, being old.


# GEORGE MEREDITH/1828-1909

### *"I Play for Seasons"*

"I play for Seasons: not Eternities!"
  Says Nature, laughing on her way. "So must
  All those whose stake is nothing more than dust!"
  And lo, she wins, and of her harmonies
  She is full sure! Upon her dying rose
  She drops a look of fondness, and goes by,
  Scarce any retrospection in her eye;
  For she the laws of growth most deeply knows,
  Whose hands bear, here, a seed-bag—there, an urn.
  Pledged she herself to aught, 'twould mark her end!
  This lesson of our only visible friend
  Can we not teach our foolish hearts to learn?
  Yes! yes!—but, oh, our human rose is fair
  Surpassingly! Lose calmly Love's great bliss,
  When the renewed for ever of a kiss
  Whirls life within the shower of loosened hair!

## Am I Failing?

Am I failing? For no longer can I cast
A glory round about this head of gold.
Glory she wears, but springing from the mould;
Not like the consecration of the Past!
Is my soul beggared? Something more than earth
I cry for still: I cannot be at peace
In having Love upon a mortal lease.
I cannot take the woman at her worth!
Where is the ancient wealth wherewith I clothed
Our human nakedness, and could endow
With spiritual splendour a white brow
That else had grinned at me the fact I loathed?
A kiss is but a kiss now! and no wave
Of great flood that whirls me to the sea.
But, as you will! we'll sit contentedly,
And eat our pot of honey on the grave.

## Mark Where the Pressing Wind

Mark where the pressing wind shoots javelin-like
Its skeleton shadow on the broad-backed wave!
Here is a fitting spot to dig Love's grave;
Here where the ponderous breakers plunge and strike,
And dart their hissing tongues high up the sand:
In hearing of the ocean, and in sight
Of those ribbed wind-streaks running into white.
If I the death of Love had deeply planned,
I never could have made it half so sure,
As by the unblest kisses which upbraid
The full-waked sense; or failing that, degrade!
'Tis morning: but no morning can restore
What we have forfeited. I see no sin:
The wrong is mixed. In tragic life, God wot,
No villain need be! Passions spin the plot:
We are betrayed by what is false within.

### Their Sense Is with Their Senses All Mixed In

Their sense is with their senses all mixed in,
Destroyed by subtleties these women are!
More brain, O Lord, more brain! or we shall mar
Utterly this fair garden we might win.
Behold! I looked for peace, and thought it near.
Our inmost hearts had opened, each to each.
We drank the pure daylight of honest speech.
Alas! that was the fatal draught, I fear.
For when of my lost Lady came the word,
This woman, O this agony of flesh!
Jealous devotion bade her break the mesh,
That I might seek that other like a bird.
I do adore the nobleness! despise
The act! She has gone forth, I know not where.
Will the hard world my sentience of her share?
I feel the truth; so let the world surmise.

### Thus Piteously Love Closed

Thus piteously Love closed what he begat:
The union of this ever-diverse pair!
These two were rapid falcons in a snare,
Condemned to do the flitting of the bat.
Lovers beneath the singing sky of May,
They wandered once; clear as the dew on flowers:
But they fed not on the advancing hours:
Their hearts held cravings for the buried day.
Then each applied to each that fatal knife,
Deep questioning, which probes to endless dole.
Ah, what a dusty answer gets the soul
When hot for certainties in this our life!—
In tragic hints here see what evermore,
Moves dark as yonder midnight ocean's force,
Thundering like ramping hosts of warrior horse,
To throw that faint thin line upon the shore!

### Lucifer in Starlight

On a starred night Prince Lucifer uprose.
Tired of his dark dominion swung the fiend
Above the rolling ball in cloud part screened,
Where sinners hugged their spectre of repose.
Poor prey to his hot fit of pride were those.
And now upon his western wing he leaned,
Now his huge bulk o'er Afric's sands careened,
Now the black planet shadowed Arctic snows.
Soaring through wider zones that pricked his scars
With memory of the old revolt from Awe,
He reached a middle height, and at the stars,
Which are the brain of heaven, he looked, and sank.
Around the ancient track marched, rank on rank,
The army of unalterable law.


# CHRISTINA ROSSETTI/1830–1894


### A Dirge

Why were you born when the snow was falling?
You should have come to the cuckoo's calling,
 Or when grapes are green in the cluster,
 Or, at least, when lithe swallows muster
     For their far off flying
     From summer dying.

Why did you die when the lambs were cropping?
You should have died at the apples' dropping,
 When the grasshopper comes to trouble,
And the wheat-fields are sodden stubble,
     And all winds go sighing
     For sweet things dying.

# RICHARD WATSON DIXON/1833–1900

## *Dream*

### I

With camel's hair I clothed my skin,
   I fed my mouth with honey wild;
And set me scarlet wool to spin,
   And all my breast with hyssop filled;
Upon my brow and cheeks and chin
   A bird's blood spilled.

I took a broken reed to hold,
   I took a sponge of gall to press;
I took weak water-weeds to fold
   About my sacrificial dress.

I took the grasses of the field,
   The flax was bolled upon my crine;
And ivy thorn and wild grapes healed
   To make good wine.

I took my scrip of manna sweet,
   My cruse of water did I bless;
I took the white dove by the feet
   And flew into the wilderness.

### II

The tiger came and played;
Uprose the lion in his mane;
The jackal's tawny nose
And sanguine dripping tongue
Out of the desert rose

And plunged its sands among;
The bear came striding o'er the desert plain.

Uprose the horn and eyes
And quivering flank of the great unicorn,
And galloped round and round;
Uprose the gleaming claw
Of the leviathan, and wound
In steadfast march did draw
Its course away beyond the desert's bourn.

I stood within a maze
Woven round about me by magic art,
And ordered circle-wise;
The bear more near did tread,
And with two fiery eyes,
And with a wolfish head
Did close the circle round in every part.


### III

With scarlet corded horn,
With frail wrecked knees and stumbling pace
The scapegoat came:
His eyes took flesh and spirit dread in flame
At once, and he died looking towards my face.


### Both Less and More

I rode my horse to the hostel gate,
    And the landlord fed it with corn and hay:
His eyes were blear, he limped in his gait,
    His lip hung down, his hair was grey.

I entered in the wayside inn;
    And the landlady met me without a smile;

Her dreary dress was old and thin,
  Her face was full of piteous guile.

There they had been for threescore years:
  There was none to tell them they were great:
Not one to tell of our hopes and fears;
  And not far off was the churchyard gate.


# ALGERNON CHARLES SWINBURNE
## 1 8 3 7 – 1 9 0 9


*Chorus from* ATALANTA IN CALYDON

When the hounds of spring are on winter's traces,
  The mother of months in meadow or plain
Fills the shadows and windy places
  With lisp of leaves and ripple of rain;
And the brown bright nightingale amorous
Is half assuaged for Itylus,
For the Thracian ships and the foreign faces,
  The tongueless vigil, and all the pain.

Come with bows bent and with emptying of quivers,
  Maiden most perfect, lady of light,
With a noise of winds and many rivers,
  With a clamour of waters, and with might;
Bind on thy sandals, O thou most fleet,
Over the splendour and speed of thy feet;
For the faint east quickens, the wan west shivers,
  Round the feet of the day and the feet of the night.

Where shall we find her, how shall we sing to her,
  Fold our hands round her knees, and cling?
O that man's heart were as fire and could spring to her,
  Fire, or the strength of the streams that spring!
For the stars and the winds are unto her

As raiment, as songs of the harp-player;
For the risen stars and the fallen cling to her,
   And the southwest wind and the west wind sing.

For the winter's rains and ruins are over,
   And all the season of snows and sins;
The days dividing lover and lover,
   The light that loses, the night that wins;
And time remembered is grief forgotten,
And frosts are slain and flowers begotten,
And in green underwood and cover
   Blossom by blossom the spring begins.

The full streams feed on flower of rushes,
   Ripe grasses trammel a travelling foot,
The faint fresh flame of the young year flushes
   From leaf to flower and flower to fruit;
And fruit and leaf are as gold and fire,
And the oat is heard above the lyre,
And the hoofèd heel of a satyr crushes
   The chestnut-husk at the chestnut-root.

And Pan by noon and Bacchus by night,
   Fleeter of foot than the fleet-foot kid,
Follows with dancing and fills with delight
   The Maenad and the Bassarid;
And soft as lips that laugh and hide
The laughing leaves of the trees divide,
And screen from seeing and leave in sight
   The god pursuing, the maiden hid.

The ivy falls with the Bacchanal's hair
   Over her eyebrows hiding her eyes;
The wild vine slipping down leaves bare
   Her bright breast shortening into sighs;
The wild vine slips with the weight of its leaves,
But the berried ivy catches and cleaves
To the limbs that glitter, the feet that scare
   The wolf that follows, the fawn that flies.

## A Forsaken Garden

In a coign of the cliff between lowland and highland,
  At the sea-down's edge between windward and lee,
Walled round with rocks as an inland island,
  The ghost of a garden fronts the sea.
A girdle of brushwood and thorn encloses
  The steep square slope of the blossomless bed
Where the weeds that grew green from the graves of its roses
      Now lie dead.

The fields fall southward, abrupt and broken,
  To the low last edge of the long lone land.
If a step should sound or a word be spoken,
  Would a ghost not rise at the strange guest's hand?
So long have the grey bare walks lain guestless,
  Through branches and briars if a man make way,
He shall find no life but the sea-wind's, restless
      Night and day.

The dense hard passage is blind and stifled
  That crawls by a track none turn to climb
To the strait waste place that the years have rifled
  Of all but the thorns that are touched not of time.
The thorns he spares when the rose is taken;
  The rocks are left when he wastes the plain.
The wind that wanders, the weeds wind-shaken,
      These remain.

Not a flower to be pressed of the foot that falls not;
  As the heart of a dead man the seed-plots are dry;
From the thicket of thorns whence the nightingale calls not,
  Could she call, there were never a rose to reply.
Over the meadows that blossom and wither
  Rings but the note of a sea-bird's song;
Only the sun and the rain come hither
      All year long.

The sun burns sere and the rain dishevels
   One gaunt bleak blossom of scentless breath.
Only the wind here hovers and revels
   In a round where life seems barren as death.
Here there was laughing of old, there was weeping,
   Haply, of lovers none ever will know,
Whose eyes went seaward a hundred sleeping
      Years ago.


Heart handfast in heart as they stood, "Look thither,"
   Did he whisper? "look forth from the flowers to the sea;
For the foam-flowers endure when the rose-blossoms
    wither,
   And men that love lightly may die—but we?"
And the same wind sang and the same waves whitened,
   And or ever the garden's last petals were shed,
In the lips that had whispered, the eyes that had lightened,
      Love was dead.


Or they loved their life through, and then went whither?
   And were one to the end—but what end who knows?
Love deep as the sea as a rose must wither,
   As the rose-red seaweed that mocks the rose.
Shall the dead take thought for the dead to love them?
   What love was ever as deep as a grave?
They are loveless now as the grass above them
      Or the wave.


All are at one now, roses and lovers,
   Not known of the cliffs and the fields and the sea.
Not a breath of the time that has been hovers
   In the air now soft with a summer to be.
Not a breath shall there sweeten the seasons hereafter
   Of the flowers or the lovers that laugh now or weep,
When as they that are free now of weeping and laughter
      We shall sleep.

Here death may deal not again for ever;
  Here change may come not till all change end.
From the graves they have made they shall rise up never,
  Who have left nought living to ravage and rend.
Earth, stones, and thorns of the wild ground growing,
  While the sun and the rain live, these shall be;
Till a last wind's breath upon all these blowing
      Roll the sea.

Till the slow sea rise and the sheer cliff crumble,
  Till terrace and meadow the deep gulfs drink,
Till the strength of the waves of the high tides humble
  The fields that lessen, the rocks that shrink,
Here now in his triumph where all things falter,
  Stretched out on the spoils that his own hand spread,
As a god self-slain on his own strange altar,
      Death lies dead.

# WILFRID SCAWEN BLUNT/1840–1922

## The Old Squire

I like the hunting of the hare
  Better than that of the fox;
I like the joyous morning air,
  And the crowing of the cocks.

I like the calm of the early fields,
  The ducks asleep by the lake,
The quiet hour which Nature yields,
  Before mankind is awake.

I like the pheasants and feeding things
  Of the unsuspicious morn;
I like the flap of the wood-pigeon's wings
  As she rises from the corn.

I like the blackbird's shriek, and his rush
   From the turnips as I pass by,
And the partridge hiding her head in a bush
   For her young ones cannot fly.

I like these things, and I like to ride
   When all the world is in bed,
To the top of the hill where the sky grows wide,
   And where the sun grows red.

The beagles at my hõrse heels trot
   In silence after me;
There's Ruby, Roger, Diamond, Dot,
   Old Slut and Margery,—

A score of names well used, and dear,
   The names my childhood knew;
The horn, with which I rouse their cheer,
   Is the horn my father blew.

I like the hunting of the hare
   Better than that of the fox;
The new world still is all less fair
   Than the old world it mocks.

I covet not a wider range
   Than these dear manors give;
I take my pleasures without change,
   And as I lived I live.

I leave my neighbours to their thought;
   My choice it is, and pride,
On my own lands to find my sport,
   In my own fields to ride.

The hare herself no better loves
   The field where she was bred,
Than I the habit of these groves,
   My own inherited.

I know my quarries every one,
   The meuse where she sits low;
The road she chose to-day was run
   A hundred years ago.

The lags, the gills, the forest ways,
   The hedgerows one and all,
These are the kingdoms of my chase,
   And bounded by my wall;

Nor has the world a better thing,
   Though one should search it round,
Than thus to live one's own sole king,
   Upon one's own sole ground.

I like the hunting of the hare;
   It brings me, day by day,
The memory of old days as fair,
   With dead men past away.

To these, as homeward still I ply
   And pass the churchyard gate
Where all are laid as I must lie,
   I stop and raise my hat.

I like the hunting of the hare;
   New sports I hold in scorn.
I like to be as my fathers were,
   In the days e'er I was born.


THOMAS HARDY/1840-1928


*In Tenebris, I*


Wintertime nighs;
But my bereavement pain

It cannot bring again:
   Twice no one dies.


   Flower-petals flee;
But since it once hath been,
No more that severing scene
   Can harrow me.


   Birds faint in dread:
I shall not lose old strength
In the lone frost's black length:
   Strength long since fled!


   Leaves freeze to dun;
But friends cannot turn cold
This season as of old
   For him with none.


   Tempests may scath;
But love cannot make smart
Again this year his heart
   Who no heart hath.


   Black is night's cope;
But death will not appall
One who, past doubtings all,
   Waits in unhope.


### The Convergence of the Twain

*Lines on the Loss of the* Titanic


  In a solitude of the sea
   Deep from human vanity,
And the Pride of Life that planned her, stilly couches she.

Steel chambers, late the pyres
Of her salamandrine fires,
Cold currents thrid, and turn to rhythmic tidal lyres.


Over the mirrors meant
To glass the opulent
The sea-worm crawls—grotesque, slimed, dumb, indifferent.


Jewels in joy designed
To ravish the sensuous mind
Lie lightless, all their sparkles bleared and black and blind.


Dim moon-eyed fishes near
Gaze at the gilded gear
And query: "What does this vaingloriousness down
    here?" . . .


Well: while was fashioning
This creature of cleaving wing,
The Immanent Will that stirs and urges everything


Prepared a sinister mate
For her—so gaily great—
A Shape of Ice, for the time far and dissociate.


And as the smart ship grew
In stature, grace, and hue,
In shadowy silent distance grew the Iceberg too.


Alien they seemed to be:
No mortal eye could see
The intimate welding of their later history,


Or sign that they were bent
By paths coincident
On being anon twin halves of one august event,

Till the Spinner of the Years
    Said "Now!" And each one hears,
And consummation comes, and jars two hemispheres.


## *Wessex Heights*


There are some heights in Wessex, shaped as if by a kindly
    hand
For thinking, dreaming, dying on, and at crises when I stand,
Say, on Ingpen Beacon eastward, or on Wylls-Neck
    westwardly,
I seem where I was before my birth, and after death may be.

In the lowlands I have no comrade, not even the lone man's
    friend—
Her who suffereth long and is kind; accepts what he is too
    weak to mend:
Down there they are dubious and askance; there nobody
    thinks as I,
But mind-chains do not clank where one's next neighbor is
    the sky.

In the towns I am tracked by phantoms having weird
    detective ways—
Shadows of beings who fellowed with myself of earlier days:
They hang about at places, and they say harsh heavy things—
Men with a frigid sneer, and women with tart disparagings.

Down there I seem to be false to myself, my simple self that
    was,
And is not now, and I see him watching, wondering what
    crass cause
Can have merged him into such a strange continuator as this,
Who yet has something in common with himself, my
    chrysalis.

I cannot go to the great gray Plain; there's a figure against the
    moon,
Nobody sees it but I, and it makes my breast beat out of
    tune;
I cannot go to the tall-spired town, being barred by the forms
    now passed
For everybody but me, in whose long vision they stand there
    fast.

There's a ghost at Yell'ham Bottom chiding loud at the fall of
    the night,
There's a ghost in Froom-side Vale, thin lipped and vague, in
    a shroud of white,
There is one in the railway-train whenever I do not want it
    near,
I see its profile against the pane, saying what I would not
    hear.

As for one rare fair woman, I am now but a thought of hers,
I enter her mind and another thought succeeds me that she
    prefers;
Yet my love for her in its fulness she herself even did not
    know;
Well, time cures hearts of tenderness, and now I can let her
    go.

So I am found on Ingpen Beacon, or on Wylls-Neck to the
    west,
Or else on homely Bulbarrow, or little Pilsdon Crest,
Where men have never cared to haunt, nor women have
    walked with me,
And ghosts then keep their distance; and I know some liberty.


### In Death Divided

I shall rot here, with those whom in their day
    You never knew,

And alien ones who, ere they chilled to clay,
    Met not my view,
Will in your distant grave-place ever neighbour you.


No shade of pinnacle or tree or tower,
    While earth endures,
Will fall on my mound and within the hour
    Steal on to yours;
One robin never haunt our two green covertures.


Some organ may resound on Sunday noons
    By where you lie,
Some other thrill the panes with other tunes
    Where moulder I;
No selfsame chords compose our common lullaby.


The simply-cut memorial at my head
    Perhaps may take
A rustic form, and that above your bed
    A stately make;
No linking symbol show thereon for our tale's sake.


And in the monotonous moils of strained, hard-run
    Humanity,
The eternal tie which binds us twain in one
    No eye will see
Stretching across the miles that sever you from me.


## The Going


Why did you give no hint that night
That quickly after the morrow's dawn,
And calmly, as if indifferent quite,
You would close your term here, up and be gone
    Where I could not follow
    With wing of swallow
To gain one glimpse of you ever anon!

Never to bid good-bye,
    Or lip me the softest call,
Or utter a wish for a word, while I
Saw morning harden upon the wall,
      Unmoved, unknowing
      That your great going
Had place that moment, and altered all.


Why do you make me leave the house
And think for a breath it is you I see
At the end of the alley of bending boughs
Where so often at dusk you used to be;
      Till in darkening dankness
      The yawning blankness
Of the perspective sickens me!


      You were she who abode
      By those red-veined rocks far West,
You were the swan-necked one who rode
Along the beetling Beeny Crest,
      And, reining nigh me,
      Would muse and eye me,
While Life unrolled us its very best.


Why, then, latterly did we not speak,
Did we not think of those days long dead,
And ere your vanishing strive to seek
That time's renewal? We might have said,
      "In this bright spring weather
      We'll visit together
Those places that once we visited."


      Well, well! All's past amend,
      Unchangeable. It must go.
I seem but a dead man held on end
To sink down soon. . . . O you could not know

That such swift fleeing
No soul foreseeing—
Not even I—would undo me so!

## An Ancient to Ancients

Where once we danced, where once we sang,
  Gentlemen,
The floors are sunken, cobwebs hang,
And cracks creep; worms have fed upon
The doors. Yea, sprightlier times were then
Than now, with harps and tabrets gone,
  Gentlemen!

Where once we rowed, where once we sailed,
  Gentlemen,
And damsels took the tiller, veiled
Against too strong a star (God wot
Their fancy, then or anywhen!)
Upon that shore we are clean forgot,
  Gentlemen!

We have lost somewhat, afar and near,
  Gentlemen,
The thinning of our ranks each year
Affords a hint we are nigh undone,
That we shall not be ever again
The marked of many, loved of one,
  Gentlemen.

In dance the polka hit our wish,
  Gentlemen,
The paced quadrille, the spry schottische,
"Sir Roger."—And in opera spheres
The "Girl" (the famed "Bohemian"),
And "Trovatore," held the ears,
  Gentlemen.

This season's paintings do not please,
           Gentlemen,
Like Etty, Mulready, Maclise;
Throbbing romance has waned and wanned;
No wizard wields the witching pen
Of Bulwer, Scott, Dumas, and Sand,
           Gentlemen.

The bower we shrined to Tennyson,
           Gentlemen,
Is roof-wrecked; damps there drip upon
Sagged seats, the creeper-nails are rust,
The spider is sole denizen;
Even she who voiced those rhymes is dust,
           Gentlemen!

We who met sunrise sanguine-souled,
           Gentlemen,
And wearing weary. We are old;
These younger press; we feel our rout
Is imminent to Aïdes' den,—
That evening shades are stretching out,
           Gentlemen!

And yet, though ours be failing frames,
           Gentlemen,
So were some others history names,
Who trode their track light-limbed and fast
As these youth, and not alien
From enterprise, to their long last,
           Gentlemen.

Sophocles, Plato, Socrates,
           Gentlemen,
Pythagoras, Thucydides,
Herodotus, and Homer,—yea,
Clement, Augustin, Origen,

Burnt brightlier towards their setting-day,
      Gentlemen.

And ye, red-lipped and smooth-browed; list,
      Gentlemen;
Much is there waits you we have missed;
Much lore we leave you worth the knowing,
Much, much has lain outside our ken:
Nay, rush not: time serves: we are going,
      Gentlemen.


ROBERT BRIDGES / 1844 – 1930


*Who Has Not Walked upon the Shore*

Who has not walked upon the shore,
And who does not the morning know,
The day the angry gale is o'er,
The hour the wind has ceased to blow?

The horses of the strong south-west
Are pastured round his tropic tent,
Careless how long the ocean's breast
Sob on and sigh for passion spent.

The frightened birds, that fled inland
To house in rock and tower and tree,
Are gathering on the peaceful strand,
To tempt again the sunny sea;

Whereon the timid ships steal out
And laugh to find their foe asleep,
That lately scattered them about,
And drave them to the fold like sheep.

The snow-white clouds he northward chased
Break into phalanx, line, and band:
All one way to the south they haste,
The south, their pleasant fatherland.

From distant hills their shadows creep,
Arrive in turn and mount the lea,
And flit across the downs, and leap
Sheer off the cliff upon the sea;

And sail and sail far out of sight.
But still I watch their fleecy trains,
That piling all the south with light,
Dapple in France the fertile plains.


## A Passer-By

Whither, O splendid ship, thy white sails crowding,
    Leaning across the bosom of the urgent West,
That fearest nor sea rising, nor sky clouding,
    Whither away, fair rover, and what thy quest?
    Ah! soon, when Winter has all our vales opprest,
When skies are cold and misty, and hail is hurling,
    Wilt thou glide on the blue Pacific, or rest
In a summer haven asleep, thy white sails furling.

I there before thee, in the country that well thou knowest,
    Already arrived am inhaling the odorous air:
I watch thee enter unerringly where thou goest,
    And anchor queen of the strange shipping there,
    Thy sails for awnings spread, thy masts bare;
Nor is aught from the foaming reef to the snow-capped,
        grandest
    Peak, that is over the feathery palms more fair
Than thou, so upright, so stately, and still thou standest.

And yet, O splendid ship, unhailed and nameless,
   I know not if, aiming a fancy, I rightly divine
That thou hast a purpose joyful, a courage blameless,
    Thy port assured in a happier land than mine.
    But for all I have given thee, beauty enough is thine,
As thou, aslant with trim tackle and shrouding,
    From the proud nostril curve of a prow's line
In the offing scatterest foam, thy white sails crowding.

## On a Dead Child

Perfect little body, without fault or stain on thee,
   With promise of strength and manhood full and fair!
    Though cold and stark and bare,
The bloom and the charm of life doth awhile remain on thee.

Thy mother's treasure wert thou;—alas, no longer
   To visit her heart with wondrous joy; to be
    Thy father's pride;—ah, he
Must gather his faith together, and his strength make
   stronger.

To me, as I move thee now in the last duty,
   Dost thou with a turn or gesture anon respond;
    Startling my fancy fond
With a chance attitude of the head, a freak of beauty.

Thy hand clasps, as 'twas wont, my finger, and holds it:
   But the grasp is the clasp of Death, heartbreaking and stiff;
    Yet feels to my hand as if
'Twas still thy will, thy pleasure and trust that enfolds it.

So I lay thee, thy sunken eyelids closing,—
   Go lie thou there in thy coffin, thy last little bed!—
    Propping thy wise, sad head,
Thy firm, pale hands across thy chest disposing.

So quiet! doth the change content thee?—Death, whither
    hath he taken thee?
   To a world, do I think, that rights the disaster of this?
     The vision of which I miss,
Who weep for the body, and wish but to warm thee and
    awaken thee?

Ah! little at best can all our hopes avail us
   To lift this sorrow, or cheer us, when in the dark,
     Unwilling, alone we embark,
And the things we have seen and have known and have heard
    of fail us.


### The Evening Darkens Over

     The evening darkens over.
     After a day so bright
     The windcapt waves discover
     That wild will be the night.
     There's sound of distant thunder.

     The latest sea-birds hover
     Along the cliff's sheer height;
     As in the memory wander
     Last flutterings of delight,
     White wings lost on the white.

     There's not a ship in sight;
     And as the sun goes under
     Thick clouds conspire to cover
     The moon that should rise yonder.
     Thou art alone, fond lover.

## Nightingales

Beautiful must be the mountains whence ye come,
And bright in the fruitful valleys the streams, wherefrom
  Ye learn your song:
Where are those starry woods? O might I wander there,
 Among the flowers, which in that heavenly air
  Bloom the year long!

Nay, barren are those mountains and spent the streams:
 Our song is the voice of desire, that haunts our dreams,
  A throe of the heart,
Whose pining visions dim, forbidden hopes profound,
 No dying cadence nor long sigh can sound,
  For all our art.

Alone, aloud in the raptured ear of men
We pour our dark nocturnal secret; and then,
  As night is withdrawn
From these sweet-springing meads and bursting boughs of
 May,
 Dream, while the innumerable choir of day
  Welcome the dawn.

## Winter Nightfall

The day begins to droop,—
 Its course is done:
But nothing tells the place
 Of the setting sun.

The hazy darkness deepens,
 And up the lane
You may hear, but cannot see,
 The homing wain.

An engine pants and hums
 In the farm hard by:

Its lowering smoke is lost
    In the lowering sky.

The soaking branches drip,
    And all night through
The dropping will not cease
    In the avenue.

A tall man there in the house
    Must keep his chair:
He knows he will never again
    Breathe the spring air:

His heart is worn with work;
    He is giddy and sick
If he rise to go as far
    As the nearest rick:

He thinks of his morn of life,
    His hale, strong years;
And braves as he may the night
    Of darkness and tears.

### Low Barometer

The south-wind strengthens to a gale,
Across the moon the clouds fly fast,
The house is smitten as with a flail,
The chimney shudders to the blast.

On such a night, when Air has loosed
Its guardian grasp on blood and brain,
Old terrors then of god or ghost
Creep from their caves to life again;

And Reason kens he herits in
A haunted house. Tenants unknown

Assert their squalid lease of sin
With earlier title than his own.

Unbodied presences, the packed
Pollution and remorse of Time,
Slipped from oblivion reënact
The horrors of unhouseld crime.

Some men would quell the thing with prayer
Whose sightless footsteps pad the floor,
Whose fearful trespass mounts the stair
Or bursts the locked forbidden door.

Some have seen corpses long interred
Escape from hallowing control,
Pale charnel forms—nay ev'n have heard
The shrilling of a troubled soul,

That wanders till the dawn hath crossed
The dolorous dark, or Earth hath wound
Closer her storm-spredd cloke, and thrust
The baleful phantoms underground.


# GERARD MANLEY HOPKINS/1845-1889


### God's Grandeur

The world is charged with the grandeur of God.
It will flame out, like shining from shook foil;
It gathers to a greatness, like the ooze of oil
Crushed. Why do men then now not reck his rod?
Generations have trod, have trod, have trod;
And all is seared with trade; bleared, smeared with toil;
And wears man's smudge and shares man's smell: the soil
Is bare now, nor can foot feel, being shod.

And for all this, nature is never spent;
There lives the dearest freshness deep down things;
And though the last lights off the black West went
Oh, morning, at the brown brink eastward, springs—
Because the Holy Ghost over the bent
World broods with warm breast and with ah! bright wings.


### The Windhover:

#### To Christ Our Lord

I caught this morning morning's minion, king-
        dom of daylight's dauphin, dapple-dawn-drawn Falcon,
            in his riding
        Of the rolling level underneath him steady air, and
            striding
High there, how he rung upon the rein of a wimpling wing
In his ecstasy! then off, off forth on swing,
        As a skate's heel sweeps smooth on a bow-bend: the
            hurl and gliding
        Rebuffed the big wind. My heart in hiding
Stirred for a bird,—the achieve of, the mastery of the thing!

Brute beauty and valor and act, oh, air, pride, plume, here
        Buckle! AND the fire that breaks from thee then, a
            billion
Times told lovelier, more dangerous, O my chevalier!

        No wonder of it: sheèr plòd makes plow down sillion
Shine, and blue-bleak embers, ah my dear,
        Fall, gall themselves, and gash gold-vermilion.

*Pied Beauty*

Glory be to God for dappled things—
 For skies of couple-color as a brindled cow;
  For rose-moles all in stipple upon trout that swim;
Fresh-firecoal chestnut-falls; finches' wings;
 Landscape plotted and pieced—fold, fallow, and plow;
  And all trades, their gear and tackle and trim.

All things counter, original, spare, strange;
 Whatever is fickle, freckled (who knows how?)
  With swift, slow; sweet, sour; adazzle, dim;
He fathers-forth whose beauty is past change:
     Praise him.


*Andromeda*

Now Time's Andromeda on this rock rude,
With not her either beauty's equal or
Her injury's, looks off by both horns of shore,
Her flower, her piece of being, doomed dragon's food.
Time past she has been attempted and pursued
By many blows and banes; but now hears roar
A wilder beast from West than all were, more
Rife in her wrongs, more lawless, and more lewd.

Her Perseus linger and leave her tó her extremes?—
Pillowy air he treads a time and hangs
His thoughts on her, forsaken that she seems,
All while her patience, morselled into pangs,
Mounts; then to alight disarming, no one dreams,
With Gorgon's gear and barebill, thongs and fangs.

## *Felix Randal*

Felix Randal the farrier, O he is dead then? my duty all
    ended,
Who have watched his mould of man, big-boned and hardy-
    handsome
Pining, pining, till time when reason rambled in it and some
Fatal four disorders, fleshed there, all contended?

Sickness broke him. Impatient he cursed at first, but mended
Being anointed and all; though a heavenlier heart began some
Months earlier, since I had our sweet reprieve and ransom
Tendered to him. Ah well, God rest him all road ever he
    offended!

This seeing the sick endears them to us, us too it endears.
My tongue had taught thee comfort, touch had quenched thy
    tears,
Thy tears that touched my heart, child, Felix, Poor Felix
    Randal;

How far from then forethought of, all thy more boisterous
    years,
When thou at the random grim forge, powerful amidst peers,
Didst fettle for the great gray drayhorse his bright and
    battering sandal!

## *Spring and Fall:*

### To a Young Child

    Márgarét are you grieving
    Over Goldengrove unleaving?
    Leáves, líke things of man, you
    With your fresh thoughts care for, can you?
    Ah! ás the heart grows older
    It will come to such sights colder
    By and by, nor spare a sigh

Though worlds of wanwood leafmeal lie;
And yet you wíll weep and know why.
Now no matter, child, the name:
Sórrow's springs áre the same.
Nor mouth had, no nor mind, expressed
What heart heard of, ghost guessed:
It ís the blight man was born for,
It is Margaret you mourn for.


### Inversnaid

This darksome burn, horseback brown,
His rollrock highroad roaring down,
In coop and in comb the fleece of his foam
Flutes and low to the lake falls home.

A wind-puff bonnet of fáwn-fróth
Turns and twindles over the broth
Of a pool so pitchblack, féll-f,fówning,
It rounds and rounds Despair to drowning.

Degged with dew, dappled with dew
Are the groins of the braes that the brook treads
    through,
Wiry heathpacks, flitches of fern,
And the beadbonny ash that sits over the burn.

What would the world be, once bereft
Of wet and wildness? Let them be left,
O let them be left, wildness and wet;
Long live the weeds and the wilderness yet.

### Thou Art Indeed Just, Lord

*Justus quidem tu es, Domine, si disputem tecum: verum-tamen justa loquar ad te: Quare via impiorum prosperatur? &c.*

Thou art indeed just, Lord, if I contend
With thee; but, sir, so what I plead is just.
Why do sinners' ways prosper? and why must
Disappointment all I endeavour end?
Wert thou my enemy, O thou my friend,
How wouldst thou worse, I wonder, than thou dost
Defeat, thwart me? Oh, the sots and thralls of lust
Do in spare hours more thrive than I that spend,
Sir, life upon thy cause. See, banks and brakes
Now, leavèd how thick! lacèd they are again
With fretty chervil, look, and fresh wind shakes
Them; birds build—but not I build; no, but strain,
Time's eunuch, and not breed one work that wakes.
Mine, O thou lord of life, send my roots rain.

# ROBERT LOUIS STEVENSON/1850–1894

### Requiem

Under the wide and starry sky
Dig the grave and let me lie:
Glad did I live and gladly die,
    And I laid me down with a will.

This be the verse you grave for me:
*Here he lies where he longed to be;*
*Home is the sailor, home from sea,*
    *And the hunter home from the hill.*

### In the Highlands

In the highlands, in the country places,
Where the old plain men have rosy faces,
  And the young fair maidens
   Quiet eyes;
Where essential silence chills and blesses,
And for ever in the hill-recesses
  *Her* more lovely music
   Broods and dies—

O to mount again where erst I haunted;
Where the old red hills are bird-enchanted,
  And the low green meadows
   Bright with sward;
And when even dies, the million-tinted,
And the night has come, and planets glinted,
  Lo, the valley hollow
   Lamp-bestarred!

O to dream, O to awake and wander
There, and with delight to take and render,
  Through the trance of silence,
   Quiet breath!
Lo! for there, among the flowers and grasses,
Only the mightier movement sounds and passes;
  Only winds and rivers,
   Life and death.

### Blows the Wind To-Day

Blows the wind to-day, and the sun and the rain are flying,
 Blows the wind on the moors to-day and now,
Where about the graves of the martyrs the whaups are crying,
 My heart remembers how!

Grey recumbent tombs of the dead in desert places,
 Standing stones on the vacant wine-red moor,

520   A. E. HOUSMAN

Hills of sheep, and the howes of the silent vanished races,
    And winds, austere and pure:

Be it granted me to behold you again in dying,
    Hills of home! and to hear again the call;
Hear about the graves of the martyrs the peewees crying,
    And hear no more at all.

A. E. HOUSMAN/1859–1936

*1887*

From Clee to heaven the beacon burns,
    The shires have seen it plain,
From north and south the sign returns
    And beacons burn again.

Look left, look right, the hills are bright,
    The dales are light between,
Because 'tis fifty years tonight
    That God has saved the Queen.

Now, when the flame they watch not towers
    About the soil they trod,
Lads, we'll remember friends of ours
    Who shared the work with God.

To skies that knit their heartstrings right,
    To fields that bred them brave,
The saviors come not home tonight:
    Themselves they could not save.

It dawns in Asia, tombstones show
    And Shropshire names are read;
And the Nile spills his overflow
    Beside the Severn's dead.

We pledge in peace by farm and town
    The Queen they served in war,
And fire the beacons up and down
    The land they perished for.

"God save the Queen" we living sing,
    From height to height 'tis heard;
And with the rest your voices ring,
    Lads of the Fifty-third.

Oh, God will save her, fear you not:
    Be you the men you've been,
Get you the sons your fathers got,
    And God will save the Queen.


### Loveliest of Trees

Loveliest of trees, the cherry now
Is hung with bloom along the bough,
And stands about the woodland ride
Wearing white for Eastertide.

Now, of my threescore years and ten,
Twenty will not come again,
And take from seventy springs a score,
It only leaves me fifty more.

And since to look at things in bloom
Fifty springs are little room,
About the woodlands I will go
To see the cherry hung with snow.


### When Smoke Stood Up from Ludlow

When smoke stood up from Ludlow,
    And mist blew off from Teme,
And blithe afield to ploughing
    Against the morning beam
    I strode beside my team,

The blackbird in the coppice
    Looked out to see me stride,

And hearkened as I whistled
  The tramping team beside,
And fluted and replied:

"Lie down, lie down, young yeoman;
  What use to rise and rise?
Rise man a thousand mornings
  Yet down at last he lies,
  And then the man is wise."

I heard the tune he sang me,
  And spied his yellow bill;
I picked a stone and aimed it
  And threw it with a will:
  Then the bird was still.

Then my soul within me
  Took up the blackbird's strain,
And still beside the horses
  Along the dewy lane
  It sang the song again:

"Lie down, lie down, young yeoman;
  The sun moves always west;
The road one treads to labour
  Will lead one home to rest,
  And that will be the best."


### On Moonlit Heath

On moonlit heath and lonesome bank
  The sheep beside me graze;
And yon the gallows used to clank
  Fast by the four cross ways.

A careless shepherd once would keep
  The flocks by moonlight there,[1]

[1] Hanging in chains was called keeping sheep by moonlight.

And high amongst the glimmering sheep
    The dead man stood on air.

They hang us now in Shrewsbury jail:
    The whistles blow forlorn,
And trains all night groan on the rail
    To men that die at morn.

There sleeps in Shrewsbury jail to-night,
    Or wakes, as may betide,
A better lad, if things went right,
    Than most that sleep outside.

And naked to the hangman's noose
    The morning clocks will ring
A neck God made for other use
    Than strangling in a string.

And sharp the link of life will snap,
    And dead on air will stand
Heels that held up as straight a chap
    As treads upon the land.

So here I'll watch the night and wait
    To see the morning shine,
When he will hear the stroke of eight
    And not the stroke of nine;

And wish my friend as sound a sleep
    As lads' I did not know,
That shepherded the moonlit sheep
    A hundred years ago.

### When I Watch the Living Meet

When I watch the living meet,
    And the moving pageant file

Warm and breathing through the street
    Where I lodge a little while,

If the heats of hate and lust
    In the house of flesh are strong,
Let me mind the house of dust
    Where my sojourn shall be long.

In the nation that is not
    Nothing stands that stood before;
There revenges are forgot,
    And the hater hates no more;

Lovers lying two and two
    Ask not whom they sleep beside,
And the bridegroom all night through
    Never turns him to the bride.


### To an Athlete Dying Young

The time you won your town the race
We chaired you through the market-place;
Man and boy stood cheering by,
And home we brought you shoulder-high.

Today, the road all runners come,
Shoulder-high we bring you home,
And set you at your threshold down,
Townsman of a stiller town.

Smart lad, to slip betimes away
From fields where glory does not stay
And early though the laurel grows
It withers quicker than the rose.

Eyes the shady night has shut
Cannot see the record cut,

And silence sounds no worse than cheers
After earth has stopped the ears:

Now you will not swell the rout
Of lads that wore their honours out,
Runners whom renown outran
And the name died before the man.

So set, before its echoes fade,
The fleet foot on the sill of shade,
And hold to the low lintel up
The still-defended challenge-cup.

And round that early-laureled head
Will flock to gaze the strengthless dead,
And find unwithered on its curls
The garland briefer than a girl's.

### The Welsh Marches

High the vanes of Shrewsbury gleam
Islanded in Severn stream;
The bridges from the steepled crest
Cross the water east and west.

The flag of morn in conqueror's state
Enters at the English gate:
The vanquished eve, as night prevails,
Bleeds upon the road to Wales.

Ages since the vanquished bled
Round my mother's marriage-bed;
There the ravens feasted far
About the open house of war:

When Severn down to Buildwas ran
Coloured with the death of man,

Couched upon her brother's grave
The Saxon got me on the slave.

The sound of fight is silent long
That began the ancient wrong;
Long the voice of tears is still
That wept of old the endless ill.

In my heart it has not died,
The war that sleeps on Severn side;
They cease not fighting, east and west,
On the marches of my breast.

Here the truceless armies yet
Trample, rolled in blood and sweat;
They kill and kill and never die;
And I think that each is I.

None will part us, none undo
The knot that makes one flesh of two,
Sick with hatred, sick with pain,
Strangling—When shall we be slain?

When shall I be dead and rid
Of the wrong my father did?
How long, how long, till spade and hearse
Put to sleep my mother's curse?

### On Wenlock Edge

On Wenlock Edge the wood's in trouble;
　His forest fleece the Wrekin heaves;
The gale, it plies the saplings double,
　And thick on Severn snow the leaves.

'Twould blow like this through holt and hanger
　When Uricon the city stood:

'Tis the old wind in the old anger,
  But then it threshed another wood.

Then, 'twas before my time, the Roman
  At yonder heaving hill would stare:
The blood that warms an English yeoman,
  The thoughts that hurt him, they were there.

There, like the wind through woods in riot,
  Through him the gale of life blew high;
The tree of man was never quiet:
  Then 'twas the Roman, now 'tis I.

The gale, it plies the saplings double,
  It blows so hard, 'twill soon be gone:
To-day the Roman and his trouble
  Are ashes under Uricon.


### The Immortal Part

When I meet the morning beam
Or lay me down at night to dream,
I hear my bones within me say,
"Another night, another day.

"When shall this slough of sense be cast,
This dust of thoughts be laid at last,
The man of flesh and soul be slain
And the man of bone remain?

"This tongue that talks, these lungs that shout,
These thews that hustle us about,
This brain that fills the skull with schemes,
And its humming hive of dreams,—

"These to-day are proud in power
And lord it in their little hour:

The immortal bones obey control
Of dying flesh and dying soul.

" 'Tis long till eve and morn are gone:
Slow the endless night comes on,
And late to fulness grows the birth
That shall last as long as earth.

"Wanderers eastward, wanderers west,
Know you why you cannot rest?
'Tis that every mother's son
Travails with a skeleton.

"Lie down in the bed of dust;
Bear the fruit that bear you must;
Bring the eternal seed to light,
And morn is all the same as night.

"Rest you so from trouble sore,
Fear the heat o' the sun no more,
Nor the snowing winter wild,
Now you labor not with child.

"Empty vessel, garment cast,
We that wore you long shall last.
—Another night, another day."
So my bones within me say.

Therefore they shall do my will
To-day while I am master still,
And flesh and soul, now both are strong,
Shall hale the sullen slaves along,

Before this fire of sense decay,
This smoke of thought blow clean away,
And leave with ancient night alone
The steadfast and enduring bone.

## Be Still, My Soul

Be still, my soul, be still; the arms you bear are brittle,
  Earth and high heaven are fixt of old and founded strong.
Think rather,—call to thought, if now you grieve a little,
  The days when we had rest, O soul, for they were long.

Men loved unkindness then, but lightless in the quarry
  I slept and saw not; tears fell down, I did not mourn;
Sweat ran and blood sprang out and I was never sorry:
  Then it was well with me, in days ere I was born.

Now, and I muse for why and never find the reason,
  I pace the earth, and drink the air, and feel the sun.
Be still, be still, my soul; it is but for a season:
  Let us endure an hour and see injustice done.

Ay, look: high heaven and earth ail from the prime
      foundation;
  All thoughts to rive the heart are here, and all are vain:
Horror and scorn and hate and fear and indignation—
  Oh why did I awake? when shall I sleep again?


## Hell Gate

Onward led the road again
Through the sad uncoloured plain
Under twilight brooding dim,
And along the utmost rim
Wall and rampart risen to sight
Cast a shadow not of night,
And beyond them seemed to glow
Bonfires lighted long ago.
And my dark conductor broke
Silence at my side and spoke,
Saying, "You conjecture well:
Yonder is the gate of hell."

Ill as yet the eye could see
The eternal masonry,
But beneath it on the dark
To and fro there stirred a spark.
And again the somber guide
Knew my question and replied:
"At hell gate the damned in turn
Pace for sentinel and burn."

Dully at the leaden sky
Staring, and with idle eye
Measuring the listless plain,
I began to think again.
Many things I thought of then,
Battle, and the loves of men,
Cities entered, oceans crossed,
Knowledge gained and virtue lost,
Cureless folly done and said,
And the lovely way that led
To the slimepit and the mire
And the everlasting fire.
And against a smolder dun
And a dawn without a sun
Did the nearing bastion loom,
And across the gate of gloom
Still one saw the sentry go,
Trim and burning, to and fro,
One for women to admire
In his finery of fire.
Something, as I watched him pace,
Minded me of time and place,
Soldiers of another corps
And a sentry known before.

Ever darker hell on high
Reared its strength upon the sky,
And our footfall on the track
Fetched the daunting echo back.
But the soldier pacing still

The insuperable sill,
Nursing his tormented pride,
Turned his head to neither side,
Sunk into himself apart
And the hell-fire of his heart.
But against our entering in
From the drawbridge Death and Sin
Rose to render key and sword
To their father and their lord.
And the portress foul to see
Lifted up her eyes on me
Smiling, and I made reply:
"Met again, my lass," said I.
Then the sentry turned his head,
Looked, and knew me, and was Ned.

Once he looked, and halted straight,
Set his back against the gate,
Caught his musket to his chin,
While the hive of hell within
Sent abroad a seething hum
As of towns whose king is come
Leading conquest home from far
And the captives of his war,
And the car of triumph waits,
And they open wide the gates.
But across the entry barred
Straddled the revolted guard,
Weaponed and accoutred well
From the arsenals of hell;
And beside him, sick and white,
Sin to left and Death to right
Turned a countenance of fear
On the flaming mutineer.
Over us the darkness bowed,
And the anger in the cloud
Clenched the lightning for the stroke;
But the traitor musket spoke.

And the hollowness of hell
Sounded as its master fell,
And the mourning echo rolled
Ruin through his kingdom old.
Tyranny and terror flown
Left a pair of friends alone,
And beneath the nether sky
All that stirred was he and I.

Silent, nothing found to say,
We began the backward way;
And the ebbing luster died
From the soldier at my side,
As in all his spruce attire
Failed the everlasting fire.
Midmost of the homeward track
Once we listened, and looked back;
But the city, dusk, and mute,
Slept, and there was no pursuit.

### Epitaph on an Army of Mercenaries

These, in the day when heaven was falling,
  The hour when earth's foundations fled,
Followed their mercenary calling
  And took their wages and are dead.

Their shoulders held the sky suspended;
  They stood, and earth's foundations stay;
What God abandoned, these defended,
  And saved the sum of things for pay.

# RUDYARD KIPLING/1865–1936

### Recessional

God of our fathers, known of old,
   Lord of our far-flung battle-line,
Beneath whose awful Hand we hold
   Dominion over palm and pine—
Lord God of Hosts, be with us yet,
Lest we forget—lest we forget!

The tumult and the shouting dies;
   The Captains and the Kings depart:
Still stands Thine ancient sacrifice,
   An humble and a contrite heart.
Lord God of Hosts, be with us yet,
Lest we forget—lest we forget!

Far-called, our navies melt away;
   On dune and headland sinks the fire:
Lo, all our pomp of yesterday
   Is one with Nineveh and Tyre!
Judge of the Nations, spare us yet,
Lest we forget—lest we forget!

If, drunk with sight of power, we loose
   Wild tongues that have not Thee in awe,
Such boastings as the Gentiles use,
   Or lesser breeds without the Law—
Lord God of Hosts, be with us yet,
Lest we forget—lest we forget!

For heathen heart that puts her trust
   In reeking tube and iron shard,
All valiant dust that builds on dust,
   And guarding, calls not Thee to guard,
For frantic boast and foolish word—
Thy mercy on Thy people, Lord!

## Danny Deever

"What are the bugles blowin' for?" said Files-on-Parade.
"To turn you out, to turn you out," the Colour-Sergeant said.
"What makes you look so white, so white?" said Files-on-
          Parade.
"I'm dreadin' what I've got to watch," the Colour-Sergeant
  said.
      For they're hangin' Danny Deever, you can hear the
          Dead March play,
      The Regiment's in 'ollow square—they're hangin' him
          today;
      They've taken of his buttons off an' cut his stripes away,
      An' they're hangin' Danny Deever in the mornin'.

"What makes the rear-rank breathe so 'ard?" said Files-on-
          Parade.
"It's bitter cold, it's bitter cold," the Colour-Sergeant said.
"What makes that front-rank man fall down?" said Files-on-
          Parade.
"A touch o' sun, a touch o' sun," the Colour-Sergeant said.
      They are hangin' Danny Deever, they are marchin' of 'im
          round,
      They 'ave 'alted Danny Deever by 'is coffin on the
          ground;
      An' 'e'll swing in 'arf a minute for a sneakin' shootin'
          hound—
      O they're hangin' Danny Deever in the mornin'!

" 'Is cot was right-'and cot to mine," said Files-on-Parade.
" 'E's sleepin' out an' far to-night," the Colour-Sergeant said.
"I've drunk 'is beer a score o' times," said Files-on-Parade.
" 'E's drinkin' bitter beer alone," the Colour-Sergeant said.
      They are hangin' Danny Deever, you must mark 'im to
          'is place,
      For 'e shot a comrade sleepin'—you must look 'im in the
          face;
      Nine 'undred of 'is county an' the Regiment's disgrace,
      While they're hangin' Danny Deever in the mornin'.

"What's that so black agin the sun?" said Files-on-Parade.
"It's Danny fightin' 'ard for life," the Colour-Sergeant said.
"What's that that whimpers over'ead?" said Files-on-Parade.
"It's Danny's soul that's passin' now," the Colour-Sergeant
    said.
      For they're done with Danny Deever, you can 'ear the
          quickstep play,
      The Regiment's in column, an' they're marchin' us away;
      Ho! the young recruits are shakin', an' they'll want their
          beer to-day,
      After hangin' Danny Deever in the mornin'!


## The Sea and the Hills

Who hath desired the Sea?—the sight of salt water
    unbounded—
The heave and the halt and the hurl and the crash of the
    comber wind-hounded?
The sleek-barrelled swell before storm, grey, foamless,
    enormous, and growing—
Stark calm on the lap of the Line or the crazy-eyed hurricane
    blowing—
His Sea in no showing the same—his Sea and the same
    'neath each showing:
               His Sea as she slackens or thrills?
So and no otherwise—so and no otherwise—hillmen desire
    their Hills!

Who hath desired the Sea?—the immense and contemptuous
    surges?
The shudder, the stumble, the swerve, as the star-stabbing
    bowsprit emerges?
The orderly clouds of the Trades, the ridged, roaring sapphire
    thereunder—
Unheralded cliff-haunting flaws and the headsail's low-
    volleying thunder—

His Sea in no wonder the same—his Sea and the same
    through each wonder:
                  His Sea as she rages or stills?
So and no otherwise—so and no otherwise—hillmen desire
    their Hills.
Who hath desired the Sea? Her menaces swift as her
    mercies?
The in-rolling walls of the fog and the silver-winged breeze
    that disperses?
The unstable mined berg going South and the calvings and
    groans that declare it—
White water half-guessed overside and the moon breaking
    timely to bare it—
His Sea as his fathers have dared—his Sea as his children
    shall dare it:
                  His Sea as she serves him or kills?
So and no otherwise—so and no otherwise—hillmen desire
    their Hills.

Who hath desired the Sea? Her excellent loneliness rather
Than forecourts of kings, and her outermost pits than the
    streets where men gather
Inland, among dust, under trees—inland where the slayer
    may slay him—
Inland, out of reach of her arms, and the bosom whereon he
    must lay him—
His Sea from the first that betrayed—at the last that shall
    never betray him:
                  His Sea that his being fulfils?
So and no otherwise—so and no otherwise—hillmen desire
    their Hills.


### The Way Through the Woods

They shut the road through the woods
    Seventy years ago.
Weather and rain have undone it again,
    And now you would never know

There was once a path through the woods
  Before they planted the trees:
It is underneath the coppice and heath,
  And the thin anemones.
  Only the keeper sees
That, where the ring-dove broods
  And the badgers roll at ease,
There was once a road through the woods.
Yet, if you enter the woods
  Of a summer evening late,
When the night-air cools on the trout-ringed pools
  Where the otter whistles his mate
(They fear not men in the woods
  Because they see so few),
You will hear the beat of a horse's feet
  And the swish of a skirt in the dew,
  Steadily cantering through
The misty solitudes,
  As though they perfectly knew
The old lost road through the woods . . .
But there is no road through the woods.

### Song of the Galley-Slaves

We pulled for you when the wind was against us and the sails
    were low.
      Will you never let us go?
We ate bread and onions when you took towns, or ran aboard
    quickly when you were beaten back by the foe.
The Captains walked up and down the deck in fair weather
    singing songs, but we were below.
We fainted with our chins on the oars and you did not see
    that we were idle, for we still swung to and fro.
      Will you never let us go?
The salt made the oar-handles like shark-skin; our knees were
    cut to the bone with salt-cracks; our hair was stuck to
    our foreheads; and our lips were cut to the gums; and
    you whipped us because we could not row.
      Will you never let us go?

But, in a little time, we shall run out of the port-holes as the
water runs along the oar-blade, and though you tell the
others to row after us you will never catch us till you
catch the oar-thresh and tie up the winds in the belly of
the sail. Aho!
    Will you never let us go?


# WILLIAM BUTLER YEATS/1865-1939

### The Wild Swans at Coole

The trees are in their autumn beauty,
The woodland paths are dry;
Under the October twilight the water
Mirrors a still sky.
Upon the brimming water among the stones
Are nine and fifty swans.

The nineteenth autumn has come upon me
Since I first made my count.
I saw, before I had well finished,
All suddenly mount
And scatter wheeling in great broken rings
Upon their clamorous wings.

I have looked upon those brilliant creatures,
And now my heart is sore.
All's changed since I, hearing at twilight,
The first time on this shore,
The bell-beat of their wings above my head,
Trod with a lighter tread.

Unwearied still, lover by lover,
They paddle in the cold
Companionable streams, or climb the air.
Their hearts have not grown old;

Passion or conquest, wander where they will,
Attend upon them still.

But now they drift on the still water
Mysterious, beautiful.
Among what rushes will they build,
By what lake's edge or pool
Delight men's eyes, when I awake some day
To find they have flown away?

## In Memory of Major Robert Gregory

### I

Now that we're almost settled in our house
I'll name the friends that cannot sup with us
Beside a fire of turf in th' ancient tower,
And having talked to some late hour
Climb up the narrow winding stair to bed:
Discoverers of forgotten truth
Or mere companions of my youth,
All, all are in my thoughts to-night being dead.

### II

Always we'd have the new friend meet the old
And we are hurt if either friend seem cold,
And there is salt to lengthen out the smart
In the affections of our heart,
And quarrels are blown up upon that head;
But not a friend that I would bring
This night can set us quarrelling,
For all that come into my mind are dead.

### III

Lionel Johnson comes first to mind,
That loved his learning better than mankind,
Though courteous to the worst; much falling he
Brooded upon sanctity
Till all his Greek and Latin learning seemed
A long blast upon the horn that brought
A little nearer to his thought
A measureless consummation that he dreamed.

### IV

And that enquiring man John Synge comes next,
That dying chose the living world for text
And never could have rested in the tomb
But that, long travelling, he had come
Towards nightfall upon certain set apart
In a most desolate stony place,
Towards nightfall upon a race
Passionate and simple like his heart.

### V

And then I think of old George Pollexfen,
In muscular youth well known to Mayo men
For horsemanship at meets or at race-courses,
That could have shown how pure-bred horses
And solid men, for all their passion, live
But as the outrageous stars incline
By opposition, square and trine;
Having grown sluggish and contemplative.

### VI

They were my close companions many a year,
A portion of my mind and life, as it were,
And now their breathless faces seem to look
Out of some old picture-book;
I am accustomed to their lack of breath,
But not that my dear friend's dear son,
Our Sidney and our perfect man,
Could share in that discourtesy of death.

### VII

For all things the delighted eye now sees
Were loved by him; the old storm-broken trees
That cast their shadows upon road and bridge;
The tower set on the stream's edge;
The ford where drinking cattle make a stir
Nightly, and startled by that sound
The water-hen must change her ground;
He might have been your heartiest welcomer.

### VIII

When with the Galway foxhounds he would ride
From Castle Taylor to the Roxborough side
Or Esserkelly plain, few kept his pace;
At Mooneen he had leaped a place
So perilous that half the astonished meet
Had shut their eyes; and where was it
He rode a race without a bit?
And yet his mind outran the horses' feet.

IX

We dreamed that a great painter had been born
To cold Clare rock and Galway rock and thorn,
To that stern colour and that delicate line
That are our secret discipline
Wherein the gazing heart doubles her might.
Soldier, scholar, horseman, he,
And yet he had the intensity
To have published all to be a world's delight.


X

What other could so well have counselled us
In all lovely intricacies of a house
As he that practised or that understood
All work in metal or in wood,
In moulded plaster or in carven stone?
Soldier, scholar, horseman, he,
And all he did done perfectly
As though he had but that one trade alone.


XI

Some burn damp faggots, others may consume
The entire combustible world in one small room
As though dried straw, and if we turn about
The bare chimney is gone black out
Because the work had finished in that flare.
Soldier, scholar, horseman, he,
As 'twere all life's epitome.
What made us dream that he could comb grey hair?

### XII

I had thought, seeing how bitter is that wind
That shakes the shutter, to have brought to mind
All those that manhood tried, or childhood loved,
Or boyish intellect approved,
With some appropriate commentary on each;
Until imagination brought
A fitter welcome; but a thought
Of that late death took all my heart for speech.


### Sailing to Byzantium

That is no country for old men. The young
In one another's arms, birds in the trees
—Those dying generations—at their song,
The salmon-falls, the mackerel-crowded seas,
Fish, flesh, or fowl, commend all summer long
Whatever is begotten, born, and dies.
Caught in that sensual music all neglect
Monuments of unaging intellect.

An aged man is but a paltry thing,
A tattered coat upon a stick, unless
Soul clap its hands and sing, and louder sing
For every tatter in its mortal dress,
Nor is there singing school but studying
Monuments of its own magnificence;
And therefore I have sailed the seas and come
To the holy city of Byzantium.

O sages standing in God's holy fire
As in the gold mosaic of a wall,
Come from the holy fire, perne in a gyre,
And be the singing-masters of my soul.
Consume my heart away; sick with desire
And fastened to a dying animal

It knows not what it is; and gather me
Into the artifice of eternity.

Once out of nature I shall never take
My bodily form from any natural thing,
But such a form as Grecian goldsmiths make
Of hammered gold and gold enameling
To keep a drowsy Emperor awake;
Or set upon a golden bough to sing
To lords and ladies of Byzantium
Of what is past, or passing, or to come.

*The Tower*

I

What shall I do with this absurdity—
O heart, O troubled heart—this caricature,
Decrepit age that has been tied to me
As to a dog's tail?
           Never had I more
Excited, passionate, fantastical
Imagination, nor an ear and eye
That more expected the impossible—
No, not in boyhood when with rod and fly,
Or the humbler worm, I climbed Ben Bulben's back
And had the livelong summer day to spend.
It seems that I must bid the Muse go pack,
Choose Plato and Plotinus for a friend
Until imagination, ear and eye,
Can be content with argument and deal
In abstract things; or be derided by
A sort of battered kettle at the heel.

## II

I pace upon the battlements and stare
On the foundations of a house, or where
Tree, like a sooty finger, starts from the earth;
And send imagination forth
Under the day's declining beam, and call
Images and memories
From ruin or from ancient trees,
For I would ask a question of them all.

Beyond that ridge lived Mrs. French, and once
When every silver candlestick or sconce
Lit up the dark mahogany and the wine,
A serving-man, that could divine
That most respected lady's every wish,
Ran and with the garden shears
Clipped an insolent farmer's ears
And brought them in a little covered dish.

Some few remembered still when I was young
A peasant girl commended by a song,
Who'd lived somewhere upon that rocky place,
And praised the colour of her face,
And had the greater joy in praising her,
Remembering that, if walked she there,
Farmers jostled at the fair
So great a glory did the song confer.

And certain men, being maddened by those rhymes,
Or else by toasting her a score of times,
Rose from the table and declared it right
To test their fancy by their sight;
But they mistook the brightness of the moon
For the prosaic light of day—
Music had driven their wits astray—
And one was drowned in the great bog of Cloone.

Strange, but the man who made the song was blind;

Yet, now I have considered it, I find
That nothing strange; the tragedy began
With Homer that was a blind man,
And Helen has all living hearts betrayed.
O may the moon and sunlight seem
One inextricable beam,
For if I triumph I must make men mad.

And I myself created Hanrahan
And drove him drunk or sober through the dawn
From somewhere in the neighbouring cottages.
Caught by an old man's juggleries
He stumbled, tumbled, fumbled to and fro
And had but broken knees for hire
And horrible splendour of desire;
I thought it all out twenty years ago:

Good fellows shuffled cards in an old bawn;
And when that ancient ruffian's turn was on
He so bewitched the cards under his thumb
That all but the one card became
A pack of hounds and not a pack of cards,
And that he changed into a hare.
Hanrahan rose in frenzy there
And followed up those baying creatures towards—

O towards I have forgotten what—enough!
I must recall a man that neither love
Nor music nor an enemy's clipped ear
Could, he was so harried, cheer;
A figure that has grown so fabulous
There's not a neighbour left to say
When he finished his dog's day:
An ancient bankrupt master of this house.

Before that ruin came, for centuries,
Rough men-at-arms, cross-gartered to the knees
Or shod in iron, climbed the narrow stairs,
And certain men-at-arms there were

Whose images, in the Great Memory stored,
Come with loud cry and panting breast
To break upon a sleeper's rest
While their great wooden dice beat on the board.

As I would question all, come all who can;
Come old, necessitous, half-mounted man;
And bring beauty's blind rambling celebrant;
The red man the juggler sent
Through God-forsaken meadows; Mrs. French,
Gifted with so fine an ear;
The man drowned in a bog's mire,
When mocking muses chose the country wench.

Did all old men and women, rich and poor,
Who trod upon these rocks or passed this door,
Whether in public or in secret rage
As I do now against old age?
But I have found an answer in those eyes
That are impatient to be gone;
Go therefore; but leave Hanrahan,
For I need all his mighty memories.

Old lecher with a love on every wind,
Bring up out of that deep considering mind
All that you have discovered in the grave,
For it is certain that you have
Reckoned up every unforeknown, unseeing
Plunge, lured by a softening eye,
Or by a touch or a sigh,
Into the labyrinth of another's being;

Does the imagination dwell the most
Upon a woman won or woman lost?
If on the lost, admit you turned aside
From a great labyrinth out of pride,
Cowardice, some silly over-subtle thought
Or anything called conscience once;

And that if memory recur, the sun's
Under eclipse and the day blotted out.


### III

It is time that I wrote my will;
I choose upstanding men
That climb the streams until
The fountain leap, and at dawn
Drop their cast at the side
Of dripping stone; I declare
They shall inherit my pride,
The pride of people that were
Bound neither to Cause nor to State,
Neither to slaves that were spat on,
Nor to the tyrants that spat,
The people of Burke and Grattan
That gave, though free to refuse—
Pride, like that of the morn,
When the headlong light is loose,
Or that of the fabulous horn,
Or that of the sudden shower
When all streams are dry,
Or that of the hour
When the swan must fix his eye
Upon a fading gleam,
Float out upon a long
Last reach of glittering stream
And there sing his last song.
And I declare my faith:
I mock Plotinus' thought
And cry in Plato's teeth,
Death and life were not
Till man made up the whole,
Made lock, stock and barrel
Out of his bitter soul,
Aye, sun and moon and star, all,
And further add to that

That, being dead, we rise,
Dream and so create
Translunar Paradise.
I have prepared my peace
With learned Italian things
And the proud stones of Greece,
Poet's imaginings
And memories of love,
Memories of the words of women,
All those things whereof
Man makes a superhuman
Mirror-resembling dream.

As at the loophole there
The daws chatter and scream,
And drop twigs layer upon layer.
When they have mounted up,
The mother bird will rest
On their hollow top,
And so warm her wild nest.

I leave both faith and pride
To young upstanding men
Climbing the mountain side,
That under bursting dawn
They may drop a fly;
Being of metal made
Till it was broken by
This sedentary trade.

Now shall I make my soul,
Compelling it to study
In a learned school
Till the wreck of body,
Slow decay of blood,
Testy delirium
Or dull decrepitude,
Or what worse evil come—
The death of friends, or death

Of every brilliant eye
That made a catch in the breath—
Seem but the clouds of the sky
When the horizon fades;
Or a bird's sleepy cry
Among the deepening shades.


## Among School Children

I walk through the long schoolroom questioning;
A kind old nun in a white hood replies;
The children learn to cipher and to sing,
To study reading-books and history,
To cut and sew, be neat in everything
In the best modern way—the children's eyes
In momentary wonder stare upon
A sixty-year-old smiling public man.

I dream of a Ledaean body, bent
Above a sinking fire, a tale that she
Told of a harsh reproof, or trivial event
That changed some childish day to tragedy—
Told, and it seemed that our two natures blent
Into a sphere from youthful sympathy,
Or else, to alter Plato's parable,
Into the yolk and white of the one shell.

And thinking of that fit of grief or rage
I look upon one child or t'other there
And wonder if she stood so at that age—
For even daughters of the swan can share
Something of every paddler's heritage—
And had that color upon cheek or hair,
And thereupon my heart is driven wild:
She stands before me as a living child.

Her present image floats into the mind—
Did Quattrocento finger fashion it

Hollow of cheek as though it drank the wind
And took a mess of shadows for its meat?
And I though never of Ledaean kind
Had pretty plumage once—enough of that,
Better to smile on all that smile, and show
There is a comfortable kind of old scarecrow.

What youthful mother, a shape upon her lap
Honey of generation had betrayed,
And that must sleep, shriek, struggle to escape
As recollection or the drug decide,
Would think her son, did she but see that shape
With sixty or more winters on its head,
A compensation for the pang of his birth,
Or the uncertainty of his setting forth?

Plato thought nature but a spume that plays
Upon a ghostly paradigm of things;
Solider Aristotle played the taws
Upon the bottom of a king of kings;
World-famous golden-thighed Pythagoras
Fingered upon a fiddle-stick or strings
What a star sang and careless Muses heard:
Old clothes upon old sticks to scare a bird.

Both nuns and mothers worship images,
But those the candles light are not as those
That animate a mother's reveries,
But keep a marble or a bronze repose.
And yet they too break hearts—O Presences
That passion, piety or affection knows,
And that all heavenly glory symbolize—
O self-born mockers of man's enterprise;

Labor is blossoming or dancing where
The body is not bruised to pleasure soul,
Nor beauty born out of its own despair,
Nor blear-eyed wisdom out of midnight oil.
O chestnut tree, great rooted blossomer,

Are you the leaf, the blossom or the bole?
O body swayed to music, O brightening glance,
How can we know the dancer from the dance?

## The Statues

Pythagoras planned it. Why did the people stare?
His numbers, though they moved or seemed to move
In marble or in bronze, lacked character.
But boys and girls, pale from the imagined love
Of solitary beds, knew what they were,
That passion could bring character enough,
And pressed at midnight in some public place
Live lips upon a plummet-measured face.

No! Greater than Pythagoras, for the men
That with a mallet or a chisel modelled these
Calculations that look but casual flesh, put down
All Asiatic vague immensities,
And not the banks of oars that swam upon
The many-headed foam at Salamis.
Europe put off that foam when Phidias
Gave women dreams and dreams their looking-glass.

One image crossed the many-headed, sat
Under the tropic shade, grew round and slow,
No Hamlet thin from eating flies, a fat
Dreamer of the Middle Ages. Empty eyeballs knew
That knowledge increases unreality, that
Mirror on mirror mirrored is all the show.
When gong and conch declare the hour to bless
Grimalkin crawls to Buddha's emptiness.

When Pearse summoned Cuchulain to his side,
What stalked through the Post Office? What intellect,
What calculation, number, measurement, replied?
We Irish, born into that ancient sect
But thrown upon this filthy modern tide

And by its formless spawning fury wrecked,
Climb to our proper dark, that we may trace
The lineaments of a plummet-measured face.


LIONEL JOHNSON/1867–1902


*By the Statue of King Charles
at Charing Cross*

Sombre and rich, the skies,
Great glooms, and starry plains;
Gently the night wind sighs;
Else a vast silence reigns.

The splendid silence clings
Around me: and around
The saddest of all Kings,
Crowned, and again discrowned.

Comely and calm, he rides
Hard by his own Whitehall.
Only the night wind glides:
No crowds, nor rebels, brawl.

Gone, too, his Court: and yet,
The stars his courtiers are:
Stars in their stations set;
And every wandering star.

Alone he rides, alone,
The fair and fatal King:
Dark night is all his own,
That strange and solemn thing.

Which are more full of fate:
The stars; or those sad eyes?

Which are more still and great:
Those brows, or the dark skies?

Although his whole heart yearn
In passionate tragedy,
Never was face so stern
With sweet austerity.

Vanquished in life, his death
By beauty made amends:
The passing of his breath
Won his defeated ends.

Brief life, and hapless? Nay:
Through death, life grew sublime.
*Speak after sentence?* Yea:
And to the end of time.

Armoured he rides, his head
Bare to the stars of doom;
He triumphs now, the dead,
Beholding London's gloom.

Our wearier spirit faints,
Vexed in the world's employ:
His soul was of the saints;
And art to him was joy.

King, tried in fires of woe!
Men hunger for thy grace:
And through the night I go,
Loving thy mournful face.

Yet, when the city sleeps,
When all the cries are still,
The stars and heavenly deeps
Work out a perfect will.

# EDWARD THOMAS/1878–1917

### The Owl

Down hill I came, hungry, and yet not starved;
Cold, yet had heat within me that was proof
Against the North wind; tired, yet so that rest
Had seemed the sweetest thing under a roof.

Then at the inn I had food, fire, and rest,
Knowing how hungry, cold, and tired was I.
All of the night was quite barred out except
An owl's cry, a most melancholy cry

Shaken out long and clear upon the hill,
No merry note, nor cause of merriment,
But one telling me plain what I escaped
And others could not, that night, as I went in.

And salted was my food, and my repose
Salted and sobered, too, by the bird's voice
Speaking for all who lay under the stars,
Soldiers and poor, unable to rejoice.


### When I First Came Here

When I first came here I had hope,
Hope for I knew not what. Fast beat
My heart at sight of the tall slope
Or grass and yews, as if my feet

Only by scaling its steps of chalk
Would see something no other hill
Ever disclosed. And now I walk
Down it the last time. Never will

My heart beat so again at sight
Of any hill although as fair

And loftier. For infinite
The change, late unperceived, this year,

The twelfth, suddenly, shows me plain.
Hope now,—not health, nor cheerfulness,
Since they can come and go again,
As often one brief hour witnesses,—

Just hope has gone forever. Perhaps
I may love other hills yet more
Than this: the future and the maps
Hide something I was waiting for.

One thing I know, that love with chance
And use and time and necessity
Will grow, and louder the heart's dance
At parting than at meeting be.

### The Green Roads

The green roads that end in the forest
Are strewn with white goose feathers this June,

Like marks left behind, by someone gone to the forest
To show his track. But he has never come back.

Down each green road a cottage looks at the forest.
Round one the nettle towers; two are bathed in flowers.

An old man along the green road to the forest
Strays from one, from another a child alone.

In the thicket bordering the forest,
All day long a thrush twiddles his song.

It is old, but the trees are young in the forest,
All but one like a castle keep, in the middle deep.

That oak saw the ages pass in the forest:
They were a host, but their memories are lost,

For the tree is dead: all things forget the forest
Excepting perhaps me, when now I see

The old man, the child, the goose feathers at the edge of the
    forest,
And hear all day the thrush repeat his song.


*The Gallows*

There was a weasel lived in the sun
With all his family,
Till a keeper shot him with his gun
And hung him up on a tree,
Where he swings in the wind and rain,
In the sun and in the snow,
Without pleasure, without pain,
On the dead oak tree bough.

There was a crow who was no sleeper,
But a thief and a murderer
Till a very late hour; and this keeper
Made him one of the things that were,
To hang and flap in rain and wind
In the sun and in the snow.
There are no more sins to be sinned
On the dead oak tree bough.

There was a magpie, too,
Had a long tongue and a long tail;
He could both talk and do—
But what did that avail?
He, too, flaps in the wind and rain
Alongside weasel and crow,
Without pleasure, without pain,
On the dead oak tree bough.

And many other beasts
And birds, skin, bone, and feather,
Have been taken from their feasts
And hung up there together.
To swing and have endless leisure
In the sun and in the snow,
Without pain, without pleasure,
On the dead oak tree bough.


# JAMES JOYCE/1882–1941


### All Day I Hear the Noise of Waters

All day I hear the noise of waters
    Making moan,
Sad as the sea-bird is, when going
    Forth alone,
He hears the winds cry to the waters'
    Monotone.

The grey winds, the cold winds are blowing
    Where I go.
I hear the noise of many waters
    Far below.
All day, all night, I hear them flowing
    To and fro.


### I Hear an Army Charging upon the Land

I hear an army charging upon the land,
  And the thunder of horses plunging, foam about their
    knees:
Arrogant, in black armour, behind them stand,
  Disdaining the reins, with fluttering whips, the charioteers.

They cry unto the night their battle-name:
   I moan in sleep when I hear afar their whirling laughter.
They cleave the gloom of dreams, a blinding flame,
   Clanging, clanging upon the heart as upon an anvil.

They come shaking in triumph their long, green hair:
   They come out of the sea and run shouting by the shore.
My heart, have you no wisdom thus to despair?
   My love, my love, my love, why have you left me alone?

## JAMES STEPHENS/1882–1950

### The Goat Paths

The crooked paths go every way
Upon the hill—they wind about
Through the heather in and out
Of the quiet sunniness.
And there the goats, day after day,

Stray in sunny quietness,
Cropping here and cropping there,
As they pause and turn and pass,
Now a bit of heather spray,
Now a mouthful of the grass.

In the deeper sunniness,
In the place where nothing stirs,
Quietly in quietness,
In the quiet of the furze,
For a time they come and lie
Staring on the roving sky.

If you approach they run away,
They leap and stare, away they bound,
With a sudden angry sound,

To the sunny quietude;
Crouching down where nothing stirs
In the silence of the furze,
Crouching down again to brood
In the sunny solitude.

If I were as wise as they,
I would stray apart and brood,
I would beat a hidden way
Through the quiet heather spray
To a sunny solitude;

And should you come I'd run away,
I would make an angry sound,
I would stare and turn and bound
To the deeper quietude,
To the place where nothing stirs
In the silence of the furze.

In that airy quietness
I would think as long as they;
Through the quiet sunniness
I would stray away to brood
By a hidden, beaten way
In the sunny solitude,

I would think until I found
Something I can never find,
Something lying on the ground,
In the bottom of my mind.

### The Snare

I hear a sudden cry of pain!
There is a rabbit in a snare;
Now I hear the cry again,
But I cannot tell from where.

But I cannot tell from where
He is calling out for aid!
Crying on the frightened air,
Making everything afraid!

Making everything afraid!
Wrinkling up his little face!
As he cries again for aid;
—And I cannot find the place!

And I cannot find the place
Where his paw is in the snare!
Little One! Oh, Little One!
I am searching everywhere!

### In Waste Places

As a naked man I go
Through the desert, sore afraid;
Holding high my head, although
I'm as frightened as a maid.

The lion crouches there! I saw
In barren rocks his amber eye!
He parts the cactus with his paw!
He stares at me, as I go by!

He would pad upon my trace
If he thought I was afraid!
If he knew my hardy face
Veils the terrors of a maid.

He rises in the night-time, and
He stretches forth! He snuffs the air!
He roars! He leaps along the sand!
He creeps! He watches everywhere!

His burning eyes, his eyes of bale
Through the darkness I can see!
He lashes fiercely with his tail!
He makes again to spring at me!

I am the lion, and his lair!
I am the fear that frightens me!
I am the desert of despair!
And the night of agony!

Night or day, whate'er befall,
I must walk the desert land,
Until I dare my fear, and call
The lion out to lick my hand!


# D. H. LAWRENCE/1885–1930


### Love on the Farm

What large, dark hands are those at the window
Grasping in the golden light
Which weaves its way through the evening wind
   At my heart's delight?

Ah, only the leaves! But in the west
I see a redness suddenly come
Into the evening's anxious breast—
   'Tis the wound of love goes home!

The woodbine creeps abroad
Calling low to her lover:
   The sun-lit flirt who all the day
   Has poised above her lips in play
   And stolen kisses, shallow and gay
Of pollen, now has gone away—
   She woos the moth with her sweet, low word;

And when above her his moth-wings hover
Then her bright breast she will uncover
And yield her honey-drop to her lover.

Into the yellow, evening glow
Saunters a man from the farm below;
Leans, and looks in at the low-built shed
Where the swallow has hung her marriage bed.
  The bird lies warm against the wall.
  She glances quick her startled eyes
  Towards him, then she turns away
  Her small head, making warm display
  Of red upon the throat. Her terrors sway
  Her out of the nest's warm, busy ball,
  Whose plaintive cry is heard as she flies
  In one blue stoop from out the sties
  Into the twilight's empty hall.

Oh, water-hen, beside the rushes
Hide your quaintly scarlet blushes,
Still your quick tail, lie still as dead,
Till the distance folds over his ominous tread!

The rabbit presses back her ears,
Turns back her liquid, anguished eyes
And crouches low; then with wild spring
Spurts from the terror of *his* oncoming;
To be choked back, the wire ring
Her frantic effort throttling:
  Piteous brown ball of quivering fears!
Ah, soon in his large, hard hands she dies,
And swings all loose from the swing of his walk!
Yet calm and kindly are his eyes
And ready to open in brown surprise
Should I not answer to his talk
Or should he my tears surmise.

I hear his hand on the latch, and rise from my chair
Watching the door open; he flashes bare

His strong teeth in a smile, and flashes his eyes
In a smile like triumph upon me; then careless-wise
He flings the rabbit soft on the table board
And comes toward me: ah! the uplifted sword
Of his hand against my bosom! and oh, the broad
Blade of his glance that asks me to applaud
His coming! With his hand he turns my face to him
And caresses me with his fingers that still smell grim
Of the rabbit's fur! God, I am caught in a snare!
I know not what fine wire is round my throat;
I only know I let him finger there
My pulse of life, and let him nose like a stoat
Who sniffs with joy before he drinks the blood.

And down his mouth comes to my mouth! and down
His bright dark eyes come over me, like a hood
Upon my mind! his lips meet mine, and a flood
Of sweet fire sweeps across me, so I drown
Against him, die, and find death good.

## Piano

Softly, in the dusk, a woman is singing to me;
Taking me back down the vista of years, till I see
A child sitting under the piano, in the boom of the tingling
    strings
And pressing the small, poised feet of a mother who smiles as
    she sings.

In spite of myself, the insidious mastery of song
Betrays me back, till the heart of me weeps to belong
To the old Sunday evenings at home, with winter outside
And hymns in the cozy parlor, the tinkling piano our guide.

So now it is vain for the singer to burst into clamor
With the great black piano appassionato. The glamor
Of childish days is upon me, my manhood is cast

Down in the flood of remembrance, I weep like a child for
    the past.


### Hymn to Priapus

My love lies underground
With her face upturned to mine,
And her mouth unclosed in a last long kiss
That ended her life and mine.

I dance at the Christmas party
Under the mistletoe
Along with a ripe, slack country lass
Jostling to and fro.

The big, soft country lass,
Like a loose sheaf of wheat
Slipped through my arms on the threshing floor
At my feet.

The warm, soft country lass,
Sweet as an armful of wheat
At threshing-time broken, was broken
For me, and ah, it was sweet!

Now I am going home
Fulfilled and alone,
I see the great Orion standing
Looking down.

He's the star of my first beloved
Love-making.
The witness of all that bitter-sweet
Heart-aching.

Now he sees this as well,
This last commission.

Nor do I get any look
Of admonition.

He can add the reckoning up
I suppose, between now and then,
Having walked himself in the thorny, difficult
Ways of men.

He has done as I have done
No doubt:
Remembered and forgotten
Turn and about.

My love lies underground
With her face upturned to mine,
And her mouth unclosed in the last long kiss
That ended her life and mine.

She fares in the stark immortal
Fields of death;
I in these goodly, frozen
Fields beneath.

Something in me remembers
And will not forget.
The stream of my life in the darkness
Deathward set!

And something in me has forgotten,
Has ceased to care.
Desire comes up, and contentment
Is debonair.

I, who am worn and careful,
How much do I care?
How is it I grin then, and chuckle
Over despair?

Grief, grief, I suppose and sufficient
Grief makes us free
To be faithless and faithful together
As we have to be.

### Quite Forsaken

What pain, to wake and miss you!
  To wake with a tightened heart,
And mouth reaching forward to kiss you!

This then at last is the dawn, and the bell
  Clanging at the farm! Such bewilderment
Comes with the sight of the room, I cannot tell.

It is raining. Down the half-obscure road
  Four laborers pass with their scythes
Dejectedly;—a huntsman goes by with his load:

A gun, and a bunched-up deer, its four little feet
  Clustered dead.—And this is the dawn
For which I wanted the night to retreat!

## WILFRED OWEN/1893–1918

### Disabled

He sat in a wheeled chair, waiting for dark,
And shivered in his ghastly suit of grey,
Legless, sewn short at elbow. Through the park
Voices of boys rang saddening like a hymn,
Voices of play and pleasure after day,
Till gathering sleep had mothered them from him.

About this time Town used to swing so gay
When glow-lamps budded in the light blue trees,
And girls danced lovelier as the air grew dim,—
In the old times, before he threw away his knees.
Now he will never feel again how slim
Girls' waists are, or how warm their subtle hands;
All of them touch him like some queer disease.

There was an artist silly for his face,
For it was younger than his youth, last year.
Now, he is old; his back will never brace;
He's lost his color very far from here,
Poured it down shell-holes til the veins ran dry,
And half his life-time lapsed in that hot race,
And leap of purple spouted from his thigh.

One time he liked a blood-smear down his leg,
After the matches, carried shoulder-high.
It was after football, when he'd drunk a peg,
He thought he'd better join.—He wonders why.
Someone had said he'd look a god in kilts,
That's why; and maybe, too, to please his Meg;
Aye, that was it, to please the giddy jilts
He asked to join. He didn't have to beg;
Smiling, they wrote his lie; aged nineteen years.
Germans he scarcely thought of; all their guilt,
And Austria's, did not move him. And no fears
Of Fear came yet. He thought of jewelled hilts
For daggers in plaid socks; of smart salutes;
And care of arms; and leave; and pay arrears;
*Esprit de corps;* and hints for young recruits.
And soon he was drafted out with drums and cheers.

Some cheered him home, but not as crowds cheer Goal.
Only a solemn man who brought him fruits
*Thanked* him; and then inquired about his soul.

Now he will spend a few sick years in Institutes,
And do what things the rules consider wise,

And take whatever pity they may dole.
Tonight he noticed how the women's eyes
Passed from him to the strong men that were whole.
How cold and late it is! Why don't they come
And put him into bed? Why don't they come?


### Wild with All Regrets

To Siegfried Sassoon

My arms have mutinied against me—brutes!
My fingers fidget like ten idle brats,
My back's been stiff for hours, damned hours.
Death never gives his squad a Stand-at-ease.
I can't read. There's no use. Take your book.
A short life and a merry one, my buck!
We said we'd hate to grow dead-old. But now,
Not to live old seems awful; not to renew
My boyhood with my boys, and teach 'em hitting,
Shooting, and hunting,—all the arts of hurting!
—Well, that's what I learnt. That, and making money.
Your fifty years in store seem none too many,
But I've five minutes. God! For just two years
To help myself to this good air of yours!
One Spring! Is one too hard to spare? Too long?
Spring air would find its own way to my lung,
And grow me legs as quick as lilac shoots.

Yes, there's the orderly. He'll change the sheets
When I'm lugged out. Oh, couldn't I do that?
Here in this coffin of a bed, I've thought
I'd like to kneel and sweep his floors forever,—
And ask no nights off when the bustle's over,
For I'd enjoy the dirt. Who's prejudiced
Against a grimed hand when his own's quite dust,—
Less live than specks that in the sun-shafts turn?
Dear dust—in rooms, on roads, on faces' tan!
I'd love to be a sweep's boy, black as Town;

Yes, or a muckman. Must I be his load?
A flea would do. If one chap wasn't bloody,
Or went stone-cold, I'd find another body.

Which I shan't manage now. Unless it's yours.
I shall stay in you, friend, for some few hours.
You'll feel my heavy spirit chill your chest,
And climb your throat on sobs, until it's chased
On sighs, and wiped from off your lips by wind.

I think on your rich breathing, brother, I'll be weaned
To do without what blood remained me from my wound.

## Index of Titles and First Lines

(Titles are in italics)